FORMS OF FEELING

TO MARJORIE

and also to Margaret

ROBERT F. HOBSON

FORMS

The Heart of
Psychotherapy

OF

FEELING

TAVISTOCK PUBLICATIONS · London & New York

First published in 1985 by
Tavistock Publications Ltd
11 New Fetter Lane,
London EC4P 4EE

Published in the USA by
Tavistock Publications
in association with Methuen, Inc.
29 West 35th Street, New York,
NY 10001

Printed in Great Britain at the
University Press, Cambridge

*British Library Cataloguing in
Publication Data*

Forms of feeling:
the heart of psychotherapy. −
(Social science paperback; 304)
1. Psychotherapy
I. Title   II. Series
616.89′14   RC480

ISBN 0−422−78870−8
ISBN 0−422−78880−5 Pbk

*Library of Congress Cataloging in
Publication Data*

Hobson, Robert F.
Forms of feeling.
Bibliography: p.
Includes indexes.
1. Family psychotherapy.
I. Title.
RC488.5.H59 1985   616.89′156   85−16966

ISBN 0−422−78870−8

CONTENTS

ACKNOWLEDGEMENTS

Growing up is a matter of engaging in a never-ending personal conversation. Ideas, intellectual formulations, and love emerge from a shared 'space'. We cannot split dialogue into 'I' and 'others'.

This book has unfolded *in-between*: a 'getting to know' which has happened between me and countless friends, patients, and professional colleagues, some of whom have been 'enemies for friendship's sake'. My ideas are 'my own' but I do not 'own' them. In expressing my gratitude I cannot construct a hierarchy, an order of importance. Each relationship is unique.

The problem of 'acknowledging' has troubled many sleepless nights. I wish that I could express a heart-felt 'thank you' to many, many persons, most of whom have been labelled 'patients'. There is not enough space. I shall mention only a few friends who, as well as sharing in the growth of germinal ideas, have helped (and sometimes bullied) me in the preparation of a manuscript.

My life and views as a psychotherapist have evolved in exciting conversations, and in shared hardships, with my friend Russell Meares.[1] He will not agree with all I say but he and I stand together on the foundations of the Conversational Model. It is a joint creation.

It is salutory to discover, in reading forgotten journals, how much of this book was written by a young seasick Surgeon-Lieutenant on the

Arctic convoys in 1943. We cannot avoid change, but we do not change very much! Maybe all that I have to say was latent in the stories that arose between my brother, Alan, and me when we shared a double-bed in a Lancashire cotton valley during the gloomy 1920s. Alan[2] listened and responded. Later, he opened up to me the world of William Wordsworth.

Before our war I met Sam Burton.[3] We came together in a rare moment, as we shared a look at a game of cricket from a train window. Sam enlarged my 'knowing' of literature and life. Without his expertise in writing and, much more important, our rare friendship, this book could never have been written. As a teacher of, and writer on, English language and literature, he made me feel that what I wished to say was of some importance and might be heard by at least some persons outside the world of psychotherapy and psychiatry.

A central theme in the book is the meaning of 'persons' as distinct from 'people' and 'things'. Meetings with Herbert McCabe[4] and Ian Ramsey[5] opened up new vistas about language and life. Over many years my views have grown in sympathetic and critical dialogues with close friends who are also experts in different fields, especially David Jenkins[6], Miller Mair,[7] and my son, Peter.[8] Nina Coltart[9] opened up to me worlds within worlds.

Careful research method, applied with sympathetic understanding, has compelled me to take a more honest look at what I do and why I do it, and ask whether or not I am wasting my time. I shall always be grateful to David Shapiro[10] who many years ago, at great personal cost, courageously and generously began this difficult task. More recently, David Goldberg[11] has given me a very great deal in very many ways, not least in directing research on the clarification, teaching, and examination of the Conversational Model.

Margaret Towse[12] and Frank Margison[13] have contributed very much more than expert assistance on neurological aspects of psychotherapy and the enlightening experience of preparing videotapes for teaching.

I do not know how to thank Margaret Wilson. After more than twenty-five years at the Mecca of scientific psychiatry, the Bethlem Royal and Maudsley Hospitals, and involvement in the Society of Analytical Psychology and other London psychotherapeutic bodies, I came to Manchester. I was confronted not only with the high academic standards of the University but also with the urgent needs of the North West Region, where there were few trained therapists. I could not have coped without Margaret's firm support, challenging honesty, and sensitive understanding. I am grateful to her for tireless work on the preparation of this book, but far more for her unwavering faith that I had something worthwhile to write.

Unselfishly, my friend Jim Seddon has given long hours to studying and making suggestions about the mode of presentation, the details of my personal style, and to correcting my very curious punctuation. But, more important, over many years I have learned from his wide-ranging knowledge and shared with him exciting explorations into the world of spiritual values.

I have been very fortunate in finding, and being found by, Gill Davies of Tavistock Publications. She has been a person to write for. That is a large statement.

I shall now contradict myself. I said that there is no hierarchy. I was wrong.

One name stands far above all others: Marjorie, my typist, my wife. My Friend.

INTRODUCTION

'The principal object, then, which I proposed to myself . . .
was to choose incidents and situations from common life,
and to relate or describe them throughout, as far as was
possible, in a selection of language really used by men; and
at the same time to throw over them a certain colouring of
imagination whereby ordinary things should be presented
to the mind in an unusual way; and further, and above all,
to make these incidents and situations interesting by
tracing in them, truly though not ostentatiously, the
primary laws of our nature . . . truth, . . . not standing
upon external testimony but carried alive into the heart by
passion.'

(W. Wordsworth, Preface to *Lyrical Ballads* 1805)

This, dear Reader, is a covering letter. It underlines my belief that it is
the stories that matter — and how they are told. The real introduction is
Chapter 1. If you turn to the stories of Sam and Stephen (pp. 1 and 9) you
should know whether or not this book is for you.

I write primarily for those who wish to learn how to engage in psychotherapy: for beginners, for experienced practitioners, for disciplined research workers, and for myself. For me, the word 'psychotherapy' has a very broad meaning. I hope that much of what I say will be of value to each of you who, wishing to help others within a personal relationship, takes the risk of discovering yourself. I write for anyone who hopes to respond to a close friend, a student, or a little-known neighbour asking for help with a problem. The 'heart beat' of therapy is a process of learning how to go on becoming a person together with others. That learning never ends.

I try to describe, and to present, what I do in psychotherapy and why I do what I do. I try.

There are very many ways of giving accounts: verbatim transcripts, observations of videotapes, tales of long-lasting relationships, and would-be poetic expressions of personal experience. I am concerned with the 'facts', but there are no facts without frameworks, no data without meaning. So I tell stories in various ways for different purposes. Most moving events cannot be talked about, they can be *shown*. You may wish to see something of what I do. If so you can compare what I write with video-recordings.[1]

Every psychological statement is, to a greater or lesser degree, a personal confession — however subtly it is disguised by conventional shibboleths of 'objectivity'. We choose our subject, we select our evidence, we draw upon our own experience, and (trimming our sails to the scientific and political Establishment) we decide what are the 'facts'.

This book is very personal, but that does not mean that what I have to say is idiosyncratic. I have attempted to re-write my autobiography as a psychotherapist in such a way as to formulate a method, a Conversational Model, with specified skills which can be learned, practised, and tested out by others.

When I speak of an 'autobiography' I mean the development of ideas, attitudes, and meanings which have arisen and been transformed through joy, sorrow, chaos, and relative tranquillity in a journey of forty years through the world of academic psychiatry, of analytical psychotherapy, of scientific research, and of life in a therapeutic community. To a large extent this book is an expression of individual experience. But it is not only that.

In the labour of writing, I am concerned with formulations and skills which cut across the existing 'schools' of psychotherapy. I do not propound a coherent, final synthesis, nor elaborate an eclectic compromise. I seek for a growing-point which might lead on to closer cooperation, further discovery, and more effective ways of helping others.

I seldom use the impersonal passive style, the convention of modern 'scientific' papers. Resisting a temptation to launch an attack on what is often an evasion of personal commitment, I shall quote Samuel Taylor Coleridge. He sees the avoidance of 'I' as an expression of concealed egotism and of the 'watchfulness of guilt':

> 'With what anxiety every fashionable author avoids the word *I*! – now he transforms himself into a third person, – "the present writer" – now multiplies himself and swells into "*we*".'[2]

I believe that my viewpoint, my personal opinion, has some general significance.

The word 'heart' in my subtitle can be understood in at least two senses. I am concerned with the centre, the basis, of my approach to psychotherapy: a developing relationship. What I say and do in therapy is aimed at promoting understanding: a 'conversation', a meeting between two experiencing subjects (an I and a Thou), here and now, in such a way that the learning can be effective in other relationships. If, as I believe, psychotherapy is a matter of promoting a personal dialogue, then we need to know how to receive, express, and share feeling: how to learn a language of the heart in its 'minute particulars'.

In his clinical practice a psychotherapist is a kind of hybrid or half-caste: a quasi-scientist, quasi-artist. As a *scientist*, I do my best to formulate general theories on the basis of hard evidence and, however crudely, to test hypotheses derived from them. I make predictions about what will be the consequences of what I say and I look for facts which will show me that I am wrong. But the important therapeutic factor is not so much *what* is said but rather *how* it is said. In an unrepeatable moment, I hope to respond to my unique client by sharing in an on-going act of creation, expressing and shaping immediate experience in the making and re-making of a verbal and non-verbal language of feeling. It is not only a matter of 'knowing about' someone but also, and mainly, of sharing a language of 'knowing'. Personal knowing has a 'logic' but it is not discursive, not set out in straight lines; it is an artistic all-at-once presentation of 'forms of feeling'. The psychotherapist must also be something of an *artist*. Like all of us in our personal relationships, he needs to speak, however hesitantly, two different and yet related languages: the language of science and the language of art. He needs the help of proper scientists and of great artists.

I seek aid from academic and experimental psychologists but my main theme is day-to-day therapy in personal conversations. In the task of learning *how* to say what I have to say, I took to Shakespeare, Wordsworth, Coleridge, Conrad, Rilke, and the authorized version of the Bible.

There are many different ways of reading this book. I have

said that the stories are most important. In Chapter 1 I try to present two dialogues in therapy. Long ago, they had a profound impact upon me, and, in retrospect, I see my development as a psychotherapist as an effort to explore the mysteries and the wider practical applications of those transforming meetings.

As students, we have different needs. Some of us wish to be told what to do, now. Whilst being interested in the stories, you may become bewildered, frustrated, and irritated by some apparent digressions in Book I. I recommend you to enjoy the tales and, without guilt, to move on to the more obviously practical and well-known parts of Book II, perhaps using the published videotapes.[3]

Other students are different — not better, not worse, but different. You, like me, may have no use for techniques unless they arise from, or are at least consistent with, a coherent theoretical, philosophical ground; and, indeed, a metaphysical world-view.

Theory and practice fertilize each other. They are inseparable. But a book must have some straight-line order. The difficulty is that my imposed 'logic' may not be the same as yours.

In 1949 I adopted Wordsworth's manifesto about poetry (the epigraph to this Introduction) as a clarion call to psychotherapists. 'Let us say what we mean in the "language really used by men"' – and women. 'Away with jargon,' I cried. I have not succeeded. In the last three highly condensed paragraphs there are a number of significant words such as 'persons', 'conversation', 'experience', 'feeling', and 'language'. Over the years, they have gained special meanings.

In Book I, I begin (and it is only a beginning) to explore what I mean when I use these loaded terms. As I shall argue, words are not isolated things which can be exhausted by scrupulous definition. They move together in manifold relations. I hope that meanings will emerge as repetitive, interpenetrating themes are embodied in stories within varying contexts.

Inevitably, I am led into fields of philosophy and metaphysics in which, not being an expert, I may lose my way. If you, my Reader, are preoccupied with what you are going to say tomorrow morning to Ms Flabbergast or Mr Freezeby, you may not welcome my enthusiasm for exploration of ideas. Perhaps, unlike me, you do not feel that the logic of signs and the cosmic reverberations of the living symbol are immediately relevant to the minute particulars of a brief interview.

In Book II, I outline a teachable and researchable Conversational Model of psychotherapy. It embodies the more far-flung reflections of Book I but is concerned with day-to-day practicalities related to simplified expositions of more familiar work done by others in the field.

Perhaps the rather long, schematic Chapter 12 is a key. It is a general summary which points backwards and forwards. You, my doubtful Reader, might well try Chapters 1, 2, and 3. Then, wondering what it is all about, you could turn to 'Towards a Model of Psychotherapy' (Chapter 12) and decide how or whether to proceed.

Book III is an intimate statement: an invitation to a conversation should you and I ever meet. It is an effort to convey some of my central values which arise from the loneliness which lies at the heart of psychotherapy and, indeed, of all personal relationships.

The theme of the whole book is an attempt to explore crucial factors which, as yet, we cannot specify: a few 'words' in the language of a person-in-relationships. I state, rather than argue, my view of *some* fundamentals of psychotherapy. There are glaring omissions. I do not have space to record and evaluate my experience of group situations, small meetings, and therapeutic communities.[4] Nor is there room for discussion of psychological, sociological, economic, and political factors that are of very great importance. The heart of the matter is a two-person relationship, a friendship which throughout life emerges from the 'conversation' of a 'mother' (who could be male) and child. That must always remain the focus for a psychotherapist, a counsellor in any field, and, I believe, a politician.

Facts lie in how stories are told. 'Truth' is an elusive word. It emerges and is refined in and between persons. If a story is objectivized, as if it were a final statement of what 'really' happened (e.g. *merely* in terms of reliable and valid observations), then it is false. Experimental science is a help in detecting some of our timid falsehoods, but if there is any truth in this book it is embodied in the stories written in a selection of language really used by men and women.

As persons we draw life from roots that lie deep in our language. I hope that my examples drawn from cricket and from the Lancashire dialect will not be too individual and too parochial for you, my Reader. I trust that they will resonate with other games and with other languages in Seattle and in Bangkok. General formulations are, at worst, flat and lifeless; and at best, 'sounding brass', unless they have a local habitation and a name. Stories in a book *about* the 'heart' should come *from* the heart.

When I was very young I was moved in my middle by a story. It spoke to my condition and it is still 'real'. Every year I discover new levels of meaning. It has long been a music-hall joke and, for many centuries, versions have been told in many languages in many parts of the world. You will be acquainted with the 'what', the content, but maybe a personal tone of voice may evoke freshened meanings. At the age of ten I *knew* that it had actually happened in Oswaldtwistle, a Lancashire village. Perhaps it.did. I wish I could speak it to you in the language of my feeling. The footnote translations are inadequate.

In 1930 Oswaldtwistle had only one street lamp.

It is a dark night when George, taking his regular stroll to the 'Royal Oak', sees Joe on hands and knees groping in the light of the solitary lamp.

'Wot's up lad?' George says. 'As ti lost summat?'*

'Aye. A pound note.'

'Oh! Aye! Ah'll 'elp thi find it.'

George joins Joe in the November mud. They search together. A quarter of an hour goes by. Half an hour. As the hour approaches George, weary and thirsty, asks plaintively:

'Ah corned find nowt. Are ti sure tha lost it 'ere?'†

'Oh no!' replies Joe. 'Ah dropped it up t'street, but there's no leet up theer.'

There is no light up there.

'Old men ought to be explorers.'[5]

* 'What is wrong my friend? Hast thou lost something?.'
† 'I can't find anything. Art thou sure that thou lost it here?'

BOOK · I ·
THE TRUE VOICE
OF FEELING

'All real living is meeting'
(Martin Buber, *I and Thou*)

'WHAT COMES FROM THE HEART
THAT ALONE GOES TO THE HEART.'
(S.T. Coleridge, 'Essays on the
Principles of Method', *The Friend*)

TWO MEETINGS

Thirty-three years ago, I met Sam. I was young and inexperienced. An expensive medical training and a year or two in general medicine and surgical practice had taught me a great deal about the brain, lungs, and kidneys, with a little about academic psychology and the diagnosis of mental illness. But it was Sam who began my education in psychotherapy.

I classified him, with a certain satisfaction, as a case of 'behaviour disorder in an introverted adolescent', but this gratification was short-lived. As time went by, I found myself forced out of the secure haven of the formulated phrase and compelled to experience the fear and joy of a unique personal relationship.

My conversation with Sam, over a period of months, contained in embryo the central principles of a method of psychotherapy which is the subject of this book.

A PEARL OF GREAT PRICE

Sam was fourteen when he was referred for treatment because of disturbed behaviour at home and at school. Although previously he had been a dutiful and obedient son to his widowed mother, in the last year he had become aggressive and wayward. He wandered alone all night and flew into violent rages with his mother, from whom he stole money to buy cigarettes. At school, he had acquired a reputation for surly, uncooperative behaviour. He often played truant, would do no work, and had been caught passing round papers on which lewd stories were written in the coarsest possible language. Punishment and moral exhortation had no effect and psychiatric help was sought by his mother and the education authority after an episode of thieving at school.

An only child, Sam was seven when his father died and he was brought up by his hard-working, conscientious, liberal-minded mother, whose main concern was to give Sam 'a really good start in life'. He had always been shy and rather solitary but there had been no serious problems before the apparently inexplicable onset of his behaviour disorder.

Sam sat rigidly in his chair and glowered at me – a picture of dumb insolence. Determined to play the part of a sympathetic adult, I set about showing an interest in his life. I tried to explore his attitudes to his teachers, schoolmates, and mother. I encouraged him to talk about what I supposed to be his interests – films, games, and girls. I even asked him if he had any dreams and, with the help of a textbook, tried some interpretations of unconscious fears. All he gave me was a surly frown and the very occasional favour of a short, grudging answer.

He was compelled to come and I was compelled to see him. So it went on week after week, until I felt that I could stand it no longer. I do not suppose I would have persisted if I had not seen hints of an unhappy, frightened, lonely boy behind the sulky, aggressive mask.

It was a glorious summer in 1947 – perfect for cricket. One day, just before seeing Sam, I had been listening to a radio commentary on the Test Match at Lords where England was playing South Africa. I forget the details now, but the position was exciting and I was full of it when Sam came in. For some minutes I spontaneously and unreservedly poured out my opinions and feelings about the state of the game – an irresponsible piece of behaviour. Then I asked him what he thought about the state of play and at that moment – this is the vital point – I really needed a response.

Sam smiled. For the first time. Then we began to talk together. Together. I felt some months later that there was a vital step, a turning-point, when I, as a person, valued what Sam gave. He felt that he had something good to give.

During the next few weeks there was a complete change in the atmosphere of our interviews. I forgot about divining Sam's complexes, about plumbing the depths of his guilt, or probing into his sexual fantasies. We talked cricket. Devotees do not talk *about* cricket. They do not 'describe'. They 'show', they 'present', they 'disclose'. I demonstrated my classic hook and he expressed his bodily joy in fast bowling. It was very much a case of give and take. Now, I thoroughly enjoyed our sessions and Sam said that he looked forward to his visits.

Then, one day, he came in wearing a strange expression and sat down slowly without his usual 'Hello'. He was not interested in the county championship results or the selection of the Test team. We sat in silence. It was a very different sort of silence from the tense closed-upness of the first few weeks. Neither of us seemed either to fight against, or to withdraw into it; we sat in it each alone and yet together.

Eventually Sam spoke with a new seriousness and decisiveness and I sensed a note of confidence and trust in me, and in himself.

'I had a dream the other night,' he said.

He had told me before about a few dreams, in a casual way, but now he spoke with a strange intensity, akin to awe.

'I was by a dark pool. It was filthy and there were all sorts of horrible monsters in it. I was scared but I dived in and at the bottom was a great big oyster and in it a terrific pearl. I got it and swam up again.'

I felt myself caught up in mystery, in a sense of otherness. At the time, my few words seemed very lame, but I was right to reply in the present tense.

'That's good. Brave, too. You've got it, though, and pearls are pretty valuable.'

We said nothing more about the dream, then, but this interview was followed by another important step. Sam began to express his feelings and thoughts, his hopes and fears, and I was able to use my book knowledge in formulating his problems. He wanted to leave school as soon as possible, against his mother's wishes. He hated himself for becoming violently angry when she treated him as a child, and yet, at times, he feared that she did not really love him and he was terrified by the thought of leaving her.

On several occasions he wept with grief and rage about the loss of his father, though when it happened, he had been a 'good boy' and 'kept a stiff upper lip'. As might be expected, for some months he experienced me as a wonderful father but, as his confidence grew he became able to be critical and angry and I became nearer life-size. Hesitantly, he talked about masturbation and about sexual and violent fantasies which he felt to be dangerous and wicked (the monsters in the pool). He warily let me know about feelings that he called 'silly and soppy' – his romantic love for a girl, and his attempts to write poetry.

In discussing these ideas, wishes, and impulses, and finding that I still accepted and liked him, he lost much of his hate for himself. He came to see that, hidden in these 'bad' feelings, were positive values which intimated possibilities of rewarding achievements in his developing sexuality and independence. He aspired to leave the world of childhood and become an adult. It was possible for him to experiment in thought and action and test his fantasies against external reality.

He emerged from isolated loneliness.

Becoming more able to love himself he was able to discover what he felt to be a new 'self', and a new attitude to his home and school life. There were marked changes in his activities with a new orientation to his future, to his social milieu and, like many adolescents, he struggled to make sense of the cosmos.

Only once did Sam refer to the dream. It was many months later.

'It's queer about that pearl. I suppose it's me in a *sort of way.*'

'Mm,' I responded, wondering about 'me' and 'myself' and what Wordsworth meant by:

'The calm existence that is mine when I/Am worthy of myself!'[1]

Then (as now) I found in Wordsworth and other poets so much that was absent from academic and dynamic psychology. Today, when I am asked by beginners in psychotherapy what they should read first, I often reply 'The Bible and Shakespeare'.

Adolescence is the phase of development from a state of childhood dependence to one of adult autonomy. It is one stage in growth from infancy to old age: unfolding potentialities are realized in a process of becoming a unique person in relation to the demands and opportunities of the outer world of people and things. Sam's personal growth was inhibited by fear and conflict.

The adolescent is in a state of conflict. On the one hand he wishes to maintain the secure state of a protected child, and on the other he aspires to an independent life in an adult world. He is faced with a problem. For Sam, the problem was magnified by the extremely strong bond with his 'good' protective mother and the absence of a father who could serve as a model. It was further complicated by guilt. Partly because of pressure of a social stereotype (the 'brave boy') and partly owing to disturbing, but largely unrecognized, anger associated with the loss, Sam had not adequately mourned his father's death. Anger added to his unadmitted resentment of being imprisoned by his mother, whom he loved deeply. He was bewildered by his sudden outbursts of aggression, together with feelings of guilt which were inextricably mixed with, and augmented by, sexual stirrings at puberty. There were hints of sexual desires which were bound up with his devotion to his mother (who in some ways treated him like a husband) but we did not explore these disturbing fantasies in detail.

Sam hated himself and defiantly set out to prove how bad he was – one way of striving for independence. His minor delinquencies only served to increase his sense of guilt, and his view of himself was reinforced by teachers and other worthy citizens. He could not trust or like himself, nor trust others to respect and value him. Perhaps most important of all, he felt that he had nothing valuable to give. He became more and more lonely and alienated.

The above schematic and somewhat naive formulation omits many complexities. Indeed, the themes were never spelled out in detail with Sam. The important process was not 'talking about' the problems but an enactment of them with a testing out of solutions within a conversation of mutual trust. It was not so much an elucidation of the causes of the problems, but rather a matter of discovering conditions in which personal growth could occur.

The vital factor was the mutual creation and expansion of a common 'feeling-language'. The meaning of 'feeling' (elaborated throughout this book) is intimated by the vital significance of cricket for Sam and for me – alone and together. In a moving cricket conversation, our immediate experience was shared and shaped in verbal and non-verbal symbols of a language which emerged between us. It was not merely a matter of talking about events. It was a dialogue, a meeting, a talking-with in mutual trust – a personal conversation. A simultaneous giving and receiving. A finding and being found.

We discovered cricket by luck – or by grace. But the topic was not the important thing. With another therapist the content might well have been different. A feeling-language is constantly created, modified, and endowed with value, within a unique developing relationship. It involves processes which we habitually separate as 'thinking', 'emotion', and 'action'. Such watertight compartments are inappropriate to an experience which is apprehended as a 'whole'; an experience that is created in the 'space' between persons.

It might be suggested that the cricket talk was merely a matter of establishing a preliminary 'rapport' – a word that trips easily from the tongue but covers a world of ignorance. In psychotherapy the *what* (the content) is of vastly less importance than the *how* (the manner of discovering, exploring in, and mutually developing a feeling-language). Learning how to engage in a personal conversation: that is the heart of psychotherapy.

I do not suggest that the content (the material) of a conversation is of no importance. That would be absurd. I am saying that in order to explore Sam's problems we had to learn to understand each other, to use many kinds of language, many universes of discourse which were different and yet related. The language of day-to-day practicalities is not that of cricket which, again, is not that of the dream and of its parallels in widespread myths and folktales.

I have emphasized the importance of mutuality, of my involvement with Sam as a person. The meeting with him called forth echoes from somewhere deep within 'myself'. Before my meeting with another boy, Stephen, I had an experience which has stayed with me. It comes alive now.

A BIG DREAM

Often, reflecting in solitude, I 'listened' again and again to Sam's story of the pearl. I listened until I felt that I shared it – really shared it, I mean, in my head, in my bowels, and in my heart. Then, nine months after that moving interview I was visited by a dream. Since then, the dream has returned repeatedly as a day-vision, especially in times of crisis. Each time it is the same and yet each time it is fresh. No associations can exhaust its meaning. It always says something new. It cannot be put into other terms. It cannot be translated. It can only be extended, enriched, and amplified as new meanings body forth.

I 'see' the dream all at once in a picture, but I must put words end to end. It was 'then' but it is also 'now'.

I am a medical student dissecting a cadaver, carefully tracing delicate nerves and ramifying arteries in the left arm. Intellectually absorbed, I mutter a string of Latin anatomical names.

Resting a moment, I stand back to admire my handiwork. Suddenly, in a moment of horror, the corpse sits up and looks at me. He looks into my eyes.

'Jesus Christ,' I blaspheme.

He picks up the scalpel with his left hand and thrusts it into his side. A river of clear water flows towards me.

I awakened to find myself asking 'Where is the river going?' and saying 'It is my own dream but I don't own it.' I thought of Sam's pearl and said 'The corpse is alive ... me ... in a sort of way.'

The dream happened on Holy Saturday, the void between Good Friday and Easter Sunday, but I only realized that much later. For me, that weekend was merely a blessed relief from the pressures of a sound training in critical, scientific psychiatry. 'Jesus Christ' was a casual phrase of my day-to-day war-time naval vocabulary. The faded blasphemy came alive.

My purpose in telling this dream is not to elaborate my idiosyncratic conflicts but only to intimate the deep reverberations of a psychotherapeutic meeting. In our conversation, Sam changed and I changed.

The dream presents its own meaning; a meaning which I hope will expand throughout this book. Here, I mention only one image that it brought to mind immediately. I remembered a distinguished physician of the Manchester Royal Infirmary, who during the early years of the war was recalled from retirement. On my first day on the wards as an undergraduate, the aged doctor pointed his monaural stethoscope at me to emphasize his words of advice: 'Young man, a good doctor knows that he can't cure anybody; he can only hope to assist the *vis medicatrix naturae*'.

About a year after the dream I met Stephen.

A BOY AND A RAINBOW

Stephen was fifteen when first brought for treatment by his mother – a determined and masterful woman who had always said 'Now Stephen, you go out and do what you please.' He *had* gone out and done what *she* pleased. That is, until three months previously when he had ceased to do anything – even speak. The ominous diagnosis of 'schizophrenia' had been made by a psychiatrist and I was asked to see him.

For many weeks he sat motionless, never looking at me. During this period I had been trying to understand what Stephen was experiencing and striving to express what my imagination produced in response to his barely detectable body-language: slight changes of posture, tension, and so on. I had made metaphorical statements such as: 'I reckon that you are all screwed up inside'; 'I feel that you are really scared. It is terrible to be locked up with a volcano inside but terrified to emerge'; 'Just now I sensed that you felt really mad, but scared . . . I wonder if you are scared of hurting . . . or being hurt'.

All these remarks say something about Stephen; but, in my use of the word 'I' ('I reckon', 'Just now I sensed') they refer to him *in relation to* me. Furthermore, they carry more than one message; there is a communication about a communication – a meta-communication:[2] that is, an implicit statement about how the main message is to be received and understood. This overtone, or undertone, is expressed verbally and non-verbally by gestures and tones of voice. It can be translated, roughly, as: 'I wish to understand if you will help me, and so I am making the best guesses I can.' It is certainly not a matter of stating 'This is what you are feeling'. There is no interrogation or 'throwing back'. I am hoping for a conversation; a dialogue in which I am involved. I seek a 'togetherness' whilst respecting Stephen's 'aloneness'; not wishing either to intrude on his personal space or to promote alienation. Although all the suggestions that I made were subsequently shown to be reasonably 'accurate', at that time they were wrong because I could not find an appropriate feeling-language which he and I could share, here and now.

The word 'empathy' (*Einfühlung*) is commonly used for the

communication of an appreication of what another person is experiencing at this moment. The term was first used to refer to the appreciation of an inanimate work of art, and, whether used of personal encounters or of aesthetic experience, it refers to a one-way activity. In personal conversation, it is a first step towards mutuality, a 'feeling with', for which I prefer the terms 'understanding' or 'sympathy'. Regrettably, the latter word often carries an unfortunate suggestion of patronizing 'pity'.

A description of a conversation in terms of 'A said this' and then 'B said that' is inevitable but inadequate. It ignores the fact that both persons are always saying something at the same time. While a person is speaking he is modifying, and often radically changing, a communication at the time he is making it. He responds to an everchanging 'feedback' which is usually non-verbal. Conversation is not like writing prose, nor is it a matter of talking at or to someone. It is a 'talking with' – one feature which distinguishes a relationship between *persons* from an attitude towards, and a manipulation of, *things*. 'Understanding', as used in this book, puts the emphasis upon an appropriate response to everchanging dialogue with a mutual correction and adjustment of messages and meanings.

One Thursday Stephen and I met. Since I wish to *present* rather than to describe what happened on that afternoon, I change the tense.

It is 4.30. Thursday. Stephen sits. I sit. I have run through all my repertoire of techniques. I have tried hard. But I give up. The sun is shining, but now, as I look out of the window, a dark cloud is moving up. Right over the cricket pitch too. I converse silently with myself: 'I hope our badly drained pitch will be fit for play on Saturday. Play? Enjoyable play is a very serious matter. But I *must* concentrate on my job.'

Stephen is twisting his fingers. That is something new. I see, but I cannot see *into* his finger-language. No *in*sight. I burst out:

'It's bloody.'

I think he moves towards me. I think so – but I am not sure. We are stuck.

Suddenly I am visited by an impulse that begins to expand into an idea. I take an old envelope out of my pocket and put it on the table which stands in front of and between us. Picking up a pencil I casually draw a line (*a* in *Figure 1*).

'Do you know that party game, Stephen?' I say. 'Someone draws a line and then someone else goes on with the picture. There's a line. Let's play together and see what comes out of it.'[3]

The phrase 'see what comes out of it' suggests a 'symbolical attitude' as described by Jung.[4] It is an invitation to explore the unknown, an

Figure 1

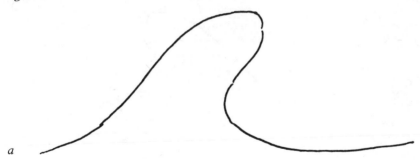

a

adventure which calls for courage. It can only be undertaken by Stephen in the security of a relationship which involves *trust*.

Stephen slowly turns his head and looks at the line. I hold out the pencil (I feel that we must use the same pencil). Hesitatingly, he takes it and draws what is clearly a ship (*b* in *Figure 2*).

Figure 2

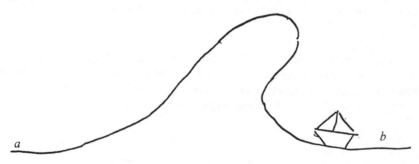

a   b

I now discover what I have drawn. A terrifying tidal wave. Psychotherapy is mainly a matter of mutual exploration of emerging meanings. Most techniques are means of diminishing fear and of promoting courage to engage in a joint exploration in which two or more people venture into the unknown alone and yet also together. I take the pencil and draw *c* (*Figure 3*) saying 'A landing stage'. Maybe I need the firm feel of dry land and Stephen tells me, non-verbally, that is not now what he is seeking. He quickly takes the pencil and draws a man or boy waving goodbye (*d* in *Figure 3*).

Many exciting possibilities are opened up to me. But I do not stop to make a deliberate choice. I quickly draw a woman waving goodbye (*e* in *Figure 3*).

Figure 3

At this point, though without deliberation, I am acting on the basis of a hypothesis that Stephen's problem is associated with an emotional separation from his mother. But there is a danger; for I know that I, myself, share this problem. I need to remember that his problem is his and mine is mine. We are together yet alone. I can only hope that we are on the right lines for Stephen. Perhaps he is a little less lonely.

By now we are absorbed in a serious playful conversation, and the rest of the picture is completed very quickly – although I shall take it slowly.

Stephen's face has begun to move whilst drawing, but now it is once more mask-like. Yet, as he draws (*f* in *Figure 4*) he speaks. For the first time.

'A flying fish.'

I suppose that all sorts of phallic fishes and clinging, devouring mothers are playing games in the periphery of my awareness but I do not stop to 'explain'. I am absorbed in the unfolding drama.

'An octopus,' I say, drawing *g* (*Figure 4*).

Figure 4

Stephen's shoulders droop as he slowly marks lines (*h* in *Figure 5*).

'It is raining,' he says, with a sigh of sad resignation. Maybe I can't stand it. Or maybe . . . Well, I tell myself, 'There must be some hope of a game of cricket on Saturday.' Silently I draw the sun with its rays conflicting with the rain (*i* in *Figure 5*).

Figure 5

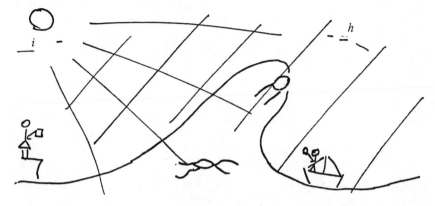

Stephen pauses. It seems an age-long pause though I suppose that it is only a few seconds if we are to believe the clock. Then he looks at me.

He looks at me. Or *with* me. For the first time I notice that Stephen has brown eyes. With a sweeping hand he draws embracing lines (*j* in *Figure 6*).

Figure 6

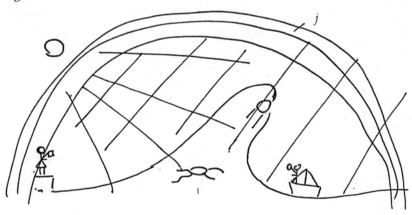

'A rainbow.'

Stephen smiles. I smile. We smile. A moment in and out of time.

I think it was important that after the heart-felt expletive 'bloody' I 'gave up' on that Thursday. Perhaps the swear-word was appropriately expressive. I do not know what it conveyed but, at least, I did stop trying too hard. My tension fell and I became more able to let things happen. Perhaps, also, I conveyed a new kind of openness – patience to wait with what St John of the Cross terms 'loving attentiveness'. By this phrase I mean maintaining an active receptiveness; an alert and yet free-floating attention whilst beginning to play with my own fantasy, and feeling. The tale illustrates three phases in the development of imagination, termed by Jung passive fantasy, active fantasy, and imaginative activity.[5]

In *passive fantasy* an image appears in a dream, in a fantasy, or out of a line on a piece of paper. *Active fantasy*, promoted by an expectant intuitive attitude (an active willingness to allow images to emerge), moves later into *imaginative activity* as the process is made the focus of concentrated attention and viewed more critically; a 'union of deep feeling with profound thought'.[6] When I said, 'See what comes out of it', I implied: 'Let us see what emerges from the unknown dimension in and behind that line on a piece of paper.' It is a line that I have drawn. Yet it can intimate what is as yet unknown; the mysterious regions of 'myself' and 'yourself'.

The movement from fantasy to imagination is a special instance of how psychotherapy involves a discovery of activity in apparent passivity. Sam and Stephen emerge from overt negative withdrawal. They become active responsible persons. The corpse sits up.

In 'giving up' I left space between Stephen and me where we could come together in serious play. From time to time, in the mutuality of our drawing, there were times of retreat into isolated loneliness, and periods in which our identities seemed to fuse as we used the same pencil. But between these extremes, there was a rhythm of intimacy and distance, as we returned again and again to what I term aloneness-togetherness (the hyphen is important). Stephen and I could only be alone (as distinct from lonely) in so far as we were together, and we could only be together (as distinct from fusion without distinction) in so far as we could be alone. But both loneliness and fusion played their part – a needful part – in the creative relationship.

The rainbow arose in a conversation in-between Stephen and me. It transcended and reconciled the conflicting discordant elements of rain and sun-rays. Combining all colours, it could be seen as a bridge over the separation between Stephen and his mother, as well as between him and me. Perhaps it was a message of hope intimating the possibility of a new kind of relationship emerging from a chaos of warring emotions. The picture represented, or rather presented, the progressive integration of meaningful symbolic forms (wave, ship, flying fish) within the 'commanding form' of a shared feeling-language. Each element could be reduced to other terms (e.g. the fish as a phallus) but the whole picture has, or is, its own meaning within a unique relationship.

Later, Stephen referred to Noah, the Flood, and the Covenant. Privately, I reflected upon the 'natural symbol' of the rainbow as part of the grammar of a language of mankind.

When a rainbow appears, the pygmies of Africa shoot arrows at it because it is a sign that God wishes to communicate with them. In some ancient writings, the ark preserves order in the 'lower waters' as does the rainbow in the 'upper waters', both completing the circle of Oneness corresponding to the two halves of the ancient notion of 'the world egg'. In China, the rainbow denoted the union of heaven and earth, and for the Greeks it was Iris, the messenger of the gods. The crock of gold lies at the end of the rainbow and the multicoloured rainbow is related to the 'peacock's tail' in alchemy.

Recalling Sam's dream, I wondered about the many myths of the hero and his dangerous quest for the treasure hidden in the Otherworld; and about how the basic themes of separation – transition – re-incorporation, of loss – disorganization – re-organization, have been enacted in diverse rites at puberty.[7] What a lot of odd and different languages men use to get together, I thought; a psychotherapist needs to learn to play many different 'language-games'.[8]

Stephen remained in therapy for just over a year. That Thursday was a turning-point, but it was only the beginning of a tedious-exciting process of exploration, of repeated talking and feeling through complex conflicts, resolution of defences, and avoidance activities, with vivid expression of loss, sexual fears, and violent aggression expressed in many different 'logics'. The mundane practical choices of everyday life were related to the vicissitudes, illusions, and sincerity of his relationship with me. Psychotherapy is not mainly a matter of revealing numinous pearls, rainbows, and living corpses. The spectacular vision of a rainbow was certainly not a miracle cure. It was, however, an important step – an evocative 'phrase' in a developing conversation.

The stories of Sam and Stephen are fragments of an autobiography. Although they stay close to full notes written at the time, in commenting (and to some extent interpreting) I have introduced many words and concepts which are central in my conversational approach today. At this point we can note a few general themes.

1   I conceive of psychotherapy as a process of learning, and learning how to learn, within a personal conversation. The central feature of this relationship is the mutual creation or discovery of a feeling-language – a language of the heart.

2   Immediate personal experience is shared and developed. It is

expressed now. It is 'disclosed' or 'presented' rather than 'talked about'.

3 Understanding is achieved, here and now, by an imaginative exploration in different but related languages between persons who are at once alone and together. Learning how to correct misunderstandings is one (and, perhaps, *the*) most important therapeutic factor.

4 As a climate of trust develops, fear and avoidance activities diminish. Problems, usually involving conflicts in intimate relationships, are enacted and explored. Solutions are applied to situations outside therapy. It is a matter of learning how to be with *persons*, as distinct from relating to and manipulating *things*.

5 A conversation involves providing conditions for on-going growth as a person. Moments of insight are steps in a progressive realization of potentialities. A relatively unknown 'myself' extends beyond 'I'.

This first chapter embodies the message of the whole book. In what follows I attempt to unfold the significance of certain key words, notably 'persons', 'experience', 'action', 'languages', 'metaphor', 'symbols', 'feeling', 'seeing', 'insight', and 'myself'. In Book II, I spell out some basic psychotherapeutic skills, techniques, and theories in relation to a theoretical model of conversational psychotherapy. Book III is a personal statement.

I shall begin with 'persons'.

· 2 ·
PERSONS

A cloud of boredom closes around me. I feel bad about it.

Freda's monotonous voice goes on and on. All about her 'agoraphobia'.

I try to hear what is being said 'beneath' and 'between', as well as 'in' and 'by' the words. I try hard. I strive to focus my attention on a verbose, repetitive, and seemingly interminable catalogue of panic attacks, palpitations, sweating, fears of fainting, and the dubious effects of tranquillizers.

Freda hardly moves. Her face shows little change of expression, and I detect no inflection in her droning voice. The monologue goes on; Freda talking *about* her symptoms – as if they are 'out there'.

She is treating herself as if she were only a thing, and talking at me as if I were a thing, not talking with me as a person. We are trapped in a world of things.

I want to know Freda, not only to know about her.

The distinction between a relationship with a person and a relation to a thing is crucial in psychotherapy.

PERSONS AND THINGS

Roberts is an umpire. He wears his carefully-laundered white coat with a dignity which befits his office as administrator of the canonical laws of cricket. A new batsman is taking guard and Roberts, with dignity, moves a directing finger. Then, in a flash, the world changes. The anonymous batsman is George Ashworth, a close friend of Fred Roberts in his schooldays. Their eyes meet, they smile and, with shocking impropriety, Fred cries 'George!'. An impersonal situation has become 'alive'. It has taken on a new depth – there is a new 'discernment', a new 'disclosure', a new 'insight'. A communication between a 'batsman' and an 'umpire' has become an encounter between two persons, 'Fred' and 'George'. There is a meeting.

Martin Buber, re-interpreting an age-old distinction, begins his book *I and Thou* with a series of cryptic, yet pregnant, aphorisms.

'To man the world is twofold, in accordance with his twofold attitude.

The attitude of man is twofold, in accordance with the twofold nature of the primary words which he speaks.

The primary words are not isolated words, but combined words.

The one primary word is the combination *I-Thou*.

The other primary word is the combination *I-It*; wherein, without a change in the primary word, one of the words *He* and *She* can replace *It*.

Hence the *I* of man is also twofold.

For the *I* of the primary word *I-Thou* is a different *I* from that of the primary word *I-It*.'[1]

The following discussion arises out of these sayings, elaborated by the work of modern philosophers, notably I.T. Ramsey, D.W. Hamlyn, R.S. Peters, and H. McCabe.[2] I shall change the word *I-It* into *I and It* since, for me, the hyphen implies a reciprocity, a togetherness; and I shall modify much of Buber's subsequent elaboration. My aim is to present the central feature of a Conversational Model – learning within, and by means of, a personal relationship.

There is a radical difference between a man's attitude to persons and his attitude to things. In a personal relationship one subject, 'I', confronts another subject, 'Thou'. Fred, an experiencing being, meets George, another experiencing being. In a relation to things, a subject experiences an object: Roberts looks at the bat, the wickets, and directs the 'batsman' (a human being can be a thing). 'Fred' and 'George' are both subjects.

The two attitudes represent the basic twofold situation of human life; the 'world of the *Thou*', and the 'world of the *It*'. In these two worlds the quality of experience is radically different ('the *I* of man is also twofold'). The difference is suggested by my use of 'Roberts' as distinct from 'Fred'.

The world of objects or things presupposes a single centre of consciousness, an 'I' which experiences, arranges, and appropriates. It is the world of the scientist, the economist, and the man of practical commonsense. Things are related *to* as objects which are distinguished, observed, and classified in categories; especially as regards qualities and traits in terms of space, time, causality, and usefulness. The object, an It, is divorced from the subject, the I.

I observe a jam jar as one thing among many other different things in the kitchen. It is one instance of a class, 'jam jars'. Although jam jars come in different shapes and sizes, they are used for the same purpose. I relate to the jar but it is quite distinct and separate from me. I inspect it from 'outside'. I can point to, and define, a 'jam jar' in such a way that someone who has never seen one will be able to recognize it readily. In talking about jam jars my logic is 'linear' and 'literal'. The symbolism is discursive.

Freda talks about her bodily sensations and her agoraphobia and, indeed, about herself, in 'jam jar' language. The fact that experience is called 'inner' does not necessarily make it less of a thing. It all depends upon the attitude taken towards it and how it is talked about. Much introspection about experiences, emotions, ideas, and other 'contents' of the mind remains in the world of things. So does a psychology which only conceives of a man as a bundle of traits, or a collection of drives and complexes.

A relationship with a person is very different. A meeting happens *between* persons. They are unique. Fred, in the moment of encounter with George, is the sole member of a class, 'Fred', not one instance of the class 'umpire'. A meeting is a simultaneous acting and being acted upon. It is a sharing, a dialogue, which cannot be reduced to 'I say this' and 'Thou saith that'. There is a hyphen between I and Thou. Regrettably, in recent translations of Buber, the primary word has been rendered 'I-You' with a serious loss of the force of the intimate second person singular.

The hyphen in no way implies a lack of distinction. There is not a fusion ('IThou') nor a divorce ('I/Thou'). There is separation with mutuality. I have termed this personal meeting a state of aloneness-togetherness. I can only be together with another in so far as I can be alone. I can only be alone (as distinct from being isolated and lonely) in so far as I can be together with a Thou.

A Thou is 'known' in the relationship itself. Knowing, in this sense, is not a matter of recognizing qualities. The Thou is not one thing amongst other things. The Other cannot be appropriated or bounded by me but only 'met'.

'When *Thou* is spoken, the speaker has no thing for his object. For where there is a thing there is another thing. Every *It* is bounded by others; *It* exists only through being bounded by others. But when *Thou* is spoken, there is no thing. *Thou* has no bounds.'[3]

The Thou has no bounds but yet there is a sense of a centre: analogous, perhaps, to the visual field, a 'seeing'. A meeting is experienced as total – as a whole.

Buber stresses the importance of 'speaking' primary hyphenated 'words'. He is not referring merely to speech but rather to ways of living, of relating, in different 'worlds'.

'Primary words do not signify things, but they intimate relations . . . .
Primary words do not describe something that might exist inde-
pendently of them, but being spoken they bring about existence . . . .
Primary words are spoken from the being . . . The primary word *I-
Thou* can only be spoken with the whole being.'[4]

Following Wittgenstein, I shall term these two 'languages' *forms of life*, which I regard as akin to some existentialist notions such as modes of 'being-in-the-world' or 'being-towards-others'.[5]

'Knowing' a person and 'knowing about' a thing are distinct forms of life. They are realized, or to put it more dramatically, are 'incarnated' in different languages. If I describe a jam jar to a visitor from a sour, jamless, far-distant planet he will very soon be able to say 'That is a jam jar.' It is a very different matter with a word like 'love'. Love is a growing word. We only 'grow' into further apprehensions of its meaning. It would not only be meaningless but also inappropriate to say 'I love you' to a jam jar.[6]

The language of the world of things is literal and discursive whereas person-talk calls for a 'language of the heart', which I term feeling-language. In order to 'disclose' to someone what I mean by 'I love you', I would have to tell stories: first one story, then another story, and another, and another, until the 'ice breaks' or 'the penny drops'. The 'disclosure' or 'discernment' calls for a language which is more akin to an art form, with symbols which do not merely point to discrete things, but rather 'present' a mode of being. A language not of 'facts' but of feeling.

The cricketers stroll off the field at the tea interval. Fred walks up to George, pokes him in the midriff, and with a chuckle asks 'How're things, Georgie Porgy, you old crate-egg?' His question involves two common features of feeling-language, a personal name and a shared metaphor.

The logic of names will be discussed in Chapter 5. Here, it is to be noted that, except in those social groups where the use of first names has become a mere convention, 'George' is more personal than 'Mr Ash-worth'. The nickname 'Georgie Porgy' is much more so. Maybe, it has some factual reference:

Georgie Porgy pudding and pie
Kissed the girls and made them cry;
When the boys came out to play
Georgie Porgy ran away.

It could be that George had a taste for fattening foods and was shy with girls. But, the nickname is not a means of extending the range of facts. It is person-logic, giving depth to a characteristically personal situation. Almost factually empty names such as 'Chick' and 'Honeybunch' can disclose love. It was an important turning-point in the therapy of Helen, a very seriously disturbed girl, when, for her, I changed from 'Dr Hobson' to 'Uncle Bob'.

The cricket match was being played on the ground of an upper-class club somewhere near Surbiton, far away from the Lancashire valley where Fred and George had played in childhood. None of the southerners could discern the meaning of 'crate-egg'. It was private to the two friends. The metaphor, no doubt implying the inferiority of packed eggs to those fresh from the hen, suggests that someone is a little 'cracked', and rather foolish. But, Fred does not use it as a term of abuse; the metaphor discloses its significance in a constellation of words and non-verbal statements (chuckle, 'poke'), which evoke memories of moors and mill chimneys.

Often a disclosure of, and insight into, a personal situation occurs as a sudden revelation. A chat, an interview, a friendship, or the process of psychotherapy often moves not by a gradual progression but in steps. A marked change in the interview with Freda occurred with the emergence of a metaphor. The interview was recorded on videotape and independent observers have had no difficulty in agreeing about the striking difference between two phases of the conversation before and after three vital minutes.

The last sentence highlights the difficulties of giving an accurate account of interpersonal events. A recording can be inspected from 'outside' with a reliable description of defined behaviours and patterns of communication. This is the language of the It. Maybe observers can infer that a personal meeting has occurred and note its effects. But an attempt to express the disclosure-experience of I-Thou calls for a different language, one spoken from 'inside'. In the following story I shall adopt an uneasy compromise by using a verbatim transcript together with a few comments about my own understanding and feelings.

A therapeutic dialogue involves the use of varied languages. Buber stresses that every human Thou must become an It; but to speak of, and to act towards, another as if their reality consisted only in his or her being simply a He or a She (an It) is disloyalty to the truth of the meeting with the Thou. Then, there is alienation with a loss of mutuality, trust, and personal exploration. For Buber, knowing a person is what it means to be a human being: 'All real living is meeting', 'Where there is no sharing, there is no reality'.[7]

At the same time, it is essential to study a human being as an It, by means of inspection and classification. The fabric of a relationship is a tapestry woven by the weft of person-language and the warp of thing-language. A psychotherapist needs to learn to work the loom of language.

AN EMPTY HEART

Almost in passing, Freda, who is forty-eight, casually mentions that her mother died a week previously. She will miss her because she needs a companion – but, of course, that is only because of the 'agoraphobia'. I catch a shaded note of anger. I am not sure. I say that I suppose her mother's death must have affected her deeply.

Imperturbably, Freda confesses that her mother's death was a 'shock', and ends a long circumstantial account with the words:

Freda   'It just seems to be bottled up. And I feel guilty over that, as though there's something wrong with me – that I should be crying and yet I just can't cry.'

R.F.H.   'Well, I think you *are* feeling a lot *inside*.'

As I say these words, I move towards her speaking with my hands. My fingers move back and forwards between my tummy and hers. I then point to the space between us.

Freda   'Inside, yes, but I . . . I just can't cry. It was the same when my dad died, and my husband. I found him dead in bed, although it was an unhappy marriage, and, er, my mother, and, er, I just can't cry. I want, I feel as though I should, but I can't.'

There is a tremor in Freda's voice – just a trembling hint of emotion. I respond, wondering what she is experiencing right now. Here, with me. Now.

R.F.H.   'Mm. Yes.'

A transcript cannot do justice to the infinite varieties of 'Mm' and the multitude of meanings that are born from them. I remember when *I* was not able to weep, and scenes from the past are joined together in complex shapes with profound feelings of loss and guilt. I can only hope that my 'Mm', will convey the 'tone' of these imaginary forms which are re-creating my own autobiography in response to Freda, as a person. Now. Perhaps it might strike a chord – call forth an echo – somewhere deep down inside her. I remember other occasions in therapy, when a long drawn-out 'Ah' has been heard as something like a melody, or even a fugue with a harmonizing of different verbal, tonal, and non-verbal 'voices'. In conversation we use many channels of communication hoping for a resolution of discords. A psychotherapist needs assiduous practice in using the wide-ranging language of 'Mm'. It can be a highly imaginative creation.

Freda's words come slowly and softly with an eloquent sigh.

Freda   'There's . . . this terrible empty feeling I've got inside.'

Freda moves. For the first time, she moves fluently. Her hand now rests on her chest. She pauses. Only for a moment – a brief but rare silence. I speak with my hands, gently moving them up and down with palms towards her. Trying to say something like, 'Let's stay with that feeling. Just stay with it. Let it happen and see what emerges.' When I feel that I know what it could feel like in my own heart, then I speak quietly.

R.F.H.   'Sort of . . . empty.'

I repeat her word 'empty', and yet it is not a mere repetition. There is a different inflection contributed by me. My tone is more 'empty'. In responding, I am amplifying, not merely reflecting.

Freda's lips tremble. I hear sadness in her hesitant words.

Freda   'Empty. Just empty.'

We now share a feeling-image.

I must not allow the silence to last too long. I sense that Freda is becoming tense – scared perhaps; going over the top of the stress curve. She is finding it hard to bear and she might block. By now, I have become aware of recurrent patterns, especially of how she switches to long descriptions of her precious 'agoraphobia' whenever the topic becomes tinged with emotion and her anxiety mounts. Avoiding fear I suppose.

I discover that my right hand is over my heart.

R.F.H.   'You put your hand about here.'

Freda repeats my movement and her words come with a new gentleness.

Freda   'Just about here. Emptiness.'
R.F.H.   'Mm.'

I pray that the 'Mm' expresses sympathy – a feeling-with.

I seem to hear the first chord of an emerging theme – a body-word metaphor 'empty heart'. The 'commanding form' of a symphony can be suggested by the first phrase of the first movement.

We speak at the same time. A meeting is disclosed. Alone and together, looking into a void.

Freda   'Just empty.'

R.F.H.   'Just as if there is nothing there at all.'

My phrase 'just as if' is more an analogy than a metaphor. But, I am 'seeing' a system forming from a constellation of messages ('I can't cry', 'I feel guilty') together with a host of slight non-verbal cues which convey sadness, frustration, and anger. I decide to try out my hunch. It is, perhaps, too pretentious to speak of 'putting an hypothesis to the test' but, as well as hoping for mutuality, I maintain a quasi-scientific attitude.

R.F.H.   'Let me make a guess . . . er . . . I think that there are times . . . when you feel bad . . . that you can't love people enough.'

I introduce a new, odd, indefinable word 'love' which means whatever it means in the context of a particular, unique developing conversation of a few moments or of a lifetime.

Freda   'That's just it.'

Freda's tone of voice and expression suggest that the word 'love' has been 'carried alive into the heart'. There is some non-verbal amplification (extension) of what I say; but I am cautious. By this time there is ample evidence that she is a person who is prone to placatory agreement. I pursue that metaphor, albeit wrongly.

R.F.H.   'You see . . . you say there's a gap in your heart.'

Freda has not said that at all . . . not yet. Her words were 'as if I've no heart'. Here, I am intruding my own idiosyncratic image and forcing it by 'You see . . . you say'. I have not listened.

Fortunately, Freda does not block. Later, she speaks of an 'empty heart' but, at this point, she takes up the word 'love' and extends it with the words 'fear' and 'guilt'.

Freda   'I feel as though there's no love here somehow [hand over heart]. And my husband or my mother, although we got on very well, and I thought a lot of her but I just feel as though I've no love. And, er, it's a horrible fear. I feel terribly *guilty* about it . . . terribly guilty about it. It's just as though here it's just empty. Absolutely empty. And I keep thinking . . . well there must be something wrong with me. I mustn't be normal 'cos I should be crying and I'm not. And I feel as though I should be crying and I'm not and yet I don't seem to be able to show them love.'

Freda's voice becomes more musical as it changes pitch, rhythm, and tempo. Her words fail, but she continues to 'talk' by moving her hands and arms offering something to me. Some sort of gift. I am slow to understand the language and my response is vague.

R.F.H.   'No, but you were wanting to show something then, with your hands.'

Freda   'Yes, I wanted to, I want to show them love and yet I don't feel love *here*, and I know I should do. It doesn't seem natural. It's not natural is it?'

As Freda says 'I don't feel love here' she once more puts a hand on her heart, repeating the metaphor non-verbally.

Later in this session Freda's tears flow as she 'sees' me looking 'just like' her beloved 'Dad'.

BEING A PERSON

That fragment of my conversation with Freda illustrates a number of technical points introduced in Chapter 1: the importance of non-verbal language, staying with feeling, the maintenance of optimum anxiety (stress), the correction of mistakes, the 're-writing of an autobiography', amplification, togetherness in the space-between, and the formulation of hypotheses which call for the attitudes and skills of both scientist and artist. These all occur within the context of a personal meeting.

I shall summarize by a brief recapitulation of six qualities of a personal relationship which are at the heart of conversational therapy: it happens between experiencing subjects, it can only be known from 'within', it is mutual, it involves aloneness-togetherness, its language is a disclosure of private 'information', and it is shared here and now.

A Relationship Happens between Two Experiencing Subjects

The important distinction is between Freda talking *with* me as a person and Freda talking *about* things (remembering that 'inner' events can be related to as things).

To 'know about' a thing is a very different matter from 'knowing' an experiencing being. I could say to Freda 'I really don't know what is going on inside you – where you are,' but it would be very odd for me to address these words to a jam jar, or even to a computer. Two quite distinct attitudes, two 'worlds', are embodied in different languages: person-language (I-Thou) and thing-language (I and It).

In Order to Know What a Person Is, I Must Be a Person

That is to say, the meaning of 'personal' can only be apprehended by experiencing a relationship.

To talk about a relationship from 'outside': to describe and classify it as, say, 'dependent' or 'sadomasochistic', may be of some help in pointing to a way for exploration. But, an infant, a lover, a patient, or a therapist can learn to relate more fully to another person only from within a relationship. One can learn that there is a word 'friendship' but yet be puzzled about what a 'friend' is.[8] I can only know Freda by engaging in a personal conversation with her.

The above statements are at once obvious and puzzling. How does the notion of a person arise in the first place, and why is it absent in some human beings, such as autistic children? How do we apprehend someone else's experience: what is the nature of empathy? We shall be forced to consider these and other enigmas.

In order to be able to engage in personal problem-solving, I need to know through experience what it is to be in a situation which involves feeling which we call 'personal'. In order to perceive Freda as a person, as distinct from a thing, I must have a prior notion (idea, conception, construct, or schema) of what a person is, and what kind of relationship can exist between Freda and me.

Knowing Is Mutual

In a personal relationship, there is a shared commitment – mutual action, a simultaneous acting and being acted upon. Words are inadequate. We need body-language. The struggle to discover a mutual language in a ten-year psychoanalysis, in a chat in a pub, or being together in building a sand-castle, is what it means to engage in a relationship.

To Know a Person Is to Be Alone and Yet Together

A personal dialogue both expresses and promotes a relationship of aloneness-togetherness. There is an apprehension of distinction and of mutuality, of autonomy and of reciprocity, of identity and of sharing.

In egocentric pre-rational thinking there is no clear separation: no togetherness, no recognition of, and sensitivity to, the feelings and point of view of the other. A childlike sense of 'fusion', of non-differentiated union, is very different from being an individual-in-relationship; an encounter over and against, as well as a sympathetic feeling-with, another. There are times when we need to say 'Do be my Enemy for Friendship's sake.'[9]

Aloneness-togetherness involves explicit and implicit rules. Every intimate relationship has special requirements and necessary limits which vary from situation to situation. The relationship of psychotherapy is not more nor less intimate than a friendship: it is different. The rules are not immutable: they are modified in negotiation by persons genuinely choosing, and adjusting.

There Is a Mutual Private Disclosure

In aloneness-togetherness two experiencing subjects commit themselves to a meeting. They disclose themselves in a shared language.

In a personal conversation, there is a communication of private information. Confidences, not usually made public, are exchanged. We tell our close friends about secret hopes, fears, and sexual escapades and are open to receive their stories. In psychotherapy, for the most part, such confessions are one-way: there is an asymmetry. It is not the job of a therapist to burden a patient with details of his or her problems.

But, confession does not in itself make a personal relationship. Indeed, the topic might be very public: such as the details of the Test Match debated with Sam (Chapter 1). But, there is a sharing of 'feeling-information' – a mutuality. The 'how' is more important than the 'what'. A personal conversation means a two-way disclosure of feeling.

Dialogue arises and grows in the space between persons. By an act of imagination, the experiences of a lifetime are dissolved and re-created in a reciprocal language of feeling which is presented and shared now, at this moment. The episode with Freda is a life-story in a few moments. A conversation, in which I know and am known, needs a special language with forms of feeling akin to those of art – poetry, painting, music, and dance.

In my conversation with Freda, disparate images, sensations, emotions, and actions come together. A vague sensation in her chest, movements of our hands, 'no heart', 'no love', are integrated in a new form – a voice of feeling, for which I have used the analogies of music and poetry. Freda and I share the word 'empty'. It is a mutual creation; meeting in a private world, looking into a void. Together, and yet alone. New shapes, new wholes are created in figurative language. A fresh metaphor, a living symbol, 'Dad', is expressed in a flow of tears.

I can only try to express a state of feeling by telling 'stories'. 'We stand on the edge of a void in one gaze'. If that does not 'click' I can try another: 'our empty hearts beat together, lonely in a darkness'. I may need another, another, and another, in the hope that the penny may drop. Poor and purple poetry, perhaps, but it is the language of psychotherapy. A central form is the fresh metaphor.

A psychotherapist may or may not be a hard scientist; but, he cannot avoid trying to be a kind of artist. His task is to assist in discovering a precise expression for personal feeling, for a 'felt-meaning' in, and between, himself and his client.

In my talk with Freda I am concerned with relating words to the evocative language of the body, but that does not mean translating one into the other. To speak of 'figurative language' does not imply that the 'real' meaning lies somewhere else in a 'literal' definition.

Wittgenstein writes of his relation to a friend:

> 'My attitude towards him is an attitude towards a soul. I am not of the *opinion* that he has a soul .... The human body is the best picture of the human soul.
>
> And how about such an expression as: "In my heart I understood when you said that", pointing to one's heart? Does one, perhaps, not *mean* this gesture? Of course one means it. Or is one conscious of using a *mere* figure? Indeed not. – It is not a figure that we choose, not a simile, yet it is a figurative expression.'[10]

To speak of Freda's gesture as 'putting her hand on an empty heart full of tears' is a figurative expression and yet it is not a 'mere' figure consciously chosen as adornment. It is a symbol which both points to and shares in a relatively unknown 'experiencing'.

The word 'intimated' appears again and again in this book. In the brief clinical example, we can catch a glimpse of how an 'empty feeling inside', 'bottled up' tears, and pregnant words such as 'guilt' and 'fear' about not being able to give love, progressively relate to each other in a personal dialogue and evoke a new insight.

The meaning of insight, with a sense of 'seeing as a whole', cannot be expressed in any language but, in a rare moment, its significance can be 'disclosed'. As stories interweave, it might happen that the 'light dawns', 'the ice breaks', and 'the penny drops'. Discernment of personal experience, disclosure of meaning, and an act of commitment are features of a mutual feeling-language.

Although the significance of feeling-language cannot be exhausted by objective description and definition it does have an important empirical reference. It is tied to observable 'facts'. Using the language of communication, independent observers can come to a measure of agreement about how Freda and I behave, and describe this in terms of cues ('Freda's lips tremble') and of messages ('I hear sadness in her hesitant words'). Changes can be observed in the nature of an interview as, for example, before and after the few minutes described above. Indeed, an observer who has himself experienced a personal relationship can make a guess about whether or not others are involved in a meeting. But, the vocabulary of communication (as that term is used here) is very different from that of dialogue.

There is communication in a game of chess with a computer, but it would be hardly appropriate for the player to address the machine as 'darling' except with a humorous use of an explicit and far-flung metaphor. In the conversation with Freda there was communication in the first part of the interview. This led on to dialogue and provided conditions for a moment of meeting.

I-Thou; I and It. Both are necessary. In order to become persons we need jam jar language, but we cannot become persons *in* it.

All too often, well-meaning, spontaneous 'humanism' becomes an avoidance of disciplined observation. Thing-language (such as is provided by careful inspection and measurement of videotapes by independent observers) provide illuminating signposts and necessary, salutory checks. But it can never define what it means to be a person-in-relationship.

Experiencing a Personal Relationship Is Always Here and Now

The topic, the 'what', might be past events but accounts are reformed and enlivened in a present that is always moving into the future.

This book is an amplification of the theme of learning and growing in a personal conversation. That is the heart of psychotherapy. Psychodynamic formulations and explanatory interpretations can be learned in a few weeks, but to master the minute particulars of a feeling dialogue is the unattainable ideal of a lifetime.

Problems, the roots of which lie in disturbances of personal relationships, can only be detected, explored, and healed *within* a mutual relationship of two experiencing subjects who are alone and together. Inspection and classification are essential to provide possibilities, checks, and limits, but can never create conditions for the solution of personal problems. If I am to discover what it means to go on becoming a person I must *be* a person sharing, and failing to share, a language of feeling with another, here and now.

A crucial phrase is 'experiencing subjects'. It calls for elaboration.

· 3 ·
EXPERIENCE

The Hasidic leader, Rabbi Hanokh, retold an old jest.

'There was once a man who was very stupid. When he got up in the morning it was so hard for him to find his clothes that at night he almost hesitated to go to bed for thinking of the trouble he would have on waking. One evening he finally made a great effort, took paper and pencil and as he undressed noted down exactly where he put everything he had on. The next morning, very well pleased with himself, he took the slip of paper in his hand and read: "cap" – there it was, he set it on his head; "pants" – there they lay, he got into them; and so it went on until he was fully dressed. "That's all very well, but now where am I myself?" he asked in great consternation. "Where in the world am I?" He looked and looked, but it was a vain search; he could not find himself. And that is how it is with us.'[1]

I remember the rabbi's story as I wonder how I can join in a conversation with Joe Smith, a successful shop steward. My mind wanders away from the long psychiatric history, from the catalogued 'caps' and 'pants' of clinical signs, behaviour patterns, and introspective formulations. 'Where is Joe and where in the world am I . . . where am I myself?'

It is my first meeting with Mr Joseph Smith. For the last few months he has been depressed and has had fainting attacks for which no organic cause has been found. But just now, I do not want to make a list of so-called 'facts' about him. I want to begin to know a person.

Our handshake is very one-sided. His fingers are limp and there is no answering pressure to my slight squeeze. There is no conversation. That does not mean that Mr Smith has not said anything. He has said a great deal, and his body-language becomes more eloquent as he sits down rigidly erect with arms tightly folded, and stares out of the window. I want to achieve and to express some understanding of what he is experiencing *now* – at this moment. Seeing him perched on the edge of his chair, I try out a crude metaphor.

'I feel you are all on edge,' I say. 'It's an odd situation, coming to see a chap like me.'

He shifts slightly but that is all. I try again.

'I reckon it's not easy to put into words but I'd like to know something about the problem . . . about the sort of thing you would like help with.'

Perhaps it is too early to enquire 'about' a problem but I hope also to convey my wish to understand something, however little, of what it is like to *be* him now.

Mr Smith shuts his eyes, screws up his face, drops his head, and, unfolding his arms, twists his fingers on his forehead as if trying to bore a hole.

His gestures are eloquent but there are no words. I note signs of increasing tension. He seems to be getting into a panic, and I do not want his fear to block him. Hoping to lower his anxiety by communicating my wish to understand, I make a guess at what he is experiencing.

'It's hell when you . . . when you just can't get anything out,' I suggest.

He puts me right, speaking with desperation.

'No . . . no . . . There's nothing . . . nothing there. They say I do my job . . . but it's not *my* job. Like a machine getting the figures right. A thing moving about. I can't carry on – there is no "me". Nothing inside . . . I am nowhere.'

Mr Smith drops his hand and looks at me. He looks for a response.

I now feel that a conversation has begun. But I am unsure how to proceed.

'Mm,' I respond.

I do not know what I am saying, but it is something like 'Well, I reckon I know something of how that feels.'

Joe Smith sighs.

'I feel . . . queer.'

The word 'queer' has a puzzled, tentative sound. Perhaps it expresses an important experience which we could explore in a personal conversation.

In this chapter, amplifying the notion of 'personal', I shall consider the words 'experiencing', 'experience', 'action', and 'act'. The argument and terminology are greatly influenced by the work of E.T. Gendlin,[2] R. Schafer,[3] L. Wittgenstein,[4] J.L. Austin,[5] S. Hampshire,[6] and R. Harré and P.F. Secord.[7] I have borrowed freely, but at many points my formulation differs radically from all of these writers.

EXPERIENCING

Sit in silence for one minute and ask yourself, 'What am I experiencing?' 'How am I now, at this moment?' Do not try to answer in words. Just let things be. Feel what is happening – now.

How can I express my immediate experience? I cannot – not all of it. A multitude of changing sensations, emotions, concrete and elusive images, words, phrases, memories, ideas, and thoughts emerge. There are also 'felt-meanings'. Some are relatively explicit, others hazy or emerging. And there is an overall sense of what it means to be 'I'. Living now in a flow of experiencing. J.C. Powys imagines this 'life-sensation in itself' as a baffling, evasive fish which is never caught,

> 'the slippery, quivering, darting, doubly-electrified salmon-trout-nerve of the 'Richard is Richard, Annie is Annie' self – that loving-hating, spring-heel Jack within us that makes the world go round!'[8]

Yet, despite the multiplication of adjectives and hyphens, he cannot say what he means; and nor can Joe Smith.

I shall list four features of experiencing: it is pre-conceptual; it is a body-feeling; it is 'in relation to'; and it moves in time.[9]

1 Experiencing is incommunicable. No words, gestures, or actions can exhaust it. It is *pre-conceptual*. Units and patterns can be differentiated endlessly – my fuzzy head, this room, the sensations in my chest, worries about yesterday and tomorrow, fleeting memories, and indistinct emotions. Trains of thought, words, movements, pictures, or even phrases of music might emerge out of it. But, no verbal or non-verbal expression of the complexity and interrelatedness of such particular experiences can convey the immediacy of the raw, sensed-and-felt stuff of awareness: the 'just there-ness'.

Although particular delineated experiences, such as I have just pointed to, are only aspects of the boundless flow of experiencing, they have a 'felt-meaning' which can intimate a greater whole. They may become symbols.

Joe Smith symbolizes felt-meaning by the words 'queer' and 'like a machine', by twisting his fingers on his forehead, and in many other ways. The word 'symbol' is used here in a very broad sense. It can be a picture, an action, a physical object, or a situation. It is anything that refers to, or expresses, a part of experience in such a way that we can attend to it. Later, I shall distinguish very different modes of symbolization, and different ways of attending.

Experiencing is a kind of knowing, and not only of oneself. Think of someone you know well, George or Jane. You get a sense of George as a whole. You do not add up separate characteristics: height, tone of voice, quick temper, and fondness for snooker. There is an awareness of George.

2   Experiencing is *felt in the body*. But, 'in' is not an adequate word. I mean a concrete sense of the 'life' of 'my' body, as felt from 'inside'. A sense of being in a place, or of knowing a person, is a 'gut' feeling. I have a vast amount of information about George which can be spelled out, at least up to a point. But no amount of catalogued description can exhaust the meaning of my felt-sense, my experiencing of 'George' in my body.

3   Experiencing is *in relation to* things, persons, and situations. I am 'afraid of', I 'hope for', I 'am angry at'. Experience is not 'inside' nor is it 'outside'. Existentialists use hyphenated phrases (such as 'being-in-the-world') in an attempt to transcend the limitations of prose, and we have already considered Buber's 'primary words', I-Thou and I-It.

4   In the flow of experiencing, the past is taken up as an experience which is *immediately present*. If I weep for a rejection of twenty years ago, it is happening *now*. But (and this is more important) it is guided by the *future*. My experience, now, is shaped by my anticipations, what I envisage: what shall be, what might be, what I hope for.

Experiencing is not static. There is movement. If I can stay awhile with raw experiencing, if I can wait attentively; then, perhaps, with luck or grace, a new possibility might emerge: a movement, a carrying forward.

THE PROCESS OF THERAPY

'I feel queer'.

'Queer' denotes an experience: it is a symbol, intimating experiencing which is felt by Joe in his body. I want him to stay with the feeling: to stay in touch with it, to rest in it.

Later, we may discover new symbols which can be amplified in relation to persons, things, and situations, here and now in the interview, and in Joe's wider life. Then, perhaps, we can carry forward.

I respond to Joe. That is my responsibility.

'Let's stay with that feeling. Maybe something will emerge.'

We sit in silence for a moment or two. Joe mutters:

'It's just strange. Mixed up like.'

Silence. Joe's body becomes more and more tense. I feel tense too. I sense fear; I am not sure where, perhaps in my chest. I shift uneasily and my hand moves to my heart. I mutter.

'I feel . . . feel . . . it is scaring.'

'Well yeah . . . yeah . . . a part of it . . . but . . . yeah, something like that.'

Joe sits back and relaxes a bit. There has been a kind of shift: just a small step of feeling.

In an interview some weeks later a similar feeling recurs.

Joe says:

'I have got something like that queer feeling, odd and a bit scaring. I am stuck with it.'

'Odd? I reckon, you are scared like you talked about when you . . . when as a lad you first went to work?' I suggest.

'Yeah, I did then and, before that, going to school leaving Mum at the door.'

Joe pauses, self-absorbed. He begins to shift uneasily. I lean forward, nearer to him, opening my fingers wide. He goes on.

'It makes me feel sort of wobbly in my middle. Now. Scared, yeah . . . but excited a bit . . . something new. Not knowing about . . . not knowing where.'

Another pause.

Joe sighs and smiles – a soft smile.

'Yeah, wobbly, that's just bang on.'

His hand moves to his tummy.

'Wobbly like trying to walk . . . like a child I mean.'

Joe sighs . . . a deep sigh. A tear trickles down as he smiles. It is not often that we get 'bang on' in therapy. When we do there is a feeling of release, a bodily – yet more than bodily – sense of significance, of meaning. Things come together in a new shape. There is 'insight' – a 'seeing into' or 'feeling into'. It is active. It carries our experience forward in a movement guided by the future. Out of 'wobbly' emerges a possibility of being able to 'walk'.

In the progress of psychotherapy, and in the growth of human relationships, there are three important activities: staying with experiencing, carrying forward, and conversation which involves action.

Staying With

A new experience, intimated by the tear trickling down Joe's cheek, emerges from the specific mode of experiencing now, as he and I share the symbol 'wobbly'. At this point, my task, as with Freda in the previous chapter, is not to explain but to attend; to remain in touch with, and to value, the experience as intimating what is as yet unknown. To be ready to receive what will emerge and lead forward. Following Jung, I have called this expectant waiting, a symbolical attitude.[10]

Carrying Forward

Goals emerge from immediate experiencing. Potentialities are realized by possibilities inherent in, and created out of, the present state of feeling.

In the short extract from the talk with Joe Smith there is a carrying-forward: 'queer' . . . 'mixed up like' . . . 'scaring' . . . 'something like that' . . . 'relaxation' . . . 'odd and a bit scaring' . . . 'leaving Mum' . . . 'wobbly'. There are steps of feeling, personal makings, within a continuous bodily-felt process of change.

In therapy and, indeed, in education, the manner in which steps are taken is more important than the content. Learning *how* to move forward is more important than learning about the 'what'. The steps must be the right 'height'. They must allow a person to remain in touch with his raw, pre-conceptual experiencing ('staying with', 'letting it happen', 'waiting with attentiveness'). Symbol formation occurs when shifts in experience are neither too big nor too abrupt, nor merely repetitive.

If Joe responds to his 'queer' feeling by saying 'Oh, I must shake it off, I feel great,' then he will probably lose touch with it. Not staying with the experience, he tries to leap ahead. If he says 'It's my illness, it's always like that, just queer,' then he distances himself from the experience. He objectifies himself – like a thing. If referred to as 'my illness' the sensation can become detached, fixed and repetitive, a state of affairs which occurs not infrequently in response to a theoretically 'correct' explanatory interpretation which is wrong if it is too 'far away'.

Joe's experiencing is the main concern. Not mine. But my own feeling plays a large part in discovering the apt verbal and non-verbal symbols – 'wobble', 'walk', the expanding fingers. The right word, sound, or gesture is one which indicates, expresses, and carries forward his specific experience. Yet symbolization happens in a relationship. Joe and I, alone and together, have been searching for the next step which will ensure both continuity and change. Carrying forward happens in a conversation.

The Therapist-in-Conversation

'It's hell when you . . . when you just can't get anything out.' 'It makes *me* feel sort of wobbly in my middle.' Such apparently simple statements, spoken with appropriate inflection and at the right time in response to Joe's language, are extremely complex. They intimate something of what I have made, and failed to make, of the experiences of a lifetime.

What Rilke says of verses applies to every understanding intervention in psychotherapy — and in friendship:

> 'verses . . . are experiences. In order to write a single verse, one must see many cities, and men and things; one must get to know animals and the flight of birds, and the gestures that the little flowers make when they open out to the morning. One must be able to return in thought to roads in unknown regions, to unexpected encounters, and to partings that had long been foreseen; to days of childhood that are still indistinct, and to parents whom one had to hurt when they sought to give some pleasure which one did not understand. . . . There must be memories of many nights of love, each one unlike the others, of the screams of women in labour, and of women in childbed, light and blanched and sleeping, shutting themselves in. But one must also have been beside the dying, must have sat beside the dead in a room with open windows and fitful noises. And still it is not yet enough to have memories. One must be able to forget them when they are many and one must have the immense patience to wait until they come again. For the memories themselves are not yet experiences. Only when they have turned to blood within us, to glance and gesture, nameless and no longer to be distinguished from ourselves — only then can it happen that in a most rare hour the first word of a poem arises in their midst and goes forth from them.'[11]

Cities and men and things; animals, birds, and little flowers opening in the morning; encounters and partings; hurting parents; nights of love; women in childbed shutting themselves in; the dying and the dead. Memories forgotten and patience in waiting for them to emerge in a new form, turned to blood within us, to glance and gesture — part of ourselves.

The therapist is a person-in-relationship. He is what he has made of his experiences. What counts is not what has happened to him but what he has created from what has happened to him. All too often the pronouncement 'In *my* experience . . .' is a justification for repeating our mistakes.

To share in a dialogue which carries forward, means that the therapist is open to immediate experiencing in relation to the patient, ready to reassess and revalue past experiences, to scrutinize them, let them go, and to have the 'immense patience' to wait until they are turned to blood. The way in which he enters into a conversation, his genuineness, is more important than his theoretical framework, his concepts, his explanations, or his classifications.

Learning in a personal relationship means knowing and being known. The therapist is committed to a relationship, and he must be willing to be lived with, now. The patient must find his own implicit steps forward but can only do so *within* a relationship in which the therapist risks himself. The discoveries are made in the act of relating – not in talking about a problem but being together in it. In a conversation, whatever *I* feel is in some way related to the other – in some way.

Those categorical statements are open to serious misunderstanding. The therapeutic relationship is mutual as regards expression of feeling. But it is also asymmetrical. The therapist is involved but also to some extent non-attached. He should enjoy himself and yet not seek gratification at the expense of his client. He is open in relation to this particular person now, at this moment, and his responses should be congruent with the goals of therapy, the agreed problems. He does not express what he does not genuinely feel. But that is not to say that he gives vent to every fleeting emotion. 'Feeling', as the word is used in this book, involves balanced judgment.

Genuineness is always related to a situation. With Joe, I am, or should be, a genuine therapist, not a genuine husband or a genuine cricketer. One of Joe's problems is that he can no longer be a genuine shop steward.

On at least one occasion, what I regard as being appropriate genuineness proves to be harmful.

Joe is going on and on about the minute details of union business. These are important matters, but I get bored. He is a good politician and can certainly talk once he gets started.

I feel out of touch, and try to help him to relate what he is saying to his immediate experiencing.

'Yeah! It's difficult to keep to the party line. I reckon you are feeling bad about it now.'

Joe reflects about the ethics of differentials. I interrupt.

'Look, Joe, I'm bored.'

I intend to say 'I feel this talk is boring, because it is not coming from your middle' but he hears 'You, Joe Smith, are a boring person'. It transpires later that he feels attacked and, for a moment, almost destroyed. My remark is persecuting.

Joe blocks and gets into a panic which does not subside by the end of the session. Next day he feels too scared to go to work.

Some weeks later, shortly before I am going on holiday, he once more begins to make a speech. This time I respond differently.

'Joe, you know this way of talking makes me feel bored. I can't get the feeling. I reckon you want to stop me getting into it.'

'Yeah', he replies. 'Yeah – yeah. I suppose there is something or other.'

'Well,' I respond. 'Let's both shut up for a bit and be quiet. Sit back and rest a bit inside. Let things happen.'

There is a need for silence. After a few minutes, he speaks.

'Sad, that's it. Sad. But now ... as the sadness *comes* ... well ... it seems different ... and ... and ... you are not going away for too long.'

It is naive and dangerous to pretend that a therapist, or a friend for that matter, can always be absolutely 'open'. An expression of anger can be devastating for some patients, and for some husbands, at certain times. Yet, our clients can often accept much more than we give them credit for, and to patronize is, perhaps, one of the worst things a therapist, or a parent, can do.

Worst of all, is when we are impelled by a moral imperative to say what we feel. Then we are likely either to give a wrong impression or to deny our experience; to avoid thinking of what we 'needs must feel'.[12] A psychotherapist has a responsibility to try to become more and more aware of himself, but that means facing the stark fact that, despite good intentions, he will always cheat himself in one way or another and, inevitably, cheat his patient.

Joe Smith is a unique person: he is also a shop steward and a patient. In order to be a person he must play all these parts. But, if he becomes encased or imprisoned by one label he progressively alienates himself from his own experiencing. He says:

'No ... no ... There's nothing ... nothing there. They say I do my job ... but it's not my job. Like a machine getting the figures right. A thing moving about. I can't carry on – there is no "*me*". Nothing inside ... I am nowhere.'

It is only when Joe becomes able to stay with, to rest in, his feelings of emptiness or nothingness that he can discover an implicit meaning. There is 'something more' and he becomes able to live beyond the void.

But the ending is not always so happy. Perhaps no amount of personal experiencing can altogether overcome the alienation arising from damage in early childhood and from life in a competitive-acquisitive society. Yet we cannot set limits to the creative potentialities of experiencing.

The conversation of psychotherapy involves doing: responsible acting with choice and commitment. There are times when it is imperative to say to Joe Smith: 'Look! You can go on just experiencing here for ever with me, but it's high time you did something about those problems with your boss and the party. I don't know what. Only you can choose.'

The interview is a part of living. The important question is how its manner is similar to, or different from, what happens, or fails to happen, in the patient's wider life; how the person *makes* himself or herself through the activity of his life: what are his actions, how does he act?

Change requires activity, action, and act.

ACTION

A serious defect in much psychological theorizing is the neglect of the first-person 'I', which is always a subject. To speak in the third-person about 'the ego' can be to treat a human being as if he were a thing-like collection of objectified structures and impulses – an It. Such formulations have profound implications for clinical practice.

A person is not a thing propelled by uncontrollable forces, whether 'inner' instincts or 'outer' conditioning. It is important to distinguish between causes and reasons.

A *cause* implies an explanation in terms of necessary and sufficient antecedents, e.g. a particular disease is caused by the invasion of germs: Joe's depression is caused by early deprivation. Although helpful as a limited formulation, causal mechanistic accounts such as these are very incomplete explanations of human behaviour. Man often initiates action with ends in view; he anticipates, he plans, he hopes. He creates a future. He does things for a *reason*.

We see a man walk down to the bottom of the garden. We can describe his behaviour at many levels: in terms of the electrical impulses of his brain, his muscular coordination, and the posture and rhythm of his walk. We can view and speculate about his action. But we can only know his reasons if we ask him about his plans. Maybe he wants to enjoy the view, to consider the loosestrife which is scattering seeds on his rockery, or perhaps he wants to put some distance between himself and his wife.

There is no one meaningful description which is true, though there are an infinite number which are false. We need both causal and final explanations.[13] It all depends on the sort of descriptive and explanatory context we are concerned with, and how consistent and coherent this is.

Up to a point Joe's disturbance can be explained in terms of what led up to it: he had a traumatic separation from his mother, and, as an adolescent, he desperately wanted to emulate his union activist father. Such formulations, if put to him, might help to suggest that there can be some sense in the apparent nonsense of his breakdown. They might reassure him by bringing some order into present chaos. But in attempting to promote a process of carrying-forward we need another way of thinking – a different language.

In talking with Joe I am not concerned with what 'actually' happened in the past, but with how he experiences himself now; as a wobbly child learning to walk forward. He is going somewhere. What are his aims, his anticipations, his intentions, his hopes? What action can he take?

All living systems are inherently dynamic systems with *activities* directed towards an end, a goal. *Action* is a special kind of human activity. Intimated by the word 'I', it means a subjective 'owning', an acceptance of responsibility, of personal commitment.

Not all activity is action. When we run, our heart-rate increases in order to achieve a goal – an increase of oxygen to the muscles. But (except perhaps in disciplines such as yoga) this is not a controlled responsible action. There is no choice, no 'mental aim' or direction. We can (and this is important) provide conditions for such activities, e.g. go to the lavatory at certain times and wait. We can 'listen' and to some extent respond to our physical functions in many ways, but choice is limited. It is a matter of 'going along with', just as we need to go along with the current of experiencing.

The emphasis that I put upon the use of the word 'I' is of immense practical significance. There is a vast difference between what happens to a person and what is done and willed by a person. For instance, it is one thing to ascribe what I experience as being due to my 'illness', which I suffer passively as if it were beyond my control; to accept responsibility, or aim to be responsible ('I am doing this' or 'this is me') is quite another matter. In the previous chapter I emphasized the importance of 'I' in personal relationships.

In Chapter 1, I stated that a vital feature of psychotherapy is the discovery of activity in passivity with a movement into action. A symbolical attitude means, at first, a passive waiting to see what emerges from experiencing. Joe Smith accepts the experience of 'queer' as his own, not merely as an illness which he suffers. He, Joe Smith, owns the experience of 'queer'. It is not now an illness from which he suffers. There is a receptive action. He, Joe Smith, on 24 January, *is* a wobbly child leaving mum and trying to walk. Choosing to become a little child he 'sees' the world anew. He re-creates his past in a fresh shape. He steps forward.

The word 'action', as used in this book, does not necessarily imply visible movement or audible speech. To say to oneself 'I think' rather than 'a thought comes to me' is action in so far as I own the thought as being mine. Of course, to think is one kind of action, to do is quite another. Action might or might not become an act.

An act is an action made public when it is brought into relation with one or more persons. In aloneness, action is private; in togetherness there is communication and perhaps an act of sharing. A personal relationship is given a meaning which ascribes purpose, intentionality, and choice to another experiencing being.

Not all acts are appropriate, and in subsequent chapters I shall discuss various ways of acting and of 'acting out'. At this point, I merely draw attention to my suggestion to Joe that acting within his relationship with me is no substitute for dealing with his boss.

The movement from apparent passivity to action means claiming responsibility for experiences and behaviour of which we are unaware. I shall use Schafer's term 'disclaimed actions' in attempting to resolve an apparent contradiction.[14] If an action is defined in terms of 'owning' and 'willing', can I, like the Ancient Mariner, act 'unaware'?

Disclaimed Actions

Albert stands before the altar.

'I, Albert, take thee Sarah Ellen as my awful wedded wife.'

After a short deathly hush, he blushes, laughs nervously and hastily stammers 'What a silly slip of the tongue . . . of course, *lawful* wedded wife!'

The phrase 'slip of the tongue' implies two things. First, that it is the tongue that has slipped and not the person. It is as if the 'tongue' had a separate activity and could use language. Second, what has happened is a senseless accident and not an intended and meaningful action.

In some situations (such as in organic conditions which lead to aphasia or a difficulty Albert has with 'l' sounds) there could be some force in such disclaimers, but in most circumstances the phenomenon can be understood in terms of action. The psychotherapist asks himself whether *in some sense* the patient means what he says although he does not say all that he means. A slip of the tongue can usually be regarded as action, in terms of:

1 something the person has done;
2 something that is intelligible in terms of wished-for actions;
3 conflicts associated with the action and the act.

Albert thinks that he was intending to say one thing, represented by 'lawful'. What he does is to say two things, 'lawful' (as demonstrated by the context) and also 'awful'. Albert may or may not recognize the fact that he sometimes regards Sarah Ellen as 'awful' as, for instance, when she has had a gin too many. He may or may not be aware of a willed effort to ward off an impulse to say something different from, or contrary to, his 'proper' purpose (when, for instance, he feels tempted to swear loudly in church). The fact is that *he*, Albert, a person – not his tongue – says 'awful'. To some degree, by his blushing apology, he owns his action but, at the same time, he disclaims responsibility for it. Owning is a matter of degree.

Perhaps, to acknowledge that he feels Sarah Ellen as 'awful' even at times, would be contrary to Albert's notion of love and would be damaging to his self-esteem; although this recognition is not necessarily incompatible with the personal and legal commitment he is making. In any case, it is inappropriate to use private informal language in a public act. Sometimes, two actions in 'slips of the tongue' are more opposite, or 'ambivalent', than in this case.

Schafer gives an example which those of us who attend many meetings are likely to have heard more than once. 'Ladies and gentlemen, it is now my pleasure to *prevent* our distinguished speaker.'[15] We can take the consciously-intended statement 'present' as being just as sincere as his desire to 'prevent' out of envy, jealousy, or a longing for a quiet snooze. Both can be genuine. Indeed we do not have a disrupted action but rather a special kind of action — a double action. The person is responsible for the whole action-act sequence, for both sides of the conflict involved and for its incomplete solution.

I have stressed that both components of the action can be 'sincere' and 'genuine' and this insistence cannot be repeated too often. It is a disease of some psychotherapists and not a few patients to assume that the hidden action (wish, impulse, motive, or whatever) is some-how the 'real' reason and is more true. It is an assault upon a client to suggest 'You don't mean that, you *really* mean this', or 'So and so is what you *really* wanted to say'. Albert 'really' means 'lawful' and also he 'really' means 'awful'. But he has not reconciled the two actions in one and in his vow (dismissed defensively as a 'slip of the tongue') he manifests both his effort to do the proper job and also the inappro-priate action which he attempts to avoid by disclaiming it.

A slip of the tongue is a relatively simple example of how experi-ences can be denied and actions disclaimed. They may be banished from awareness but yet become manifest, obviously in some slips of the tongue but more concealed in psychological symptoms and dis-turbances of behaviour. These can usually be regarded as double actions, as indeed can many of our day-to-day acts.

During three months therapy Joe Smith and I detected, with a good deal of pain, a host of disclaimed actions. For instance, unrecognized sexual and aggressive wishes, distorted and disrupted relationships with his wife, his friends, and his work-mates. At first, they were disowned by him as alien symptoms or moods over which he had no control.

Later, he was able to say 'I want ...', 'I feel ...' and own both sides of double actions.

In order to act decisively, maintaining a coherent sense of my existence, identity, and self-esteem as a person living in a relatively ordered social and material world, I can only deal with a limited amount of experience. This is especially so when the information is, or seems to be, contradictory; when I am faced with *conflict*. I can continue to create my personal world only by some degree of exclusion, by restricting what I perceive, what I feel, and what I think. I cannot cope with everything.

If I feel that the demands made upon me are too great to be met by my resources, or if my impulses are too strong to control, then I am under *stress*, a state which is most commonly characterized by what seems to be an impossible clash between different courses of action. I become anxious, I vacillate and, as the stress increases, I become progressively paralysed in the face of increasing disorder and impending chaos. Like Hamlet my enterprises 'lose the name of action'. If I am to cope, I need to reduce an overwhelming amount of information. I must take avoidance action. Appropriate and inappropriate means of avoiding disruption of psychological functioning associated with painful conflict are key notions in psychotherapy.

In facing and exploring significant problems we need to tolerate some degree of anxiety, to function at an optimum, bearable level of stress. It is necessary to avoid too much mental pain, but if we retreat too quickly or if our means of escape are too widespread, irreversible, or only partially effective, then the result can be disabling symptoms and maladaptive behaviour. Important life-problems which remain unsolved, especially if unrecognized, give rise to unease, distress, and neurosis. The creation of a climate in which the anxiety of conflict can be borne, in such a way that avoidance actions need no longer be employed, is a central feature of psychotherapy. Then, a problem can be recognized, explored, and solved to a sufficient extent, or at least recognized as unrealistic. But it may have to be faced and lived with. We cannot be aware of everything.

The elucidation of multifarious means of avoiding the pain of conflict and of responsibility of actions and acts in personal relationships is central to the Conversational Model. The above preliminary statement is made in order to stress the clinical importance of regarding experiences and avoidance manoeuvres as actions and acts (often double actions) for which a person is responsible and needs to own if he is to solve personal problems and to grow. We are responsible for what we do unaware.

Many questions remain unanswered. For instance, if I say 'I was nice to you yesterday but now I see that I wanted to hurt you,' then I am faced with the puzzle of three seemingly different 'I's. I shall return to this and other problems raised in this brief discussion in Chapter 10. At this point, I am asserting that the notion of degrees of owning and the concepts of unadmitted, disclaimed, and unconscious actions are of great practical importance.

By focusing upon, staying with and attending to raw experiencing within a personal relationship, Joe Smith was able to distinguish, to link, and to own particular experiences. Possibilities were generated which provided alternatives for choice in moving towards the future. Taking responsibility for actions hitherto hidden in the shadows he committed himself in acts within and outside therapy. Future goals were not determined by causes; the 'facts' of the past re-created and re-ordered in the present were seen in a new light of personal reasons. In this active process of making, he felt that he was becoming more whole – more himself.

The last sentence takes us back to the rabbi's story of the stupid man: 'Where in the world am I?' . . . 'where am I myself?' The reply to the riddle lies hidden in the meaning of a personal conversation. We are confronted with the mystery of language.

· 4 ·
LANGUAGES

Mr Archibald Chip, a successful technologist, protests with a note of rising irritation.

'There is something wrong with my heart. There *must* be ... whatever those heart specialists say. The pains ... I can't bear them.'

'Yes,' I reply. 'Yes, I suppose there is ... maybe, it's broken.'

He is unimpressed but icily polite.

'I really do not follow you.'

Many doctors have talked to Mr Chip, informing him in tones of authority that his heart is sound, and patiently explaining how disturbed emotions can cause pains in the chest.

Mr Chip grips the arms of his chair. I note how his lips suddenly tighten although his face remains calm and still; I hear the measured, controlled tone of his voice. I am striving to listen to the language of his body.

'Well,' I say. "You know the way people say "He died of a broken heart!"'

Mr Chip seizes on one word, petulantly.

'Died! People don't die of broken hearts. They drop down dead with coronary thrombosis.'

I feel that Mr Chip's tone of vigorous denial is saying something important. But I am in too much of a hurry. I press too hard and too quickly.

'Maybe you are scared of dropping down dead.'

Mr Chip responds with calm superiority.

'Oh no. It never occurred to me. But do tell me more about how mind affects the body. A sort of positive feedback in cybernetic terms?'

Mr Chip's voice is even and unconcerned as he pursues his customary style of tolerant, intellectual interest in machine concepts: a mechanical, 'straight-line', discursive logic. Yet, I muse, his analogy could be a pregnant one.

The skill of a psychotherapist lies in his ability to learn the language of his patient, and to help in creating a mutual language – a personal conversation. I shall return to the story of Mr Chip after a brief discussion of language.

LANGUAGE-GAMES

Language is the means by which human beings live together within the common life of a culture. In, and through, language an individual becomes more aware of himself as a unique person-in-relationships: of his distinctiveness, growth, and of varied moments of aloneness-togetherness in intimate relationships, in families, in small groups, and in society. Throughout his development a person uses, and is used by, a multitude of diverse and yet related forms of experience and action: of interrelated signals and symbols from which a more or less integrated personal language is progressively created.

Consider the following: describing a dinner party; expressing a wild, careless rapture; commanding a fielder to move two paces on a cricket field; shocking a religious gathering by shouting an obscene blasphemy. Then reflect upon such curious but important activities as praying, talking to oneself, replying to an hallucination, and composing a poem in order to throw it into the waste-paper basket.

The term 'language' is often restricted to spoken or written words. It is evident, however, that words play only a part, and often a very small part, in conveying the depth of meaning in, say, a resounding political speech, or in a confidential chat over a pint of beer. Indeed, in activities such as the dance (a symbolic form that can be termed a 'language') and the expression of some shared and conflicting passions within a group, words play no part in complex 'forms of life'. Furthermore, speech is composed of meaningful sounds which may or may not approximate to the words, phrases, and sentences of written prose.

Some disturbances in personal relationships, which result in psychological disorders, are characterized by the inability of persons to use and/or learn certain types of language. Psychotherapy is concerned with the detection, exploration, and correction of such disturbances. It is a

matter of learning how to use a new language. A therapist in action needs
to draw upon a large repertoire of different ways of 'speaking', verbally
and non-verbally.

In the present state of knowledge (or, rather, lack of it) concerning the
nature and development of language, formulations can only be tentative
and nebulous. Nevertheless, a therapist needs a general theory in order
to give direction to his practice. I shall reflect upon the phrases of my
conversation with Mr Chip ('There *is* something wrong with my heart
...', 'Maybe, it's broken ...' 'A sort of positive feedback ...', and a
variety of non-verbal messages) in terms of a notion of 'language-games'.

Ludwig Wittgenstein's concept of language-games is central to the
Conversational Model. His allusive, aphoristic, and often disjointed style,
is not always easy to follow since he seldom uses a consecutive, flowing
argument. I am indebted to him for fertilizing ideas. While attempting to
avoid misrepresentation, I shall risk quoting him out of context.

Wittgenstein insists that, primarily, language has to do with shared
activities of living: 'forms of life'. It is not so much a form of words as the
use, in action, of a form of words. It is characteristic of a large group of
activities – talking, writing, playing golf, and riding on a bus. He
comments:

> 'When I take a bus, I say to the conductor: "Threepenny". We are
> concentrating not just on the word or the sentence in which it is used –
> which is highly uncharacteristic – but on the occasion on which it is
> said ...'[1]

The important question is 'What is this language doing within a
particular situation?'

If I give a slip marked 'five red apples' to someone who is going
shopping it does not mean only a 'picture' of a number of apples with a
characteristic colour. Such an image may be useful, but in the human
activity of shopping it 'means' what a shopkeeper does when the slip is
handed to him – opening particular drawers and so on. A word has
meaning only in the context of human relationships: how it is used.[2]

A builder calls 'slab' to his assistant. The latter selects and passes a slab
from among 'blocks', 'pillars', and 'beams'.[3] A definition of a 'slab' in
terms of a stone of certain size, shape, and so on is not the effective
meaning of the spoken word 'slab' in this situation. Learning the
definition might help the assistant to act in such and such a way (and to
understand 'Bring me a slab'). But he can only act if he has had a
particular training in the use of slabs.

Wittgenstein uses the term 'language-game' to refer to the whole act,
consisting of language and the actions into which it is 'woven'.[4]

The word 'game' might give an unfortunate, unintended impression of frivolity although, as I shall suggest, play is a very serious matter. The analogy with games has many uses. Wittgenstein asks us to think of the way in which words are used as an integral part of games such as 'ring-a-ring-o'-roses'. He suggests that we can conceive of language in terms of activities, and actions which are regulated by rules.

Different games have different rules. Yet, they are related in varied ways. Golf and chess are very different kinds of activity, but they have similarities, e.g. there are opponents and there are rules. Someone might define a game as 'moving objects about on a surface according to certain rules'.[5] Such a definition can refer only to board games such as Chess, Ludo, or Backgammon. The definition of any one game is restricted for a purpose — in order to play a particular game.

If we talk of God we are playing one game, if we describe physiological changes we are playing a different game. The two are separate and yet they are, in some way, related.

Wittgenstein uses many illuminating analogies other than games. For instance, we can think of a tool-box or of families. The uses of words are as varied as that of the components of a tool kit consisting of a hammer, pliers, a saw, a screwdriver, a rule, a glue pot, glue, nails, and screws. And yet there are similarities between all tools, they are used to modify something.

The complicated network of overlapping and criss-crossing relations can also be compared to family resemblances. Similarities of build, features, colour of eyes, gait, temperament, overlap and criss-cross in a similar way. 'And I shall say: "games" form a family.'[6] Words and sentences have intimate, near, and distant relatives.

There are, then, countless different ways of using language. For example; giving orders and obeying them, describing the appearance of an object, reporting an event, forming and testing an hypothesis, play-acting, guessing riddles, asking, thanking, cursing, and greeting.[7]

Language grows. It is continually transformed. The multiplicity of forms of life is not something which is fixed, given once and for all. New language games emerge and others become obsolete, die, and are forgotten. The process of death and rebirth of language is the story of development of the individual and of culture.

I invite Mr Chip to try out a different language game. I suggest that, for the purposes of personal psychotherapy, a 'broken heart' is more useful, more meaningful, than 'coronary thrombosis'. The two 'hearts' are different. ('There is something wrong with my heart' and 'Maybe it is broken.') Yet, there is a kinship. The languages are different members of a family; they are different tools, and there are different rules for their use. They express different forms of life: different ways of being with others in intimate relationships and in a wider society. Yet both belong to an extended family. They can both be differentiated for special uses and yet also integrated in a personal language.

Just now, I want to enter into a conversation with Mr Chip. I hope to share a language of feeling, of living symbols, which resonates with his pre-conceptual experiencing, rather than listen to a discursive description of arteries in a bag of muscle. The languages are distinct and yet there is a link between them.

When Shelley writes 'Hail to thee, blithe spirit/Bird thou never wert', he asks us to play a game with rules and purposes very different from those which constrain a zoologist when he classifies a skylark. One language cannot be translated into the other, but that is not to say that they are antithetical or contradictory. Neither, in itself, is more accurate, more 'real', or more 'true' than the other. The question is which is more appropriate, more expressive with regard to what particular persons are doing together; what action, what form of life they are engaged in at a particular moment in time.

In an intimate personal conversation we are sharing a feeling language. Mr Chip and I are faced with the problem of learning a new and appropriate vocabulary.

THE HEART OF A SCIENTIST

'A sort of positive feedback in cybernetic terms.'

'Well ... er ... yes,' I muse aloud. 'Maybe a sort of ... well ... a rather dodgy negative feedback, or maybe it could ...'

'Oh come, Dr Hobson! Correcting what?'

'Well ... I don't really know ... but maybe heart talking to head.'

Fortunately, to some extent, I can share Mr Chip's language. I know that, in technical jargon, a 'positive' feedback is not a good but a bad thing. In a guided missile, information about the direction being taken is 'fed back' (a 'negative' feedback) in order to correct error and maintain the missile on a steady course. A similar mechanism is built into a thermostat so that it will maintain a constant temperature. Sometimes things go wrong and the feedback increases rather than decreases the divergence from the required constant (a 'positive feedback'). Errors are fed back which further increase the divergence.

Mr Chip is on to something important. The more palpitations he feels, the more anxious he becomes, the more his heart palpitates, and so on. It is important that I accept what he is saying and respect the language in which he says it. As I shall stress later a person always means what he says but he does not say all that he means.

A psychotherapist should never even imply 'You don't mean that, you *really* mean this,' but rather, 'Yes, you mean that, but maybe you *also* mean this.'

Mr Chip is saying something about the way in which his bag of muscle functions. As in all science, he uses an analogy. Later, this becomes more than an analogy, it becomes what I shall term 'a living symbol'. At this point, I extend the analogy.

'Well maybe, something has gone wrong with the self-regulating mechanism. Perhaps ... well ... maybe the heart can correct errors of the head.'

Mr Chip looks doubtful. I am not sure whether or not he has grasped the idea and I leave it in the air.

Many weeks later Mr Chip is still talking about his symptoms in controlled, measured phrases. He is calmly detached, but his chest pain is unchanged. He is disclaiming, not owning, his emotionally-laden experiences.

I recall my hypothesis about him being 'scared of dropping down dead'. He rejected it then but he did add something: an angry, vehement tone when he repeated the word 'die'. At the right time, perhaps, my speculation might be worth pursuing.

One day, when I am bored with his measured monologue, I decide to use a crude version of the Word Association Test. This is a procedure I rarely use but it is one which might commend itself to a technological scientist.[8] It could serve as a preliminary test of my hypothesis regarding death.

I draw up a list of fifty words which include 'death' and 'grave'. I read each word to Mr Chip asking him to respond by giving the first word that comes to mind. I predict, to myself, that forty-eight of the words will be emotionally neutral for him; that his response word will be given within a few seconds; that it will stand in some clear logical relation to the stimulus word; and that it will be repeated on re-testing. If 'death' and 'grave' are associated with a significant 'complex' (an anxiety-laden association or cluster of images and ideas which may be beyond awareness) then I expect a delay or an absence of response to these words and/or the response word may be incongruous and perhaps changed at the second reading.

Table 1 portrays some of the results. The first three responses are typical of those made to forty-seven words. The predictions regarding 'grave' and 'death' are supported but one other word, to my surprise, is not at all neutral: 'church'.

To the word 'grave' Mr Chip replies by 'marriage', substituting 'funeral' on repetition. 'Death' is followed by a long pause; he protests that his mind is blank and he only manages to say 'grave' after an interval of about a minute and a half. Repetition of the word is followed

Table 1

stimulus word	time interval (seconds)	response first	words second
mother	2	father	father
table	1	chair	chair
bed	2	sleep	sleep
grave	3	marriage	funeral
death	92	grave	churchyard
church	50	home	road

by a similar pause before he thinks of 'churchyard'. There is a long delay after the word 'church' before 'home' and 'road' are eventually given, at the first and second readings respectively. The response to all other words are produced within the expected limits of time lag, and are appropriate with regard to various types of logical association which have been described on the basis of long use of similar lists under standardized conditions.

There are problems about the introduction of a 'test situation' into a psychotherapeutic interview. It can convey an undesirable impression about the nature of the relationship. Nevertheless, this particular test can sometimes be most useful, particularly in brief psychotherapy. For the purpose of this book it serves to illustrate an attitude of *hypothesis-testing* which, in my view, is one essential component of a general attitude in a psychotherapeutic conversation. In this instance, I am valuing Mr Chip's experimental attitude and, at the same time, I hope to extend the range of conversation by a change of language-game.

There are three immediate results of this quasi-scientific procedure:

1   I formulate two new possibilities which, in subsequent sessions, increase my awareness of possible meanings. In this extension of my original hypothesis I imagine a system of interrelated themes, a 'complex' of death-grave-marriage-church-home.

2   The most important consequence is Mr Chip's reaction. He is astonished when I draw his attention to the result. His curiosity is aroused. He begins to explore in fantasy, to own disclaimed actions, and to embark upon a new type of 'experiment'.

3   He suddenly remembers that his heart symptoms first occurred in a railway carriage accompanied by a fear of being shut up, perhaps like being buried alive.

After a pause I speak.

'Graveyard . . . a funeral.'

'Yes, this fear . . . that fear somehow about death. When my parents died. Something . . . something like it was when . . . when . . . it was when my parents died.' [Silence] 'I have lost it now.'

I do not press further.

At our next meeting Mr Chip immediately begins to speak excitedly.

'A dream. I had a dream . . . In Yorkshire where I was brought up. I was on the hillside above the town looking into the town square. There was a man there with a flame-thrower shooting tongues of fire all around at the house and at the people who were streaming away down the road. Yes what was it . . .? Yes, the church. Black. A silhouette against the flames.'

Mr Chip is telling me a dream, *now*. He is speaking to me in this unique, present, situation. I do not know what he dreamed last night. Whatever it was, he is discovering a new language in which to talk with me. Using the dream-language, he is amplifying the 'church' features of the complex as being black and related to fiery destructiveness. The language is one in which he might express and further explore unowned experiences and actions.

I am concerned less with what the dream 'really' means, than with what he and I do with it in our conversation. Perhaps we might approach a language of feeling.

Just now I do not want Mr Chip to explain away the dream, or to attempt to translate it by means of discursive logic. I hope that he will stay with the vivid presentation of the picture as a whole. I attempt to convey my dim apprehension of a living symbol which means both what it says, and intimates what is as yet unknown. Shelley's skylark is what it is in the poem; Mr Chip's Flame-thrower man can be confronted, and related to as a 'person' rather than as a thing to be reduced to abstractions such as 'aggressive tendencies'.

By remaining in touch with the immediate experience, Mr Chip may catch echoes of the stream of experiencing and come to own the Flame-thrower as 'himself' (or rather, as suggested later, one of many 'selves'), to be reckoned with in action and act. In seeing, and seeing into, he might catch a glimpse of what is beyond. In encountering hitherto unknown aspects of himself in the conversation with me, he might develop an on-going conversation with a relatively unknown 'myself'.

Mr Chip does amplify the meaning of the scene, although I do not encourage him to do so. He associates the Flame-thrower with a blow-lamp he has used in his home with the danger of the 'jet igniting', going on to talk about scientific research on destructive weapons with a hint of some doubts about values in scientific work. The cold emptiness of the church contrasts with the searing flame and he recalls childhood feelings of hate for religion.

As time goes on, Mr Chip's memories are recounted with more and more emotional expression, very different in tone from that of the account he had given previously when he talked about 'hard facts'. We begin to share a new language.

During the next few months he returns again and again to his dream which serves as a kind of 'organizer', as a new story of his life unfolds: a tale very different from the detailed history 'about' Mr Chip which had been taken by a psychiatric colleague.

The movement from hard facts to broken hearts would usually be described as a change from literal to figurative or metaphorical language. The distinction is not, however, as clear as it might seem. We need to consider the meaning of metaphor. In the story of Freda (Chapter 2), I suggested how the creation of a 'moving metaphor' was an important step, a carrying forward in a therapeutic conversation.

METAPHOR AND MEANING

Metaphor is a large and complex subject, about which literary and linguistic experts disagree. It bristles with unsolved problems which raise questions about the nature of language and, indeed, of all knowledge. In making one or two brief categorical statements, I state a point of view in so far as this is relevant to the day-to-day practice of psychotherapy. Many writers have influenced me and I draw heavily on I.A. Richards, M. Mair, and A. Ortony.[9]

What is metaphor and what does it do?

I am in the public bar of a Lancashire pub. Two mill workers are sadly and seriously drowning their sorrows about the heavy defeat of the England football team. A tackler (a senior operative) gives his solemn verdict.

'An' that bloody Martin Chivers, 'ee were weighvin' beawt weft all neet.' ('. . . he was weaving without weft all night.')

As I listen, I am presented with an image of a chattering loom, and its busy shooting shuttle. There is warp (the length-wise threads) but the workman has forgotten to feed in the weft (the cross-threads); a mistake which can be made relatively easily with a mechanical loom. The 'weaving' is not weaving. No cloth forms. No pattern emerges. And, if the weaver is on piece work, he is losing much needed 'brass' (money). As I listen to the conversation I hear echoes of a vast society of similar metaphors which speak of the traditions, the personal life, and the gloomy future of a society of workers in a cotton valley. These images and constellations of meaning are put side-by-side with the behaviour of a famous footballer and we *see* a meaning which emerges *between* them, and in which they are related.

In the nomenclature of Richards a developed metaphor has three terms:

topic, vehicle, and ground.[10] The subject term, the *topic*, is what is referred to literally, e.g. the performance of a footballer, the pain in Mr Chip's heart, and the empty sensation in Freda's chest. Then there is the *vehicle*, a term which can be used literally but is now metaphorical: 'weaving without weft' and 'broken'. Footballers do not weave cloth and hearts do not literally break. The two terms have something in common; they can be compared in some respects. When put together there is a 'transaction' between them. From the 'transaction' a new meaning emerges. The added meaning is termed the *ground*. The footballer, Martin Chivers, is working hard trying to shape goal-scoring patterns but achieves nothing: Mr Chip is suffering from emotional damage which disrupts his individual integrity and his personal relationships. But no literal translations of the ground ideas, such as those given in the last sentence, can convey the colour or significance of the vivid metaphorical expressions. They open depths of felt-meaning and invite us to explore further. A crucial problem in psychotherapy is how a new insight can be realized (made real), felt, experienced, and carried alive into the heart.

Metaphor, then, is a creative relation between hitherto unrelated 'terms'. By 'term' I do not mean merely a written or spoken word or phrase but rather a pattern of meaning, an idea, a schema, a complex system. In the example of the weaver I have attempted to make this clear: the two terms represent a multitude of experiences associated on the one hand with the behaviour of a footballer in an important game and on the other hand with working a loom in a cotton mill. A single word, as used in ordinary speech, has many facets. In the therapy with Mr Chip, 'broken' was amplified in many diverse ways. A metaphor embodies and generates multiple meanings. It cannot be translated into unequivocal discursive language; but it can be extended, expanded, or amplified. I shall repeatedly stress the importance of *amplification* in psycho-therapeutic technique.

Richards stresses that a metaphor is a relation between complex conceptions, between thoughts and feelings. Using the word 'thinking' in a broad sense as the 'mind's activity', he argues that metaphor is a way of thinking of one thing in terms of another. There are small-scale instances, as in a particular figure of speech ('broken-hearted'), and large-scale ones in many personal activities such as the conduct of a friendship. As we grow up, we shift, transfer, or 'carry over' modes of loving and acting from one set of people and things (a family group) to other sets (our friends). In healthy growth, the topic and the vehicle cooperate freely and the resultant ground (the friendship) derives from both. This important suggestion has profound implications for psycho-therapy, as for example when Freda saw me (topic) as her father (vehicle).

A metaphor is not always a single phrase. Each term can be a whole sentence within which there is no anomaly. 'He is weaving without weft' in itself can be a literal statement about what is happening in a modern cotton mill. An operative is working a loom but has omitted to check the weft. Its metaphorical meaning comes when it is put in the context of the equally literal description of a football match. Similarly, 'We are hacking our way through a jungle' is a straightforward statement which becomes a metaphor only when it is inserted, for example, in an involved passage about psychological theory.

Several figures of speech, traditionally distinguished in textbooks of English grammar,[11] can be used as metaphors in the sense that the word is used in this book. I shall comment only on one, *personification*. It is of great importance in psychotherapy and in a notion, which I shall develop, of a 'society of selves' (Chapter 10).

In personification, inanimate objects, abstract concepts, and complex feelings are spoken of as if they possessed human attributes. A simple near-literal example is when we talk of a country as 'she'. In this book my main concern is with more vivid presentations in which relatively unknown 'parts' of the psyche are encountered in fantasy and dream as other 'persons'. For instance later in therapy, Mr Chip came to relate to, and converse with, various figures of whom one was the Flame-thrower man. Here we move beyond, or rather beneath, metaphor. The 'shadow' figure could be used deliberately in a contrived metaphor as a vehicle for (say) the topic of aggression. But Mr Chip experiences 'him' as much more than that. Before discussing the wider significance of figurative language I shall consider what a metaphor does, how it works.

THE WORKING OF METAPHOR

A metaphor does many things.

1 It *compares*. But the comparison is an unusual one. It brings together a 'something' and a 'something else' which according to our accustomed logical categories do not seem to fit, There is an anomaly, a clash. There is tension. What we regard as 'literal' is upset. We are surprised at the unexpected, a shock which can precipitate intense anxiety of conflict.

When I say to Mr Chip 'maybe it's broken', this phrase does not fit the context of speaking in literal terms of a bag of muscle. The meaning of 'weaving without weft' is inappropriate in the context of a football field. There are similarities between the terms. A comparison is made, but there is a literal incompatiblity between topic and vehicle.

During an early session, in trying to convey a psychological explanation of his symptom, I say 'The mind is in some ways like a computer.' I am using a simile, speaking in terms of information-processing and overloading in order to convey how anxiety can arise. I am making a comparison. I hope that something which is well-known to him will, on the basis of some similarities, help him to comprehend what is obscure and will bring forward some neglected aspects of his problem. In this computer analogy, there is little tension: for Mr Chip the anomaly is not great.

Tension is created by bringing together different languages. The degree of anxiety depends on how closely the terms are related. In Mr Chip's language, computers, brains, and minds are something like brothers and sisters, whereas heart pains and broken hearts belong to very different 'families' or, indeed, 'races'.

2 An apt, well-timed metaphor suggests the possibility of the resolution, or rather *transcendence of the anomaly*. A new ground-meaning (an apprehension of the behaviour of a footballer, a glimpse of what a heart pain might be 'saying' to Mr Chip, or a sharing of the depths of grief in Freda's chest) is 'shown' or 'presented'. It emerges, as it were, between the terms. It does not belong exclusively to either term but points beyond them. We use the old to explore the new. We discover a new language-game.

The revelation of the ground idea, which is not clear-cut and ready-made, depends upon an optimum degree of tension. For Mr Chip, the computer analogy might illuminate new facets of the topic but it is unlikely to generate the expanding third term which is intimated by a 'broken heart'.

If the anomaly is too great there is nonsense. The statement 'Despite the feedback some fear imagined the newspaper' is anomalous as regards meaning, and, in a lecture on gardening, also as regards context. If the tension is not resolvable (at least, in principle), it is not a metaphor. Yet, one man's sense is another man's nonsense. To a schizophrenic it could be a concrete literal statement. To a scientific journalist, personifying fear might be using a pregnant, albeit very far-flung metaphor, which could become evident in psychotherapy.

3 In bringing together hitherto disparate terms we create *more encompassing wholes*: new and more extended 'families', 'societies', or systems with different and yet related forms of life.

Some similes are not mere comparisons. They can be striking metaphors. As, for example, 'My Luve's like a red, red rose'. Here, if custom has not staled the familiar quotation, experience is seen in a new way. There is a disclosure of a new whole. The moving metaphor is a process in which, out of tearing tension, we cry 'Eureka!', 'I see!'

4 The colourful, vigorous, ambiguous language of metaphor generates *a sense of immediacy and life* which lures us on to explore what is dimly sensed.

5   Metaphor *breaks the rules* of existing language-games. Yet, conventions of grammar and syntax are still preserved. There is both a conservative action and a revolutionary action. We break the rules but we also keep them. In the tension between the old and the new, there is a balance between *stability and change*. We retain as much as possible of the past in exploring the future.

The use of metaphor is not a rare activity, it is the life's blood of ordinary speech ('I am high', 'my heart is heavy', 'I feel light-headed'). It is embedded in the technical language of science, philosophy, religion, and politics (notions of consciousness as an impression on wax, light as waves or particles, genetic codes, God as a king or a clock-maker, and the state as a monstrous Leviathan). In psychology, we are presented with metaphorical pictures of man as a computer, as a growing plant, or as a battleground of personified forces.

A metaphorical construction can be a means of playing on emotions in order to avoid the effort to achieve a clear unambiguous language. It can be an adornment which puts gilt on the gingerbread, an apt witty decoration, a frill of rhetoric. Yet it is an essential mode of expressing as precisely as possible obscure, shifting, and paradoxical experiences especially in personal conversations. It is central to the development of language, the process of creative thought, and the growth of a person. Living metaphors are not 'beautiful lies'.[12]

A psychotherapist is not a third-rate metaphysical poet. His job is not to think up fanciful analogies with which to ice the cake but, together with his client, to seek for 'moving metaphors'. In a language of feeling separate experiences are brought together and they disclose a new meaning which resonates with deep levels of pre-conceptual experiencing. Then, as a new and larger synthesis emerges from our middle, there is a carrying forward with a step on to new ground.

The resounding generalities in the last paragraph need to be tied to the minute particulars of what the therapist says and does when he uses figurative language.

PSYCHOTHERAPY AND METAPHOR

In clinical practice metaphor is important in many ways. I shall distinguish four.

1   *We use metaphors but all too often we are used by them.* Different language-games are identified. Figurative expressions are taken as literal statements.

Many psychoneurotic symptoms can be regarded and treated as unrealized, unrecognized, or incomplete metaphors. The bodily topics of Mr Chip's heart pain, Freda's strange feeling in her chest, and Joe Smith's

'queer' sensation are clear. The vehicles ('broken', 'empty' and 'wobbly')
are not. The literal assumption 'There *is* something wrong with my heart'
is a disguised metaphor. Owing to the disguise, one term (constellation of
meaning) is concealed: 'broken' is disclaimed and, hence, does not work
as a vehicle. If it can be recognized and owned then a ground can be
revealed and explored.

In the story of Freda, I gave an example of the mutual creation (or,
better, discovery) of a metaphor with multiple meanings – an empty
heart.

I listened to Mr Chip's symptom as a metaphorical body-language: as if
it was saying something to him, to me, and to others about what was
lacking in his life. His accustomed language was adequate for talking
about things but not for engaging in a reciprocal, personal dialogue. The
problem of therapy was one of listening to, and learning how to share, a
language of the heart: how to be together in a new form of life.

Tentatively, we tried out a different 'how' of talking: a new language-
game. We began to explore and learn to use a metaphorical feeling-
language, very different from formulating accounts or carefully defining
terms. In the on-going conversation, Mr Chip became aware of un-
acknowledged emotions and of disclaimed actions. The most important
factor, however, was not a discovery of 'contents of the unconscious' but
learning *how* to converse, how to act in a personal relationship, how to
use metaphor. It meant both distinguishing and also relating varied ways
of talking: different language-games with different rules. We needed to
learn not only a new vocabulary, but also a skill in using it: like the
experience of Wittgenstein's builder with the word 'slab'.

At first we engaged in some superficial play on words. This led on to a
more serious consideration of comparisons and analogies (feedbacks and
heart rhythms). A marked change, a step forward, occurred following the
Word Association Test.

In the associations there was a carrying over of meaning, such as from
'grave' to 'marriage'. Later, we explored complex combinations of
metaphors. Mr Chip accepted 'broken heart' as having a meaningful
ground which was subsequently amplified by a combined metaphor and
pun, 'It breaks my heart to be in a grave marriage.' Past events (e.g. the
death of parents and being shut in a railway carriage) were brought alive
in discovering a present problem.

In telling me his dream Mr Chip presented analogies in a vivid
compelling form. He was faced not merely with an abstract notion of
aggression but with a personification of fiery, murderous passion. It was
as if the Flame-thrower was a person acting now. Later, Mr Chip learned
to carry on quasi-conversations with the Flame-thrower and other
figures owned by him as his 'selves'.

In empathy there is a personal knowledge of another, an 'in-dwelling'.[13] It can be regarded as an involvement in a metaphorical process which requires an appropriate language. Richards writes:

'The psychoanalysts have shown us with their discussions of "trans-ference" – another name for metaphor – how constantly modes of regarding, of loving, of acting, that have developed with one set of things or people, are shifted to another. They have shown us chiefly the pathology of these transferences, cases where the vehicle – the borrowed attitude, the parental fixation, say – tyrannizes over the new situation ... and behaviour is inappropriate. The victim is unable to see the new person except in terms of old passion and its accidents. He reads the situation only in terms of the figure, the archetypal image, the vehicle.'[14]

There are great risks of error in such transferring as, for example, when Sam experienced me as a wonderful father and cricketer (Chap-ter 1). We can be controlled by a literal equation. But, if the metaphor is recognized as such, the 'error' becomes an anomaly which opens up possibilities for exploring a fresh ground-meaning. That is what I understand by 'analysing the transference'.

An 'interpretation' which facilitates a step forward in growth is the creation of a metaphor in which the topic is a symptom or a selected piece of verbal or non-verbal behaviour. Suppose that a patient puts his thumb in his mouth. On the basis of previous events and of general theory a psychoanalyst might suggest that he is sucking milk from a penis. Whatever it is intended to mean, such an intervention is a far-flung metaphor. If it is badly-timed, it may be heard as nonsense or as a joke. But, if it goes home, it can open up a dimly apprehended ground of meaning which lies between a literal 'thumb' and a vehicle 'nipple-penis'. It is an invitation to explore. It is important to own the metaphor as an action.

Two vital features of such interpretations are the level of reality – the balance between 'is' and 'as if' – and the use of bodily terms. The metaphor must relate to immediate experiencing.

2 *Metaphors die.* Our ordinary language is full of 'warm-hearted women' and 'hard-headed businessmen', and our scientific jargon has its 'atomic particles' and its psychological 'drives', not to mention the personified 'ego', 'id', and 'superego'.

Names of psychological symptoms can be petrified metaphors. ('I am depressed' – in a 'depression', 'a hollow.') The therapist's job is not so much to explain, to elucidate, but to help (and he can only help) to enliven significant figurative expressions, to share in creating moving metaphors which shift forward personal growth and open up new possibilities.

We can recognize a metaphor as living and yet not be deeply affected by it. 'My Luve's like a red, red rose', or 'Life's but a walking shadow' can become so familiar that although we recognize them as metaphors we are not moved by them: they do not facilitate a step of feeling. There is no carrying-forward (Chapter 3).

One reason that I have used the example of 'weaving without weft' is its originality both for me and for a friend who studied Lancashire dialect.[15] Some beautiful metaphors from the cotton trade have become moribund for those who still speak the dialect.

When I was about to get married, John Henry gave me some good advice about how to 'keep t' band in t'nick' (keep the band, rope, or thong in the groove). If a loom is to work, two pulleys must work together. They are joined by a 'band'. The wheels must work together. Sometimes, the band slips out of the groove and then the loom breaks down. 'Keeping t'band in t'nick' is, or used to be, a common phrase in which to speak of personal relationships. In a marriage it is essential to keep the 'wheels' of the two persons revolving in harmony. If the band slips out, the marital 'weaving' ceases. The metaphor is almost dead to an old Lancastrian but it can be powerful and moving to someone who has never heard it before. Furthermore, it can be brought alive for someone who knows it well when brought into relation with his or her current marriage problems.

In psychotherapy we need to learn, and to share, the language of our patient in developing a conversation. An important activity is that of giving life to significant metaphors. In the dialogue with Mr Chip the term 'feedback' became recognized as a living metaphor and later as an evocative phrase (a moving metaphor) in relating his technical activities to a longing to be 'fed' by me in the interview, to be 'fed' by his wife in bed; and was vivified by memories of not having been given substantial food by his mother in childhood.

Antique grammarians have bullied us with that *ex-cathedra* dictum of English teaching 'Do not mix metaphors'. The reply is 'Why not, if a mixture has power for both speaker and hearer?' In an exploration of sex with Stephen (Chapter 1) we came to see that the legs of the flying fish were tired by struggling through the mud of a narrow valley. Progress in psychotherapy often depends on an ability to paint a vivid mixture of metaphors which is good to eat.

3   The meaning of a metaphor is revealed within a *personal and cultural context*, within a society of other utterances. They do a job within a form of life in a particular situation within a tradition. There are systems of language-games within language-games. The figurative mean-

ing of 'feedback' emerged in how it was used in the conversation with Mr Chip within the context of a technological community. The impact of 'weaving without weft' is experienced more powerfully in a Lancashire cotton town.

The psychotherapist's concern is with moving metaphors which express pre-conceptual experiencing.

4 *Words* can properly be used as counters, as Hobbes argues, but yet they *have a history and a life* of their own.[16] We need to live *with* them. They may or may not be clearly defined, but their meanings lie in how they are used between people – and how we are used by them. Most words have 'outside' meanings but, as Rilke suggests, there is an innermost life of a language which, often, is at variance with its external behaviour. He sought for

'a language of word-kernels, a language that's not gathered, up above, on stalks, but grasped in the speech seed . . . isn't the pure silence of love like heart-soil around such speech seeds? Oh how often one longs to speak a few degrees more deeply . . . a shade further in the ground . . . but one gets only a minimal layer further down; one's left with a mere intimation of the kind of speech that may be possible there, where silence reigns.'[17]

A moving metaphor opens up depths of experiencing 'where silence reigns'. It is one kind of living symbol – a term which needs elucidating.

· 5 ·
SYMBOLS

I have repeatedly stressed the importance of 'staying with' immediate experience, ready and open to receive nascent images and ideas which emerge (p. 34). That means adopting a 'symbolical attitude', a central feature of the Conversational Model. It is vital in every initial interview, and throughout psychotherapy; indeed, it is necessary in personal growth and in all human relationships.

The word 'symbol' is difficult to define. In this rather abstract, condensed, and maybe difficult chapter, I shall make a brief incursion into philosophy. It is an attempt to formulate the activities of 'signs', 'signals', and 'symbols' as a preliminary to a more lively discussion of creative thinking, feeling, and imagination in psychotherapy (Chapters 6 and 7).

The power of a symbol is vividly expressed by an event in the life of one of the most remarkable persons of our time, Helen Adams Keller. Following a severe illness at the age of nineteen months Helen became blind, deaf, and mute. When she was about six years old her parents sought the help of Alexander Graham Bell, the inventor of the telephone who, in 1872, had opened a school for training teachers of the deaf in Boston. As a result, Helen met a twenty-year-old teacher of genius, Anne Mansfield Sullivan who, having been blind, was at that time partially-sighted.

On 2 March, 1887, there began a process of learning, which is probably unparalleled in the history of education. It happened within a personal relationship. Until her death in 1936, Anne remained a close friend of, and companion to, her highly talented pupil. Under her guidance Helen learned to speak within a month and could soon read and write. She graduated *cum laude* in 1904 and wrote many outstanding books and articles.

Many events in this deeply moving story of the power of intelligence, courage, and love are immediately relevant to psychotherapy. A famous passage from Helen Keller's *The Story of My Life*[1] is a vivid illustration of the vital significance of symbolization in the dawn of language and of self-awareness. Helen had learned many different finger movements from her teacher. These were a kind of play but without clear and continuing meaning. One day, Anne took her for a walk.

'She brought me my hat, and I knew I was going out into the warm sunshine. This thought, if a wordless sensation may be called a thought, made me hop and skip with pleasure.

We walked down the path to the well-house, attracted by the fragrance of the honeysuckle with which it was covered. Some one was drawing water and my teacher placed my hand under the spout. As the cool stream gushed over my hand she spelled into the other the word *water*, first slowly, then rapidly. I stood still, my whole attention fixed upon the motion of her fingers. Suddenly I felt a misty consciousness as of something forgotten – a thrill of returning thought; and somehow the mystery of language was revealed to me. I knew then that w-a-t-e-r meant the wonderful cool something that was flowing over my hand. That living word awakened my soul, gave it light, hope, joy, set it free! There were barriers still, it is true, but barriers that in time could be swept away.

I left the well-house eager to learn. Everything had a name, and each name gave birth to a new thought. As we returned to the house every object which I touched seemed to quiver with life. That was because I saw everything with the strange, new sight that had come to me.'[2]

Language discloses a new world. A 'living word' is a window. It awakened Helen's soul, gave it 'light, hope, joy, set it free'. She uses a metaphor of seeing – 'the strange, new sight', not only seeing anew but discovering a new way of seeing, a fresh vision: new insight.[3]

I shall use this beautiful story as a basis for a brief discussion of symbolism. My formulation is very close to that of Suzanne Langer.[4] It is influenced by Charles Morris,[5] C.K. Ogden and I.A. Richards,[6] Samuel Taylor Coleridge,[7] Carl Gustav Jung,[8] and Paul Tillich,[9] although I modify their views in many respects. A long philosophical argument would not be appropriate in a short book. I merely state, and to some extent oversimplify, my point of view.

SIGNS, SIGNALS, AND SYMBOLS

I shall amplify Helen's story in an attempt to clarify some terms. Unfortunately much confusion arises because philosophers and psychologists use the words 'sign', 'signal', and 'symbol' in very different senses. I choose to follow the terminology of Charles Morris.[10]

Symbols and meaning are inseparable. Four points from this story are relevant to a consideration of the meaning of 'meaning' which is of central importance in everyday psychotherapy.

1   Anne brings Helen's hat. The act arouses in Helen 'a wordless sensation'. It 'means' that she is going out for a walk in the 'warm sunshine'. The anticipation makes her hop and skip with pleasure, rather like a dog frisking with delight when his master takes down a lead from the hall-stand.

For an event such as bringing the hat or taking down a lead, I shall use the term *signal*.

A clever dog, 'Taffy', recognizes the name of his mistress, 'Maggie'. Maggie is out, and I am chatting with George in her house. Taffy lies on the hearthrug. I say, 'I hope Maggie is enjoying the opera.' On hearing 'Maggie', Taffy at once pricks up his ears and looks expectantly at the door. George and I go on talking. For Taffy, the word 'Maggie' in this context signals or 'means' the *immediate or anticipated presence* of his mistress and evokes appropriate behaviour.

2   Helen vividly conveys the overwhelming importance of the discovery of a name. In her new vision the word w-a-t-e-r (compounded from finger signs) is no longer a mere signal indicating a present situation or 'cool something'. There is not a simple one-to-one correspondence. The name is more than a pointer. It is an awakening, living, 'inner' symbol. She can only try to convey the importance of her discovery by a powerful metaphor of sight.

George and I go on talking. For us, the name 'Maggie' is a *conception*, which may give rise to acts more appropriate to her absence than to her presence. We talk 'about' Maggie. For George and for me, the *symbol* 'Maggie' is a means of 'thinking' about Maggie. It is not a pointer. It is a vehicle for conceiving. My symbol 'Maggie' means ideas about the person Maggie who is watching *Rigoletto*. 'Maggie' is the name of a construction, an experience which is constantly being reconstructed and developed. 'She' is part of my 'inner' personal world.

For Taffy, 'Maggie' means 'here'. For George and me the meaning is very different. Symbols enable us to *conceive* objects. To conceive of a thing or of a situation is a very different matter from pointing to it, reacting towards, or being aware of its presence. It is a vehicle in a process of thinking, of developing new thoughts. (I am here using 'thinking' in the broad sense of owned mental activity, suggested in the last chapter, p. 54.)

The word 'water' for Helen, and 'Maggie' for George and me, *denote*. They do not merely signal. The denotation, the name, is separated from the thing which is referred to. It expresses a shape, a form, a category, or a construct in thinking: a *connotation*. In Helen's words, 'each name gave birth to a new thought'.

3   Helen has lived in a world of pleasant (and unpleasant) sensations such as the fragrance of honeysuckle, the feel of cool water. This world is transformed and enlarged by the significance of the word 'water'. From pre-conceptual experiencing, experiences arise and are directly 'known' as symbols (Chapter 3).

The symbol (as distinct from a signal) comes as if it is a consciousness of something once known and forgotten – a 'thrill of returning thought'. In psychotherapy, when a new word is discovered in a conversation, an experience is created with a sense both of freshness and of recollection. For Joe (Chapter 3) the word 'wobbly' recreated a sense of childhood stumblings with a present learning how to 'walk': a new *construction* of a conception which was also a *reconstruction*.

4   Language brings power. To Helen Keller the apprehension of names as symbols sweeps away barriers to exploration in thought. The new meanings make every object 'quiver with life'. A new depth to experience, new possibilities for action, and a new 'meaning' in life, arise with what I shall call 'a freshening of the familiar'.[11]

A 'living symbol' has a significance in and for itself. Yet it remains connected with, and in a sense partakes of, pre-conceptual experiencing.

Not all symbols are 'living' and I shall first discuss points 1 and 2 with reference to the meaning patterns of signal and symbol situations.

The distinction between signals on the one hand, and different modes of symbolism on the other, is of great importance in psychotherapy. It is not a philosophical quibble. Indeed, I shall suggest that it might help in clarifying the present state of confusion evident in some debates or, more often, fruitless arguments between self-styled 'behaviour therapists' and so-called 'dynamic psychotherapists'. 'Signal therapy' and 'symbol therapy' can be employed separately or in combination. Conversational therapy embraces both but the emphasis is upon a process that I shall term 'symbolical transformation' as it occurs in personal relationships.

I recapitulate with some amplification.

Signals

A signal evokes an experience which is a response to a particular immediate situation. It is based upon past events with, perhaps, an 'anticipation' of pleasant or unpleasant consequences. Consider a rat's response to a choice point in running in a maze, anticipating a good meal. There is an activity guided by signals. A particular fork in the maze is a pointer to 'food' or to an electric shock. The rat's behaviour is conditioned by previous events: the pleasure of eating or the pain of the shock. Human beings are rats to some extent.

A signal *indicates or announces* the existence (past, present, or future) of a thing, event, or condition. It forms a pair, with a one-to-one correspondence. It announces, it *points* to a particular 'something'.

Signals can be of various kinds.

Natural signals are parts of a larger event or complex condition to which they point, e.g. drops on my window-pane 'mean' that it is raining now, dark clouds that it might rain soon. A special instance is a 'symptom', e.g. red spots signify a condition of measles.

Signals can be *intentionally correlated*, e.g. a red traffic light means 'stop' and a green one 'go'. The correlation may, however, be *unintentional*. A stomach ache following too many oysters may be associated with the sight of a balloon and, thereafter, a balloon might conceivably 'mean' and be followed by pangs in the abdomen. Such conditioned signals can, of course, be intentionally correlated by an experimenter or by an indoctrinator who contrives associations of bells with food, or of shocks with pornographic pictures. Despite a catastrophic conditioned response the subject may not be aware of the bells or shocks as signals.

Conditioned signals are important in all psychotherapy.

The main point I wish to make is about language. In signal situations there is a one-to-one correspondence between a *pair*. One member of the pair is more available and more definite (drops of water on the window, a red traffic light). The other member is more significant yet often more complex, ambiguous, or doubtful ('Is it raining?', 'Shall I go now?').

Symbols

Symbols, unlike signals, *represent* rather than point. They enable us to make shaped conceptions. In thinking we combine these shapes and create new representations which are relatively independent of immediate responses to present and past stimuli and events. Symbols inhabit, and are reconstructed in, an 'inner' world.

A signal forms a pair with an object. In symbol-situations there is a trinity. A further term, the conception or '*reference*', lies between the symbol and the object. In elaborating this highly condensed statement we are faced with the different meanings of the word 'meaning'.[12]

It is important to note that in human experience and action (in language) an object, a word, or a picture cannot simply be classified as being either a signal or a symbol. A cross on a traffic sign is intended to signal 'crossroads' with a one-to-one correspondence, but for a particular driver experiencing a religious conversion, it can also represent a complex conception centred upon the idea of what the crucifixion means to him. We are always concerned with the purposes for which language is used in different situations (Chapter 4).

In the preceding discussion I have used the word 'mean' in various ways. The bringing of her hat means to Helen going for a walk. For Taffy, 'Maggie' means the presence of his mistress. For George and me 'Maggie' means a conception of knowing a person. The discovery of language brings to Helen a new meaning in life. These different senses have one feature in common.

Meaning is a matter of relations within a pattern.

Consider a musical chord as a pattern surrounding and including 'A'.[13] We can think of the meaning of A in terms of its key position in the pattern: the written bass with the sixth, the fourth, the third notes above A. So meaning works, or 'functions' by referring one special term to a pattern which centres around it. For instance, I hope that the meaning of the word 'feeling', as used in this book, will emerge as it becomes a key term in a pattern of stories.

A term is only meaningful *to* someone. There must be an 'object' (a 'something') that is meant and a subject who uses the term.

If we take one term, 'wobbly', in the context of my conversation with Joe and ask 'What does it mean?', I answer by relating it to feelings in Joe's tummy, to 'like trying to walk ... like a child' (p. 34), to a tear flowing down his cheek, and so on. The meaning of a line drawn by Stephen is conveyed by its place in the pattern of a developing picture (p. 14f.).

In Chapter 4, I suggested that there were different ways of considering the meaning of a word such as 'slab'; either in terms of a dictionary definition or in the way it is used in building a house (p. 47). In a living language there are as many different meanings of meaning as there are forms of life: praying, demanding, expressing love, or carrying out a scientific experiment. Here I am distinguishing two extended 'families' in speaking of signal-meaning and symbol-meaning.

I shall call all meaningful patterns in language, *sign-situations*. The generic term 'sign' (which can be a sound, a gesture, a thing, or an event, distinguished from raw pre-conceptual experiencing) may be either a signal or a symbol. In signal-patterns there are two terms: signal and object. In *symbol-situations* there are three terms as portrayed in *Figure 7.*[14]

Figure 7

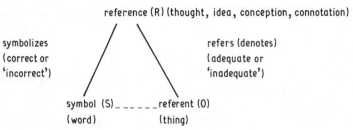

reference (R) (thought, idea, conception, connotation)

symbolizes (correct or 'incorrect')

refers (denotes) (adequate or 'inadequate')

symbol (S)_ _ _ _ _ _referent (O)
(word)   (thing)

To say that a symbol (S) denotes an object (O), a 'sense presentation' or referent, does not involve two terms only. For an experiencing person, S is coupled (correctly or incorrectly) with a conception, a reference (R). It is the conception R that fits (or fails to fit) O – a notion that O satisfies more or less adequately. If I say 'Maggie is a barrister' or 'Maggie is lively', I can ask 'Am I symbolizing correctly?'. Do the words 'barrister' and 'lively' accurately represent my own conception of Maggie? The former does not, the latter does. I might also ask whether my denotation is adequate for others and seek for evidence about whether Maggie is, or is not, a barrister and can reasonably be called 'lively'. It is evident that, in certain statements, correctness and adequacy raise major problems of criteria: of how we decide whether I am right or wrong. The word 'lively' is likely to raise more difficulties than is 'barrister'. Questions of correctness of symbolization and adequacy of denotation are crucial in both theory and practice of psychotherapy. They are posed by statements about 'testing fantasy against reality'.

It should be clear that although there is a definite relation between reference (conception) and symbol, and between reference and referent (object), that between symbol and referent is indirect (dotted line in Figure 7). That is to say that when using discursive reflective language the word must not be confused with the thing. In emotional expression this distinction is not so clear, and in magical thinking there is an identity (e.g. in pre-literate cultures, to know someone's name or to possess a piece of a fingernail, is to have power over them).

As I have emphasized above, a symbol is a vehicle for a personal conception. It can be regarded as 'internal' but, although sometimes idiosyncratic, it is in some way related to the 'external' world of things. I shall pursue the instance of names.

Naming a person (Mr Smith, Joseph Smith, Joe Smith, Joe) is vital in psychotherapy, as is naming of emotions, thoughts, and feelings. An important step forward was how Mr Smith and I came together when I called him 'Joe' and when we found a word, 'wobbly'.

Proper names are the simplest kind of symbol. They evoke and recall a conception, a construct, an image, a pattern of experiences. Because they are so obviously derived from a particular individual object, they are often supposed to 'mean' the object in the same way that a signal would. This supposition tends to be strengthened by the fact that the name 'Maggie' is also a 'call-name', or a command. I can shout 'Maggie!', implying 'Come here now'. To Taffy (that is, in the situation described – it could be different in his dreams!) it is a kind of call-name: a signal to 'look for' a footfall, smell, and so on.

For me, the name 'Maggie' *can* be used as a signal, a call-name, but it is *also* a symbol by means of which I think, feel, and imagine about a person Maggie. It represents a conception of Maggie 'as a whole'. A call-name is quite different and, in my view, is not a bridge from dog-communication to human symbolic conversation. Later, I shall stress the importance of names for our own various selves (Chapter 10).

Behavioural signal-therapy can be combined with symbol-therapy; but it is very different. Symbolization is not merely signalling. Except in special circumstances, 'Maggie' does not signal, it *denotes* Maggie. A conception 'Maggie' 'fits' a particular, unique human being.

In leading up to different ways of thinking, I shall follow Langer,[15] distinguishing discursive symbols and presentational symbols.

DISCURSIVE AND PRESENTATIONAL FORMS

It is important for the psychotherapist to distinguish two broad families of languages. One is closely knit and is characterized by discursive symbolism. The other is an extended family with many sub-families using different forms of presentational symbolism.

When I say 'A killed B', I express a succession of events. In this sentence 'A' comes first, then there is 'killing', then there is 'B'. In life, A and B were present together. They were simultaneous. But, in making the proposition we use a straight line. Discrete words are strung out in succession like beads on a thread. We cannot talk in simultaneous bunches of names. Some of our words are names (A and B) but others such as 'killed' (put between or after them) are not names, although they may be mistaken for them. Words must be put in a temporal order but they do not always represent things in temporal order.

I shall term linear, straight-line thinking and talking, 'discursiveness'.

Discursive symbolism is the language used by experimental science. It strives for clear unequivocal definition of terms, related by the syntax and grammar of syllogistic logic. As far as possible the units of meaning (the words) 'mean' their referents, the objects or operations to which they point. They have fixed equivalencies which are often one-to-one, and hence they are treated as intentionally correlated signals (p. 66). The symbolism lies in the *form* of the conception, the reference, the thought. It is an end-to-end, beads-on-a-thread pattern. Meanings are successively understood, being gathered together by discourse. The language is literal and can be translated into other terms.

Discursive thinking is linear, in straight lines. One idea, image, action, at a time, follows and is related to a previous one with reference to the aim in view. The goal is an act in the external world or at least the conclusions are tested against external reality. There is, then, a leading idea formulated in discursive symbolism. It is expressed in concepts using defined words (or occasionally substitutes motor signs), and it involves abstraction, generalization, and a causal sequence. Immediate sensory gratification, or indeed emotion, is of little importance.

The above abstract and highly condensed paragraphs raise many philosophical problems, but they are likely to be understood well enough for my purpose. That way of thinking is often called 'logical' or 'rational' but I shall extend the meaning of those words. Very little of our ordinary communication measures up to this scientific standard of 'meaning'. I shall try to convey what I mean by 'presentational symbolism'. Here a meaning is not spelled out by a serial argument, it is directly and immediately 'presented'.

Let us consider two pictures (*Figure 8*).[16]

Figure 8

A   B

'A' is a cat and 'B' is a rabbit. But neither looks at all like the animal it represents. Neither is a portrait which applies only to one particular animal. Nor is 'A' a copy of a typical cat. The pictures select and present certain salient visual features, ears and tail, which distinguish them. Such a picture is a symbol which selects and arranges certain elements in a particular form, a meaningful pattern. There is a logic.

We can recognize a house from a photograph, a painting, a sketch, an architect's drawing, or a builder's diagram – all of the front of the house. Our recognition is due to the fact that all express the same relation of parts in what I shall term a *conception*. It is the same house. There is a common pattern – the same form. What is embodied is an abstract 'concept' but we, in imagination, clothe it as a private, personal conception. We recognize the *concept*, and, with feeling, form a *conception*.

In a photograph of George's face there are areas of light and shade. If these are considered in isolation they are simply blotches. It is the indescribable combination of blotches, with complex gradations of light and colour, that conveys a total picture. Nameable features can be extracted and pointed out: a nose, an eyebrow and so on. But no description in words placed end to end can convey either the wealth of detail or the all-at-once meaningful 'presentation' of a photograph of George.

The examples I have given are all visual presentations. Later I shall discuss the great importance of seeing in personal development (Chapters 8 and 9).

'Abstractive seeing' is the foundation of reason. As far as we can tell, dogs do not see pictures. They see canvases. A representation of a cat in a drawing does not make them see one.

Our most basic experiences of perception are active processes of *formulation*. We make forms. The eye and the ear have their 'logic'. An object is not simply given. It is created by an action of perception. It is construed by a sensitive and 'intelligent' organ. Meaning is a matter of form, of relation in patterns, and a mind that works primarily with meanings must have organs that supply it with forms. Seeing is itself a creation, a formulation: an act of understanding the visible world. As a modern psychologist puts it:

'Seeing is a matter of building up an *explicit symbolic description of the scene* observed .... Sight enables us to point to things, to pick them up, to talk about them, in a word to *act* in relation to them. It does so because it makes *explicit* what the visual scene contains in a *description* cast in a language of symbols.'[17]

Direct perception of the world involves abstractions made by the ear and the eye; and, so, we apprehend the world of 'things'. Visual forms such as lines, colours, and proportions, are just as capable of articulation, of complex combination, as are words. Such visual forms are not discursive but the laws which govern their articulation are very different from the laws of syntax. In an act of vision the constituents are presented simultaneously.

Presentational symbolism is non-discursive and untranslatable. It does not allow of definitions within its own system and cannot directly convey generalities. A presentation is unique: it is what it is and means what it says (p. 8). The meanings of the symbolic elements that pose a large articulate symbol (such as Stephen's rainbow picture) can only be understood through the *meaning as a whole*: a 'seeing'. There is a simultaneous, integral presentation which is ultimately wordless. Yet words, although they must be set end to end, can be used to intimate images which, as it were, are set 'side by side'. A moving metaphor (or other 'living' figurative language) involves a kind of 'abstractive seeing'. In Chapter 7 I suggest that presentational forms are the currency of a language of feeling.

Presentational symbols cannot be broken up into basic units. Photography has no vocabulary and, here, lies a major problem in the description of a videotape. There are techniques of picturing objects but the laws governing such techniques cannot be properly called 'syntax'. There can be no dictionary, and elements have no fixed meaning apart from the context. We may pick out a line in the 'rainbow' drawing made with Stephen and say that it 'represents' some item, but in another place the same curve would have an entirely different meaning. Non-discursive symbols cannot be defined in terms of relatively fixed referents as discursive symbols can.

Whereas discursive verbal symbolism has a general reference and meaning, the non-discursive mode is a direct presentation of an individual and unique object. We can define triangles in general, but a particular drawing always presents a triangle of some specific kind and size.

A description of Joe as a patient made from 'outside' is very different from the form in which Joe presents or discloses himself in a conversation. Person-language, 'knowing', entails presentation whereas thing-language, 'knowing about' is discursive.

Imaginative thinking uses presentational symbols in a dynamic elaboration of patterned wholes. My examples so far have been of visual constructions; mental 'pictures'. I shall argue that, although vision is central, touching, hearing (as in music), and metaphor are also means of constructing meaningful, all-at-once ideas. Such representations may not be accompanied by affect (e.g. schematic diagrams) but they often are. Then they are shapes of feeling, as in works of art. These I shall consider as modes of thinking. They are ways of confronting and solving special kinds of problems – notably those within personal relationships.

Both discursive and imaginative thinking are *directed* in the sense that they are deliberate, chosen means of solving problems. But they are derived and refined from, and related to, a kind or level of mental activity which I shall term *fantasy-thinking*. This 'wild-ranging' process is evident in passive fantasy (p. 14).

In the dream-language of fantasy-thinking, images pile on images and feeling on feeling. There is a condensation of (or non-distinction between) conceptions: affects are displaced from one to another of these without a clear recognition of opposites, and with little or no distinction between subject and object. Images are vividly sensed and there is little fatigue. A great deal of the process goes on in the 'half-shadows' or unconsciously, when it can only be inferred indirectly. For adaptive purposes it is seemingly unproductive. Yet patterns form; there are nascent meanings. I relate this mode of thinking to pre-conceptual experiencing, pre-symbolical magical thinking, and pre-metaphorical language.

The emerging felt-meanings, embryonic conceptions, might be elaborated in either signal-situations or in the two forms of symbolical *directed thinking*. The quality of direction implies an executive function, a deliberate willed directedness towards a problem. Problems are of very different kinds. They call for different approaches, different languages.

Both kinds of directed thinking emerge from, and are in touch with, fantasy-thinking. Although in the latter there are fragmentary lines or trains of thought, the images and proto-symbols are mainly presentations vividly sensed and charged with affect. Fantasy-thinking corresponds to Freud's 'primary process', but his descriptions of an adapted 'secondary process' do not, in my view, do justice to the 'rationality' of differentiated imaginative thinking. The important factor in rational thought is the executive function, the willed control, the action in the face of a perceived problem.

In the light of recent work we can speculate about the relation of these three types of thinking to brain functioning – remembering that, in bringing together different language-games, we are in the realm of metaphor.

We create order in our world by selecting, relating, and giving meaning to sensations and perceptions. We elaborate, shape, and 'process' meaningful 'information' within wider systems of meaning. Modern psychological computer jargon distinguishes two different ways of processing information. One is 'sequential', an item following and related to a previous item; the other is 'parallel', when separate activities are occurring at the same time. The linear mode corresponds roughly to discursive thinking, and the 'simultaneous' one to fantasy and imaginative thinking. However, the term 'parallel' regrettably suggests straight lines which never meet and is hardly appropriate to suggest the deluge of images, fleeting ideas which join, separate and re-combine in fantasy-thinking or the complex interrelated patterns of imaginative thinking.

There is evidence to suggest that these ways of processing are carried out by different parts of the brain in different ways. Linear, 'sequential', or 'serial' processing is probably a function of the left cerebral hemisphere (in most people) and patterned or 'parallel processing' is carried out by the right hemisphere. Maybe the differentiation and integration of these is a function not only of psychotherapy but of the development of the individual and of cultures. I shall elaborate this speculation in a later discussion of 'symbolical transformation'.

If, as seems possible, linear processing is a function of the left cerebral hemisphere and parallel processing of the right hemisphere, then it could be that fantasy-thinking is closely connected with the 'lower' parts of the brain and we can wonder about complex interconnections.[18] The suggestions are important in giving direction to lines of neurophysiological investigation, a subject beyond the scope of this book. The danger lies in the elaboration of hypostatized analogies and concealed metaphors.

In fantasy-thinking lie the germs of creative thought as well as the threat of madness. Herein lies the importance of a symbolical attitude.

> 'Lovers and madmen have such seething brains,
> Such shaping fantasies, that apprehend
> More than cool reason ever comprehends.'[19]

A brief summary may be of help in orientating the reader.

I have labelled all meaningful differentiated experiences *signs*. Signs may be either signals or symbols.

1   *Signals* indicate by a one-to-one correspondence (e.g. a green traffic light means 'Go!'). Whether recognized or not, they point to something in the present and lead to immediate action.

2   *Symbols* represent. They enable us to elaborate 'inner' forms, conceptions, which can be modified, combined, and re-combined in the process of thinking and solving problems. There are two modes of symbolism which are related in different logics, different patterns of meaning.

Discursive symbolism is an arrangement of defined elements in straight lines; in sequence, like beads on a string.

Presentational symbolism is an all-at-once presentation, as a whole, as in a picture.

3   Those ways of symbolizing characterize *two modes of thinking* which are probably related to different parts of the brain.

Discursive thinking is linear with a causal sequence. It is the language aimed at by experimental science.

Imaginative thinking, more evident in art, employs presentational symbols in conveying ideas, and especially feelings in patterns, as a whole.

Both modes are 'directed' in that they are chosen, owned, and deliberate. They emerge from a third more basic form of mental activity, fantasy-thinking.

Fantasy-thinking goes on in the half-shadows or perhaps beyond awareness. There is an apparent chaos of vividly-sensed images but yet there are nascent meanings. I relate this activity to what I have termed pre-conceptual experiencing (Chapter 3). It is the source of both kinds of directed thinking.

In the next two chapters I shall be concerned with how these forms are combined in feeling and in creative thought by means of 'living symbols'. I return to stories, remembering that though the distinctions made in this chapter may be useful up to a point, they are arbitrary and ultimately artificial.

> 'But who shall parcel out
> His intellect by geometric rules,
> Split like a province into round and square? . . .
>
> In weakness, we create distinctions, then
> Deem that our puny boundaries are things
> Which we perceive, and not which we have made.'[20]

· 6 ·
FEELING

The aim, or rather hope, of a psychotherapist, is to share with his patient in the creation of a language – a language spoken with a 'true voice of feeling'. I shall try to convey something of what I mean by 'feeling' and 'feeling-language' but I cannot define my terms precisely. Their meaning should emerge from how they are used, in various living situations. The important message lies in stories.

As I talked with Mr Chip (Chapter 4), my mind wandered to John Stuart Mill, and how he felt a need for a 'culture of feeling'.

THE HEART OF A PHILOSOPHER

Mill was one of the most outstanding, mixed-up intellectuals of the last two hundred years. The details of his early education are well known. By the age of ten he could read Plato and Demosthenes; at thirteen, he had grappled with the subtleties of scholastic logic and was far advanced in the study of political economy. He had acquired many philosophical and economic ideas from his eminent father, and adopted the latter's scrupulous method of enquiry and his 'constant and anxious concern about evidence'. By the age of twenty (1826) Mill had mastered many subjects, including chemistry, botany, advanced mathematics, Roman law, psychology, and several languages, as well as engaging actively in the affairs of the East India Company. Then, not surprisingly, he became depressed.

In his autobiography Mill gives a detached, clinical and yet very moving account of his condition.[1] He was regarded by most people as 'an intellectual machine set to grind certain tunes', and, despite his moral judgement about the importance of the betterment of mankind, he 'seemed to have nothing left to live for'.
He writes:

'In this frame of mind it occurred to me to put the question directly to myself: "Suppose that all your objects in life were realized; that all the changes in institutions and opinions which you are looking forward to, could be completely effected at this very instant: would this be a great joy and happiness to you?" And an irrepressible self-consciousness distinctly answered, "No!" At this my heart sank within me: the whole foundation on which my life was constructed fell down ... The end had ceased to charm, and how could there ever again be any interest in the means? I seemed to have nothing left to live for ...

For some months the cloud seemed to grow thicker and thicker. The lines in Coleridge's "Dejection" – I was not then acquainted with them – exactly describe my case:

"A grief without a pang, void, dark and drear,
A drowsy, stifled unimpassioned grief,
Which finds no natural outlet or relief
In word, or sigh, or tear." '[2]

Books, scholarships, the betterment of mankind, and talking with others did not help. He writes: 'If I had loved any one sufficiently to make confiding my griefs a necessity, I should not have been in the condition I was.'[3] Without a personal relationship he had lost hope.

Attempting to analyse and understand his own condition, Mill adhered to his 'behaviourist' views of mind which depended upon the laws of association, 'praise and blame, reward and punishment'.[4] He came to regard his analysis as inadequate, for:

'to know that a feeling would make me happy if I had it, did not give me the feeling: ... I was thus, as I said to myself, left stranded at the commencement of my voyage, with a "well-equipped ship and a rudder, but no sail".'[5]

He thought seriously of suicide.

One day, he was reading Marmontel's *Memoires*. He reflects:

'I ... came to the passage which relates his father's death, the distressed position of the family, and the sudden inspiration by which he, then a mere boy, felt and made them feel that he would be everything to them – would supply the place of all that they had lost. A vivid conception of the scene and its feelings came over me, and I was moved to tears.'[6]

It is interesting to speculate about the significance of Mill's relationship with his own father – a stern moralist who was disillusioned about life and had a contempt for emotions which he regarded as a kind of 'madness':

'The element which was chiefly deficient in his moral relation to his children was that of tenderness . . . it is impossible not to feel true pity for a father who did, and strove to do, so much for his children, who would have so valued their affection, yet who must have been constantly feeling that fear of him was drying it up at its source . . . I was always loyally devoted to him.'[7]

Mill never mentions his mother.

It is not my purpose to make a psychodynamic formulation of Mill's depression. I note only that, although after the outburst of weeping, his symptoms persisted with fluctuations, he describes how

'my burthen grew lighter. The oppression of the thought that all feeling was dead within me, was gone. I was no longer hopeless: I was not a stock or a stone.'[8]

The story of Mill's recovery is fascinating and illuminating: his mixed pleasure and torment from music, and his realization that happiness could not be made the direct end of life. The healing 'medicine' he received was from William Wordsworth.

Mill, like Mr Chip, came to acknowledge in his head that there was a need for 'cultivation of feelings', but it was some time before he came to *know* that, in his immediate personal experience. The poetry of Wordsworth answered to his condition. He writes:

'What made Wordsworth's poems a medicine for my state of mind, was that they expressed, not mere outward beauty but states of feeling, and of thought coloured by feeling, under the excitement of beauty. They seemed to be the very culture of the feelings, which I was in quest of . . . he may be said to be the poet of unpoetical natures . . . But unpoetical natures are precisely those which require poetic cultivation.'[9]

There is an eloquent message here for all psychotherapists. In learning the basic skills of promoting a therapeutic conversation, the heart of psychotherapy, it is good to have at hand the works of a 'poet of unpoetical natures'.

Mill regards the 'culture of feelings' as being the medicine which brought about a gradual but complete recovery from his habitual depression. He was never again subject to it.

In a debate with a Utilitarian friend, Roebuck, Mill argued a case for the importance of poetry in the development of character. Yet he did not abandon his respect for deductive and experimental science. He still looked to Newton and the positivist ideas of Comte when searching for a basis for moral and social science:

> 'I urged on him that the imaginative emotion which an idea, when vividly conceived, excites in us, is not an illusion but a fact, as real as any of the other qualities of objects . . . quite consistent with the most accurate knowledge and most perfect practical recognition of all its physical and intellectual laws and relations. The intensest feeling of the beauty of a cloud lighted by the setting sun, is no hindrance to my knowing that the cloud is vapour of water, subject to all the laws of vapours in a state of suspension; and I am just as likely to allow for, and act on, these physical laws whenever there is occasion to do so.'[10]

In this passage Mill distinguishes 'feeling' not only from scientific discursive thought but also from 'mere' (unimaginative) emotion. His outburst of weeping when reading Marmontel moved on to a culture of feeling; that is, an 'imaginative emotion' which, when 'vividly conceived' generates an 'idea'. That constitutes a meaningful 'fact'. We must ask whether or not 'feeling' is in some sense 'rational'; an instance of what, in the previous chapter, I have termed imaginative thinking.

Psychotherapy involves a 'culture' in which there is a development from the expression of crude affect to refined feeling.

Forms of feeling are elaborations of presentational symbols. I shall extend the previous discussion of metaphor (pp. 53–61) in considering figurative 'poetic' language and the meaning of 'living symbol'.

FIGURATIVE LANGUAGE

In a metaphor there is an asymmetry between two terms (Chapter 3). A vehicle illuminates the main focus, the topic. Then a ground meaning is disclosed. 'Weaving without weft' extends and deepens the apprehension of the activity displayed by Martin Chivers; 'broken' conveys an extended significance of Mr Chip's 'heart' pain (Chapter 4). Yet, as I have stressed, there is always an interaction between the terms with the generation of a new meaning. That creative activity is often made more evident when the asymmetry is less marked. Two examples from poems are given by MacLeish.[11]

In Chinese poetry there are no grammatical devices to indicate the relations of words to each other: no external indications such as 'as if', 'as though', 'like'. One line translated literally from a poem of Tu Fu about an eighth-century civil war reads:

BLUE ... SMOKE ... BEACON-FIRES ... WHITE ... BONES ... MEN

The connections supply themselves: blue is the smoke of beacon-fires, white is bones. This line can make us *see*. As smoke blows *now* we see it as blue. The white bones of men killed long ago are *then* in an endless war. MacLeish comments:

> 'The characters, each of them representing a root idea, stand there side by side with their graphic backgrounds, like imaginary shadows, off behind them ... the verbal meaning is divined, not, as in English, by solving the syntax, but by letting these root ideas take their places in a pattern they compose together ... it is the two images that hold that tragedy of time and war between them.'[12]

In the above commentary 'now' and 'then' are written in succession. In the poem it is as if they stand, or are *presented*, side by side. The root ideas are part of a wider pattern, a presentational symbol.

I suggest that felt-meanings emerge in the development of language from root patterns which are experienced in the body.

A beautiful English song is another example:[13]

> 'O westron wind when wilt thou blow
> That the small rain down can rain?
> Christ that my love were in my arms
> And I in my bed again.'

Two scenes, one of wind and weather, another of love and bed, are put together. In their relationship, they 'mean'. The verse is not about the weather. Nor is the poem just about making love (although 'love' is perhaps more the topic, and 'wind' more a vehicle). The meaning is where love and time cross. The sensed images convey much more than the prose question: 'When will the wind go west and the spring rain come to bring her back to me and me to her?'. We cannot adequately describe in discursive prose the sad, bodily pain when we recognize the obstacle of time; or the new life brought by the 'small rain' and by 'my love'. We can only speak off one side and then off the other, by leaving a space between one sensed image and another where what cannot be said can be 'known' by feeling. We are like a man at the helm of a ship who looks from starboard to larboard in order to see, eventually, the channel marker in the darkness ahead.[14]

If these poems work their magic, hitherto disparate images are brought together, and out of the tension of their relation a greater whole is disclosed. Separate experiences are united in such a way as to intimate a groundswell of pre-conceptual experiencing which enlivens a new pattern of meaning. We see the minute particulars of distinct objects, ideas, and feelings; we bring them together and, in a new synthesis with echoes from our middle, we see beyond – into 'the life of things'.[15] There is a new vision and a new way of seeing. That is insight.

A psychotherapist needs to be a poet if, with Coleridge, we mean by poetry 'the best words in the best order'.[16] remembering his caveat that all men are poets but most are 'damned bad ones'.

Poetry is not an activity divorced from everyday living. Its forms are a vital part of ordinary language. The process of creation of fresh meanings by a combination of root ideas is a central feature of personal development. In psychotherapy, metaphors which carry experience forward are those which disclose a meaning which is beyond, or prior to conceptual thoughts and formulated words. The significance is 'Felt in the blood, and felt along the heart'[17] and the figurative expressions usually employ clear bodily terms, e.g. Joe Smith's 'wobbly', Mr Chip's 'broken heart' and Freda's 'empty heart'. As I suggested in Chapter 3, to say that life and movement is felt 'in the body' does not mean referring to the body or its parts as physical things 'out there'. It is the body as sensed from within.

In our everyday language there are some 'double-function' terms. They can refer to either physical or psychological phenomena as, for example, 'sweet', 'hard', 'cold', 'soft', 'bright', 'deep', 'warm', and 'crooked'.[18] They can be applied both to things and to persons: 'she is cold', 'he is hard', and so on. Some research evidence, supported by clinical experience, suggests that such double-aspect words, referring to both body and mind, often lead to effective insight when used in psychotherapy. For instance, a word such as 'strength' can imply strength of body and strength of character.[19] The terms are frequently moribund metaphors. Their power depends on how far they are brought to life in a particular linguistic, social, and interpersonal context.

At first, perhaps, there is an undifferentiated mode of experiencing. During development, an infant learns progressively to differentiate and to integrate perceptual and motor activities. For instance, he sees, touches, sucks, shakes, and hears a rattle. These actions are distinguished and related as he comes to know what a rattle is. As the child grows they have double or multiple aspects. Later there is clearer differentiation, and disparate activities are organized in greater wholes. When verbal language emerges this process is evident in, and promoted by, figurative language of which one instance is metaphor. Sight, touch, and hearing are integrated in phrases with double-aspect terms such as 'a hard look', 'a quiet gaze'. An important feature of the infant's development is a growing distinction between subject and object, between the subject 'I' and people or things in the environment.

The non-differentiated mode of experiencing is not something we grow out of, although we can lose touch with it. It is the source of creative thought and a feature of the 'in-dwelling' of empathy. A moving metaphor creates new wholes, whilst remaining in touch with undifferentiated experiencing and its pre-conceptual, pre-metaphorical bodily language. The jolt of an anomaly shakes us out of our customary, and maybe neurotic habits of perceiving, feeling, and thinking. The resulting tension is resolved by a return to the ground of experiencing with its multiple, unrealized, potential meanings. Controlling and refining this 'regression', an effective metaphor points a way towards a new creation with a resolution of contradiction and conflict (Chapter 4).

To speak of figurative language can give a false impression, as is suggested by Wittgenstein's reflection on the action-statement ' "In my heart I understood when you said that", pointing to one's heart' (p. 28). It is a figurative expression but not a *mere* figure, not a simile nor a figure that we choose. To say 'My heart is broken, I feel the pain here' can be more than a fanciful figure of speech, indeed, more than an 'as if'. It is a metaphor but is also an expression of pre-symbolical, pre-metaphorical language in which 'literal' and 'figurative' are not yet distinguished. It intimates a root idea from which language is born.

I shall speculate about a mystery: the roots of symbolism in personal relationships.

STONES

The great psychologist Wolfgang Köhler studied and loved chimpanzees. Tschego, an adult female, treasured a single stone; smooth, round, and polished by the sea. She sat gazing at it, fondled it, and took it to bed with her. She would never part with it. Tschego would greet a young monkey by pressing his/her hand to her lap as she did to Köhler and some other humans.

> 'She will press our hand to just that spot between her upper thigh and lower abdomen where she keeps her precious objects. She herself, as a greeting, will put her huge hand to the other animal's lap or between their legs and she is inclined to extend this greeting even to men.'[20]

The stone had no obvious practical usefulness, such as for throwing at other offending monkeys or cracking nuts. It had *significance*. It was more than a signal. There was a suggestion of an 'inner' reference since

Tschego, when alone, behaved as if it were a precious treasure. Furthermore, it was a currency in social situations. Perhaps, here, we see something of the beginning of symbolism and of a language of feeling in relationships.

Betty was tortured by a compulsion to touch every gas tap 153 times. After eighteen months of psychotherapy she could get by with just a few touches when, sitting alone, she was able to get a warm feeling that, in some way, I was immediately present. But, now I was going away for two weeks – an eternity.

I did not know what to do. Betty was in an agony of panic.

My hand was in my trouser pocket and there was a stone I had picked up on the driveway. As a boy, all my pockets bulged with wet stones. They kept company with crumpled bits of paper on which I had jotted down disjointed notes about 'bumping against people's outsides' and never 'getting inside them'. I felt sorry for some stones lying lonely in the cold rain.

I offered the stone to Betty. It was light grey with a white star.

'Keep this,' I muttered with some embarrassment.

'Thank you,' Betty murmured.

That was twenty years ago. Now Betty's compulsions trouble her only when things in her life go badly wrong. Then she holds that grey stone with a white star, and she can cope.

The shape, the texture, the touch – the 'feel' – of a stone, can have a 'personal' quality. It can be an emerging symbol of togetherness.

A vital feature in a child's achievement of separation from, and yet continued intimacy with, the mother is by means of such 'charged' and significant 'transitional objects', to use D.W. Winnicott's term.[21] The bit of rag that must be clutched in bed, the battered teddy bear (or in arrested growing up, a beloved pipe), have a significance which has a kinship with meanings attributed to persons. Indeed sometimes such 'personal things' are addressed in a language of feeling. At this level, when there is little distinction between 'inside' and 'outside', the symbol is not clearly distinguished from the object or thing. There is a primal, magical form of meaning.

The word 'magical' does not necessarily imply 'bad' or 'unreal'. It all depends on how we talk: on the context, and the agreement about our 'language-game'. Maybe, for Tschego, thing and reference are inseparable: we can only speculate.

In an emotional bond, embodied in the stone which 'joined' Betty and me, there is an intermediate (not quite literal, not quite figurative) pre-metaphorical language.

That mode of experience is vital in achieving a transforming insight. It is a necessary phase of development which we never grow out of. If clung to, it becomes a feature of psychopathology. When concealed in 'scholarly' debates about the one true meaning – 'What is personality?', 'What is mental illness?', or 'What does "psychotherapy" *really* mean?' – then it is pernicious. But it can be creative and lead on to growth.

The stories of Tschego and Betty can be regarded as a phase in symbolical transformation.

SYMBOLICAL TRANSFORMATION

Experiencing is a spontaneous activity in which elementary shapes emerge, are related, dissolved, and re-combined. They are elaborated in diverse forms. I shall term that process symbolical transformation. It is essential to thought and is prior to it. Only certain products of symbol-making can be used according to the rules of discursive reasoning. Some of the vast body of symbolic material is put to obvious use, but much (manifest in Tschego's stone, Sam's dream, Stephen's drawing, and Joe's word 'wobbly') forms a reserve of potential ideas. There is a surplus of mental wealth, both within and without awareness.

The brain is in a state of constant activity and does not lie dormant because there is no clear, immediate, willed purpose. To speak of 'brain activity' is one way of referring to a process which can be pictured in another language as streams, fountains, cataracts, and deluges of ideas which have no clear purpose. Following its own laws, the mind is satisfying a basic need, translating experiencing into symbols. The sheer expression of ideas or forms of thought is a spontaneous human activity. It is a need as fundamental as the needs for food, bodily exploration, and sex.

Ideas are created or constructed from sense-impressions from eyes, ears, nose, skin, and vague visceral rumblings, as well as more organized perceptions. Associations are made by contiguity and similarity, but I must also conceive of *elementary inborn ideas* (forms or 'structures' in a language of mankind). These 'ideas' or pattern-making tendencies shape experiencing and experiences as symbols. Some ideas, akin to the 'form' of crystals when 'filled out'[22] can be differentiated, combined, disrupted, and re-integrated in reasoning. Others find expression in dreams, fantasies, myths, and religion. The mind (brain) is a kind of transformer of symbols converting the flow of raw experiencing into everchanging experienced forms.[23]

As I have suggested (Chapter 4), the variety of actions and language-games associated with them is both bewildering and exciting. We laugh, weep, preach sermons, conduct experiments, cross ourselves, consult horoscopes, create works of art, and make scientific discoveries. Some of our practical activities are mediated by signals related in a one-to-one manner to things and activities in the world of commonsense. Such signals indicate present states of emotion, commands or calls for help. But much, and perhaps most, of our activity is the making of simple and highly complex patterns which have no practical purpose other than to carry on a symbolical process. A child plays alone and chatters to himself with a gusto which is difficult to explain in terms of the social development of communication in order to satisfy other needs.

Speech is the expression of one kind of symbolical process. Ritual is another. Kneeling, travelling, answering questions, prostitution, and eating a part of the corpse of a dead loved one may enter into sanctioned rites. But ritual is only partly practical (e.g. promoting cohesion of a social group). It is also expressive, using a symbolical language to incarnate fundamental ideas. Human behaviour is a *language* in which each and every move is at the same time a meaningful gesture. Symbolization is both an end and an instrument. Persons are not merely utilitarians.

As I have stated perception is a creation as well as a receiving; it is action. From perceptual images (e.g. of that particular tree) we make and abstract generalities ('trees'). Calling up further images we let them fall, as it were, *between* us and objects. They are 'ours' but not in the same sense that, for instance, bodily actions are ours. Usually, if we wish, we can dismiss them. They are 'living' but not necessarily immediately 'lived'. We can reflect upon, or contemplate them. A perceptual image is a symbol. It is 'me' and yet it is not 'me'. It is the basis of figurative language and metaphor.

Fire moves, flares, warms, and colours. The feeling of being alive is active, rising, and falling, with 'multicoloured' sensations – the 'fire' of life. Perhaps, in early childhood, as bodily activities are organized by differentiation and integration, fleeting images are ordered out of a confusion of needs, fulfilments, frustrations with further needs and desires. As images are combined, dissolved and re-combined, fantasy develops and a story is envisaged. Food, touch, human nearness, patterns of sight and movement are elaborated as stories of a warm, soft 'good mother'. A 'bad mother' is elaborated out of hunger, falling, insecurity, tightness. These are the life-giving and death-dealing themes of unique personal development and of religion.

Symbolical transformation is a primary need of man. It goes on all the time throughout life, within and beyond awareness. It is the mind's recreation and re-creation, which may be expressed in crude and primitive ways or in sophisticated refinements.

The activity of symbolical transformation, with the weft and warp of discursive and presentational forms, weaves a pattern of significance, of 'meaning in life'. The key to this sense of 'meaning', especially in the dialogue of personal relationships, is the living symbol.

The process is one of *movement* in which new wholes are created. Perhaps rather than ask 'What does a symbol mean?', our question should be 'What is the symbol doing? Where does it lead us?'. Steps forward in personal development are the apprehension of new forms, which guide new action (p. 39f.). One instance is the creation of a language of feeling. In leading up to my meaning of 'feeling', I shall briefly consider an example of everyday artistic creation.

FORMS IN FLOWERS

Sonia, a vivacious married woman aged fifty-six, makes greeting cards, lampshades, candles, and wastepaper baskets adorned with designs created from pressed flowers, leaves, and grasses. I had often seen her absorbed, gripped by work which brought no personal profit in terms of money. It was only recently that she responded to my repeated questions about what it was like to sit for hours with a pin, moving the stem of a buttercup half a millimetre, first one way and then another. At the end of a long day, after a large glass of sherry, she talked. Unbeknown to her, I switched on a tape-recorder and preserved a quiet, hesitant meditation. It is a record of a process of thought – of reason.

> 'I have to get it right. The eye is carried around. You see shapes, triangular shapes, or round – in forms. You may be making a card for someone and so you want to please *them*. But . . . not only . . . Now – what I am doing now – that is different . . . the blowing of cotton-grass . . . a movement. Well, there are different ways for different people and for me – different materials, colours, but always . . . in a way it is for myself . . . like the cotton-grass and memories of mountain tops. A sort of harmony . . . like nature . . . and out there . . . copies but to some extent . . . forms from outside but . . . it is . . . well, if you have experienced a gale and cotton-grass blowing. but . . . well . . . *organized* . . . it looks arranged but is not really . . . it comes . . . well . . . out of your middle. Yes . . . if you have got it right – and you might have to fiddle for hours – you know you have got it right. It *feels* right. But it is not just me. The flowers have a "mind" of their own. You see, straight lines are no good; it is curves that take your eye around. I'm not sure . . . if it is in me or out there . . . I don't know.'

Later, she added, 'You don't always have to fiddle though . . . sometimes it comes and is there in a flash, and then it is often better.'

We shall have to remain content with a crude summary of what Sonia says, although a schematic catalogue can do scant justice to the 'wholeness' of her experience. My notes merely direct the reader back to the original text. But, then, that is the main function of a psychotherapist's interventions – to help a person (called a 'patient') to enrich an experience by seeing more.

1   The artistic creation happens in a felt, *dynamic, moving relationship* between Sonia and a bit of cotton-grass. And also, with other persons to whom she is 'speaking' in her work – for different people. She is *alone* ('it is for myself') *but not isolated*.

2   There is a sense of achieving a *'fit between "inner" and "outer"* forms'. 'The flowers have a "mind" of their own.' They draw her outward eye around, but it is much more than that; there is a shaping vision of an 'inward' eye. The picture forms 'in-between'.

3   In an *imaginative activity*, memories are combined in a new unity. She 'sees' a graceful movement of the rigid desiccated stem which recovers, renovates, and refreshes experiences of mountain gales – and, maybe, many other scenes and bodily activities, recollected and re-fashioned in tranquillity.

4   A *harmonious organization* is experienced as arising from Sonia's 'middle'. It is not merely a matter of loosely associated memories floating in passive fantasy (what Coleridge would term 'Fancy'). In a process of imagination, the memories are fused, not linked as 'artifice' by an imposition of order from 'outside' ('It looks arranged but is not really'). They are being 'organized', 'out of your middle'. A 'sort of harmony . . . like nature'. It is disclosed both 'out there' as well as 'in here' – or perhaps it is neither. She cooperates with, rather than controls, what Wordsworth calls the 'dark invisible workmanship'. Her attitude is both receptive and critical. I hear intimations of a story: a quest for a 'fit' between forms which move in her 'middle' – a curious 'myself' – and curves in the grass 'out there', 'curves that take your eye around'.

5   Minor forms which she 'fiddles with' are organized in larger 'commanding forms'. There are forms within forms, systems within systems.

6   When a 'fit' occurs, there is a *feeling-knowledge*. Sometimes it dawns, or appears, 'in a flash' of insight, a seeing into a new presentation, after hours of fiddling – although there has been, perhaps, a dim and undetermined sense that it is approaching. But, when it comes, 'you know you have got it right'. 'It *feels* right.' Yet, some fits are better than others.

It is a 'knowing' which is different from 'knowing about'; as 'knowing' a person is not at all the same as being able to catalogue his or her qualities in a personality inventory or a psychiatric history.

7   *Learned technical skills* are an integral feature of the process. They are learned only with arduous practice: the manipulation of blotting paper, presses, glue, and pins. Sonia's feeling of 'knowing' that it is

'right' (the rightness of a presentation) cannot be divorced from 'knowing about' (discursive knowledge) which classes of flowers fade and which do not.

Many features of Sonia's experience and achievement have been commented upon throughout this book – aloneness and isolation, imaginative activity, knowing and knowing about, presentational and discursive symbolism, the movement of insight, the meaning of a 'personal' (or quasi-personal) relationship with a bit of cotton-grass, and the great importance of technical skills. In the growth of a pattern, Sonia experienced a process of fitting between inner and outer forms.

In the following discussion I shall attempt to clarify the meaning of 'feeling' and 'feeling-language', terms which I have used often (e.g. p. 7). In arguing that psychotherapy is closely akin to artistic creation (as indeed are all personal relationships), I shall employ a word which is seldom found in psychology but is commonplace in some philosophical literature. The word is 'form'. I recommend the reader to refresh his or her memory of the clinical examples I have given. Perhaps the most useful might be that of Stephen (p. 9).

FEELING

There is a big difference between the meaning of my cry 'Ouch!' when I sit on a pin and when I say 'My Luve's like a red, red rose'. Yet they are related. We can say I 'felt' the pin and I 'feel' love.

The terms 'feeling', 'emotion', and 'affect' are used in many different senses in psychology. A review of more than twenty theories of emotion reveals a plethora of widely diverging technical definitions. These vary with the technique of investigation, the general theoretical framework, and the value-judgement of the psychologist. Often, they are so diverse as to defy comparison let alone synthesis. There is a babel of languages.

In everyday life, the word 'feeling' has very many meanings. Such multiple associations, although confusing, are an exciting feature of a growing language. They can be helpful in an effort to convey what I mean by feeling-language. One feature of method in experimental science is to construct a highly technical jargon of new words with relatively clear references and referents. In my view, psychotherapy has not reached that stage of development, and confusion has been more and more confounded by the proliferation of an esoteric terminology which gives a false impression of exactitude. Furthermore, it seems wise in the present state of knowledge to keep hypothetical formulations as close as possible to actual operations and aim to use everyday language, while recognizing the many pitfalls and advantages in this effort. Although the language in which we talk *about* psychotherapy differs from that used *in* therapy, it should be a very near relative of it.

In everday speech the use of the word 'feeling' can refer to apparently diverse activities. To give a few examples: examining by touching (the 'feel' of a piece of cloth), bodily sensation ('I feel dizzy'), a quest ('I feel after him and find him,' *Acts* 17.27), tenderness for others ('I feel for you'), moral judgement ('It feels the right thing to do'), or the quality of a work of art.

I wish to evoke all these and other overtones and undertones in using the word with the implication of a *movement* from a less organized to a more organized state or language. There is an increasing differentiation and integration in the creation of wider 'commanding forms'. Yet elaborated feeling always keeps in touch with the body, a level of experiencing from 'within' the body (see Chapter 5). A feeling language is not a static entity but a dynamic tendency which moves towards refined meaningful wholes.

'Feeling', then, is a growing 'family' or 'society' of meanings which range from elementary physical sensations, perceptions, and emotions, metaphors of touch, and groping exploration, to organized, vivid, and heart-felt artistic shapes. It expresses personal knowledge with a growing self-awareness in sympathetic ('feeling-with') conversations between persons. The meanings, as it were, 'ascend' from the literal body and yet remain firmly tied to it (especially the sense of touch). The characteristic of feeling-language does not lie in the final formulation (e.g. a great love poem) but in a quality of *directedness*, a growth towards an increasingly complex order – towards 'significant', 'expressive' form.[24] Examples are the evolution of Stephen's drawing within a relationship (pp. 9–14), and the few minutes of the interview with Freda which led to the discovery of a moving metaphor (pp. 22–25). Non-directed anxiety and fear gave way to an on-going feeling conversation.

A personal feeling-language means a progressive increase in mutual understanding and its form must be such as to promote that creative process within a relationship. It is not a mere matter of discharging affect ('Get it off your chest').

Feeling involves, but is not to be identified with, 'affect' or 'emotion'. The distinction is not sharp. Affect and emotion (here used almost synonymously) are characterized by, or identified with, physiological changes and are involuntary, i.e. not consciously directed, not owned. Emotion, 'a moving out', a 'stirring agitation' of pain, desire, or hope, is often contrasted with 'cognition', the faculty of knowing or consciousness ('I will not be myself or have cognition of what I feel').[25] When I speak of feeling, I do not mean a faculty of emotion *plus* a faculty of cognition. It is a kind of 'emotional knowing' or, as Mill puts it, an

'imaginative emotion' related to an 'idea'. Mill moved from an uncontrollable outburst of weeping to a culture of feeling. Emotion, acting
in isolation, can disturb directed thinking: feeling is a form of imaginative thinking.

Choice, will, and directedness are characteristics of feeling. It is not
merely a 'blowing off' of emotion. Perhaps it is better to think of a
continuum. The sentimental lyric of a popular song has form but is
nearer to expression of affect. Nevertheless, it is useful to have a name to
describe a process of development in which an outburst of undifferentiated, undirected affect is refined, formed, and organized. Feeling is a
voluntary process. It is a valuing. An individual can be swayed by
transient affects but yet have little coherent feeling.

Feeling imparts a *value* to experiences and involves a choice mediated
by like and dislike, approval and disapproval, acceptance and rejection,
approach and avoidance. It involves a *judgement* which may be more or
less concrete, discrete, personal ('Cold tripe and chips is much better than
venison with claret sauce', 'Harry is warm and a much nicer chap than
Claude'), or more or less general ('I feel that lying is always wrong',
'Christianity feels right').

Differentiated feeling is characterized by a complex ordering of
experiences. There is a judgement about, and an arrangement of, the
values of events in 'outer and inner worlds'. Discrete, individual
feelings are selected and articulated with more general previously
existing forms. They can be transient, diffuse, moods, or they can be
habitual and highly organized attitudes. An attitude is a state of expectation or readiness which regulates selection of stimuli and determines
response and action. This input, 'processing', and output, may occur
with or without awareness.

Feelings and attitudes can be visualized as dynamic systems within
which 'elements' or sub-systems are integrated into 'wholes' (Chapter
14). Such systems are more or less stable and more or less changing, and,
to differing degrees, are either 'open' or 'closed' (i.e. with a free or
limited interchange with other internal or external systems). Thus on the
one hand, an attitude can be so closed and rigid as to select and
incorporate only such feelings as do not disturb a highly integrated
stability, whilst another might be open to a wide range of feelings and be
rapidly changing. In this analogical picture (and it is no more than that)
there can be many attitude-systems, the difference between feelings and
attitudes being one of degree. It is evident that what is regarded as
constituting an 'element' or a 'whole' system is arbitrary and depends
upon the purpose for which the analogy is used. The abstraction needs to
be given a local habitation and a name – as, for instance, in phrasing an
intervention in psychotherapy by choosing a new metaphor in such a

way as to promote a balance between stability and change in personality organization.

The meaning of feeling-language cannot be defined in terms of reference to things (denotation). It lies in *expression* of connotation by means of presentational forms – pictures, music, rhythm, gesture, or metaphor. The language of art or of personal relationships cannot be translated into discursive statements. Music uses a mode of symbolism which is adapted to the presentation of 'unspeakable' things. It lacks the logical denotation which is the characteristic of discourse; and yet we can say that a certain piece of music is 'significant', and that a particular phrase lacks 'meaning', or that a violinist fails to convey the 'import' of the passage. Perhaps, however, such statements can make sense only to those people who have an understanding of the medium, those whom we call 'musical'. The problem of how far such an understanding can be cultivated raises important questions about how far psychotherapists are born and not made.

I shall consider further the word 'form'.

FORMS OF FEELING

The process of psychotherapy involves a mode of artistic creation which has affinities with literature, drama, music, painting – and making lampshades. As a partner in the creation of a shared feeling-language, the therapist needs to be a kind of artist. Being alone and yet together with his patient, he apprehends, and cooperates with, emerging forms of symbolism which are elaborated and organized as a unique personal conversation grows between them.

The conception of a work of art, whether it springs from a sudden inspiring revelation or arises out of a joyless and laboured 'fiddling', is an envisagement of a *commanding form* – an elaborated feeling as regards general structure, proportion, and rhythm: a total organization. It is not a matter of juxtaposed parts but of interacting elements which convey a pattern, a meaning, a balance which is 'felt' as a complex system. An order emerges from the differentiation and integration not only of 'psychic' phenomena but also of physiological changes in muscles, skin, heart, intestines, glands, eyes, and limbs. There is an interplay of tensions and resolutions which characterize the 'inner life', 'the sense of life' – the 'life of feeling'. Perhaps this is most apparent in music when the tensions and resolutions serve to express an *organizing idea*. It certainly is not a simple matter of pleasure or pain but of complex perceptions and systems of perceptions which are remembered, anticipated, feared, or sought. Personal growth is a shaping of forms of feeling as well as an experimental testing of hypotheses.

A commanding form is 'organic' or 'living'. The emphasis upon organic form was a great achievement of Romantic poetry. [26] It is a 'form of life' which requires a faithful, sincere expression in living symbols of the poet's personal feeling. Perhaps the first person to make a clear formulation in English of organic form was Samuel Taylor Coleridge, although he was greatly influenced by, and freely borrowed from, German Romantic writers, notably Schelling and Schlegel. [27] It is of great importance to remember that his central notion of growth in poetry and in life was shaped in an intimate personal relationship with William Wordsworth.

The word 'organic' calls up analogies with growing, living organisms: plants, and animals. There is a great difference between passive association of ideas and an active growth, a creation of a new synthesis. Most of Mr Chip's responses in the association test (p. 50f.) were automatic, customary links such as 'mother-father', 'table-chair', 'bed-sleep'. It was very different with 'grave', 'death', and 'church'. Then, there were either curious anomalies such as 'grave-marriage' and 'church-home', or else a delay which suggested some activity which was beyond his control at that time, actions which he did not own. Mr Chip was annoyed but his curiosity was aroused. The anomalies aroused tension with a drive towards resolution, a forceful drive to explore. He moved from passive fantasy to imagination. The development of a feeling-language in my relationships with Stephen, Freda, and Joe Smith, was not a loose mechanical association but an active combination and fusion of meanings with the emergence of new and significant wholes: more inclusive forms. There was growth: a creation of new wholes from differentiated elements.

An innate 'tendency to form', is evident in the act of perception, in various modes of thinking, and in complex social organizations. It is postulated by many diverse 'structuralist' approaches to anthropology, linguistics, and psychology associated with such names as Lévi-Strauss, Chomsky, Jung, and Piaget. [28] The activity of elaborate inborn pattern-making tendencies, is a speculation with a very long history in Romantic thought, and in recent years it has begun to acquire a local habitation and a name in anatomical and physiological investigations of the cerebral hemispheres.

The adjective 'organic', in this context, implies 'living' in the sense of a change in an organism from one relatively stable form to another. It is *growth by transformation*, a tendency to seek new and flexible organizations of differentiated elements as opposed to fixed geometric forms. The process is evident in the history of society, of art, of science, and of individuals. It requires living presentational symbols. Unlike directed, linear, discursive symbolism, a presentational art-symbol cannot be synthetically constructed from, or translated into, a succession of semantic units with assigned meanings. It must be seen *in toto* and 'understood' by an immediate, or anticipatory, sense of a complex whole. Sonia's lampshade and Stephen's drawing convey an intuition of a whole 'presented' feeling. The felt meaning, or expressive form, cannot be described or defined: it can only be exhibited or 'shown'.

A poem must be read, or heard, as-a-whole: appreciated as a total presentation or *Gestalt*. But poetry can die and become rhetoric – a game of wits with binding rules.[29] Such imposed super-induced shapes are very different from living emergent forms.

The title of Book I is taken from John Keats. In writing his poem *Hyperion*, Keats was searching for a new means of expressing his experience. His circumstances at that time were tragic. He was consumed with a hopeless passion for Fanny Brawne and the shadow of death darkened with each day. He wrote in a letter: 'There is an awful warmth about my heart like a load of Immortality.'[30] His established language was no longer adequate to convey his feeling and thought. So he turned to Milton. But in mimicking 'Miltonics' he lost his spontaneity and sincerity. Earlier, he had written 'if poetry comes not as naturally as the Leaves to a tree it had better not come at all'.[31] Keats always sought for a language of the heart which was tested on the poet's pulse. He abandoned the poem because he found himself unable to distinguish 'the false beauty proceeding from art' and 'the true voice of feeling' (by 'art', here, he meant 'artfulness' or 'artifice').

The *true voice of feeling* is a guiding ideal for a psychotherapist. It is not a simple emotion but a complex ordering and re-ordering of experience in growing forms, especially by means of moving metaphors. It calls for 'sincerity' – a faithful expression of personal feeling. It is an ideal to which he strives but never attains. The 'shaping spirit of Imagination' often fails, and sincerity is difficult to achieve and even harder to maintain.

Neither imagination nor sincerity are enough without style and technical skill. If sincerity or candour is absent, art is *corrupt*: if the technique or mode of expression is inadequate then art is *poor*.[32] Psychotherapy can be corrupt and it can be poor.

'Technique' is as bad a word to some philosophers of art, as it is to many present-day 'humanistic' psychotherapists who seem to imply that genuineness and spontaneity are all-sufficient. A picture, a pressed-flower composition, or a conversation with Stephen are not merely the artist's or psychotherapist's 'envisagement of feeling'. Delicate brush-strokes of selected colours create forms on a properly primed canvas, precise movements of a pin arrange cotton-grass in 'blowing' shapes, and a psychotherapist, as a result of long and arduous practice, 'spontaneously' chooses words, expressions, and gestures that express the organic forms of feeling. Painting and seeing, hearing and playing music, listening and responding in psychotherapy, are indivisible acts. There can be poor art and poor psychotherapy which, although not corrupt, fail owing to inadequate technique. An unfamiliar tool, an inadequate musical instrument, an uncontrollable hand, or a poor vocabulary can render a sincere dawning idea into a poor impotent product. To feel or to imagine is one thing, to *produce* is another. The latter requires long and arduous practice.

Those psychotherapists who are addicted to rigid technique as well as those who despise (or are afraid of) the disciplined use of tape recorders, would do well to listen to William Blake:

> 'I have heard many People say, "Give me the Ideas. It is no matter what Words you put them into", & others say, "Give me the Design, it is no matter for the Execution". These People know Enough of Artifice, but Nothing of Art. Ideas cannot be Given but in their minutely Appropriate Words, nor Can a Design be made without its minutely Appropriate Execution.'[33]

Particular skills, learned by long and arduous practice, are not to be applied in a mechanical way dictated by routine. They are selected, combined, modified, and invented as a *part* of imaginative feeling in a personal dialogue. Only then are they art, not artifice.

In the Conversational Model, therapist 'behaviours' are defined in such a way that they can be learned and measured by independent raters viewing videotapes – although there are large, and as yet unsolved, problems when it comes to some operations (such as the use of metaphor). Such skills are called for in 'personal problem-solving'. I shall elaborate my use of that term with reference to creative thinking and imagination.

· 7 ·
IMAGINATION

Psychotherapy is a process of problem-solving within, and by means of, a relationship between persons. A central action is creative imaginative thinking.

In everyday speech, the use of the word 'thinking' does not present great problems – unless we begin to think about thinking. When psychologists take 'thought' as an object of scientific study then confusion is worse confounded. The psychotherapist turning hopefully to his academic scientific colleagues discovers that significant research is sparse.[1] Yet, he is confronted by a patient who is seeking a way of re-constructing his world: organizing anew his ways of 'knowing' and 'knowing about' (p. 20).

'Thinking' is used in many apparently diverse ways in ordinary language: 'I think (believe) that now is the time to define my terms'; 'I got on to the question of definition without thinking (unintentionally)'; 'To think of (anticipate) attempting a definition is alarming'; 'I can't think (remember) what I wrote in the last chapter'; 'Brainwashing is unthink-able (unacceptable)'; 'I just can't think (imagine) what it would be like to be a normal person'; 'In my day-dreams, I think (have fantasies) about such odd things'; 'I shall always think about (dwell lovingly upon) you, my darling'.

At first sight, the word 'thinking' appears to be inordinately diffuse and hopelessly inexact. Yet, three important points can be noted.[2]

First, despite the varied meanings (belief, intention, anticipation, memory, acceptability, imagination, fantasy – and whatever 'dwelling lovingly' is about) it is usually clear what sense is intended.

Second, each 'meaning' implies a kind of 'knowing' with a sense of personal responsibility, of 'I' owning, in contrast to automatic performance.

Third, although this might be less immediately obvious with regard to fantasy, all these uses relate to some problem which engages a person.

In this limited discussion, I am concerned with the process of creative problem-solving. I shall distinguish different kinds of problems which call for different modes of thinking, different forms of symbolism, and different language-games (Chapters 4 and 5).

In order to illustrate a somewhat oversimplified argument I use only one example. It is the well-known and often-repeated story of the discovery of the chemical formula for benzene as told by the bold innovator Friedrich August Kekulé von Stradonitz. A study of the original texts suggests that there is some imaginative dramatization and maybe a degree of retrospective falsification, in a tale told by an old man many years after the event. But it remains a vivid portrayal by a genius of one kind of creative thought which could be matched by many other instances.[3]

DANCING SNAKES

In 1854 Kekulé (as he is normally called) was struggling with a difficult problem. Until that time chemists conceived of atoms but there was no agreed theory about how they were related in molecules.

There is no creation without hard work. In acquiring factual knowledge about his subject, Kekulé read a vast amount and learned to manage with three or four hours of sleep a night. Creative activity needs a mass of material to play with. Working within a tradition, Kekulé was gripped by curiosity: by the luring fascination of the unknown. The investigator must, he said,

'follow the paths of the Pathfinders; he must note every footprint, every bent twig, every fallen leaf. Then, standing at the extreme point reached by his predecessors, it will be easy for him to perceive where the foot of a further pioneer may find solid ground.'[4]

This young man of twenty-five was away from home. In a foreign land, he was worn out by his labours. He struggled with the problem of how atoms could be joined together.

'During my stay in London I resided for a considerable time in Clapham Road in the neighbourhood of the Common. I frequently, however, spent my evenings with my friend Hugo Muller at Islington, at the opposite end of the giant town. We talked of many things, but oftenest of our beloved chemistry. One fine summer evening I was returning by the last omnibus, 'outside', as usual, through the deserted streets of the metropolis, which are at other times so full of life. I fell into a reverie (*Traumerei*), and lo, the atoms were gambolling before my eyes! Whenever, hitherto, these diminutive beings had appeared to me, they had always been in motion; but up to that time I had never been able to discern the nature of their motion. Now, however, I saw how, frequently two smaller atoms united to form a pair; how a larger one embraced two smaller ones; how still larger ones kept hold of three or even four of the smaller; whilst the whole kept whirling in a giddy dance. I saw how the larger ones formed a chain, dragging the smaller ones after them ... The cry of the conductor: 'Clapham Road', awakened me from my dreaming; but I spent a part of the night in putting on paper at least sketches of these dream forms. This was the origin of the *Structurtheorie*.'[5]

Kekulé paid attention to the unspectacular fantasy which appeared *to* him when, in a state of exhaustion, his careful clear thinking failed. It might have been dismissed as an idle time-wasting day-dream, but he treated the images seriously, as being significant. Perhaps they might intimate to him something which was as yet unknown. He gave them his scrupulous attention and sat up late making sketches of them, although he had only a vague and undetermined sense of their possible meaning. He had a respect for the language of the soul.

Out of his doodles developed the *Structurtheorie* which he set out in his important paper of 1858. In this publication he proposed his famous doctrine of how atoms are linked by means of bonds termed 'valencies'. These were the 'arms' with which his whirling, dancing, playing atoms embraced and dragged each other along. He had visualized the atoms before this time. But then they had been still. Now they were in motion. They 'moved' Kekulé. There were 'moving meanings'. In his theory the atoms of any particular chemical had a fixed number of arms, a distinctive valency. On the basis of his experiments Kekulé concluded that the valency of carbon must be four.

He conceived of atoms as being arranged only in straight lines. He could not imagine how this could be if benzene contained six carbon atoms each with four bonds and six hydrogen atoms which had a valency of one. One day, feeling frustrated by this apparently insoluble problem, his work was going badly. He could not think 'straight'. The lively 'atoms' appeared once more:

> 'I was sitting, writing at my textbook; but the work did not progress; my thoughts were elsewhere. I turned my chair to the fire and dozed. Again the atoms were gambolling before my eyes. This time the smaller groups kept modestly in the background. My mental eye, rendered more acute by repeated visions of the kind, could now distinguish larger structures, of manifold conformation: long rows, sometimes more closely fitted together; all twining and twisting in snake-like motion. But look! What was that? One of the snakes had seized hold of its own tail, and the form whirled mockingly before my eyes. As if by a flash of lightening I awoke; and this time also I spent the rest of the night in working out the consequences of the hypothesis.'[6]

He awakened and immediately drew a ring formula for benzene. On the basis of the abstract drawing he made logical testable predictions most of which were later confirmed.

In his 'Memorial Lecture' Kekulé urged his audience to dream but added a warning.

> 'Let us learn to dream, gentlemen – then perhaps we shall find the truth – but let us beware of publishing our dreams before they have been put to the proof by the waking understanding.'[7]

Creative thought requires both dream thinking and the straight thinking of 'waking understanding'. As Japp says, Kekulé's

> 'work stands pre-eminent as an example of the power of ideas. A formula, consisting of a few chemical symbols jotted down on paper and joined together by lines, has, as we have just seen, supplied work and inspiration for scientific organic chemists during an entire generation, and affords guidance to the most complex industry the world has yet seen.'[8]

The formula of benzene remains a mystery. Kekulé's ring does not work in all circumstances. Yet it remains a useful, albeit now faded metaphor (see p. 59f.). He was a trained architect and he brought together two terms. The vehicle, diagrammatic plans, illuminated the topic, the qualities of benzene, with the creation of a fresh ground-meaning, the formula. The moving metaphor emerged from pre-conceptual experiencing, from a pre-metaphorical language of dancing snakes which were 'presented' to him. It was a vital happening in a process of problem-solving.

PROBLEMS

In 1910, John Dewey distinguished six stages in problem-solving.[9] His general formulation is useful if we bear in mind that the phases are seldom clear-cut and there is rarely a clear sequence. (Probably Kekulé's account was a retrospective clarification and ordering.)

1   A person aims to reach a goal, e.g. a working formula for benzene.

2   There is a *felt difficulty*. A state of frustration is accompanied by arousal and anxiety. Anxiety leads to effort; it motivates, but needs to be kept at an optimum. If the level of arousal is too great, activities might, at first, be more forceful but they increasingly become unsystematic, uncoordinated, and abortive. Later, an anxiety-laden problem may be avoided altogether, e.g. by a regression to fantasy such as happened with Kekulé.

3   The problem is *located and explored*. As investigation of the difficulty proceeds, there is a progressive clarification and definition of the relevant problem, e.g. proceeding from valency to the formula.

4   *Possible solutions* are envisaged. Tentative answers are generated by a creative action. I shall return to the mysterious process of creation.

5   The possibilities are *mulled over*, with an anticipation of the consequences of commitment to various modes of action. Often, there is conflict between antithetical activities: 'I spent the rest of the night in working out the consequences of the hypothesis.'

6   A *decision*, a commitment, is made to try out a solution. If one trial fails others are tried until the problem is solved; or else, a further choice is made to abandon the attempt. Kekulé's theory was tested by experiment.

Psychological disturbance can be related to one or other of these artibrarily distinguished activities.

The actions of goal-seeking, felt difficulty, definition, investigation, mulling over, and decision are put in very general terms. I use them in order to talk about basic features of 'thinking' but (as is evident from my story about Kekulé) I do not restrict that term to activities which are customarily labelled naively as being 'intellectual' or 'cognitive'. Quite different 'strategies' are employed in solving such varied problems as finding mislaid spectacles, gaining command of the four middle squares in a chess opening, designing this chapter within a wider context, facing an enforced retirement, finding something to say at a cocktail party, making love, or discovering a meaning in life. We need to act in many different ways. We seek varied and appropriate language-games (Chapter 4).

Intellectual strategies, akin to those used in playing chess, are appropriate in solving many practical problems of life and they play a significant part in psychotherapy. But, as I have suggested in Chapter 2, there is a radical difference between problems of manipulating things and those which arise in relationships with persons. There is a need for special forms of thinking and of language in what I shall term 'personal problem-solving'.

The action indicated under 4 ('Possible solutions are envisaged') covers many different complex activities and languages, varying from shuffling around and making new links between existing categories to the spectacular disclosure-vision of Kekulé. I shall reflect upon the latter as one instance of a progress from passive fantasy to imaginative activity.

FROM FANTASY TO IMAGINATION

In discussing the story of Stephen I indicated a progressive movement from passive fantasy to active fantasy and imaginative activity (p. 14) and amplified these terms in Chapter 5. I shall consider them with reference to the story of Kekulé and the development of Sam (pp. 1–8).

1   A fantasy image can be a visual or auditory representation, a bodily sensation, or sometimes an odd bit of behaviour. It can be very complex. Its elements, derived from memory, are combined in such a way that the new product corresponds with outer reality only in a very indirect way.

In *passive fantasy* the image occurs as an involuntary intrusion. It is unexpected. It comes *to* a person. It is presented. Often, it is unwelcome when it represents dissociated psychic elements which are not consistent with a conscious attitude. Nightmares are one instance, but the intrusion can occur when awake, sometimes in barely noticed thoughts and sometimes in frightening compelling eruptions as, for example, in the case of a non-psychotic young woman who told me that during a period of study she suddenly saw 'a sort of vision' of a decapitated head on a table.

Sam's dream of the pearl re-combined many memory images – of a pool he had played by, of a documentary film about diving for pearls, of pictures of water-snakes, and doubtless of many other experiences. These 'contents' were combined in a pattern. As Coleridge put it, the imagination 'dissolves, diffuses, dissipates, in order to recreate'.[10]

Kekulé, on top of the bus, was exhausted by his labours. Straight thinking gave way to fantasy-thinking. The important thing was the *attitude* with which he regarded his 'idle fancy'. What he did with it. How he related to it. Passive fantasy became active.

2   *Active fantasy* is promoted by an expectant, intuitive attitude.

There is an active willingness to allow images to emerge, and to accept them as 'mine'.

The starting-point can be a dream or other passive fantasy image which is deliberately selected or which arises spontaneously. A person voluntarily suspends directed thinking, adopting a receptive attitude towards the image. An expectant waiting, with 'loving attentiveness', can be adopted in irrational mood-states, such as apparently causeless depressions. The person must 'try to get his mood to speak to him; his mood must tell him all about itself and show him through what kind of fantastic analogies it is expressing itself'.[11]

Sam and I shared a receptive attitude towards the dream. We sensed a kind of revelation – an intimation of something strange and important which was happening *now*. Active fantasy developed. Maybe the talk about the 'minute particulars' of cricket had intimated a romantic otherness. (A French theologian once said of cricket that it was designed to 'give the English, a not very religious people, some understanding of eternity'.)

Kekulé not only allowed the dance of snakes to continue, he endowed it with profound significance as a pointer to the unknown. He 'spent a part of the night in putting on paper at least sketches of these dream forms'. He did more. He practised the action of 'listening' and receiving. 'My mental eye rendered more acute by repeated visions of the kind.' In Kekulé's statement there is an implication of an arduous refinement of an 'interior vision' – a suggestion which calls to mind Coleridge's description of Imagination as being put in action by the will and understanding and retained under their 'irremissive, though gentle and unnoticed, controul'.[21] Kekulé cultivated what I term a symbolical attitude: he learned to dream.

The fantasies occurred unbidden. He was tired out. Yet he discerned a quasi-personal meaning in the anthropomorphized atoms. It was as if they were 'personalities' who had some message for him. He wished to understand their language and devised means of providing and maintaining conditions in which they could 'speak' to him. Static 'things' became dancing persons and, later, as a condensation of images occurred, he saw 'snake-people' who 'lived' and 'moved' in complex patterns of 'manifold conformation'. The 'atom-snake-people' were 'real' and yet not 'real'. It was as if they had a life of their own and Kekulé chose to learn how to 'see', to 'see into', and to *relate* to the images.

3 In *imaginative activity* a person's conscious attitude remains open and receptive. But it is now more active in the sense of viewing the fantasy process critically by the use of straight-line thinking. The image is made the focus of special concentrated attention. It is fixed in the mind's eye. (This phrase intimates the frequent use of visual imagery. It

is one instance. Painting, modelling, free-flowing 'automatic' writing, and music can arise from pre-conceptual experiencing.)

Gradually or suddenly, fantasy images arise and move in forms, in shapes, which assume a dramatic character. Changing scenes can be watched objectively and critically scrutinized.

Kekulé's story expresses vividly the scrupulous attention that he gave to his fantasies, writing them down and making sketches of them as soon as possible. At first when subjected to directed thinking they did not make sense. But he was still far from the solution of his problem. It was only months later when his work was again going badly and he dozed off in front of the fire, that the atoms appeared again, this time with the appearance of the tail-eating serpent.

Kekulé progressively learned to 'dream' and to train his mental eye to be 'more acute', but at the same time he searched tirelessly for methods of putting his dreams to experimental proof by the 'waking understanding'. He says that by learning to dream *perhaps we shall find the truth* (my italics): but it is only a 'perhaps'. The revelation must be put to the test. Kekulé tirelessly searched for tests. He subjected his presented 'idea' of the snake circle to straight thinking by syllogistic logic: 'If carbon atoms are arranged in a ring and if our present knowledge is accurate, then the formula must be such and such. If so, then certain propositions follow. If we do X under conditions Y then Z must result. If Z does not occur then the formula (the hypothesis H) is false.'

Sam's imaginative activity proceeded within a relationship – a verbal and non-verbal dialogue. Following the dream, the pattern of our conversation changed. Sam did most of the exploring. My interventions were mainly limited to expressing in words my understanding; making remarks about what frightened him when he got stuck; and suggesting connections between hitherto unconnected elements, providing what Coleridge termed 'the hooks and eyes of the memory'. This involved both the re-experiencing of past events charged with emotion as well as a re-organization of these into new patterns.

With my assistance, new links were made between past and present which resulted in the realization of potentialities for the future. The fantasies were *tested out* by 'experiment' in situations within and without the therapeutic hour. This was not so much a matter of recognizing them as 'false' but of making practical sense of them.

Imaginative activity can move on to what Jung terms 'active imagination'. This is a kind of colloquy, or dialogue, with the personalized fantasy images. Mr Chip was able to carry on an inner conversation with personal 'selves', such as the Flame-thrower (p. 55). The experience of 'inner conversations' is developed in Chapter 10.

Fantasy images seem to appear from another world. The mystery of these images fascinated the great scientist, psychologist, and African explorer, Sir Francis Galton (1822–1911).

NIGHT WAVES

Galton carried out an epoch-making experiment on himself. He determined to observe his own mental processes during a walk of 450 yards down Pall Mall from the Athenaeum Club to St James's Street. He became aware that in his brief stroll his mind had travelled through experiences of his whole life. The reader should repeat the investigation following Galton's method which he expressed in clear and beautiful prose.[13] He will realize the truth of Galton's statement.

'There lies before every man by day and by night, at home and abroad, an immense field for curious investigations in the operations of his own mind.

No one can have a just idea, before he has carefully experimented upon himself, of the crowd of unheeded half-thoughts and faint imagery that flits through his brain, and of the influence they exert upon his conscious life.'[14]

This exploration of the interior can be made only with an attitude which is an ideal for a psychotherapist. There is a quiescent, blank, 'half-glance' which allows the emergence of nascent ideas, faint imagery, and unheeded half-thoughts. At the same time, there is a careful scrutiny of external objects and an awakened attention by means of which nebulous, subliminal elements can be observed, recorded, and studied. A 'free-floating attention'[15] cooperates with a focused observation of minute particulars.

The 'half-thoughts' and dim imaginings *emerge* when Galton is in touch with what I have termed the flow of pre-conceptual experiencing (p. 32f.), but they tend to be unheeded unless they are seized upon, deliberately registered, and relatively fixed as experiences.

Galton discovered that ideas that surfaced were by no means 'atomic elements of thought'. They were 'frequently glimpses over whole provinces of mental experiences' and opened 'far vistas of association, that we know to be familiar to us, though the mind does not at the moment consciously travel down any part of them'.[16]

The method used by Galton is directly relevant to daily life. It is a *sine qua non* in every psychotherapeutic situation. Indeed, it led to Freud's insistence upon free association as the 'basic rule' on which the vast edifice of psychoanalysis has been built.[17]

Galton proceeded by bringing his observations under experimental control by codifying associations to stimulus words and timing the response to them with a stopwatch. In this way he devised the Word Association Test, referred to in Chapter 4 (p. 50). One of many features of association is of special interest. He noted that emerging ideas were often personified. They

'were characterised by a vague sense of acting a part. They might be compared to theatrical representations in which the actors were parts of myself, and of which I also was a spectator.'[18]

He concluded that we would not rise above the level of idiots if our brain-work was limited to that part that lies well within our consciousness. The more he continued his experiments the less respect he felt for the part played by consciousness. Galton considered that an important quality of genius, the 'sudden inspirations' and 'flashings out', were the result of 'unconscious cerebration'. He ended one paper with an evocative moving metaphor.

'The unconscious operations of the mind may be likened to the innumerable waves that travel by night, unseen, and in silence, over the broad expanse of an ocean. Consciousness may bear some analogy to the sheen and roar of the breakers, where a single line of the waves is lashed into foam on the shores that obstruct their course.'[19]

There are different ways of thinking, of organizing, and giving meaning to diverse experiences as they are differentiated from pre-conceptual experiencing. Some of these are illustrated by Kekulé's 'dreaming' and by his 'waking-understanding', by Galton's 'night waves' and willed 'cerebration', and by the distinction between active fantasy, imaginative activity, and straight-line thinking.

In 1651 Thomas Hobbes differentiated two types of thinking:

'The first is *unguided, without design* and inconstant; wherein there is no passionate thought, to govern and direct those that follow.'[20]

It is

'without harmony; as the sound which a lute out of tune would yield to any man; or in tune, to one that could not play. And yet in this wild ranging of the mind, a man may oft-times perceive the way of it, and the dependence of one thought upon another.'[21]

Hobbes was interested in the apparently wandering 'wild-ranging' nature of this first type and how, sometimes, he could discern 'the way of it'. He noted how odd it was that when talking about the Civil War he thought of a Roman penny. He was able to follow his train of thought although, as he said, this was difficult because 'thought is quick': the war

... giving up King Charles I to his enemies ... the delivering up of Christ ... thirty Roman pence.

The second way of thinking is

'more constant; as being *regulated* by some desire, and design ... And because the end, by the greatness of the impression, comes often to mind, in case our thoughts begin to wander, they are quickly again reduced into the way ... that directs all your thoughts in the way to attain it.'[22]

Galton's work supported Hobbes's distinction and, in his experimental work, he illuminated the 'way' of unguided thought by classifying different types of association between words, images, and ideas. Since then, many psychologists have persisted in maintaining a twofold division between different, or opposite, modes of thinking: rational versus intuitive, constrained versus creative, logical versus pre-logical, reality versus associative, realistic versus autistic, fantasy versus directed, and primary process versus secondary process.[23]

Forms of life are multifarious. Many language-games do not fall neatly into any two categories, and it is not possible to make a clear classification. The mind's 'eternal recreation' defies 'puny boundaries'. The urgent question which faces all psychologists, and especially psychotherapists, is not so much how human beings revive existing patterns of experience and action, but rather how they construct new sentences, new images, new rhythms, and new acts in meeting fresh challenging problems. Recent work in cognitive psychology has done little to answer this question.[24] As a basis for consideration of creative thought in psychotherapy I have proposed a tripartite division of discursive thinking, imaginative thinking, and fantasy-thinking (Chapter 5).

The differences are largely ones of degree and the listed features of each mode are not always present. Most important, the categories are not necessarily mutually exclusive let alone opposed or antagonistic. In imaginative, creative thought and in personal relationships they co-operate. My classification has much in common with, and has been greatly influenced by, the thought of Coleridge: especially his reflection upon the 'shaping spirit of Imagination'.[25]

THE SHAPING SPIRIT

In his published writings and personal notebooks, Coleridge's thought moves from a near-behaviourist concept of association of ideas towards a notion of human development in terms of organic growth, i.e. of the mind working as a whole – a potential unity in multiplicity. This creation of a dynamic order is evident in activities ranging from perception of simple objects to the highest reaches of spirituality. All these processes are organically related, within an *organism*. Coleridge's reflections were carefully tied to the results of psychological experiments on others as well as on the workings of his own mind in dreams, fantasies, poetic activity, and philosophical thought.[26] His elucidation of method in science, as well as in art, has much to say to us today.[27] He is often obscure, but he is exploring a realm of experience which is just as cloudy now as it was in the nineteenth century.

A psychotherapist needs to observe scrupulously details of verbal and non-verbal interaction in the interview. At the same time he envisages, with feeling (Chapter 6), new possibilities, new forms, new patterns of meaning. He needs to use imagination, described by Coleridge as:

> 'the union of deep feeling with profound thought; the fine balance of truth in observing with the imaginative faculty in modifying the objects observed; and above all the original gift of spreading the tone, the *atmosphere* and with it the depth and height of the ideal world, around forms, incidents and situations of which, for the common view, custom had bedimmed all the lustre, had dried up the sparkle and the dew-drops.'[28]

In a combination of old and new we feel the riddle of the world. With a childlike sense of wonder and novelty, there is a freshening of familiar appearances and experiences.

Much more difficult is to discover a language in which we can convey to others the freshness of 'deep feeling' united with 'profound thought'. By the lethargy of custom, awful and mysterious truths lose their life and power. They 'lie bedridden in the dormitory of the soul side by side with the most despised and exploded errors.'[29]

Coleridge's ideas were developed in the vicissitudes of his friendship with William Wordsworth. Wordsworth, as a poet, aimed to present 'incidents and situations from common life' in

> 'a selection of language really used by men; and at the same time to throw over them a certain colouring of imagination, whereby ordinary things should be presented to the mind in an unusual way.'[30]

In so doing he hoped to trace 'truly though not ostentatiously the primary laws of our nature'. Wordsworth's eloquent manifesto in his preface to the *Lyrical Ballads* is a challenge to all psychotherapists. It should be on every introductory reading list.

Coleridge contrasts imagination with fancy. *Fancy* is a matter of mere passive associations; as, for example, those made by accidents of contiguity in time or similarity of form. It is an aggregation in clusters of 'fixities and definites' (in my terms, of signals and elements of discursive symbolism). Imagination is very different, it is an active shaping, fusing, uniting, creative power. In his near-private language it is 'esemplastic'.[31] He distinguishes two kinds of imagination, primary and secondary.

Primary imagination is the 'living power and prime agent of all human perception'.[32] As I have stated, our sight of the outer world is also an active creation (p. 71). Coleridge interprets this fact in a religious sense. For him the act of perception is a repetition 'in the finite mind of the eternal act of creation in the infinite I AM'.[33]

Secondary imagination is *self*-conscious. It echoes primary imagination but is different in degree and in mode of operation. It is a willed creation of new forms from hitherto unrelated disparates of experience. It is essentially a *vital* process. It dissolves, diffuses, and dissipates in an effort to 'unify'.[34]

Willing and choosing go together with a deliberate 'unknowing': the adoption of an attitude of openness, a readiness to receive what emerges from the undifferentiated stream of experiencing. There is a need for a 'willing suspension of disbelief'.[35] We actively put aside, for the time being, our customary assumptions of what is 'real' in order to explore a new reality. What Coleridge calls 'poetic faith' corresponds roughly to what I term a symbolical attitude.

During every interview I try – and usually fail – to maintain Coleridge's 'poetic faith' which, hopefully, provides conditions in which 'the whole soul of man' can be brought into activity. He writes:

> 'This power, first put in action by the will and understanding and retained under their irremissive, though gentle and unnoticed con-troul ... reveals itself in the balance or reconciliation of opposite or discordant qualities: of sameness, with difference; of the general, with the concrete; the idea, with the image; the individual with the representative; the sense of novelty and freshness, with old and familiar objects; a more than usual state of emotion, with more than usual order; judgement ever awake and steady self-possession, with enthusiasm and feeling profound or vehement; and while it blends and harmonizes the natural and the artificial, still subordinates art to nature.'[36]

But, says Coleridge, the drapery of fancy and the soul of imagination are all very well, but it is *'good sense'* that is the body of poetic genius.[37] Poetry is more than good sense, just as a palace is more than a house but, at least, it must *be* a house.[38] Good sense 'forms all into one graceful and intelligent whole';[39] it is the difficult action of maintaining a fine balance between truth in observing, and the truth disclosed by transcendent mystery. An exclusive focus upon 'hard facts' and rigorous testing only too often results in a preoccupation with experiments so well controlled that the results are trivial for a human being faced with the painful and joyous complexities of meeting another person in psychotherapy. At its worst it becomes a debunking of the most precious experiences of ordinary important people. At its best a search for objectivity is also a quest in a world of mystery.

Coleridge's concern with both disciplined description and the apprehension of the infinite 'I AM' is similar to the 'great task' that William Blake set for himself: to attend to the 'minute particulars' of nature, of the human body, and the evils of the industrial revolution, and, at the same time,

'To open the Eternal Worlds, to open the immortal Eyes
Of Man inwards into the Worlds of Thought, in Eternity
Ever expanding in the Bosom of God, the Human Imagination.'[40]

To Coleridge, imagination was always related to self-knowledge, and it was inseparable from knowing others. An entry in his notebook of the 1820s long antedates the words of Martin Buber (quoted in Chapter 2):

'only by meeting with, so as to be resisted by, *Another*, does the Soul become a *Self*. What is Self-consciousness but to know myself at the same moment that I know another, and to know myself by means of knowing another, and vice-versa, an other by means of & at the moment of knowing my Self. Self and others are as necessarily interdependent as Right and Left, North and South.'[41]

A central feature of the Conversational Model is the promotion of a symbolical attitude. I suggest to Joe Smith: 'Let's stay with that feeling. Maybe something will emerge.' I intimate to Stephen that we should wait and see what comes out of the line on a piece of paper. With disciplined practice, Kekulé's 'mental eye' was rendered more 'acute'. In these and other stories I have attempted to convey the activity of being receptive to whatever might emerge from *beyond* the image, the experience, the word, the story. It is a matter of valuing, 'noticing',[42] being attentive to and ready to explore, what emerges from immediate experiencing. Passive fantasy (fancy) moves into directed thinking and imagination.

The process of psychotherapy involves the elucidation and creation of different patterns of meaning. Many symptoms and problems can be usefully understood as conditioned signals. Significant verbal and non-verbal cues can be 'heard' and responded to as, for example, call-names or cries for help (Chapter 5). Discursive symbolism is involved in medical history-taking, in explanations, in intellectual confrontation, and in the testing of fantasy against external reality. But the dialogue of a personal relationship is characterized by a language of feeling. The important currency of this language is the living symbol which has a presentational form.

It should be clear that in a human conversation the question is not 'Is that movement, word, or piece of behaviour "really" a signal or a symbol?' but rather 'How should we use it *now*?', 'What is the most appropriate way of exploring its meaning with respect to the agreed aims of therapy?'

The conflict between behaviour therapists and psychotherapists is not about 'facts' but about attitudes. Freda's phobia of open spaces (p. 17) could be described as a fortuitously correlated signal; it could be explained discursively; it could be expressed in an expanding metaphor of 'an empty heart', or, with all the overtones of guilt in *The Rime of the Ancient Mariner* we can say

> 'Fear at my heart, as at a cup,
> My life-blood seemed to sip!'[43]

Kekulé's snake presentations could have been elaborated in very different ways. Instead of using them as a means of generating chemical experimental discourse he could have developed their meaning in terms of his unsatisfactory sex-life or perhaps painted an imaginative 'religious' picture of the age-old symbol of eternity, the tail-eating *ouroboros*. The 'meaning' of the vision depends upon how its language is used in meeting particular problems.

That is not to say that the decision is quite arbitrary. There are discursive, empirical questions such as, 'What are the consequences of understanding in this way or that way?' and, 'What kind of meaning does a symptom have in fact for this person now – whether recognized or not?' Should it be regarded as a signal or as a symptom, for our purpose? Such questions are central in choosing or not choosing to use the Conversational Model in a particular situation with a particular person. The problems of selection and decision are discussed in a later section. Here I shall attempt to convey something – and it can only be a 'something' of what I mean by a 'living symbol', of which one example is a 'moving metaphor'.

The notion of a living symbol and its relation to discursive and imaginative thinking is a central theme of this book. Whether we like it or not, abstruse philosophical and metaphysical questions are raised by every routine interview.

LIVING SYMBOLS

In his later work, Coleridge sees the meaning of a symbol as standing between literal and metaphorical language. It is not an allegory. That is 'but a translation of abstract notions into picture language', a 'proxy', an 'abstraction from objects of the senses'. Individual particulars (a blade of grass, the moon) as symbols convey, more or less dimly, general or universal truths. The minute particulars represent, but they are also part of a greater whole. Above all, the symbol is characterized by 'translucence'.

'It always partakes of the Reality which it renders intelligible; and while it enunciates the whole, abides Itself as a living part in that Unity, of which it is the representative.'[44]

Recalling Helen Keller's phrase on apprehending a symbol as a 'thrill of returning thought' (p. 63), we can ponder upon a passage from Coleridge's private *Notebooks*.

'Saturday Night, April 14, 1805 – In looking at objects of Nature while I am thinking, as at yonder moon dim-glimmering thr' the dewy window-pane, I seem rather to be seeking, as it were *asking*, a symbolical language for something within me that already and forever exists, than observing any thing new. Even when that latter is the case, yet still I have always an obscure feeling as if that new phaenomenon were the dim Awaking of a forgotten or hidden Truth of my inner Nature/It is still interesting as a Word, a Symbol! It is *Logos*, the Creator! [and the Evolver!]'[45]

A symbol both represents and is also a part of a larger whole. It throws together (*sym*, *bole*) what is known and what is (as yet) unknown. It intimates and is also a part of a mystery, a whole, (the evolving Logos). He finds himself driven to a notion of unconscious workings in the mind of a poet and of his reader.[46]

Taking Coleridge's ideas together with the thought of Carl Gustav Jung and Paul Tillich, I shall enumerate six features of a living symbol. They are directly relevant to every psychiatric, psychotherapeutic, or counselling interview.

1   It is a part of a greater whole. Like a natural signal or a symptom, it participates in that to which it points: 'a sail' represents a whole ship, 'the crown' is a symbol of monarchy, and 'the flag' of the power of a nation. But unlike a red traffic light or a mathematical sign it does not merely point, it is a 'living part' inseparable from a wider unified whole. It cannot be replaced arbitrarily for reasons of expediency. A living symbol arises spontaneously and cannot be contrived. Arising from raw experiencing, it has an unconscious component and cannot be produced intentionally.

2   It implies, 'enunciates', 'renders intelligible', and is 'translucent' to, the whole. That which is accessible and relatively known intimates

what is, as yet, unknown. The symbol opens up, and discloses (however dimly) new levels of meaning both in the external world and in the personal psyche. It is a bridge which joins 'inside' and 'outside' whilst retaining a distinction. As Paul Tillich puts it:

'Every symbol opens up a level of reality for which non-symbolic speaking is inadequate ... But in order to do this, something else must be opened up – namely levels of the soul, levels of our interior reality. And they must correspond to the levels in exterior reality which are opened up by a symbol. So every symbol is two-edged. It opens up reality and it opens up the soul.'[47]

A picture, a poem, a sonata, or a great play open up new dimensions of the world 'out there', but they also reveal hidden depths of our own being.[48]

The levels of meaning relate, or resonate between, what is unique, individual, and special, to what is general and universal. In the emergence of the rainbow between Stephen and me there were echoes of a language of mankind.

3   The living symbol is presented as a whole. My 'big dream' (p. 8f.) means what it says. It cannot be reduced to other terms. Coleridge coins a word 'tautegorical' which can be rendered as 'self-declarative'.[49] By means of analogies, multiple significant facets of a symbol can be amplified but they can never be exhausted. In confronting a living symbol there is, as it were, a centrifugal movement of evocative association and a centripetal movement of clear recognition.

4   A presentation becomes a living symbol by virtue of the attitude, the action, taken towards it. In Coleridge's words there is an act of 'personal consent', a 'willing suspension of disbelief'. A drawing of a ship, a roaring cataract, the word 'wobbly', or a safety pin can be 'seen' as a signal. It can be used as a discursive symbol. Or it can be valued and confronted as an important message which calls for an exploration of the unknown.

The word 'value' is significant. In passing, we can note with A.N. Whitehead that in all observation or in any scientific or commonsense account there is valuation:

'the element of value, of being valuable, of having value, of being an end in itself, of being something for its own sake, must not be omitted in any account of an event.'[50]

5   Symbols are born, they grow, and they die. In individual development, in personal relationships, and in societies, symbols lose their force (e.g. Christian symbols, the 'king'). They do not die because of scientific or practical criticism but because they no longer touch, and

promote a response from, the deep level of experiencing in a person or within a group.

The growth of a personal conversation means discovering living symbols that can be shared, stayed with, and developed.

6   Although, for convenience, I have referred to 'a' symbol, the units in a process of symbolical transformation cannot be clearly delineated. Symbols are always parts of larger symbols in ever-widening circles of meaning. In the shared growth of our drawing, Stephen's wave-line, ship, and rain can each, severally, be called symbols; or they can be regarded as parts of the symbol of the whole picture which presented a step in a process of symbolical transformation within our conversation (p. 14f.).

The imaginative elaboration of feeling is a feature of personal problem-solving.

PERSONAL PROBLEM-SOLVING

Exploring and solving interpersonal problems calls for special modes of thinking with appropriate languages. I term the central activity of the conversational method 'personal problem-solving'. Throughout this book I shall elaborate the following features of that process which correspond to the six general phases of problem-solving indicated in this chapter.

1   The *goal* is a reciprocal conversation with increasing mutual understanding. The important aim in personal problem-solving is the discovery of a language appropriate for the expression, exchange, and sharing of feeling.

2   The *felt difficulty* becomes evident in attempts to establish a personal dialogue – to discover a language of feeling. Avoidance activities, taken in the face of extreme anxiety, result in disturbances of intimate relationships and in psychological symptoms.

3   The *problem is located and explored* as it is manifest in the therapeutic conversation. Location and investigation of the problem require the abandonment of unadapted avoidance actions, and the maintenance of an optimum level of arousal. It usually means discovery and toleration of conflict and stress. Actions which have been denied or disclaimed are acknowledged and owned.

4   The *possible solutions* generated by imaginative acts are new languages, expanding forms of life, fresh modes of action. We need to 'stay with' raw experiencing and emerging living symbols in the hope of creating an *imaginative feeling-language*.

5 *Mulling over* occurs within the therapeutic conversation as misunderstandings are recognized and modified in fantasy and in action. The language is refined.

6 *Decisions* involving personal commitment in relationships are taken, in and out of therapy.

Problem-solving in psychotherapy involves activities of thought and feeling which are very specific (e.g. how to make a telephone call, how to talk about a difficult topic) but these are related to general problems of psychological development and of unique personal growth (e.g. the problem of negotiating adolescence which faced Sam and Stephen). The problems on which psychotherapy focuses must be neither too specific nor too general.

I emphasize *activity* which leads to committed 'actions' and 'acts'. An essential feature in psychotherapy is a transition from a state of apparent passivity to appropriate action.

Problems can be recognized at various 'levels' and formulated in various ways: in terms of the minute particulars of Stephen's non-verbal behaviour, disturbances of his complex relationships, and his struggle for a sense of identity in an adult world. A central and often difficult task in psychotherapy, is to decide what problems are to be tackled at what levels. That decision (made together with the patient and renewed at intervals) depends upon many factors such as what is practicable as regards frequency of sessions and time available.

In summary I have argued that psychotherapy is a creative process of personal problem-solving. Pre-conceptual experiencing gives rise to more discrete experiences which are owned as actions and acts (Chapter 3) in diverse languages, forms of life (Chapter 4). Fantasy-thinking is elaborated in two forms of symbolism, discursive and presentational, which are characteristic of discursive and imaginative thinking (Chapter 5). Feeling is a special instance of imaginative thinking within personal relationships (Chapter 6). All three types of thinking are features of creative problem-solving, a process of imagination which leads to a unity of the whole person in relation to the outer world and to other persons. A central feature in imagination is the adoption of a symbolical attitude and an experience of living symbols (Chapter 7) especially in the use of figurative language and moving metaphors (Chapter 4).

Two points must be borne in mind.

1 I have chosen my terms with reference to one limited approach to psychotherapy, the Conversational Model. Our present knowledge does not permit us to make many general statements about the psychology of mankind.

2   A person experiences and acts as a whole. My terms are not precisely defined. They criss-cross and overlap like the rules of games or of likenesses within a family (Chapter 4). For instance, 'feeling' and 'imagination' are sometimes virtually synonymous. They are different in that imagination is used in a broader sense. Feeling (although operating sometimes in solitude as with Sonia (p. 86f.)) is more personal, in the sense in which that word is elaborated in Chapter 2.

The condensed and somewhat abstract discussion in Chapters 2 to 7 is directly relevant to the practicalities of what we do in psychotherapy. In any personal conversation, however brief, the central features are: staying with experiencing; maintaining a symbolical attitude; sharing experiences as living symbols; carrying forward in new actions of perceiving, feeling, and imagining; 'seeing', exploring, and relating new meanings; and committing ourselves in acts, shaped by signals and by discursive and presentational forms of language. They are features of a process of personal problem-solving.

The psychotherapist is faced with the problems of being together with his patient, now, sharing a 'true voice of feeling'.

A recurrent theme has been the relation between 'I' and 'myself'. In approaching the meaning of 'myself' I shall first consider the special instance of seeing and looking as it is imaginatively developed in 'vision'.

· 8 ·
SEEING

'My task which I am trying to achieve is ... to make you hear, to make you feel – it is, before all, to make you *see*. That – and no more, and it is everything ... that glimpse of truth for which you have forgotten to ask.'[1]

In this passage, Joseph Conrad is writing about the task of the literary artist, but his words embody a profound message for all analysts, psychotherapists, and counsellors. He goes on:

'To snatch in a moment of courage, from the remorseless rush of time, a passing phase of life, is only the beginning of the task. The task approached in tenderness and faith is to hold up unquestioningly, without choice and without fear, the rescued fragment before all eyes in the light of a sincere mood. It is to show its vibration, its colour, its form; and through its movement, its form, and its colour, reveal the substance of its truth – disclose its inspiring secret: the stress and passion within the core of each convincing moment.'[2]

To rescue fragments from a passing phase of life with tenderness and faith. To hold one before our eyes with courage and sincerity: to see it as it is, without questioning. To show, to reveal, to *disclose* (not explain) through form, colour, and vibrating movement, its inspiring secret, the truth that lies within the stress and passion at the core of each convincing moment. Those are the activities of insight which, we hope, will happen in an analysis of twenty years, in a half-hour interview, and indeed in any growing friendship. In a moment of new vision, the physical outward eye and the inward eye *see* in harmony.

'Insight' is an elusive word. It is used in many different senses. When making a diagnosis, psychiatrists rate degrees of insight in terms of a patient's capacity to recognize that he is 'ill', whether or not he is making judgements 'rationally' in accordance with our local conventions of what is 'sensible'. Some analytical psychotherapists use the word to refer to the extent to which a client has a 'true' (as distinct from 'verbal') understanding of the origins and dynamics of his or her behaviour. In the jargon of Gestalt psychology, 'insight' means the 'ah-ah', 'that is it', response (*Erlebnis*) when seeing a new figure in perception, or the solution of a problem.

My use of 'insight' has affinities with the last two meanings. I discover a new pattern, a shape of meaning. Maybe I cannot explain it, but I 'see into'. With significant changes in feeling and behaviour, my experience (especially of relationships with persons) is reconstructed. It is reformed. My view of the world changes.

Seeing into is also 'seeing beyond'. The present problem is viewed with a fresh prospect, from a new level with the apprehension of a greater whole. In the presentation of a living symbol, and in the expanding ground of a moving metaphor, there is a dawning apprehension of a vaster, unknown 'myself': a sense of being.

But insight is always tied to mundane minute particulars: to visual sensation and perception and to the twitches of eye-muscles in looking at and in looking away. Before venturing into the transcendent metaphors of insight and imaginative vision, I shall begin with eyesight.

In previous chapters I have attempted to convey in stories something of what I mean by insight: Sam and the pearl, Stephen and the rainbow, Joe and 'wobbly', Freda and the 'empty heart', Mr Chip and the Flamethrower, Helen Keller's 'new sight', and Kekulé seeing the dancing snakes. Here, I shall reflect upon a courageous and enigmatic statement made by Lucy Ashworth as she reflects upon a step of insight, a turning point in her therapy.

'You know things only happened – I mean being less cut off from myself, *being myself* – when I could look and see you . . . it was a real achievement, that looking. Before, I had so often wanted to say "Look into my eyes and see what I am trying to say and can't." I suppose that the shared laugh was important too.'

'EYE' AND 'I'

Miss Lucy Ashworth does not look at me as we sit down. I can only guess what her eyes might be like. We shake hands.

We sit down in chairs placed at an angle so that we can look at each other or look away without obviously doing so. Miss Ashworth turns her head and immediately begins to talk in a dull flat monotone. She tells me about her fears of travelling and goes on with a recital of her life-story. After about forty minutes she pauses. But she does not give me any of the conventional looks or glances which indicate 'Now you can say something', or which ask 'How do you take all that?' There are none of those eye signals which regulates a conversation.

She sits, quite still.

I speak.

'I feel you are telling me a lot about yourself – a lot of important things. But you seem scared to let me know what is going on inside you *now*.'

Silence. I try again.

'Maybe it is too dangerous.'

My contributions are badly timed and, maybe, they are too direct.

She continues her monologue. At the end of an hour, she is quick to glimpse a slight movement of my feet. Abruptly, she gets up and leaves without a glance.

At her next visit, with downcast eyes, Miss Ashworth motions me to my chair. Then she sits on a couch which is directly behind me. Involuntarily, I begin to turn my chair but she speaks sharply.

'No, you sit there. I'll sit here.'

It is not easy to talk, let alone listen, staring into space with eyes boring into the back of your head. It is hard going being watched like that for two months. Week by week, my interpretations become more and more desperate.

During the second and in subsequent interviews she talks differently, with a variable tempo, pitch, and rhythm. Her voice trembles as she tells me about her fears of attacking people in public places and especially about the absences of her mother.

'She was so cold . . . dead. Well, she is really dead now. But when I was little I used to imagine she was blind . . . she wasn't really.'

One day Miss Ashworth comes in and, as usual, sits on the couch. After a few minutes she murmurs softly.

'I have got a good look at you. Now I can see you are *there*.'

Hesitantly, she moves to the chair and fixes her eyes on my face, somewhere around my mouth. A fixed stare. She does not take her eyes off me for many sessions. Not for a moment.

As time goes on, Miss Ashworth begins to express her fears of having damaged her mother. Now, at times, she looks away.

It is a difficult moment when, suddenly, she looks directly into my eyes.

'My mother wasn't really cold but she felt it. Do you *see*?'

Her look is a demand: 'Now you say something.' I cannot resist replying to that commanding look.

'I suppose . . . You are scared of all that rage and are keeping it all in control. And controlling me now . . . with your eyes I mean. Scared of losing yourself in looking *with* me. But also scared of being cut off.'

I do not know what I am saying with my eyes – a great problem for a psychotherapist.

It is Tuesday afternoon. I have just returned from a holiday, and Miss Ashworth arrives late. She is silent for the first ten minutes of the session. I see that her tension is mounting and I intervene.

'I reckon you are mad with me. Maybe about my going away.'

She has never been angry with me, not in a direct way. Now, she looks straight at me with retracted eyelids – a glare. She picks up an ink bottle that I have left on the table between us, unscrews the top and makes a move as if she is going to throw it at me. I suppose that I look alarmed. Suddenly, she puts the bottle down and blushes. Her eyes fall, her head droops and she buries her face in her arm.

I wait.

She makes a few exploratory glances, like a child peeping through its fingers at a stranger – a look of shame. Then she says:

'I am sorry.'

Trying to make contact. The hope of getting in touch is important in shyness and in shame.

'You always look so severe and never smile,' she says.

I tell myself that surely that cannot be true: not literally.

'I suppose my face would look different with ink all over it.'

Maybe my eyes have a twinkle.

Our eyes meet and she smiles. Lucy (now an 'eyedentity' – not 'Miss Ashworth') smiles.

'An eminent analyst with ink running down his face,' she says.

We burst into a laugh. Together. Looking with each other as we *see* the joke: the incongruity.

A year later, Lucy says 'You know things only happened – I mean being less cut off from myself, *being* myself – when I could look and see you . . . it was a real achievement, that looking. Before, I had so often wanted to say "Look into my eyes and see what I am trying to say and can't."'

This brief account illustrates a number of ways in which looking and seeing are central in human conversation. Initially, Miss Ashworth was afraid to look at me directly. I was an unpredictable 'stranger'. Yet, she kept her eye on me and noticed how the movement of my feet signalled the end of the session. It was the eye-to-eye contact that was dangerous.

My reference to things 'going on inside now' increased the danger and, in order to avoid any possibility of looking into my eyes, she sat behind me. Then she became more able to talk more freely about violent emotions and about the pain of being left by her cold 'blind', 'dead' mother. I felt deprived of a reassuring eye-contact and my anxiety mounted.

It was only when Miss Ashworth had got a good look at me that she could 'see-feel' that I was 'there'. Then, she could sit in a chair and look at my face but not, for a time, directly at my eyes. The first eye-to-eye look was a controlling stare. Maybe that unmoving look kept her violent anger under control and helped her to talk about fears of damaging her mother. Certainly it controlled me: I felt that I could not move. My slightest reactions were scrutinized with suspicion.

Following the period of holiday separation Lucy's violent glare of direct anger and threatened aggression ended with the facial expression characteristic of embarrassment and shame – blushing, dropping of the eyes, hiding the face together with exploratory peeping.

Self-consciousness bore the possibility of a new consciousness of 'self'.

At last, our eyes met. We came together and we parted. To and fro. I thought of the pun, 'eyedentity'. We were separate. But in a mutual smile and a laugh, we looked *with* each other. We shared a gaze. Two 'I's and 'eyes', distinct and yet together. There was a shift, a step forward, a movement of insight. It was as if it happened *to* us, from somewhere 'out there': an experience of 'I-being-myself' within a personal dialogue.

In a progressive eye-conversation we made, cut off, and re-established contact. In Lucy's talk and behaviour there were many other expressive movements of approach and avoidance. Here, I am concerned with how this conflict is embodied in eye-language: in 'peeping', 'staring', 'glaring', and 'gazing'. And how fear inhibits the dialogue of aloneness-togetherness, the meaningful, reciprocal rhythm of looking and looking away, and the sharing of a gaze.

I shall make some brief comments upon the importance of personal eye-conversations, the anxiety and taboos associated with eye-intimacy, the creative potentialities in shame, and the freshness of vision in a new look.

A competent psychotherapist is not a slave of words. In promoting a therapeutic conversation he must perceive and respond to non-verbal 'body-language': subtle changes of pitch, tone, rhythm, and emphasis of voice, nuances of body movement and gesture, and especially the dialogue of faces and eyes. As H. Magnus wrote in 1885: 'though we were as eloquent as Demosthenes and Cicero . . . yet our skills would not equal the bewitching speech of the eyes'.[3]

Perhaps, the first personal conversation in life is in a language of the eyes. Recent research has demonstrated the central importance of gazing and eye-contact in early childhood.

A psychotherapist is confronted by a person. He must venture beyond hard evidence and I shall list a few germinal, albeit speculative, ideas which guide my practice.

EYES AND EARLY CONVERSATION

Man is afraid of the dark.

More than many other, if not all other species, he relies upon his vision to order his world and to relieve his uncertainty about the nature of things. He is suspicious about objects that are poorly visualized and cannot be brought into clear focus. Any indistinct perceptions arouse anxiety, but this is particularly so with regard to sight.

> 'And the earth was without form, and void; and darkness was upon the face of the deep . . . And God said, "Let there be light."'
>
> (*Gen. I.* 2–3)

> 'The light of the body is the eye.'
>
> (*Matt. VI.* 22)

Bodily contact, the sucking mouth, and kinaesthetic sensations are doubtless the formless undifferentiated 'earth' and 'deep' of the infant's world. In the first three days of life the baby can use 'perception' in a global diffuse sense to distinguish the mother's breast from a strange breast. But the light of vision plays a central part in the creation of a world of objects. The newborn baby makes gross postural movements of the head to avoid excessively bright stimuli and bring into view light of lower intensity. Between two and five weeks, the infant begins to move his eyes and head in response to sounds and sights. There is a 'What is it?' reflex; an adaptive reaction to unexpected or unfamiliar stimuli. These primitive investigatory responses develop into an exploratory attitude towards the environment. It seems that in exploring there is an inborn preference for complexity, for three dimensions, and for the pattern of a human face.

Man is characteristically a social animal, and eyes have a unique importance in human conversation. Human beings gaze into the eyes of another in an affiliative way – as a means of promoting cooperative behaviour. Most animals stare in anger or fear.[4] Human looks communicate fear, anger, shame, and other emotions, but above all they establish emotional contact and, as exploration proceeds, they play a central part in the development of feeling: of love. Sight is associated with the capacity for speech, and a 'language of the eyes' is central in human relationships – in personal conversations.

In order to develop, or indeed to survive, a baby must establish a feeling-bond with one care-taker, usually the mother. Becoming a human being means learning a language – a mode of being with other persons in a reciprocal relationship.

By twelve to fifteen weeks (probably much earlier) normal infants can control eye movements. Looking is the only activity that is as controlled an action and act as it is with an adult. Mother and baby can both choose to look or look away, and there is a back and forth 'holding and breaking' of eye contact. There is an equality. Each can deprive or attempt to control the other – or they can share a gratifying, intimate gaze. The baby learns to be an equal partner in a dialogue.

It seems that in a mutual achievement of separateness and intimacy, of aloneness-togetherness, the 'presentation' of a human face is an evocative signal and symbol.

When two weeks old, a baby can recognize the difference between crude expressions of emotions in faces: a suggestion of a dawning distinction between persons and things. The first eye-to-eye contact is probably made at the age of about one month. As he can only see a distance of from about seven to twelve inches, it might well be that it is the mother's eyes which dominate his visual experience amidst a hazy background. The child gains a basic trust, not only by being fed, warm, dry, and free from pain but also, perhaps more importantly, by enjoying an optimum degree of visual contact within the pattern of a face.

A human face provides security by its constancy: a stable equilibrium. It promotes interest and curiosity by its ever-changing novelty: a dynamic equilibrium. As looks are exchanged, understood, and re-sponded to, continued differentiation and integration occur, with the creation of expanding 'wholes'. But, there is an optimum level of arousal between boredom and overwhelming excitement and a need for a balance between approach-looking and avoidance-looking, between togetherness and separation.

In personal conversations, from infancy onwards, there is a need for an equilibrium between stability and change, between intimacy and separ-ation, between aloneness and togetherness. The balance is upset by undue anxiety and fear. Exploring eyes, loving eyes, fearful eyes, and angry eyes all play their part. If stability is too great there is boredom; if there is too much change there is undue excitement and a threat of chaos.

In the shared look separation ceases to be isolation and alienation. Yet, there is an opposite danger. Intimacy can become non-differentiation or fusion. Then, there is a loss of distinct identity.

Seeing and touching work together. Should there be deprivation of bodily contact or too little opportunity to explore by touch, there can be a compensatory visual dependence with excessive looking, or (as in the case of Lucy Ashworth) a reaction against the compulsion by avoidance of the eye-to-eye gaze.

During the first year the infant recognizes and responds to a unique, feeling face. The face of the mother is distinguished from, and chosen in preference to, other faces. I suggest that a sense of identity, closely linked with a later confident ability to say the word 'I', begins to emerge from the eye-language of infancy when a baby recognizes the face of 'my mother'. He can control ('choose', 'will') actions and acts of looking and, in a rhythm of gratifying and frustrating aloneness and togetherness, he is an active participant. This process of discovery is often re-enacted in the conversation of psychotherapy. The pun on 'eye' and 'I' is a pregnant one. It can be made in many languages ranging from French and Spanish to a dialect of Berber.

If, as I suggest, seeing and looking are of central importance in the establishment of identity, with an ability to use the word 'I', then there should be great problems for blind babies. This prediction, made very many years ago, is supported by recent research.[5]

Vision words have a peculiar logical status in our language. The visual field (and the 'visual world') has a *centre* but fades into a penumbra of mystery. Hearing, touch, and smell are non-centred, and in the achievement of personal identity these senses become organized around sight. I shall suggest that there is great significance in the fact that in metaphors bringing together sensations, seeing-words are the topic and seldom, if ever, the vehicle; for example, 'hard eyes', 'penetrating looks', 'a quiet gaze'.[6] Furthermore, in common with touch, there is a sense of direct contact. In ordinary language, we can say 'I hear a sound coming *from* that car' or 'I smell the scent *from* that flower' whereas with seeing (or touching) we do not interpose a sight and we say 'I see the car', 'I see the flower'.[7]

Lucy Ashworth became more free to explore in 'fact', fantasy, and imagination. Human beings, when not crippled by fear, are curious. Psychotherapy is concerned mainly with the lessening of what blocks exploration and discovery in the active creation and re-creation of a world in and between persons: in personal problem-solving. A tentative adventure into the unknown can be halted by pain and resulting anxiety, with the development of neurosis.

The baby and the adult need to maintain an optimum level of anxiety.

It must not become too great or seeing can become too dangerous. Hence the taboo on looking.

Drawing heavily on the work of Silvan S. Tomkins,[8] I shall consider very briefly fears of the unpredictable stranger, of sexual intimacy, and of destructive aggression – especially related to envy. Those themes will lead on to a discussion of the positive potentialities in shyness and shame.

THE TABOO ON LOOKING

Try looking deeply and intensely into the eyes of someone you do not know well. You will become aware of the deep-seated taboo on the look of intimacy.

The face is the mirror of the emotions and the eyes are the 'windows of the soul'. In a simultaneous expression and communication, we give and receive, as our eyes convey and register the emotions of joy, interest, curiosity, anger, fear, and many complex combinations of these and other affects.

There is a mutual awareness and an awareness of mutuality.

Maybe we will adjust our communication in a shared look. If you respond to my angry look with a fearful retraction of the eyelids and protrusion of the eyeballs, I can modify my look and reassure you. If your look of excited interest causes me to lower my lids and eyes in embarrassment I might peep back in a tentative exploration, to see if it is safe to continue our exchange, and to restore the equilibrium between us. But we must not go too far. Intimate looking can lead to an escalation of emotion: an error-increasing 'feedback'. Excitement (with anxiety, anger, or sexual arousal) in A then arouses excitement in B which raises excitement in A which further excites B, and so on. This danger can be avoided by a taboo on looking.

The taboo is necessary for the maintenance of a stable society and of personal relationships, but if it is extreme then it inhibits the development of a conversation. There is a need for both distance and contact. We move towards and away from others within our personal space.

The Stranger

Human beings are lured by novelty. In coming to know another person and being known by him or her, we make an exciting venture into mystery. But the too strange is dangerous. It is risky to stare hard and long at strangers and, in man and other animals, the look is cut off if the face or its expression are too unfamiliar and threaten undue excitement or dangerous self-exposure. We need a reassuring face.

The taboo on the stare is perhaps biologically based, built in by evolution. It is undoubtedly reinforced by those social pressures which maintain the cohesion and stability of a human group.

The Sexual Look

'Lust not after her beauty in thine heart; neither let her take thee with her eyelids.'

(*Prov.* VI. 25)

Perhaps Clement of Alexandria was thinking of 'making eyes', 'bedroom eyes', 'the glad eye', and 'undressing her with his eyes' when he made the somewhat exaggerated suggestion that 'it is impossible for one who looks not to lust'. In courtship, flirtation, seduction, and foreplay (if rarely in intercourse) the eye works closely together with the hand and the genitals. In so far as there is a taboo upon or fear of sexual behaviour there is an inhibition of the searching, penetrating mutual look of mounting sexual excitement. There is a conflict between desire for the joy of intimacy and the recoil from a threatened loss of identity in orgasmic fusion.

The association between looking and genital sexuality is complex as illustrated by social differences in behaviour, epitomized by a man who had intercourse with a different woman every night without a qualm but was shocked beyond measure when he saw one of them undress. The sexual look is certainly not merely a substitute or 'symbol' for other bodily activities in adult sexual behaviour.

The taboo is complicated and the interrupted look can be used to defeat its own end, as when excitement is increased by the modest lowering of the eyes which 'says' seductively, 'It is naughty but wouldn't it be nice?'

Perhaps the most intimate and exciting of all statements is to look deeply into the eyes of another.

It is not always easy for some psychotherapists to avoid using, wittingly or unwittingly, sexual attractiveness (heterosexual and/or homosexual) as a gratifying, collusive means of avoiding unpleasant significant conflicts. The sexual look and the taboo are very open to manipulative exploitation.

The Damaging Look and the Envious Eye

In many animals, the stare can express a threat of attack as well as a fear of being attacked. So too in man. Indeed, the glare can be experienced literally as an attack. It can evoke bodily sensations of damage, which is perhaps often the case in early childhood. The taboo guards against mutual destruction.

I shall confine myself to one theme which is of special importance in psychotherapy: the evil, envious eye.

According to a Moroccan proverb, the evil eye 'owns two-thirds of the graveyard' and the belief in its power still exists amongst hard-headed farmers in Devon. In the following brief comment I shall ignore many interesting features such as its relative frequency among women, the test of witchcraft by an inability to weep, and the bride's veil which protects her and others from the damaging (and sexual) look.

The power over another by looking, especially by holding his look, has been associated with contagion. It is related to touch but as Francis Bacon put it 'fascination is ever in the eye'. The eyes of John Wesley, Adolf Hitler, and other charismatic leaders are said to have had this fascinating power. It can be for good or evil but is usually assumed to be the latter. Martin Delrio, a Jesuit of Louvain, wrote in 1603:

> 'Fascination is a power derived from a pact with the devil, who, when the so-called fascinator looks at another with an evil intent, or praises, by means known to himself, infects with evil the person at whom he looks.'[9]

Witches with the evil eye were frequently the poor, old, ugly, and malformed. Their deprived hostility might be a danger to the more fortunate who (perhaps like the successful Devon farmer of today) feared the destructive power of their envious look. As Bacon put it:

> 'Envy emitteth some malign and poisonous spirit which taketh hold of the spirit of another ... Deformed persons, and eunuchs, and old men, and bastards are envious.... For he that cannot possibly mend his own case will do what he can to impair another's.'[10]

An important, widespread, but often neglected, theme is fear of the envious dead.

Lucy was most afraid of her mother's 'dead look' which she occasionally saw in my eye. The 'deadness' was not merely an absence. It was also malevolent destruction. It was only when she had got a good look at me, and recognized her own envy, that she could 'see-feel' that I was 'there'. Lucy's look of intimacy, with the possibility of dialogue, was blocked by the fear of the look of envious destructiveness: the eyes of a 'dead' mother, whom Lucy felt she had blinded and killed.

A highly intellectual young man, Martin, feels that he has cancer and is unfit to be alive. His anxiety and feelings of persecution have been related to his intense envy and fear of envious attacks by which he will be damaged or destroyed. He depends desperately upon my physical presence and my 'goodness' with which he feels able to fuse, thereby maintaining a precarious identity. Yet, there have been more than a few hints of a destructive envy of the 'good' things in me. (It is to be noted that in this envy lies the possibility of a separate identity, for one cannot envy without a distinction between oneself and the other.) Martin is terrified of death which, to him, means being shattered, mutilated, or isolated by personified Death.

We are beginning to deal with Martin's persecutory anxiety – an intense fear of an attack which he experiences, with a dim awareness, as being damaged or destroyed in a near-literal bodily sense. His difficulties in social situations have been linked, tentatively, with the fear of his own envy experienced in others, as being 'out there': 'I must stay empty or they will want to take away what I have got.'

One day, Martin is talking to me quietly. Suddenly, he shrinks away with an expression of horror, gazing fixedly at my eyes as if helpless and trapped. He sees my face change. Later he says: 'I actually saw you different, especially your eyes. Evil. Boring into me. The Devil. The Death Man and me going out of existence.'

Although much had to be done over many years, Martin still vividly recalls the moment as a transforming experience. The 'curse in a dead man's eye' recalls the case of Samuel Taylor Coleridge.

A modern psychiatrist would probably diagnose Coleridge, a great and lovable man, as a psychopathic borderline personality. His meandering, brilliant, battered death-in-life voyage through the world is disclosed in *The Rime of the Ancient Mariner*. It is a kind of prospective autobiography, but it is also a great poem and, as such, is much more than an individual statement. The sea journey, the wanton murder of the friendly white bird, the ravages of guilt, the isolated abandonment, and the hope of redemption are universal experiences. They call forth echoes in all of us – albeit in some more than in others.

The theme of envy in Coleridge's works and life merits detailed study. Here, I wish only to throw out a hint. I do so not as a venture into literary criticism but because it was the 'Ancient Mariner' that brought home to me the importance of a dead man's eye and helped me to see more in my patients' lives, and in my own. I shall make only one or two comments from an analysis of the poem.[11]

After the killing of the albatross by the Mariner, a period of exciting adventure ends in a weary time of stagnant, tortured depression. A strange skeleton ship appears and, in a game of dice, the Mariner's soul is won by a leprous woman, LIFE-IN-DEATH.

Coleridge was haunted by terrifying nightmares. They are portrayed in his poem 'The Pains of Sleep', but more vividly in his private *Notebooks*. He carefully recorded his dreams and associations to them. Often, they included terrifying and large spectre-women:

'Friday Night, Nov 28, 1800, or rather Saturday Morning – a most frightful Dream of a Woman whose features were blended with darkness catching hold of my right eye & attempting to pull it out – I caught hold of her arm fast – a horrid feel – Wordsworth cried out aloud to me hearing my scream – heard his cry & thought it cruel that he did not come ... When ~~my~~I awoke my right eyelid swelled –

'I was followed up & down by a frightful pale woman who, I thought, wanted to kiss me, & had the property of giving a shameful Disease by breathing in the face.'[12]

I am sceptical about pretentions to analyse writers long dead, and it is not my aim to make a formulation of the psychodynamics of Coleridge, although he does provide us with more material than most. It is not possible, however, to ignore the profound split between the two women in his personal world. Over here is the dark, leprous, destructive harlot and over there is the Queen of Heaven, Mother Mary, and the Moon in her benign aspect (the Moon in the poem is both 'good' and 'bad'). The divorce is evident in the poem. It is amplified in the *Notebooks* and other writings and in his idealized love for Sara Hutchinson.

The terrible woman (suggestively associated in Coleridge's notes with Wordsworth's sister, Dorothy) threatens to pull out his eye. The Oedipus myth is about blinding. Freud had great guilt-feelings about seeing his mother naked and, in his letters to Fliess, he could only write about it forty years later in Latin.[13]

Coleridge went through life as a deprived child – and a very envious child with an envious eye. Intense envy is often seen out there: projected. A rejected child feels he has no right to be alive and is persecuted by the envious dead, especially the dead mother, whom he feels that, by his rage, he has destroyed.

The Mariner's shipmates die as a result of his destructive deed. The cruel moon looks on. Yet 'looks on' is not right: we feel that it is 'she' who is in control.

The Mariner lives in the curse of the dead man's eyes, an abandoned, guilt-ridden orphan. Coleridge often spoke of himself as having no family – as being a spiritual orphan.

'An orphan's curse would drag to hell
A spirit from on high;
But oh! more horrible than that
Is the curse in a dead man's eye!
Seven days, seven nights, I saw that curse,
And yet I could not die.'[14]

When I was very young – about five I suppose – I had a dread of pennies. My mother had once said to me 'Now, Bobby, don't put that penny in your mouth' (I always liked sucking and biting things), 'it might have been on a dead man to close his eyes.' I have often felt that I was an 'accident' and have no right to be alive. A brother died in infancy. The stare of the envious dead is very hard to bear.

A survivor of the Hiroshima nuclear holocaust, recollecting the scene of devastation said:

> 'The most impressive thing was the expression in people's eyes – bodies badly injured which had turned black – their eyes looking for someone to come and help them. They looked at me and knew I was stronger than they.... It was very hard to be stared at by those eyes.'[15]

The avoidance of the 'curse in a dead man's eye' is evident in many funeral rituals. It is often clearly associated with a fear of vengeance from the departed person who envies the mourners who still possess life, strength, and material goods. The survivors feel guilty about remaining alive.

Unresolved and unrecognized envy, often experienced in projection, is frequently a clinically important feature of persistent bereavement reactions.

The expanding look of intimacy, of aloneness-togetherness, can (if not blocked by extreme, unreal fear) lead to insight: a new look. Psychotherapists can only hope to be window-cleaners.

A NEW LOOK

In his desolation the Mariner is visited by a fresh vision, expressed in one of the most simple and beautiful passages of English poetry.

> 'The moving Moon went up the sky
> And no where did abide:
> Softly she was going up,
> And a star or two beside –'[16]

He sees anew the water-snakes, 'the thousand, thousand slimy things'. He 'watches' their beauty in glossy green, velvet black, and a 'flash of golden fire'. A spring of love gushes from his heart and he blesses them 'unaware'. At last he can sleep, and the ship 'moves onward from beneath'.

Sometimes – only sometimes – that is how it is in psychotherapy. There is a new look. We sense, and move with, unaware, an obscure something which we 'know', but do not 'know about'.

I was losing hope of ever being able to help Fiona, a middle-aged woman with chronic depression and an uncontrollable habit of blinking.

We had 'analysed' sexual fears and envious rage. But it all stayed in our heads. There was no moving conversation – no vibration, no colour, no living form. We were stuck.

Then one day, I do not know 'why', she gazes at me. Or rather *with* me, for the first time.

After a few moments she looks away, as if emerging from a wide, wide sea. She speaks quietly.

'The other day . . . was it only yesterday? . . . I am not sure. Well, I saw a beggar . . . You don't see beggars these days . . . and I suppose he was really an alcoholic going down skid-row looking for cheap spirits. But asking . . . straight out. "Just a few coppers," he said. It was queer though. He asked and I saw him different. He really looked different. Changed.

'Or maybe, I changed my eyes . . . I see what it means; to look and beg without blinking. Not just ask roundabout . . . sort of . . . doctors to cure my eyes. But it's so frightening to see things different.'

Insight. Not so much seeing something new but a new way of seeing – a freshening of what is familiar. To Coleridge this is one quality of 'genius':

'To carry on the feelings of childhood into the powers of manhood, to combine the child's sense of wonder and novelty with the appearances which every day for perhaps forty years had rendered familiar. . . . And so to represent familiar objects as to awaken the minds of others to a like freshness of sensation concerning them.'[17]

We can't make it happen; but, maybe, we can cultivate attitudes and skills of being open to receive what comes. Learning to 'watch', to 'notice' with 'loving attentiveness', means owning and cleansing (if only a little) the fearful envious eye.

Re-birth? Yes and no. Our glimpses of wholeness are never realized. Fiona's symptoms did not change much. Her vision often seemed to be lost but, from time to time, it came alive and brought new courage. For the Mariner, the outer accusing eyes become the internal eyes of acknowledged guilt. The curse is relieved but not removed, by confession to, and shriving by, the holy Hermit. The Mariner remains a homeless wanderer, passing like night from land to land. When his agony reaches a climax he is compelled to tell his tale over and over again. By his glittering eye he compels strangers to listen.

We see the ageing, flabby, corpulent Coleridge a lodger at Hampstead, pretending to give up opium and wracked by grandiose self-reproach. His brilliant talk could hold such men as Keats, Hazlitt, De Quincey, Lamb, Gilman, and many others. But his prodigious torrent of scintillating words was not seldom exasperating and even boring. He talked *at*, he could never talk *with*. He was never at home, either literally or metaphorically.

Yet, like so many borderline persons I have failed to help, Coleridge had vision. Maternal deprivation and psychotic splitting are not explanations of the great poem. They do not exhaust the meaning of the spring of love that gushes unbidden, unaware, nor the succeeding stanzas which express the blending of sight and sound in a vision of the Many and the One.[18]

'I' and 'myself' unfold in personal growth as the outward eye and the inward eye combine, separate, and re-combine in the creative process of imaginative vision: Joseph Conrad's 'glimpse of truth', 'within the core of each convincing moment'. In a shared look and in 'seeing' a shared joke, Lucy felt that she was more able to 'be herself'.

In the next chapter I shall reflect upon the looks of 'inner faces' in shame, self-disgust, and guilt, in an attempt to make some sense of the movement of insight and of the curious word 'myself'.

In the hope of learning a little more about how to use my eyes, I return to the lonely, depressed, misanthrope Joseph Conrad who, more than most, looked into the 'Heart of Darkness'. He strove to descend within himself to that 'lonely region of stress and strife' and to

> 'arrest, for the space of a breath, the hands busy about the work of the earth, and compel men entranced by the sight of distant goals to glance for a moment at the surrounding vision of form and colour, of sunshine and shadows; to make them pause for a look, for a sigh, for a smile – such is the aim, difficult and evanescent, and reserved only for a very few to achieve. But sometimes, by the deserving and the fortunate, even that task is accomplished. And when it is accomplished – behold! – all the truth of life is there: a moment of vision, a sigh, a smile – and the return to an eternal rest.'[19]

And perhaps – if only for a moment – seeing through the darkness of our fear and envy, we might *share* a gaze, with a new vision.

· 9 ·
VISION

In the last chapter I moved between 'eyesight' and 'insight'. I shall expand the metaphor in an attempt to disclose what I mean by 'vision'. Insight is a central notion in 'Romantic psychotherapy', of which the Conversational Model is one example. 'Romantic' is often a bad word for hard-headed scientists but, as Ellenberger[1] has clearly shown, the roots of dynamic psychotherapy and psychiatry (including the theories and practice of Freud and Jung) lie deep in the Romantic tradition.

I have repeatedly stressed that a personal relationship means a state of aloneness-togetherness. To be alone means the discovery of an inner world. It is a world of 'my own' but I do not own it: I live *in* it. Perhaps this cryptic saying will become clearer as the following discussion develops from the inner faces of shame and self-disgust to Imagination which William Blake experienced as 'Ever expanding in the Bosom of God'.[2]

In a new look, Lucy Ashworth felt more able to be 'herself' (Chapter 8). An important movement, a shift, a carrying forward, happened in the looking and not-looking of shame. There was an angry glare, a blush, a dropping of eyes and head and, most important, a peep through her fingers. The peep was a look at, with, into, and beyond me: an outward-inward look. In shyness and shame there is a resonance between 'outer' and 'inner' faces.

SHYNESS AND SHAME

I have seen Mr and Mrs Boardman twice because of a marital problem. They have talked about their daughter, Katy, an only child aged seven. I go into the waiting room and find that they have brought Katy with them.

I make a serious mistake. I smile and say 'Hello Katy,' but I move towards her too quickly and look at her too directly. I invade her personal space.

Katy's eyes drop. Her eyelids droop. She flushes, hangs her head, covers her face with her hands, and retreats behind her mother.

Mrs Boardman blushes, drops her hand on to her daughter's shoulder. 'Say "Hello" to Dr Hobson. There's a good girl,' she urges.

Mr Boardman's head goes back and up and his lips curl in contempt. 'Now Katy!' he barks, sharply and coldly.

I chat with the parents about the weather and in a few minutes, out of the corner of my eye, I catch a glimpse of Katy peeping at me through her fingers.

Three faces: the face of shyness, the face of shame, and the face of disgust.

In situations of extreme novelty, such as an unexpected change in another's face, exploratory enjoyment is inhibited. Surprise moves into fear and the look is broken off. The avoidance is especially marked if there are other distressing or frightening circumstances. But in shyness and shame there is a continued interest in the object – the peep.[3]

Shame is a complex act in which facial communication is interrupted by a lowering of the eyes, hanging the head, and covering the face. It is on a continuum with shyness. Both are ambivalent. There is a wish to look and yet a wish not to look too hard: a desire to be looked at and yet a desire to avoid being seen too intensely. Yet, there is a taboo on looking away too obviously. 'Katy, it is rude to stare at visitors but it is bad manners to avoid them.' The peep between the fingers is a sign of continued interest: a 'looking for' with the possibility of a new 'looking at', and 'seeing' – a fresh vision.

The ambivalence is revealed by one striking feature of shyness and shame – the blush. The face is hidden but it is also made more obvious. The blush attracts attention and so defeats the aim of not being looked at. More important perhaps, it draws the attention of the person who blushes. He or she becomes more aware of her/his own face, the site of the emotions. In becoming self-conscious I become more conscious of myself. In a smile, our attention is focused on the other's face and in fear it is directed to the object. In shame we look inward.

We become ashamed of shame and learn to conceal or modify its overt expression by adopting a mask-like face, an expression of fixed humility, a penetrating stare, a forced smile. But often, on close inspection (or the use of high speed photography) it is possible to observe slight, barely detectable signs of casting down of eyes and lids with a heightening of colour. If discerned they can provide important cues in psychotherapy.

Hiram P. Pitcher was a highly successful, middle-aged, American businessman. A disciple of Hemingway and a former top-league foot-baller, he rhapsodized about the pioneers who conquered the wide-open spaces of the West. Suddenly, one day, he developed a compulsive throwing back of his shoulders and raising of the face: a caricature of the he-man keeping his chin up in the face of the whooping Sioux horde closing in on Custer's last stand. When we touched on the topic of sex the symptom became more marked, but now and then his eyes dropped and I could detect a slight blush. After many weeks, he hesitantly told me about having been impotent one night shortly before the onset of his distressing symptom. For some minutes he sat drooping with hanging head, avoiding my gaze. Then, his contortion returned with renewed vigour. 'I had had too much Bourbon that night,' he said dismissively. There was a good deal of evidence from associations and dreams to support an hypothesis that he was avoiding intense feelings of inadequacy and fears of weakness. Above all, he had a terror of the mocking laughter of his peers. But, he could not recognize and own the timid child within him. He ceased to see me and he kept his symptoms. Maybe, my formulation was wrong; it is difficult to learn from our many failures. However, there can be little doubt that he was ashamed of shame.

Real dangers are avoided in the tabooed look of shame. But in the taboo on looking outward there are positive potentialities. As I look inward, I may become more aware of 'myself'.

INTERNALIZED SHAME AND SELF-DISGUST

As psychological development proceeds, the faces of others are, as it were, taken into an 'inner' world and combined as internalized 'faces' – the lowering negative face of anger, shock, contempt, or disappointment and the smiling positive face of affection, admiration, and under-standing.

The 'looks' of these inner faces are closely related to our physical visible face and there is much truth in Abraham Lincoln's dictum that at forty a man becomes responsible for his own face. For the most part, we are not aware of what the symbolical movements and patterns of our face show, and this is a matter of great importance for the psychotherapist.

We always 'say' much more than we know. The metaphorical, symbolical transformation of inner faces is a powerful component of what we call 'conscience'.

Closely following Tomkins,[4] I make a distinction which is of great importance in psychotherapy. It is between internalized shame-humiliation, on the one hand, and internalized contempt-disgust on the other.

Recall Mr Boardman's face, contemptuously lifted away from Katy. Disgust is characterized by an expression which is very different from that of shame. There is a pulling away of the face, the upper lip is raised and the head is drawn back. It is particularly associated with food which is spat out with nausea or avoided as evil-smelling, but also with touching (e.g. slimy objects which stick to the skin). Disgust is a response to things which are noxious, disorderly, and messy. It is a rejection of the object, and increase of distance, an alienation. There is no continued interest in the object, as in the peep of shame. Hence there is less possibility of further exploration. This important difference is represented in the experience of internalized shame and internalized disgust.

In *internalized shame* there is a heightened consciousness of 'me' with a temporary withdrawal. The relation between me and myself is broken off, for a time, but there is the possibility of a new look, a peeping between the inner fingers. What I recognize as my actual behaviour is discrepant with my hitherto relatively unexamined conception of myself. There is a diminution of self-esteem, a sad break in the inner conversation with myself; yet there is the possibility of a new contact with, and increased knowledge of, the face (or faces) of 'myself' – a self-consciousness which is potentially a wider consciousness. Shame can function as an error-reducing mechanism: a 'feedback' which corrects the discrepancy between what I see I am and what I could be, leading to a new state of equilibrium. It is a recognition of incompleteness and, provided the discrepancy is not too great, can result in a drive to creation. We achieve 'insight' and perhaps, like Lucy Ashworth, 'see' the point of the incongruous joke.

The degree of discrepancy is important. If, as with Hiram Pitcher, the gap is too great, then there is the threat of a complete collapse of self-esteem; a fall into depression can only be prevented by avoidance actions which cut off the inner look. One of the most important processes in psychotherapy is the achievement of an optimum distance between what I feel I am and what I aspire to be: the re-creation of self-esteem, in which I am at ease with 'myself'. I emphasized this movement in the story of Sam (Chapter 1).

Self-disgust moving into self-contempt is very different from internalized shame. The rejection results in alienation – a getting rid of the poisonous substance and a renouncing of the hope of communion. In shame I maintain contact and continuity with yesterday's myself but, in the remorse of self-contempt, I totally reject the 'me' that behaved as I did. What I have done is always irreparable. There can never be a return to the *status quo ante*, whereas in shame the separation of me from myself can lead to creation, to a new kind of inner conversation.

When Sartre says 'the Other is the indispensable mediator between myself and me. I am ashamed of myself as I appear to the Other,' he uses a capital 'O'.[5] The 'Other' is all those other people with whom I relate. I can only find myself in and between me and my fellows in a human conversation.

When someone looks at me with disgust and contempt I can react in very different ways. One of the most common is by shame. So, too, in the dialogue between me and myself. I can be shamed by the contempt of myself or I can reject myself with contempt. In either case reconciliation is difficult so long as contempt is present. In shame, judge and offender are the same 'me', in self-disgust I am split from a part of myself which is alienated as an object – maybe as a thing. The dialectic can only be re-established by means of a mediator – the Other. The 'Other' always refers to, but is not exhausted by, another person. The term extends beyond a single other to a community of individuals.

To adapt Blake's phrase, shame cleanses the doors of perception: of myself and hence of others.[6] I become aware of my face – aware that it does not fit – that is to say that there is a discrepancy between how I see myself (in concrete fact or in imagination) and how strangers see me. 'Strangers' might be very familiar people who are seen anew. As they give me a new look which I do not fully apprehend I become aware of my inadequacy. There is a loss, a sadness. A mounting escalation of contempt-shame-increased contempt-increased shame can lead to despair or to neurotic avoidance activities. But, in shame, there is the possibility of a new 'look into' and, I might achieve *in*sight.

In simple ways shame, if not too great, can lead to correction of gaffes in social behaviours, but its significance is more profound. It can lead to growing awareness, although (or because) it implies a loss of the uninterrupted blissful union of the primal scene of Eden.

'And they heard the voice of the Lord God walking in the garden in the cool of the day [i.e. daylight]: and Adam and his wife hid themselves from the presence of the Lord God amongst the trees of the garden.
    And the Lord God called unto Adam, and said unto him,

"Where art thou?"

And he said, "I heard thy voice in the garden, and I was afraid, because I was naked; and I hid myself."

And he said, "Who told thee that thou wast naked?"'

(Gen. III. 8ff)

The loss is often experienced as catastrophic. The achievement of a new look of insight can mean the revolutionary destruction of an established order of personal experiences and social behaviour.

'And the Lord God said, "Behold, the man is become as one of us, to know good and evil . . ." So he drove out the man.'

(Gen. III: 22, 24)

'You have learnt something. That always feels at first as if you had lost something.'[7]

Sometimes – but only sometimes – if we can accept and rest in the sadness of loss and the loneliness of forsakenness and abandonment, we are visited by moments of vision in which we dimly sense and yet 'know' a larger 'myself'.

WHOLENESS AND BEING

In earlier chapters, I have emphasized the importance of responsible actions and acts. I have suggested also that it is crucial to stay with, and remain open to, what is 'beyond': an unknown, which is intimated by living symbols.

The Chinese teacher Lao Tzu said 'The way to do is to be . . . . Rather abide at the centre of your being; for the more you leave it the less you learn.'[8]

Within a developing personal relationship, Joe Smith became more able to feel 'himself', to be more in contact with his 'middle' (Chapter 3). Carrying forward, distinguishing, and linking experiences, taking responsibility for actions hitherto hidden in the shadows, creating steps of feeling, and committing himself in acts, he discovered a sense of being more 'whole'.

Questions about the 'centre' of being and 'wholeness' are often dismissed as being too vague for psychology. Yet they underlie, or are embodied in, the simple procedures of the Conversational Model.

In commenting upon the meeting with Joe, I wrote of my wish to understand something of 'what it is like to *be* him now', and, when discussing experiencing, I drew attention to the sense of knowing myself and George 'as a whole'.

It is not possible for me to stay in touch with, and own, all the experiences in my world, let alone express them. Yet in Rilke's 'most rare hour' (p. 36) I can apprehend, and to some degree remain with, a 'wholing' feeling, when memories turn to blood and are no longer distinguished from myself. In staying with experiencing, I sense, more or less dimly, a coherent 'myself' extending beyond my 'I' and giving a felt direction to my life. This movement is very different from that of abstract notions based upon discrete observations.

I am trying to intimate something about those occasions when I am in touch with, and speak from, my 'middle' in response to the language of another. The 'how', the manner of psychotherapy, can be prepared for but never commanded by technical procedures.

My experience can never be the whole of me, but yet there are times when it seems appropriate to speak of knowing, acting, and relating 'as a whole'. That is what it means to be in a personal relationship. It implies not only my wish to feel into Joe's limited experience at this moment, but also to face him, to 'be' with him 'as a whole': to value and respect his potentialities for growth towards a state of being-himself, of going on becoming a person. It means approaching an ideal which is never reached; as a curve moves towards, but never touches, an asymptote.

Symbols, such as moving metaphors, can intimate or disclose a whole. Poetry is one form of language which can suggest how a process of feeling can progressively combine units of experience into new wholes. William Wordsworth writes:

'Dust as we are, the immortal spirit grows
Like harmony in music; there is a dark
Inscrutable workmanship that reconciles
Discordant elements, makes them cling together
In one society. How strange that all
The terrors, pains, and early miseries,
Regrets, vexations, lassitudes interfused
Within my mind, should e'er have borne a part,
And that a needful part, in making up
The calm existence that is mine when I
Am worthy of myself!'[9]

The sense of a hidden, shaping, organizing workmanship, the *vis medicatrix naturae* (see Chapter 1), can be used as a faded metaphor in elaborating psychological theories. Later I apply notions of general system theory and the integrative activity of the nervous system to observations of human development. At this point I am concerned with experience.

Joe Smith, staying with his state of emptiness, became a 'wobbly' child. He ceased to be merely 'a machine getting the figures right'. Living beyond the void he was able to feel more – if only a fraction more – worthy of himself.

To hope to be oneself means to experience, to move into action, to act. Yet every act means to choose this and not that. It means a recognition of ambiguity with an acceptance of limitations. The solution of the most banal and immediate problem is an act of 'I'. But it is made against a background of what, for Wordsworth, required an initial capital: 'Being'.

> 'I felt the sentiment of Being spread
> O'er all that moves and all that seemeth still;
> O'er all that, lost beyond the reach of thought
> And human knowledge, to the human eye
> Invisible, yet liveth to the heart . . .'[10]

In rare moments of personal meeting I sense a wider myself which expands into what I shall call Being or Self. But terms and definitions are of little value, we need stories which disclose a meaning. Moments of vision do not always, indeed do not usually, happen in the immediate company of others but they do have a quality of personal relatedness and, I suggest, have something of the quality of the intimate look and gaze between mother and baby.

The outward eye works in harmony with an inward eye. Meister Eckhart said 'The eye with which I see God is the same eye with which God sees me.' In the *Upanishads* it is written 'Verily oneself is the Eye, the endless Eye.'[11] It is my eye and yet not mine. I do not possess the Buddha eye: the self which is the unseen centre of my many many inward eyes. Maybe, with it, like the Ancient Mariner, I see and act 'unaware'.

Maybe? I can only hope so, as I look back over thirty years of analytical and psychotherapeutic work, trying to use words which have been largely wasted.

MOMENTS OF DISCLOSURE

We have all known times of intense experience which stand out in relief against the more usual uniform background of our lives, and which at the time, and when recollected in tranquillity, charge our existence with special meaning and significance. As a lover of mountains I shall follow Abraham Maslow and term these moments of creative vision 'peak experiences'.[12] Many years ago I was nearing the summit of Scafell Pike, groping from cairn to cairn in a dense mist. Suddenly, to my amazement and wonder, a cloud-window opened and for an instant the beautiful green valley of Wasdale was revealed nearly three thousand feet below. The mist closed and I was left with a memory.

Artists, mystics, and some creative scientists in all ages and in diverse cultures have been able to express something of their value-laden insights, but most of us remain inarticulate about the glimpses of a visionary gleam which, in Wordsworth's terms, we 'half-perceive and half-create'. Nevertheless, we are profoundly affected by peak experiences when we are in love, when we are carried away by a theatrical performance, when our whole body is coordinated in a perfectly timed off-drive, when we take LSD, and when we have an aura before an epileptic fit. For better or for worse, they affect us profoundly.

The bright idea of the original scientist in his laboratory often does not seem to be essentially different from the vision which seized the Old Testament prophets; the 'Human Imagination' which William Blake experienced as 'the expanding Bosom of God'; the 'discernment-commitment' situation which Ian Ramsey sees as the heart of religion and morality;[13] the disclosure of a new significance in life apprehended by a schoolboy (or ageing psychotherapist) who falls in love; or from transforming moments of meeting in 'ordinary' friendships. The scientist, the poet, the theologian, the philosopher, the lover, and some 'vandals' on football terraces share an experience with some similar characteristics. But the understanding and elaboration, the developed insight, are very different.

The sense of mystery, wonder, and revelation cannot be exhausted by descriptive language. Although the process and conditions of creativity can be studied empirically, most scientific psychologists understandably ignore, or perhaps dismiss as 'mystical' and unworthy of consideration, such nebulous experiences which are difficult or impossible to study by controlled experimental methods. Yet, the clinical psychiatrist who must assess the pathological significance of ecstatic raptures is faced with the difficulties of communicating with persons who are in love. He cannot but agonize about the significance of insight in a psychotherapeutic conversation. All men are faced with the problem of making sense of moments of vision.

The disclosure-language of art, of stories employing presentational symbolism, is most appropriate for intimating ineffable and often paradoxical experiences. An attempt to describe by talking 'about' is fraught with pitfalls but there might be some value in abstracting some features of 'moments' or peak experiences. The following tentative list of characteristics is influenced by Maslow.[14]

Concreteness and Abstraction

Much of the time we abstract. Our perceptions are highly selected in terms of classifications and categories. That man is a bishop, this woman is a schizophrenic, that hard thing is a piece of limestone, this green object is a blade of grass. We enumerate the general characteristics of bishops, schizophrenics, limestone, and grass. As abstraction increases, the concrete image becomes emptied of raw experiencing.

In the immediacy of a peak experience, the person or thing ceases to be an instance of a larger category and becomes the sole member of a class. The bishop or schizophrenic is encountered as a unique person and there is an awareness of the blade of grass as a thing in itself – an intricate organization fearfully and wonderfully made. It will never occur again. There is no comparison: no better or worse, no higher or lower, no greater or less. It is as if the 'object', be it a beloved person, a leaf, a painting, or a fantasy image, claims our exclusive and full attention – it fills or rather *is* the world.

Yet, in a peak experience the ability to abstract discursively is not lost; it remains together and is interwoven with the concrete particularity of direct experience. There is a marriage between presentational and discursive symbolism, between imaginative thinking and directed thinking.

Unity and Diversity

The vision of a peak experience is unlike an act of casual observation, in that the object is seen with a 'caring minuteness' which reveals a richness of detail within a total field. The perception is highly differentiated and yet highly integrated and there is no contradiction between the parts and the whole. Nor is the vision static, there is a dynamic harmony, with many changing organizations and a continuous appearance of novelty. Continued exploration does not bring boredom; custom does not stale the infinite variety of the face of a deeply loved person or of the intertwining themes within *King Lear*.

Many thinkers, such as Butler, Kant, Ruskin, and Whitehead, have regarded moral insight as akin to aesthetic appreciation. Ruskin[15] analyses the qualities of a painting under two heads: the life and vitality of the parts and the unity of the whole, and considers that in the composed unity of a work of art the orderly balance and arrangement of the parts within the whole is heavenly in its nature and contrary to the violence and disorganization of sin. There is a sense of value.

Reconciliation of Contraries and Ambiguities

The more we apprehend the organization of greater wholes, the more we are able to discern patterns in which there is an integration of elements, experiences, and attitudes, which at other levels appear to be ambiguous, inconsistent, opposite, or flatly contradictory. Conflicts of opposing tendencies throw up new coalitions.

For Coleridge, imagination is a 'shaping spirit' which constantly breaks up established forms, by selecting and organizing the elements, resolving or transcending conflicts between them, and bringing to birth new modes of being. It achieves a 'balance or reconcilement of opposite and discordant qualities' of old and new, external and internal, natural and artificial.[16]

Bruner[17] studied a group of inventors and attempted to describe some of the phenomena of creativity. He found himself met by paradox and antinomy. There is both *detachment and commitment* – a disengagement from conventional accustomed ideas with a deep engagement and involvement in the emerging construction which will replace them. There is *passion and decorum* – a vitality, passion, and willingness to let impulses express themselves in life through the work, and yet a taming of the impulse, a love of form, an etiquette toward and a respect for materials. The exciting, turbulent speculations of the physicist give rise to the courtesy of an equation. There is *freedom from and yet a domination by the object*. We become free from the defences that keep hidden from us the deeper parts of ourselves. Yet we are the servant of the model, poem, or scientific paper which 'takes over' – for a time at least. There is *immediacy and deferral* – the creator yields to the fascination of an immediate urge and passionate conjecture and yet he resists the temptation to make a hurried closure and to exploit the idea prematurely. To Bruner's list could be added a sense of the *humour of incongruity*, which it seems correlates highly with original thinking. In a laugh, seriousness and absurdity can be reconciled and a problem can be looked at from a new angle. No doubt Einstein had fun when, in his 'combinatory play' during the initial stages of his investigation into relativity, he wondered what it would be like to run after a ray of light or ride on a sunbeam.

The Known and the Unknown

Figurative language and moving metaphor bring together, blend, and point beyond, hitherto unrelated images. They intimate a significant experience, a ground, which cannot be expressed in descriptive language. They communicate a freshness of vision. We are accustomed to describe grass as green and to look at sun-rays, but when we are confronted by such strange juxtapositions as Andrew Marvell's 'green thoughts in a green shade', or the picture of Einstein riding on a sunbeam, we are shaken out of our familiar mental sets or shapes and apprehend new possibilities.

In chapter 7, I wrote of a 'living symbol' as a presentation which re-combines images of things that are relatively familiar (although regarded, often, as contradictory or mutually exclusive) in such a way that there is an intimation of what is as yet unknown. I have stressed again and again the importance of a symbolical attitude in which a person is receptive and attentive to what might emerge from an immediate experience. Joe Smith listened to the word 'wobbly'. Kekulé had a sense of the significance of the dancing snakes and, without knowing what would come of the fantasy, he tuned in by sharpening his 'inward eye'. The presentation can be the concrete images of dream or fantasy; the perception of a person, a tree, a stone; or, for some people, the scandalous idea of Jesus Christ who was, and is, wholly man and wholly God.

The moment of insight, the 'Aha, I see it now,' is often experienced at first, as being more a discovery of something 'out there' rather than something 'I have done'. Fiona 'saw' the beggar (p. 129); Sonia, fiddling with the cotton-grass, felt a coincidence, a fit, between an 'inner' idea and a form in outer reality (p. 86f.). Persistent exploration and active attentiveness is, paradoxically, accompanied by a 'letting-be' – a receptiveness to what is 'given' in and beyond what is heard, seen, and sensed. It entails something akin to Coleridge's 'willing suspension of disbelief'.[18] There is an openness to receive what is novel, a counteraction to the more usual tendency to confirm our assumptions and presuppositions.

The combination of concentrated attention to detail, together with a nebulous receptiveness, is the unattainable ideal of a psychotherapist.

Creative thought means re-organizing and re-structuring the universe of understanding. It brings a new look in which hitherto unrecognized possibilities are apprehended. Much of the time we select what gives us immediate satisfaction and continue to justify our own beliefs. That is why I suggest to students of psychiatry that they should, in imagination, hang a text on the wall of their consulting room, 'Experience is what confirms a man in his errors', and to be on their guard when their teachers begin a sentence with 'In my experience . . .'.

In the most profound states of self-forgetfulness when we are most engrossed in the object it sometimes happens that we seem to see into 'the life of things'. This experience, which carries with it an intimation of meaning beyond the visible appearances, is the theme of Romantic poetry. Wordsworth remains firmly in the concrete world of things but his personal 'here and now' of bodily activity, of crags, of lakes, and of precipices, expands into a universe of grandeur which transcends and yet is in touch with us. There is an 'intermingling of Heaven's pomp on ground which British Shepherds tread' and 'Jerusalem is builded here in England's green and pleasant land.'[19]

By associating simple sensible experiences with some undefined order of things the Romantics have enriched our appreciation of the familiar world – awakening an awe and wonder at it; and in their living metaphors the unseen world is more vividly present just because it is made manifest in the minute particulars of a single actual case. But the poets only express and draw attention to experiences which come to most, if not all, men in everyday life.

The sense of a mysterious otherness is often disclosed with an overwhelmingness which evokes a sense of humility in the face of the enormity of the experience. The sense of wonder and awe (what Rudolph Otto calls the sense of the 'numinous',[20] a word often used by Jung) involves a blending of attraction and repulsion, of love and fear. 'I can't stand it; it is more than I can bear' is often accompanied by a sense of completion associated with dying. 'If I could die now it would be all right.' A characteristic of such experiences (which should not be beyond experimental investigation) is the changed experience of space and time which can amount to disorientation. The person not infrequently feels himself to be 'outside of' time – a state in which a day can be like a minute or a minute like a day. A moment in and out of time.

Persons and Things

The important distinction between the reciprocal relation with persons and the one-way observation of things has been discussed earlier (Chapter 2). I have suggested that material objects, such as Wordsworth's crags, a light-grey stone with a silver star, or a teddy bear, can be experienced in a 'personal way' and, conversely, that people must for some purposes be observed as things. The two attitudes complement each other in peak experiences, especially in personal relationships, and their interplay is of great importance in psychotherapy.

There is an important difference between 'objectivity', which can be defined in terms of agreement between observers, and 'objectification' – an attempt to eliminate completely the subjective personal involvement and bias of the scientist. In order to achieve reliability and consensus, the psychiatrist and psychotherapist resort to techniques such as observation through one-way screens, analysis of videotapes, self-administered questionnaires, and statistical analysis of public records. Important contributions can be made by use of these methods, given care in generalizing the findings and applying them to the face-to-face situation of the interview. Objectification goes together with a depersonalizing attitude towards human beings. (A method of psychiatric diagnosis based upon observations and classification is necessarily associated with judgements about what is valuable in human life.) Although we can tell scientific, poetical, and mythical stories about knowing a person, this knowledge cannot be caught in the net of thought or words – any more than we can explain to someone what cold tripe and chips tastes like without eating that delicious dish.

Courage and Openness

During a peak experience there is a temporary, although perhaps momentary, loss of anxiety and restraint. Fear inhibits the drive to risk the adventure of exploring the unknown. In a peak experience we are less afraid of ourselves, of being overwhelmed by our impulses towards pleasure, emotion, and aggression. We become more open to the external world and more in touch with the unknown depths in ourselves.

The tendency to cling to established habits and presuppositions is strengthened by fear of change. We can fear the loss of esteem (and income) in departing from current fashions, the pain of disappointing those we love, and be imprisoned by the inner faces of shame and disgust. Inhibiting fears of the unknown are legion, but basic to all is the threat of the disintegration of our ordered, structured world and a fall into meaningless chaos. A central theme of this book is the function of psychotherapy in lessening fear which blocks exploration and creative thought. It calls for courage – courage to be. [21]

Although love casts out fear it is perhaps more important to emphasize the fact that fear inhibits altruistic object-centred love and leads to possessiveness and jealousy with their underlying anxieties about loss, deprivation, insanity, and death.

Fact and Value

In the visionary gleam, the relationship of love, the creative leap, and the colour of the world revealed by the innocent eye of the child, there is no separation of fact from value. The 'isness' of the object carries its own value and exerts a claim upon the person. At that time, the experience is valuable in and for itself and there is little or no distinction between ends and means. That which 'is' is good in the light of a hope – an apprehension of what a whole and unified world might be like if present potentialities could be realized. There is a glimpse of 'heaven'. Pain and evil can appear unreal in the sense of being partial. The growth of a cancer can be seen as a beautiful thing in itself, intricate, awe-inspiring, and potentially good in the context of a larger whole. We become more in one piece, and there is a reconciliation of discordant elements including the impulses and wishes which we usually regard as being bad, inferior, neurotic, or infantile. Occasionally we can apprehend a pattern in our lives in which all our past joys and pains, successes and mistakes, are seen as parts of the creation of a unique shape which is right because it is what it is. Then I am worthy of myself.

Maybe, as Maslow suggests, if we could remain on the summit (which we certainly cannot) we would never blame and condemn others nor be disappointed or shocked by them. Kindness, tolerance, and perhaps sadness would be our only reactions with no comparison, exclusiveness or competition.

In moments when we are less aware of, and more detached from, our personal changing needs in relation to particular circumstances, values seem to be more universal, and timeless. We feel that the worthwhileness must be apparent to others and not only desire others to share our attitudes, but expect them to do so. An object can, however, be seen relatively in one moment and absolutely in the next. A Celtic brooch can be seen both as a typical produce of the first century AD and as having an aesthetic value for all time.

It is not only those insights which are usually regarded as specific disclosures of ethical values that 'guide and guard our moral being'.

> 'One impulse from a vernal wood
> May teach you more of man,
> Of moral evil and of good,
> Than all the sages can.'[22]

The above meditation has suggested that at times of creative insight there is a merging of the qualities of the factual, the beautiful, and the valuable – Wordsworth perceives 'the vernal wood' as a concrete reality, also as aesthetically satisfying and as exerting a moral claim – there is a coincidence of truth, beauty, and goodness. Maslow attempted to carry out an empirical study of the correlation of what is regarded as good, true, and beautiful. He reports that in 'normal' persons these are only fairly well correlated with each other and in the neurotic, even less so except in rare moments of love, of sex, of creativity, of aesthetic perception, of religious or mystic experience, of insight and understanding. But, he suggests that in some 'fully functioning people' they are 'so highly correlated that ... they can be said to fuse into a unity'.

I hope that Maslow is right, but I have never met a 'fully functioning' person and, in the face of torture, ugliness, and deceit cannot share his implied optimism. Some cloud-windows open into hell; there, too, can be a glimpse of the truth for which we have forgotten to ask. Nevertheless, the notion of 'insight' must carry some implicit idea of truth and value. The central value asserted in this book, and apprehended in moments of meeting, is Conrad's hope of a

> 'solidarity that knits together the loneliness of innumerable hearts ...
> which binds men to each other, which binds together all humanity.'[23]

It is a hope but certainly not an expectation. Conrad asserted the importance of solidarity and sincerity of feeling against a background of pessimism. He was ultimately, deeply, and compassionately involved and yet he could write:

> 'The mysteries of a universe made of drops of fire and clods of mud do not concern us in the least. The fate of a humanity condemned ultimately to perish from cold is not worth troubling about. If you take it to heart it becomes an unendurable tragedy. If you believe in improvement you must weep, for the attained perfection must end in cold, darkness and silences.'[24]

That, too, is insight.

· 10 ·
MYSELF

'I talk to myself' – 'I am not myself today' – 'I was beside myself when I said that' – 'When I did that I wasn't my real self' – 'I daren't show myself to people' – 'I wish I could be my real self and speak from my middle'.

We feel that we know what we mean by these, and similar statements. But when we detach ourselves, look at them critically, and reflect discursively, then they become more and more mysterious. What does it mean to say 'we detach ourselves'?

Richard III, in Shakespeare's play, is fighting a bloody war. The kingdom is divided. On the night before the decisive battle of Bosworth Field, Richard awakens from a nightmare. He soliloquizes:

> 'It is now dead midnight.
> Cold fearful drops stand on my trembling flesh.
> What do I fear? Myself? There's none else by:
> Richard loves Richard; that is, I am I.
> Is there a murderer here? No – yes, I am:
> Then fly. What, from myself? Great reason why –
> Lest I revenge. What, myself upon myself!
> Alack, I love myself. Wherefore? For any good
> That I myself have done unto myself?

> Oh, no! Alas I rather hate myself
> For hateful deeds committed by myself!
> I am a villain; yet I lie, I am not.'[1]

'I am I'; 'I am a villain; yet I lie, I am not'; 'Lest I revenge. What, myself upon myself! Alack, I love myself'; 'Alas I rather hate myself'. And later in the same speech: '... I myself Find in myself no pity to myself.'[2]

Most of us say immediately 'Yes, I know how it feels'. Shakespeare, the calm participating observer of human nature, realizes, in a vivid 'presentation', a split society of 'selves' engaged in an inner civil war.

Yet, pausing for a moment, I am perplexed. I enter Richard's world but there is more than one Richard: 'Richard loves Richard'. Speaking the lines again, I ask 'How many "I" "s and "myself's" are there in this lonely chaos?' I recall a short poem written by Sonia the cotton-grass lady (Chapter 6):

> 'How many of them are me?
> Were they all there in the womb?'

Was there ever a oneness – a lost Golden Age? Can there ever be peace and unity of a personal kingdom?

Wordsworth wrote of feeling: 'The calm existence that is mine when I/Am worthy of myself!'[3]

I recall Sam's discovery of the dream-pearl as 'me *in a sort of way*' (p. 6) and the question of Rabbi Hanokh's stupid man: 'Where in the world am I – where am I myself?' (p. 30).

In the last chapter I wrote of 'inner faces' and of how self-disgust and shame interrupt or promote an 'inner conversation with myself' (p. 134). I tried to convey how, in personal relationships and in creative thought, there can be moving moments of vision. Then living symbols bring a deeper knowing of a greater wholeness, perhaps with the 'disclosure' of a 'transcendent Self': Being. I sense one potentially coherent 'myself' and yet I 'see' a multitude of faces. There are many 'selves', and yet there is a hint of oneness.

There is a vast literature on the different usages of the word 'self' in psychology and psychotherapy.[4] Much confusion has arisen from a lack of distinction between 'logics' (different language-games, see Chapter 4) and from quasi-technical terms which neglect concealed metaphors. In this chapter I am concerned mainly with the expression and 'presentation' of experience in such a way as to intimate the inarticulate flow of experiencing. I use the words 'I', 'myself', and Self as the coinage of feeling-language. But, at times, I use a different framework which, formulated in discursive language, objectifies the 'mind' in terms of systems and sub-systems (further elaborated in Chapter 14). The two language-games must be distinguished, yet they are related.

Phrases such as 'my real self' are embedded in our language. They have profound, if elusive, meanings in everyday life and are central in the personal conversation of psychotherapy. Yet, in my view, every psychological and philosophical attempt to put forward a consistent coherent theory of identity and self has failed. In the following discussion I am thinking aloud and often get lost. My formulations (which are not necessary features of the Conversational Model) are unsatisfactory but they do have practical implications.

I shall tell one story, then another, and another, hoping that the meaning of 'myself' will be disclosed from in-between them. It is the ground of a metaphor.

If peak experiences are to be moving moments there is need for an interplay, a kind of conversation between I and myself in a state of aloneness. The sense of separate identity, associated with a willing, choosing 'I', is necessary for sanity in face of boundless Being.

A LAD AND THE COSMOS

I shall always remember one spring morning thirty-five years ago. 'Bedlam' (or Bethlehem), now called the Bethlem Royal Hospital, was beautiful when the daffodils opened.

Harold came into my room. He gazed at me – a direct gaze, not at all like his usual darting look that shifted away with a nervous laugh. He wasn't twitching his arms either, nor shifting in his chair. Harold was a different lad.

'I am myself now,' he said, with quiet calm. 'I have your head on my shoulders.'

Today, I should be worried by his words but they did not disturb me on that spring day. 'Harold is better,' I said to myself. 'Psychotherapy really works.'

'Great', I replied. 'So you're going home the day after tomorrow.'

'Yes. Manchester is a long way and I shan't see you any more. You come from there, don't you?'

'Well, not far away. The Rossendale valley.'

No doubt, I spoke of my home valley with a note of affectionate nostalgia.

I arrived early on the following morning. Harold stood in the ward corridor rigid and unmoving. His arms stretched wide and his head was thrown back, mouth gaping and eyes staring.

As a psychiatrist I knew a catatonic stupor (a term for a form of schizophrenia) when I saw one.

During the next few days Harold did not speak. He remained either as he was on that Wednesday morning, or else he crouched low, curled in a ball, hands across his chest, and eyes screwed tightly shut. Either 'expanding' or 'contracted'. Passively, he would allow us to move his body, but after an interval he slowly returned to one of these two positions.

It was hard to bear. I was fond of Harold. I could not understand. He had said 'I am myself now.' I had talked to 'myself' about psychotherapy.

For some months, I had seen Harold several times a week. He had been inspected at a case conference when renowned experts had concluded that 'this' was not a 'case' of schizophrenia but an adolescent crisis with crippling anxiety in an eccentric personality. So, I had been told to 'give' psychotherapy – as if it was some kind of 'thing' apart from a relationship of two unique persons. I did not really mind that, because I was reading Freud, Jung, and Adler and, anyhow, I liked Harold. He was a Lancashire lad.

I wrote voluminous notes. I tried all sorts of interpretations. Harold became fascinated by my pipe. Just having read Melanie Klein I told him that he wanted to take my penis in his mouth. He did not seem to care. We got on well together.

I shall not attempt to give an account of the mass of material that I recorded in the heavy case notes. But I must mention his father, whom I had not seen. From Harold's descriptions, I had constructed a picture of a harsh, powerful, vast, and overwhelming figure. Then, one day, Father came to visit, all the way from Manchester – a meek, inoffensive, little man, so anxious to please and to do what was best for Harold. 'Ah,' I murmured to myself. 'Now I know what "projection" means!'

Harold 'improved'. He became less twitchy, less scared of people, and it was possible to make sense of his disrupted, staccato talk. So, we arranged for his discharge, telling him of this six weeks before the arranged date. Later, I wrote about this period in careful measured phrases:

'Within a period of a few weeks, after Harold's discharge had been planned, he produced a series of dreams and drawings involving clear mandala forms. During this phase his anxiety symptoms became less marked but, retrospectively, it was apparent that there had been a restriction of the range of his interests and activities and that he had alternated between expressions of reluctance to leave hospital and denial of his fears about this. He was faced with separation from me and loss of the stable hospital environment.'

What I meant, I suppose, was that he was terrified of leaving me and of leaving Bethlem. He had glimpses of chaos and tried desperately to bring some order into his world – into 'himself'. I should say something about what I meant by 'mandala forms'.

I was absorbed in Jung at that time. He had described the appearance of patterns in his own, and his patients' fantasies and dreams which, he suggested, were symbols of 'wholeness' – of a transcendent 'self' with a centre beyond that of the limited 'ego'.[5] The typical form was a circle together with a fourfold motif – maybe a cross within a circle. He noted that such mandalas were used for meditation, not only in the East but throughout the world and that they appeared at a significant point in psychological development especially in middle age, when a person was 'individuating'. That is to say, reconciling the 'discordant elements' in the personality and becoming more of a whole individual 'worthy' of 'myself'.

Harold could never join in the kind of mutual creative drawing which happened with Stephen (Chapter 1). He made up scruffy sketches of his own separate from me – bits of motor cars with lines between them and, then, a drawing of a whole car; and of parts of bodies, which were joined together as one body – often with a large penis, like my pipe. I was pleased. 'The bits are coming together,' I said to myself.

At that time, I smoked 'Four-Square' tobacco and the 'mandala series' began when Harold became fascinated by the sight of the lid of my tobacco tin with its four coloured squares set in a circle. He drew the pattern, gazed at his drawings repeatedly and carefully, and began to call me 'four-square Hobson'. Later, the content of the mandalas and dreams became very varied – a host of circles and crosses. I foolishly took Harold's mandalas to be favourable indications and I have little doubt that, by my interest, I encouraged him to perceive, imagine, and draw these forms.

One day, when Harold was standing silent and outstretched I acted upon an impulse. I put my arms around him. But, I must try to convey *how* I did it. That is important. Not an embrace. A fixed, firm circle with fingers interlocked. The way in which you put your arms around a child when he or she is going to pieces in chaotic rage. Providing a boundary to bump against. A division between 'me' and 'not me'.

Harold had not spoken for three weeks. Now, he talked incessantly, so long as he was within the ring of my arms.

'Now I can be *me*. But, at other times . . . my body . . . either it all . . . the trees, houses . . . and the moon . . . crowd into me. I have to keep them out . . . and shut everything out . . . or else I have to *get* them out of my mouth . . . when they are in me.'

What Harold said would fill a book. I quote my summary written in 1951:

'He could only speak or move when I firmly put my arms around him. He said that, at other times, he had to maintain his rigid posture in order to keep the surface of his body intact and to prevent it from either expanding to the bounds of the cosmos or shrinking to a point.'

I wanted to go on talking with Harold but I could not. I carried out orders like a well-trained naval officer. Harold was given electric convulsive therapy and the stupor was broken. He developed ideas of persecution and is now in a mental hospital.

I often think of Harold. I wonder what he meant: 'I am myself now . . . I have your head on my shoulders.' 'I' and 'myself'?

SELF OR SELVES

For many centuries, especially since the Reformation, we have emphasized the importance of individuality.[6] We must work out our own salvation. Usually when I speak of 'me' I imply that there is only one 'me', one 'I', one 'myself'. Maybe we should think again. In his self-exploration, Jung glimpsed other possibilities.

Although he had made previous attempts to fathom his own unconscious processes it was on 12 December, 1913 during a period of severe disturbance[7] that Jung began in earnest to undertake this task in a systematic way. He actively stimulated the upsurge of imagery by writing down his dreams every morning, relating them to his mistress, and telling stories to himself. He found that he was beginning to converse with 'sub-personalities'. In Jung's terms, the psyche can 'personate', i.e. form 'complexes' which can be encountered as if they are people in a dialectic akin to a personal relationship. In this 'colloquy' the subject no longer behaves as if he were sitting in a theatre. Light dawns: it is *his* drama. He is no longer looking on but realizes that he is an active suffering figure personally involved in the play. He enters in as himself (the 'I' that he knows). He intervenes by reacting as if the situation is real, taking note of the relation that the other actors and the plot have to his conscious situation. He answers back. Listening to the 'other' voice he has it out with his 'alter ego' in a conversation – sometimes a furious argument. The alter ego is not necessarily right. The important matter is the 'relationship' – the colloquy relieves the sense of isolation.

The 'solitary' colloquy is not easy to describe and seems to occur in adult life only in exceptional people – of whom William Blake was an outstanding example.[8] I suggest, contrary I think to the view of most analytical psychologists, that it occurs commonly in pre-adolescence and early adolescence – as in my own case, when I talked for hours with little men who lived in subterranean regions beneath the lavatory. (As far as I am aware, the relation of the adult colloquy to imaginary playmates in childhood has yet to be worked out.)

It was about the beginning of 1919 that Jung felt himself emerge from what had seemed to be a long night in which he had experienced the discovery of the most intimate elements of his personality. He sensed a synthesis of his No.1 and No.2 personalities and his 'inner' and 'outer' worlds, in a process which he later termed individuation. It is during the dialogue that compensatory self-regulatory mechanisms come into play, i.e. unconscious 'contents' oppose and modify restricted conscious attitudes. In the 'inner' conversation between two 'selves' with equal rights a balance is struck or, at least, a compromise is made. By the continuing 'conversation' in individuation a person becomes progress-ively more complete and attains a renewed sense of significance in life. The process is portrayed by Jung more by metaphor and by telling stories than by denotative definition.

Jung's story suggests a way of conceiving of, and relating to, my own world in which 'I' am one of a number of selves who might, in Wordsworth's phrase, 'move in one society'. In the following discussion I am specially indebted to Miller Mair who has developed the Personal Construct Theory of George Kelly.[9]

Mair confronts us with the perennial question of how we should regard man – as a fallen angel, as a developed ape, as an empty organism dancing to the barrel-organ of stimuli, or as a mechanical super-computer. All of these metaphors can be of value in suggesting new, albeit limited approaches to a mystery. Mair suggests another metaphor: a community of selves.

The smallest community is one of two persons. We are often in 'two minds', we 'battle' with ourselves. By an act of imagination we can pay attention to, and perhaps 'get inside' one or other of them, rather than merely being aware of the two contenders as an outsider. Then we can become more aware of the incompatibilities, the assumptions, the suspicions, the tactics, the civil war, and the treaties of two 'persons' and their allies.

The word 'allies' broadens the context. It suggests that there are other dimly recognized, or unknown selves or sub-personalities working in groups. These may be weak and transitory, or more powerful and permanent.

That way of elaborating experience is often valuable in self-understanding and in therapy. Mr Chip came to 'know' and, at times, to identify with the Flame-thrower man and with a strange woman. When he was able to 'get inside' the man, he experienced the rage of a rejected person who had been deeply hurt and was repaying persecution with wild destructiveness. Mr Chip then felt himself as being very different from his customary everyday identity. Mandala forms (e.g. a roundabout with eight arms) appeared in his dreams. Jung in his self-analysis encountered and got to 'know' various personalities whom he later labelled by names such as the 'shadow', the 'anima', and the 'Old Wise Man'.[10]

Mair has developed a method of therapy for some clients in which he outlines the idea of a community of selves and encourages his patients to personify, to get to know imaginary figures as if they were persons. I shall summarize his reports of two stammerers, Peter and John. I choose them because, as a stammerer myself, I have found them of great personal value.[11]

Peter imagined the 'selves' as a troupe of actors (the Conversationalist, the Business man, the Country Bumpkin, the Adventurer, the Sentimental Lover, the Metropolitan Smooth Man, and the Dreamer) with a vacillating and not very effective Producer. He said how 'real' these characters seemed to be and a central theme of therapy was getting 'inside' the characters and experiencing their personal concerns. By means of an 'inner' dialogue, understanding and communication was fostered and the troupe came to work together with the Producer.

John talked as if he was composed of a number of political factions: 'Hard Liners', 'Soft Liners', and a 'Middle Group'. They were involved in continuous confusions of warfare, appeasement, and withdrawal. The Speaker in John's 'Parliament' had the unenviable job of trying to present to the world the view of the whole 'community' despite continued conflict of strident claims and counter-claims. Neither the Hard Liners nor the Soft Liners wanted to admit that the other side was there at all, the former never acknowledged that there was a stammer whereas the latter were eager to admit stammering in everything and anything. During therapy, in which these inner groups were personified, and related to his life situation, the Middle Group, at first a loose collection of individuals, became a more integrated 'Relaxed and Uncommitted Group' which belonged to a larger, tolerant 'Friendly Group'. Through long and hard battles there emerged a clustering of 'Relaxed', 'Friendly', and 'Free and Easy' groups. John began to develop more active involvement with people at work and at home.

Mair emphasizes that 'self as a community' is a metaphor within which some persons can express many aspects of experience in relation to themselves and others. Although not everyone can readily use the method it has some generality. The metaphor, which is by no means new in psychology,[12] can utilize varied concepts and methods in opening up new perspectives. Emphasizing interrelationships and responsibility for the acts of various selves, it is an invitation to explore ourselves in terms of personal meetings and of social events. Vehicles for the metaphor can be in the language of group processes, politics, industrial organizations, trade, law, games, and theatre. For instance, the community of another client was a Cabinet with a Foreign Secretary, a Home Secretary, and so on.

I shall use the metaphor of a society of selves in elaborating the symbolization of experiences of 'myself'.

IDENTITY AND SELF

I suggest that it is useful to conceive of a number of selves. These separate 'identities' can be more or less related or they can be divorced. There is, however, a tendency towards an harmonious organization: a whole with an integrated activity of differentiated parts. I think of 'myself' not as being one self amongst others but as an experience of a group process, a community, a 'moving' society.

My use of the word 'identities' in the last paragraph raises profound problems. It implies a conscious, willing subject, an 'I' which (or who) can never be an object. We ask then whether, when Peter 'got inside' a character in the unfolding drama, he came to experience some state of awareness which had in some sense been 'there' before his imaginative act. Can there be many distinct, choosing, acting 'I's? There are immense philosophical and logical puzzles but the question is of great practical importance as regards attitudes taken in psychotherapy. How far can Mr Chip's relation with the Flame-thrower have the characteristics of a personal relationship listed in Chapter 2; can it be between two experiencing subjects? Let us consider briefly a more objectivized discussion by John Bowlby.[13]

Reviewing experiments on subliminal perception and hypnosis, Bowlby suggests that we can conceive of a number of systems and sub-systems which interact to a greater or a lesser degree. A programme carried out by Hilgard[14] is of special interest. Pain was produced by placing the subject's hand and forearm in ice water for forty-five seconds. Usually this caused him to show many signs of discomfort such as restlessness and grimacing. He reported that he was experiencing great pain and distress. In addition, changes occurred in his heart-rate, blood-pressure, and other physiological measures – changes, most of which he was well aware. When, under hypnosis, it was suggested that he would feel no pain the physical signs of discomfort disappeared. Yet, the physiological changes occurred just as in the unhypnotized subject. Was 'pain' being 'experienced' somewhere?

Hilgard considered that during hypnosis an 'Executive Ego' assigns control to 'Subordinate Systems'. One of the latter receives, processes, and acts upon the sensory inflow from pain-endings and autonomic activity but excludes awareness of this activity from the Executive Ego.

Communications could be received from a third system by means of automatic writing and automatic talking. While the left hand and forearm were kept in the ice water without any discomfort, the right hand was placed in a box arranged for automatic writing, or for reporting pain on a scale through key pressing. The hypnotized subject was then told that 'the hand would tell us what we ought to know, but that the subject would pay no attention to this hand and would not know what it was communicating or even that it was doing anything at all'. (It is of interest that Jung used automatic writing in detecting autonomous complexes.)

Hilgard terms this third system the 'hidden observer'. This system is 'aware' of both pain and autonomic changes. (Can a 'system' be 'aware'?)

In the following account given by one of the subjects, automatic talking occurred when the subject had felt the experimenter's hand on his shoulder.

'In hypnosis I kept my mind and body separate, and my mind was wandering to other places – not aware of the pain in my arm. When the hidden observer was called up, the hypnotized part had to step back for a minute and let the hidden part tell the truth. The hidden observer is concerned primarily with how my body feels. It doesn't have a mind to wander and so it hurt quite a bit. When you took your hand off my shoulder I went back to the separation and it didn't hurt any more, but the separation became more and more difficult to achieve.'[15]

It was very apparent from the subject's facial expressions and movement that he was feeling intense pain whenever the experimenter's hand was on his shoulder. When, however, her hand was removed, his face relaxed and he appeared to be comfortable again.

Hilgard emphasizes that the interruption of communication between systems during hypnosis is rarely complete. Often one system has some 'knowledge' of what is going on in the other even if the second has no 'knowledge' of what is going on in the first.

Only a minority of people can be hypnotized and even fewer are also capable of automatic writing. Yet these findings suggest that at least in some persons there can be different systems with different states of consciousness.

A further finding is very relevant to the story of Richard III. Whenever the Subordinate System receives an order that it would be unethical to obey, he refuses to comply. Perhaps, this implies that there is another system which can also be segregated.

Richard, a deformed deprived child, had determined 'to prove a villain'.[16] He adopted a persona, a mask, of a powerful, fearless, conscienceless tyrant. For a short time, following the dream, he is afflicted with a 'coward conscience'. The conscience (perhaps what psychoanalysts would term a 'repressed superego', and others a 'moral self') which has been disclaimed, disowned, and denied, now delivers judgement:

> 'My conscience hath a thousand several tongues
> And every tongue brings in a several tale
> And every tale condemns me for a villain.'[17]

Then, as promptly as he emerges, the judge disappears again. In an important contribution to literary criticism, Alan Hobson relates the story of Richard to the observations of John Bowlby.[18]

Bowlby poses, but leaves unanswered, a question raised long ago by Jung and many others. Can we conceive of more than one 'system' as being capable of self-perception?

It can be argued that hypnosis is an artificial state and that those of us who recognize ourselves in Richard III are abnormal personalities. I act on the notion that Mair's suggestion is more than an analogy. We are many 'selves', each with a degree of consciousness. Our various selves may be quite dissociated and autonomous, they may be at war, or they may be more or less related and, in an inner dialogue, move towards an harmonious community. When I speak of my 'real' self I do not refer to one particular system among other 'unreal' ones. I have a sense of an integrated group, a vision of a wholeness which is an unattainable ideal: a movement in one society. 'Myself' is a developing relationship between members of a community in relation to the communities of other persons.

That view has implications for technique, in some instances; but I stress once more, it is not a necessary part of the Conversational Model. For some people the 'real' self is felt as a very solid centre of the body. We need to respect varied picture-languages. No one can give a satisfactory general formulation of the mystery of 'I' and 'self'.

INNER AND OUTER

Harold lost a sense of 'I', which was intimately bound up with a sense of a body-boundary. He could only talk when he was contained in the circle of my arms. In the preceding weeks his drawings had expressed an effort to keep together disintegrating fragments: arms and legs, parts of motor cars, and so on. The highly integrated figure of the mandala brought some coherence. It was apprehended as closely related to me: 'Four-square' Hobson. Harold maintained a precarious identity by experiencing my head on his shoulders. The synthesis broke down when physical separation was imminent.

In previous chapters I have suggested that in infant development an important theme is the growing capacity to distinguish 'me' and 'not me'. The capacity to be separate and yet also alone arises in a bodily and symbolical conversation in a bonding relationship with the mother. An ordered inner world is progressively created: a sense of myself as distinct from other selves. We can assume that for whatever reason (genetic or defective mothering) Harold's ability to make the distinction was precarious. He was unable to cope with the anxiety of separation and could not survive a severe loss. Perhaps a baby first experiences myself 'out there', e.g. in the mother's face.

In some people labelled 'schizophrenic', separate selves act as partial personalities, as for example when in hallucinations alien voices comment or mock. The understanding of such psychotic phenomena (which also demonstrate a loss of the capacity to symbolize and use figurative language) is beyond the scope of this book.[19] I mention them only to suggest how in confronting a mad patient as a person, the notion of many selves can be of some help. A person develops and grows as he anticipates, explores, acts, and moves forward in relationships. My notion of 'myself' is not a thing, not a structure somewhere inside me, but an activity, a mode of living, a personal creation: my own 'world'. And I live through many selves.

As Mair points out my selves are vantage points.[20] When 'I' act from one of these I am not able to identify and characterize the base. 'I' is always a subject and cannot be objectified and described in third-person terms such as 'the ego'. But if I step away as it were to another base, another self, I can perhaps get a different view within the society of myself. Then my previous base is 'other'.

Within a person then there are many 'internal others', a term used by Russell Meares whose thought has greatly influenced my ideas.[21] Many psychotherapists conceive of 'internal objects' but, in my view, this gives a wrong impression.[22] It would perhaps be more apt to speak of 'internal subjects'. The word 'internal' raises problems.

There is nothing absolute about the separation of inner and external worlds. In Kelly's terms 'self' and 'other' are personal constructions, ways in which we select, sort, and order events. The notion of a society of selves blurs the distinction between an inner subjective self, and an outer objective world. My personal world is related to the sense of experiencing from 'within my body', but as suggested in Chapter 3 (p. 33) the word 'body' here extends beyond the literal. Myself is not contained within the fixed envelope of my skin nor is it confined to an unchanging patch of personal space. Personal space is vital in relationships but it varies in extent. To recognize 'space' in psychotherapy is essential if we are to avoid either intruding or alienating.[23]

At a particular time I might relate few events to myself and be faced with a vast otherness. At other times I experience that tree outside my window as growing in my inner world. It is sometimes useful to conceive of a boundary between me and other so long as the metaphor includes pictures of expansion, contraction, and permeability.

As phenomenologists point out, in our experiencing we are not aware of a divorce between subject and object, between inner and outer.[24] There is a 'seeing' of that tree. Only when I reflect and construct a sentence do I, here, see that tree over there. The *capacity* to distinguish is vital. As I stressed in Chapter 8 the visionary who experiences a transcendent Oneness needs to be able to reflect discursively. In his stupor Harold was unable to achieve a clear boundary when it was necessary. He could not confidently say 'I' and 'Thou' (or 'It').

My notion of the hyphen in aloneness-togetherness is a rhythm of losing and establishing an expanding and contracting space. Whether I use presentational or discursive symbolism in a personal conversation depends upon my aim: the purpose that I intend my language to serve at a particular time.

The distinction between self and other is too simple. There are different kinds of 'other'. Mr Chip's shadow figure was 'other' but not in the same sense that a table was 'other'. Hence, with some hesitation, I shall speak of internal others and external others which may be related to either as persons or as things. 'Internal' and 'external' refer to the action of owning or disowning events as belonging to 'myself'. It is to be remembered however, that it is a matter of degree. An old familiar pipe is nearer myself than is my mini-computer. Furthermore, the distinction is not fixed. I suggest that the ability to sort events and to attribute them in different ways appropriate to different situations is a feature of healthy growth. Harold became unable to sort actions on any self/other dimension.

BECOMING A PERSON

I have suggested that we can think of many 'I's within a more or less divided and more or less whole society of myself. Each 'I' has a limited view of other selves in a wider community. But all do not have the same power of willing and acting. One of the characters in John's community was the Producer and in another instance there was the Speaker in a Parliament. Using a more depersonalized language, Hilgard speaks of an Executive Ego and Bowlby of Principal Systems A and B.

There is, then, a hierarchy. Except in grossly disorganized states, there is one usual vantage point, an 'I' aware of and acting in, and on, a socially accepted world. It is the 'identity' to which we are most accustomed, and which is developed in early life in order to adapt within the family and in the limited culture of our particular society. In periods of change with widening experience, especially in adolescence and middle life, it becomes important to recognize and relate to other selves, other internal subjects. I become more nearly myself, a member of a personal community.

Different selves usually do not work in harmony and hence there is a sense, and indeed danger, of disorganization. Moreover the relative loss of a well-established vantage-point means relinquishing an assumption that it is the only possible one. Growing up is a cycle of loss, relative disorganization, and re-organization. Loss is associated with fear, and the anxiety might be so great that it cannot be tolerated. Then I seek means of avoiding the chaos of civil war and of total disintegration. I maintain my accustomed position at all costs as being my 'real' identity, the whole of myself. Various modes of conflict between selves and ways of avoiding them are elaborated in Chapter 14.

When myself is identified with a limited 'I', we can use Donald Winnicott's term 'false self'.[25] The word 'false' can however be misleading.

The vision and action of 'I' is always necessary and valid. It is only false when it is assumed to be the only possible identity. It is partial. It restricts the forward movement of exploration in the aloneness of myself and in togetherness with other persons. Usually the maintenance of this limited self, which may be expressed in an efficient social and professional life style, often accompanied by apparent self-knowledge, conceals a chaotic non-society of other selves. That way madness lies.[26]

What I say and do, how I speak and act, in psychotherapy cannot but embody deep fundamental values. These have been intimated, and perhaps sometimes incarnated, in the way in which I have told many stories in previous chapters. I have spoken of 'seeing into the life of things' and of Being. I have referred to the *vis medicatrix naturae* and to Wordsworth's 'dark invisible workmanship' working towards harmony at a level of experiencing which is beyond concepts. Sometimes I think of 'a Self' with a capital 'S'. One day I hope to discover what I mean. Myself is constantly expanding as many selves move in one larger society. If, as A.N. Whitehead suggests, consciousness arises with increasing organization,[27] can there be a wider transcendent Self, a centre of consciousness? In most religions the Self is not only 'within' but also wholly Other and often is personalized. The metaphor, if it is only a metaphor, is a topic for another book.

Before returning to practicalities in Book II I shall make a quasi-religious confession. In becoming a person 'I' am more nearly myself in those relationships with other persons which intimate a Self which transcends and yet embraces all other selves, both inner and outer.

BOOK · II ·
THE MINUTE PARTICULARS

'He who would do good to another must do it in Minute Particulars: General Good is the plea of the scoundrel, hypocrite, & flatterer,
For Art & Science cannot exist but in minutely organized Particulars.'

(William Blake, *Jerusalem* III, 55: 60–8)

· 11 ·
THE FIRST FIVE
MINUTES

A nurse enters my office to tell me that a patient has arrived ten minutes late. I have never seen Mr Jones before and all I know about him is that he is single, is aged twenty-seven and is living in a YMCA hostel. I am going to see a patient. I hope to meet a person.

AN OPENING CONVERSATION

I go out into the crowded waiting hall and discover that Mr John Jones is the young man perched on a chair in a corner, huddled in a large overcoat.

I go up to him and hold out my hand:

'Mr Jones? Hello! I am Dr Hobson.'

He jumps to his feet, takes a step backward, glances at me quickly, and then looks away, hesitantly holding out his hand about four inches away from mine. I take his hand. He does not squeeze first (I give him this opportunity) but when I do so he responds by returning my grip in a half-hearted way for a second before withdrawing his arm.

Mr Jones looks at me again for a moment – this time more directly – shuts his eyes, looks at my feet, and follows me upstairs to my room. There are two identical chairs set at an angle so that we can look at each other or look away without having to do so too obviously.

'Would you like to hang up your coat?' I say, pointing to a hook. Mr Jones shakes his head. I indicate a chair and he sits down, pulls up his collar and shrinks behind it.

I wait for a few seconds. When I see his knuckles whiten as he grips the arm of his chair I break the silence.

'Maybe you could tell me something about your problem.'

I now completely lose sight of his long tangled hair, but I note that he begins to clasp and unclasp his hands with a quick rhythmical movement. His tension is mounting and I go on.

'It is not easy to know how to begin. Some things are not easy to put into words.'

Silence. He peers over his collar only to retreat again quickly.

In this chapter I want to present what happened in the first few minutes of an interview, in a busy psychiatric clinic. I do not know how I can do it. What does it mean, I wonder, to describe 'objectively'? What are the 'facts'?

There is a recording on audiotape. I have written an account of non-verbal activities, actions, and acts. But what about the shapes of feeling? Should I say 'his eyebrows rose three-and-a-half millimetres', or 'he looked surprised'? I see an infinity of 'facts' and realize that every description is also always an interpretation: a fact only has a meaning within a pattern (p. 67).

I have raised the question of 'facts' and 'objectivity' in parenthesis. It is an urgent problem for those of us who are engaged in experimental research. In the following account I shall repeatedly change my way of talking, the level of discourse, the language-game. Language is a matter of doing things with persons. I choose my language for my purposes.

I took this unspectacular example almost at random from hundreds of recordings. I decided that it would do for the following reasons.

It illustrates many fundamental attitudes, skills, and techniques to which I have referred in Book I, and introduces a point of view which is formulated in the next chapter.

For me, *some* features of the Conversational Model are of value in beginning *any* interview whether it be an assessment for psychotherapy, a psychiatric diagnostic session, a visit to a GP's surgery, a publisher's lunch with an anxious author, a teacher's lunch-break chat with a failing pupil, or the response to a friend who rings up saying 'Have you got a few minutes, Bob, I'm in a mess?'

A very great deal can happen within a very few minutes. Great revelations are rare, and even profound insights can never be fully lived out in a long lifetime. Yet a step, just a little step, forward can be an important movement in growth; it can open up a new path to explore.

An initial conversation is an important base from which to consider 'diagnosis'. I am concerned about the elucidation of the problem and making a decision about the appropriateness of conversational therapy for this particular person. The Conversational Model is not a panacea for all mankind.

The important focus is *how* a conversation is developed in its 'minute particulars'. Broad psychodynamic theories are all very well: indeed, inevitably, they guide what we observe. But any formulation of the problem which faces a unique person must emerge from the manner of *this* conversation, here and how.

We return to Mr Jones.

I should have followed my usual practice of using the word 'I' in attempting to convey to Mr Jones my understanding of his feelings about coming to a hospital and meeting a psychiatrist: perhaps something simple like 'I reckon that it feels strange to find yourself in a place like this and talking with a psychiatrist.' Such a simple statement can be crucial in beginning an interview. By lessening fear it can help someone to say what he wants to say. Maybe I am too direct in asking a question about his problem.

Mr Jones and I have already exchanged a great deal of information. I begin to discern repeated meaningful patterns. Fortunately, in a continued conversation if the therapist is blind and deaf to a message his patient will offer it again. Unless the interviewer conveys by words, gestures, or tones of voice that he really does not want to hear, he will be given many more chances to respond.

As I listen to Mr Jones's repetitive non-verbal and verbal statements, meanings emerge; some clearly and others dimly. A pattern of approach and avoidance is evident in his behaviour. I do not jump to a conclusive explanation of the fact that he has asked for an urgent appointment and yet arrives late. This act gradually gains significance as I register how he looks at me and looks away, how he responds to my grip yet abruptly terminates the hand-shake, and how he peeps over his collar only to retreat quickly. Each action acquires meaning within a developing pattern. The components of the second 'eye-conversation' are more differentiated; they are more pronounced, as Mr Jones looks at me more deliberately and directly and then shuts his eyes. The message is becoming clearer. The avoidance, by retreat into isolation, is more evident than the approach as he sits concealed in his overcoat (which he refuses to hang up), as he steps back hurriedly keeping space between us, and as he withdraws after my remark about his problem. During the subsequent progress of the interview, his anxiety and fear diminish and the disjointed components of his behaviour become more integrated. A rhythm develops.

I want to convey to Mr Jones my wish to enter into a *conversation* with him. I go out to meet him. I bring our names together with a 'Hello', and the arrangement of two identical chairs implies that I hope for a flexible verbal and non-verbal dialogue, a suggestion which would have been strengthened by subsequent use of 'I'. As yet, however, we are strangers.

A meeting with a stranger arouses curiosity and fascination, but also trepidation occasioned by the unfamiliar (p. 123). A balance of approach and avoidance, of contact and distance, of exploration and withdrawal, of 'aloneness' and 'togetherness', depends upon many factors, especially the maintenance of an optimum degree of 'arousal' or anxiety. The fluctuations of this state are indicated by changing bodily tension. I want to listen, to be receptive, and to respond appropriately. I hope – and it can only be a hope – for an attitude akin to Wordsworth's 'wise passiveness', a waiting with 'loving attentiveness'. I do not wish to intrude on Mr Jones's privacy but I cannot wait too long. He is afraid and if his anxiety rises too high he will retreat more and more into his isolation, into loneliness.

Registering the cues of rising tension, I make an attempt to establish a communication by means of words, trying to convey a meaningful message that I have received. I hope that my words will be consistent with my tone of voice, my facial expression, and my movements. I do not wish to give contradictory information by giving discrepant messages which will increase Mr Jones's conflict and uncertainty. My spoken sentence needs to be part of a coordinated, differentiated, and integrated communication – a harmonious system.

I do not ask a question. In a conversation I am not an interrogator. I make a statement. As a first step I aim to communicate in the hope of promoting a dialogue. By a 'communication' I mean an event in which one person recognizes from verbal and non-verbal cues that a message has been received, registered, understood, and responded to by at least one other person. I say, 'It is not easy to know how to begin; some things are not easy to put into words.' I am putting forward an 'hypothesis', and perhaps I am mistaken. Hence, I look for evidence that I am wrong. But, first and foremost, at this point I try to convey my wish to communicate. I am communicating about communicating.

In effect, by the way in which I speak, I am saying 'Look Mr Jones, I want to talk with you, if you also want to. As far as I am able I will let you know how I have seen and heard your messages – even when you don't realize you are saying very much. I am trying to enter into what you are experiencing now, at this moment. I am feeling my way. Maybe I am not on the right track; but I feel that you want to tell me about yourself and if we get together we can come to understand more about what is going on. But it is not easy for you. Something stops you. It is hard to express feelings in words. If what I say doesn't sound right I want you to correct me.'

It would have been better if I had prefixed my statement with 'I reckon . . .' or 'I suppose . . .', thereby emphasizing the tentative nature of my idea and inviting Mr Jones to negotiate with me in a dialogue. I hope for much more than just accurate communication. I hope for a personal meeting. I could spell out all this to him but I do not want to 'speechify'. I hope that I say it all by my tone of voice, by the mobility of my face, and by expressive gestures.

I am trying to be empathic: to feel into how he is experiencing the world *now*, and, as far as possible, to convey my 'in-dwelling' in appropriate language. At the same time, I am encouraging him to respond so that we can adjust our modes of communication *and move towards mutual understanding*. I constantly ask myself, 'What is happening now – at this moment?' For the most part, the question is on the fringe of my awareness but I focus upon it when in doubt and when the conversation flags. I assume that concealed in apparent passivity there is meaningful activity. And I remember that 'nothing never happens'. Despite his hasty retreat Mr Jones encourages me to persist.

A human being, whether therapist or patient, is constantly noting, formulating, and modifying what he is doing, while he is doing it. He 'monitors' his own performance and can monitor his monitoring. A psychiatrist needs to be attentive, absorbed, and spontaneous while at the same time observing, evaluating, and modifying his behaviour 'from a distance'. When he is working well he is, at one and the same time, both intensely involved and yet also detached – an impossible ideal. The tone of this account might well give a false impression of the way in which I habitually work. In focusing attention upon the minute details of behaviour, a therapist is in danger of becoming paralysed like the proverbial centipede deliberating about which leg to move next. In this case, for the purpose of a pilot research, I am attempting to register as many as possible of those events and inferences which go unnoticed in most spontaneous conversations. A similar mental set is valuable in learning psychotherapy with the use of special recording techniques.

'I feel that you want to tell me about it all,' I say, 'but you are not sure how I am going to react or perhaps you wonder what I am going to do.'

'You . . .' he replies with a strained note, ending with a marked glottal stop. Then he bursts out:

'I suppose you *are* a doctor.'

He looks at me – more searchingly now. Maybe I give a slight smile. I am not sure. What I am trying to do is to feel myself into his situation with my middle – perhaps a better word would be 'guts'.

'I suppose' (I note that I repeat his phrase) 'that's what holds you back – wondering if I am what I pretend to be. That's scaring if you have something important to talk about.'

He comes out in an urgent rush, speaking fast but with abrupt breaks.

'I suppose I *am* scared. There are all sorts of disguises. And people forcing you to do all sorts of things – but you don't see them at it and you don't know what they are up to at all. I can't stand it at home, so I left for good.'

He puts a hand on his middle as if it aches. Then he looks at my unlit pipe on the small table.

'Will you let me smoke . . . and not write things down? I am going to smoke anyhow.' His tentative question ends on a note of defiance.

I pick up my pipe and light up: no doubt with an accustomed ritual.

There is now a different sort of silence for a few moments before he gets up and takes off his overcoat. Resuming his seat he looks at me, moves as if about to curl up in the chair, and inhales deeply from his cigarette.

'I can't explain it at all,' he says, but looks at me expectantly.

'I suppose that just now you were feeling all mixed up inside like when your parents quarrel. As if it was happening inside you here.'

He relaxes, inhales, and watches the smoke as it rises.

'Oh, mum is all right even if she does get moods. We have some good times, but dad – my father. Oh, he is a doctor, by the way. But I find myself doing things I don't want to and everything is always wrong for him. But I am no good for life. Perhaps if I didn't get these stomach aches, it might be better.'

A slight smile flickers across his lips.

'You smile,' I say.

A mistake. I am wrong to draw attention to a cue without some indication of my understanding. It can be threatening just to be told what you have done, especially as here when you are not aware of your action.

'Oh, did I?'

At first his tone is guarded, then his voice becomes irritable.

'I wish you would say what you mean, you talk about how you will react and what you might do . . . they are different . . . what people feel and what they do.'

'You told me how you do things you don't want to, and that you never know that people expect. Your father for instance – '

He interrupts.

'Stop a minute . . . not too many things at once . . . too many to sort out. Yeah, I suppose it is like people fighting inside. It does feel something like that. I'm in a mess though and I am scared too. I must get out of it somehow and go somewhere.'

He looks at the door, tenses, and then looks at my pipe.

'Yeh, I suppose I need help.'

'Let's see where we can go. I'd like to know you better.'

The sentence 'Let's see where we can go' might sound puzzling without seeing the non-verbal 'statements' that accompany it. It means 'Let's see how you and I can get on' but also implies that in a relationship we are moving into the future: giving a hopeful meaning to his statement 'go somewhere'.

With little prompting, Mr Jones who later becomes 'Joe' for me, goes on to talk in a connected way about his unhappy schooldays and details of his disastrous work history. The interview enters a new phase.

'I never could get on at school . . .'

While attending to the meaning of what Mr Jones is saying I am registering the minute particulars of his behaviour. I now feel together with him in a personal relationship, I am also formulating tentative hypotheses and trying to test them. I am using different ways of thinking with different languages.

HYPOTHESES

My main aim is to help Joe to be able to explore in a conversation. Despite his reluctance, I assume that deep down he wishes to talk with me, and my hunches, somewhat grandly termed 'hypotheses', are about factors that prevent him from doing so. My responses are appropriate in so far as they facilitate communication, exploration, and a personal meeting. This purpose is achieved in two main ways.

1   By tentatively suggesting hypotheses, I am hoping to promote a dialogue. My inner action of empathy is phrased in statements about his experience 'now', which I hope will convey an openness to be corrected – a wish for negotiation, for mutual understanding. Furthermore, they intimate the importance of getting in touch with and 'staying with' his experiencing. I term such interventions *understanding hypotheses*. As understanding (feeling with) develops, the barriers of fear are lowered. There is an intimation of the possibility of a trusting relationship.

2   I offer him a 'model'. By showing that I am exploring I invite him to join with me in an exploration. Non-verbal behaviour is of the greatest importance: the groping gesture, the questing look and the tentative and yet definite tone of voice. The use of the word 'I' in making statements rather than asking questions is vital.

To be tentative does not mean to be vague. I am definite about my hypothesis, for example: '. . . you are not sure how I am going to react . . . going to do'. His tense, glottal stop and emphasis upon the word 'are' ('I suppose you *are* a doctor') support my suggestion about his suspiciousness and together we extend our view of the situation. At this point, we do not explain; we amplify. Joe tells me about his fears of secret goings-on behind his back, probably at home, and about being controlled against his will. In talking about his situation he directly expresses the anxiety associated with it. The pattern of his attempt to cope with the problem is enacted in his relationship with me. His request 'Will you . . . not write things down' is a plea: 'Please don't write things down to use behind my back,' and then he makes a defiant challenge: 'I am going to smoke anyhow,' implying 'You can't stop me.' Following my non-verbal response he relaxes, unbuttons his coat, and opens up literally and metaphorically. He becomes willing to explore. Now, for the first time, he asks me for help, at first by a look and later in words.

As I listen, meanings are forming. Links are made which bring together units of Mr Jones's speech and movements. Patterns emerge. I try to give him the benefit of my ideas. I put forward *linking hypotheses*. Throughout this process I am registering a vast amount of information without being aware of doing so. Perceptions take shape subliminally, beyond my conscious reflection, and often appear later as intuitions.

In my description of the interview, I have introduced wider categories of meaning as well as a hint of my own 'inner' experience. When I notice 'a searching look' I am saying much more than would be conveyed by a description of how Mr Jones's eyes move. My 'observation' involves an interpretation – a creation of meaning. When I say that I 'feel into' with 'my guts', I am symbolizing my experiencing: a happening in my body. I do have a physical sensation in my abdomen – but the visceral sensation is also an apprehension of meaning. The metaphor 'in the pit of my stomach' is more apt than 'in my abdomen'. There is an experience in which my 'body' expands beyond the literal. The notion of 'felt-meaning' has been elaborated in Chapter 3. Here it is necessary to note that the phrase 'forming hypotheses' means far more than what is usually meant by 'taking thought'. It is not merely an intellectual operation and it might be better to say that hypotheses 'arise' or are 'apprehended'.

A very important feature of the developed Conversational Model is 'staying with' immediate 'bodily experiencing' and waiting for 'living symbols' to emerge. Such symbols intimate possibilities which are as yet unknown, inexpressible. This condensed statement suggests the way in which I 'listen to myself' in formulating hypotheses. I hope to convey this attitude to the patient – often by the way in which I talk, but sometimes very directly, as in the interview with Joe.

He moves his hand to his abdomen and murmurs:

'That aching feeling ... I don't know what it means.'

I point to his middle and direct him, firmly.

'Just stay with it. Stay with the feeling. Wait and see.'

After a ten-second pause Joe goes on quietly.

'Fighting ... mum and dad ... tearing me apart ...'

Joe goes on to amplify the images and formulates a number of hypotheses for himself.

In so far as my formulations involve letting Mr Jones know that I have received messages which he has not been aware of sending, the procedure approximates to the more technical meaning of 'interpretation' as used by analytical therapists, i.e. the process of making conscious what hitherto has been 'unconscious'.

There is one point at which I make an injudicious intuitive leap, although no damage appears to have been done. I make a number of links. I notice the association between his feelings of being attacked, the movement of his hand to his abdomen, and his look at my pipe. Rightly, I relate this complex of 'elements' to what is 'happening inside you here'. Nevertheless, I cannot point to evidence which is readily available to Mr Jones to justify my statement, 'I suppose that just now you were feeling all mixed up inside – like when your parents quarrel.' There are at least three dangers in making such a leap.

1   I might suggest a wrong track to explore. Perhaps he will be too afraid to correct me openly and will play along with what he thinks I want, rather than express his immediate experience. I hope to be alert to evidence of my mistake as, for example, if he simply repeats my words without amplifying my suggestion or if he is puzzled and blocks.

2   If I am right, in the sense that Mr Jones feels, 'Yes, that is just what it is like,' he might idealize me as the all-knowing God-like therapist and 'the only person who understands me'. It can encourage childlike dependence. This is particularly damaging if, for one reason or another, I cannot continue with therapy myself. It is all too easy to be a clever interviewer at the expense of the patient, especially in a diagnostic session.

3   Perhaps the greatest danger is that the intervention, if correct, might be felt as potentially destructive magic. We are concerned with the notoriously difficult problem of fear of 'persecution'. This term requires extended discussion and I can give only a few pointers. Mr Jones readily feels attacked, controlled, and possibly fears being destroyed in a well-nigh literal sense. To be understood is reassuring but to be penetrated by means of someone else's mysterious knowledge of my 'inside', with the danger of possession and damage, is a threat to my identity. In 'togetherness', contact is experienced as a meeting in a 'space-between'

in contrast to a state of non-differentiation or 'fusion'. The sense of fusion with the loss of 'distinction' between oneself and other people or things can be a valuable experience and is a necessary feature of much creative activity, as was suggested in the story of Stephen's drawing, but I have a need to be able to regain and maintain the 'boundaries' of my own living space. If I am understood too completely and too quickly, I feel invaded. A therapist should respect his patient's need for privacy.

I hope for a rhythm of aloneness-togetherness which, at times, can fall into loneliness on the one hand or into a sense of fusion on the other.

Mr Jones accepts the link between feelings in his stomach and his parent's quarrels. If the links do not 'hold' I hope that he will put me right. By 'acceptance' I do not mean mere agreement. My suggestion is received and amplified, explicitly in his remark 'It is like people fighting inside', and implicitly by reference to his stomach aches. Yet, although he relaxes, there is a suggestion of fear of me as a dangerous person. He is irritated because I say 'different things' and he is confused by 'too many things at once'. He tells me that I am going too quickly and I suspect that my intervention has been premature. He glances at the door as if to escape from danger but is reassured by a look at my pipe.

I have mentioned only one or two of the multitude of links that occur. There are many more suggestive hints. For example, I note how he 'transfers' on to me his attitude towards his father, a critical doctor. He registers accurately some of the ways I behave but at times, especially when afraid, he selects his perceptions in such a way as to misinterpret. He behaves towards 'Dr Hobson' as if he were 'Dr Jones', his father. Such misinterpretations, which may amount to illusions, or even delusions, can portray modes of disturbance in relationships in many areas of life. Some recognition by Mr Jones of the falseness of his expectations of what I will do or think is apparent even in this brief episode. Such a realization is an important basis for further therapy. (It is important to recognize that the interviewer can misinterpret in just the same way.)

Other connections which could be significant are suggestions of 'symbolic meaning' in his attention to my pipe, and the masturbation-like clasping and unclasping of his hands. I notice such possibilities, and then mentally put them on to one side. Others of which I am not immediately aware will later arise as hunches.

There is a third kind of testable hunch which I term an *explanatory hypothesis*. There is a movement from understanding to linking, to explanation, with a return to understanding. The distinctions are arbitrary but useful. An explanatory hypothesis is a formulation of the problem in terms of reasons. When I say, 'like when your parents quarrel', I am approaching an explanation such as 'you feel like that now *because* your parents quarrel'. But it is not a full explanatory hypothesis. The latter, directed towards clarifying the avoidance of a deep-seated problem, usually involves two 'because' clauses, e.g. 'I reckon that you get that pain because you want to avoid thoughts of your parents quarrelling, and that is too scaring for you because if they damaged each other your whole world would be in chaos.'[1] The timing of such explanations is discussed in a later chapter. At this point, I suggest only that it would be too early in the relationship with Mr Jones to intervene in this way. Indeed, it might not be necessary at all. My view is that understanding, amplified by linking, is the necessary operation and often sufficient, in itself. Explanation is not an end. It is a means to promote understanding in a personal relationship.

I must not make up my mind about the significance of the 'embryonic' constellations which form in my consciousness and which intimate emergent meanings. I allow them to remain 'open', ready to join with other analogous messages should these occur – like Coleridge's 'hooks and eyes of the memory'. In my imaginative vision, they float as constellations in the space around and between Joe and me. When they do generate clear formulations these are still only possibilities. A pipe, a clasp of the hands, a slip of the tongue, a dream; I do not know what they mean. Ideas can form around them and from ideas hypotheses arise. To repeat, when I do act in accordance with these formulations I do not look first for supporting evidence; I search around for evidence to show that I am wrong. Indeed, I wish to be corrected.

When engaging in a therapeutic conversation I hope for the courage to commit myself wholeheartedly while remaining in doubt and uncertainty. I settle for a formulation or hypothesis and try it out, striving to remain open to register evidence that it may be false. But it is much more difficult, frightening, and hazardous to commit myself to a personal relationship in which, in an unknown way, I shall be changed. Perhaps, the involvement will mean only minor and barely noticeable alteration in my attitudes and ideas. Perhaps, it will result in a painful loss of cherished theories and values. Perhaps, there will be damage to my self-esteem or disillusionment about my career. Obscurely underlying every intimate encounter involving matters of ultimate concern, are fear and trembling in the face of a challenge to my being, my existence as a person.

Yet, there is hope; perhaps I might grow – a large 'perhaps'. To enter into a mutual conversation is an act of faith, a leap in the dark, which is very different from a tenacious clinging to a belief. The risks and the potentialities are intimated by my dream after meeting Sam (p. 8).

PROBLEMS AND DIAGNOSIS

In the first few minutes of our talk Mr Jones discloses some central problems in his life.

I shall consider psychotherapy in terms of problem-solving (outlined in Chapter 7). A person aims to reach a goal, there is a felt difficulty with frustration and arousal, the problem is located and explored, possible solutions are envisaged, the possibilities are mulled over, and a decision is made to try out possible solutions. In psychotherapy we are concerned with a special instance: the solution of interpersonal problems (p. 110f.).

Although the Conversational Model is being developed for use in on-going therapy, its principles are intimately bound up with my work as a general psychiatrist. As an undergraduate, long before I met Sam, I had written in my diary 'Mad patients are persons.' There, I suppose, lay my early attraction to Carl Jung. He was proud of being a 'real alienist' and of having spent long hours talking with persons labelled as cases of *dementia praecox*. But the familiar exhortation to 'treat patients as persons' can be an empty fashionable cliché. I want to know what it means.

Mr Jones came to see a psychiatrist and expected a diagnosis.

Psychiatric diagnosis is a large and thorny problem. The heat of current debate often serves only to make confusion more confounded amid practical, logical, and sectarian muddles. My limited concern in this context, is to state my view that the notion of personal problem-solving, with its associated attitudes and techniques, is always involved in diagnosis. That is not to maintain that it is the whole story.

However useful it might be to classify Mr Jones as an instance of a diagnostic category, he is a person with a problem. Notwithstanding 'mysteries, uncertainties, doubts', I commit myself to a form of interview which can have a profound and lasting effect on his life. The commitment and treatment has begun before I see Mr Jones and it is established when our eyes first meet. The few minutes talk with him discloses some essential features of the 'diagnosis' of the nature of the problem.

I do not always practise what I teach.

Mrs Smith had arrived as an emergency twenty minutes before I was due to leave the hospital to take the chair at an important meeting about psychotherapy. Using practised skill and a natural intuitive flair, I quickly elicited the symptoms and signs of a 'neurotic depression with marked anxiety'.

Predicting with confidence that this 'condition' would respond to a monoamine oxidase inhibitor together with a tranquillizer, I stole a surreptitious glance at my watch and with a smile handed her a prescription for Phenelzine mgm 15 tds, and Chlordiazepoxide mgm 10 tds. (The dangerous side-effects of the latter drug were not known then. I was well abreast of the current fashion.) Mrs Smith took the prescription, scanned it sadly for a few seconds, turned to gaze fixedly at me and, without a flicker of emotion, said:

'Who was that *handsome* doctor who was on the television last Thursday? *What* was it he said?'

The significant look, the dismissive gesture, and the contemptuous tone conveyed quite clearly that 'handsome' also meant 'not at all like you'. Too late, I realized that I had failed to hear something important. I had no idea what it was.

Mrs Smith went on:

'Oh yes, about depression not being a thing . . . and something about growing up.'

She suddenly stood up and left the room. The door slammed.

My first reaction was 'What has Dr X got that I haven't got?' I had seen the programme, which had suggested that there was a great gulf fixed between those psychiatrists who claim to cure all psychological maladies by the use of drugs with awe-inspiring names such as Chlordiazepoxide, and those who labour for years trying to help disturbed people to become persons. Although I did not agree with the suggestion of a necessary gulf, I recalled a fleeting sense of envy as I had watched and listened to Dr X. I could not have talked so fluently.

Dr X and I enjoyed a complicated relationship. A mutual respect was coloured by a keen competition about who was the better showman. In this documentary, he had suggested that we should not conceive of depression as a 'thing' which infects people, but rather think in terms of persons who are depressed. He related depressive illness to the periods of sadness which are necessary and often fruitful accompaniments of psychological development, and pointed out that people who use the same label 'depression' are often making quite different diagnoses.

Before giving her the prescription I had arranged another interview with Mrs Smith. I wondered if she would come. She arrived early and began to speak before sitting down.

'Those pills did me a world of good. I managed to find a chemist open last Monday after seeing you. I took the bottles home – such nice colours – red, green, and black. I showed them to George, my husband, and then put them down the lavatory. George was furious. He shouted "You don't *want* to get better and you just goad me all the time." He has never said anything like that before. We never have rows. It was terrible.' Mrs Smith barely concealed a satisfied smile.

By luck, things did not turn out too badly. Mrs Smith was the sort of person who eventually forced me to hear what she had to say, but it could have been otherwise. Looking back I could see how in subtle ways she had told me again and again how she was angry with her husband. She had insisted on seeing me personally, expecting that I would be on Dr X's side of the gulf and wanted me to play the part of an omniscient father-lover-husband. Indeed, the way in which she perceived and reacted towards me was an eloquent statement of her personal problem with her husband George. We both failed to fulfil the ideal roles set for us.

The problem was one of marital disharmony. The pair could not communicate about important topics, failing to listen to each other in much the same way as I had not allowed myself to hear what Mrs Smith was trying to convey at our first meeting. By jumping to a diagnostic label in order to do something quickly, and relieve my uncertainty, I had failed to register the minute particulars of her communication. The problem became evident at a subsequent joint interview with the couple, and progress towards a solution began as they learnt to talk with each other.

Diagnosis emerges in a conversation between persons.

Diagnosis is always treatment.

Diagnosis embodies a statement about fundamental values.

The last three paragraphs apply to all diagnoses made in an interview, whether it be of 'neurosis', 'schizophrenia', or 'general paralysis of the insane'. I shall limit myself to a few observations which are relevant to this chapter.

The principles, attitudes, and techniques, illustrated by the few minutes with Mr Jones, represent my approach at the beginning of any interview, whether it be an assessment for psychotherapy, a diagnostic session in a general psychiatric case conference, or a chat with a deteriorated patient in the back ward of a mental hospital. Of course, this way of conversing may only continue for a very short time. The continuation of the interview is not the same if I wish to assess the nature of dementia in an elderly patient as it is when my aim is to explore the vicissitudes of a state of marital disharmony. A battery of questions may be necessary but, in my experience (as I have said, a dangerous phrase which cries out for a rigorous testing), the answers are more likely to be valid and reliable if the initial conversation is aimed at 'knowing' a person rather than 'knowing about' him. Maybe one sentence is enough.

A pilot investigation revealed that a very large number of people visiting a general practitioner's surgery leave without having revealed what is worrying them. For instance, the dreaded word 'cancer' prevents Mrs Shuttleworth from mentioning the small hard lump on her breast, or Mr Ashworth from divulging his hurried and repeated visits to the lavatory. The initial evidence suggests that patients are much more likely to talk about what frightens them, if the doctor does not immediately make enquiries such as 'What's the matter?' If he sits back, looks at his patient and says 'I reckon it's a bit scaring to talk to a chap like me,' he expresses his *wish* to understand the fear, now, using the word 'I'. That and no more. Our findings suggested that many more patients were able to say what they needed to say. Dr Softheart is a mild-looking gentleman but he is often seen by frightened patients as 'Dr Cancer'.

Undergraduate and postgraduate students are given the hackneyed precept: 'Make a good relationship.' It is usually hastily passed over. Nothing is said about how to achieve it. In this book, I am certainly trying to elaborate vague terms such as 'establishing rapport', using 'a bedside manner', and hoping to elucidate the meaning of so-called 'non-specific factors'. But I am saying far more than that. The form of a developing conversation often *is* the diagnosis and also the treatment.

It is one thing to state that conversation *can* be therapy but quite another to say that it is always treatment. It is the current custom to distinguish the treatment (e.g. antibiotics, tranquillizers, electric convulsive therapy) from 'management'. In this chapter, I baldly state my view. It is an illogical (as well as inhuman) howler to think of a person as *having* a disease, an alien 'thing'; and, hence, to 'manage' one and 'treat' the other.

That is not to say that conversation in itself is the whole or main treatment. It may be. If diagnosis reveals that it is not, then no harm will have been done by the attempt to establish a personal conversation. Damage can be done by a different sequence. To begin by interrogation, by enquiring 'about', with a psychiatric or behavioural history, makes it much more difficult to establish a conversational psychotherapeutic approach later on. The physician's main job is not to do harm.

A 'diagnosis' of any kind is made for a purpose. Language is concerned with what we do and to what end. The end is a matter of values: ultimately, what we accept as being the 'good' life.

Value judgements are made, explicitly or implicitly, in all aspects of psychiatry. When he asks a significant question, when he labels a patient as a case of schizophrenia, or when he makes, or refrains from making, an interpretation, a psychiatrist cannot avoid expressing his own experience of love and his attitude towards death. A psychiatrist, a psychologist, a social worker, a detached experimentalist, a priest, or a helpful friend who formulates a problem inevitably makes a statement about the meaning of life and the mores of existing society. This book is concerned with individual psychotherapy but, inevitably, it is a statement about morals and politics.

PERSONAL PROBLEMS

In the first few minutes with Mr Jones his problems are expressed in different ways: in different and yet related languages.

He wishes to communicate with me (goal). There is a felt-difficulty with frustration as initial attempts fail. His anxiety is evident in mounting tension and disjointed communication. A problem of attaining openness in face of fear of attack, criticism, and rejection is progressively elucidated in terms of an approach-avoidance conflict. Some lines of investigation are begun by trying out different languages (such as images of parents fighting inside) and testing whether I do, in fact, reject him. Possibilities (indicated by my comments on the interview) are envisaged. Mr Jones and I seek various ways of establishing communication and dialogue. At the end of the short episode, he makes a decision; he commits himself to seek help by telling his story.

In the later part of his interview (not described here) these and other specific problems, intimated in these few minutes, were expanded in terms of more general problems: for example, anxiety and awkwardness in any important personal conversations, powerful mixed emotions related to his father, a wish to become independent of his parents, and fears regarding sex with uncertainty about his identity as a man. Some months later, after he and I had established a feeling dialogue he chose to abandon unrealistic academic ambitions and commit himself to an intimate relationship with a girl.

In the interview with Mr Jones, we can formulate problems at different 'levels': in terms of the minute particulars of his non-verbal behaviour, the disturbances of his complex relationships, and his struggle for a sense of identity in an adult world. A central and often difficult task in psychotherapy is to decide which problems are to be tackled at what levels. That decision (made with the patient after a few sessions and reviewed at intervals) depends upon many factors, especially regarding what is possible and practicable, e.g. frequency of sessions and time available. It is a matter of 'diagnosis'.

The main point is that although what a patient says 'about' his problem is always important, he almost invariably directly presents or demonstrates it now, here, in this interview. The procedures of the Conversational Model are designed to promote a verbal and non-verbal enactment which is more telling (and ultimately more therapeutic) for most patients, than a description by a list of symptoms or a detailed account of a life-history either from themselves or from 'objective' witnesses. The problem is vividly revealed in the immediate relationship where it can be observed, shared, and, one hopes, modified.

The interviewer's job is to hear and to notice what is being 'said'. A person always means what he says. But he does not always say all that he means, nor always act upon what he says. Nor does he know everying he is saying. And he often says different and sometimes contradictory things at the same time. Everything he says, verbally or non-verbally, deserves respect and asks for a response. In any interview or, indeed, in any conversation, each person is always saying something relevant to:

(i) himself and his life situation;
(ii) the other person;
(iii) the nature and setting of the interview (its structure, its purpose, the non-human environment).

The setting of the interview (e.g. in a hospital, type and angle of chairs) and the actions and personal characteristics of the interviewer can reveal important ways in which the patient relates to other significant people in his life – especially those close to him or her (e.g. spouse, parents, children). How, for example, he deals with closeness, distance, and eye-contact. If I am able to 'hear' what he is 'saying', Mr Jones clearly manifests his problem in many ways – overtly in words and more or less overtly in his hand-shake, his postures, his body movements, his quality of speech, his ways of changing the topic, and his silences. The way in which he talks directly expresses some important aspects of his relationships with his father-doctor, with his mother, and indeed his general mode of being with other people. At the same time, he is conveying something of his perception and evaluation of me as well as his attitude towards the situation of the interview.

A useful technical point in listening is to make possible 'translations'. What is said with reference to any one of the situations, may also refer to one or more of the others. For example, when the patient refers to someone in his life ('him' or 'her') he may also be saying something about 'you'; or in expressing attitudes about the interview-setting he can convey important feelings about his home situation. The interviewer's task is to register the cues, to attempt to understand the messages, and to respond appropriately. In the interview with Joe Jones I am concerned, first and foremost, with diagnosis. What is the problem? But, also, is there evidence here and now, in this conversation, that the problem can be explored and modified, if not solved, within a conversation?

The first few minutes of any initial interview are of vital importance. Significant personal problems are often disclosed most clearly in the anxiety-arousing encounter with a stranger (especially if he is endowed with authority and power). More important is that, by the way in which he responds, the interviewer can begin to create a relationship which will either encourage or discourage the subsequent progress not only of this session but also of all subsequent therapy.

PROBLEMS AND DIAGNOSIS

Problem-solving, whether it takes place in everyday life, in psycho-therapy, or in physical science, is a highly complex process. It is far from being a mere intellectual exercise. It involves emotion and, in problems of intimate relationships, the discovery of a language appropriate for the mutual understanding of feeling. Furthermore, it always expresses philosophical assumptions about what constitutes 'knowledge'. It asserts fundamental values, especially about what it means to be a person living and growing in relation to a physical environment, to other persons, and to the cosmos.

Any conversation involves a progressive, ever-varying exchange of information conveyed by successive and highly complex combinations of action and perception. The participants learn each other's language. In the changing rhythms of the beginning, middle, and end of an interview, there is a mutual clarification of problems and goals. There is an adjustment of communication habits and conventions (ways of talking), of meanings, and of purposes. If a personal dialogue develops, a new language emerges and, however slightly, each person changes. They see the world anew – for better or for worse.

However 'objective' an interviewer tries to be, any account must involve some comment about the psychiatrist's individual patterns of behaviour. He is always saying something about himself, about the patient, and about the immediate situation. I chose to use the conventional 'Hello!' rather than the equally conventional 'How do you do?' which would have carried a different meaning about the way in which I wish to relate to Mr Jones. The patient and doctor are faced with the problem of learning each other's language. However flexible, un-structured, or non-directive he might seem to be, any psychiatrist conveys his expectations and wishes about the direction of the inter-view. He leads the patient to talk in certain ways and about certain topics. That is his job.

The therapist is faced, first and foremost, with the problem of learning to talk his patient's language. We need to remain aware of our peculiar modes of listening and of talking. In subtle, unadmitted ways we seek to satisfy our own needs and to avoid situations that frighten us. I can only hope to respond appropriately: to be responsible.

A therapist should enjoy himself – so long as he does not seek his own gratification at the patient's expense. Recorded interviews clearly reveal our fascination with certain topics and our dislike of others. It is a chastening experience to see ourselves on a television screen as a peeping tom, an autocrat, a prosecuting counsel, an oracle, or a saviour who washes the disciples' feet. We only come to know our own mind as we become more aware of how we talk verbally and non-verbally. I repeat, our first concern is not to do harm. Yet we need to convey our joy in conversation.

Psychiatrists and psychotherapists are persons.

The account of my meeting with Mr Jones, taken together with the short stories and theoretical discussion in Book I, illustrates some features of the Conversational Model of Psychotherapy. I have developed this approach in close collaboration with many colleagues and friends over a period of thirty years and it is now being used in clinical practice and research in a number of centres in the United Kingdom and abroad.[2]

In the next chapter I shall summarize, and to some extent repeat, what has gone before. I hope that the preliminary formulation will be sufficiently coherent to enable others to examine, evaluate, and test out some of my suggestions.

· 12 ·
TOWARDS A MODEL
OF PSYCHOTHERAPY

A method of psychotherapy which can be learned quickly is needed by a wide variety of professionals and non-professionals: psychiatrists, social workers, nurses, clergy, teachers, counsellors in many spheres of life, and indeed by anyone who is consulted by a friend with a personal problem.

A formulation of fundamental principles, specified procedures, and methods of learning is essential for disciplined research, so badly needed in this field. We cannot begin to study the results of such a nebulous process as 'psychotherapy' in any meaningful way unless we can first state unambiguously what is done and for what reasons.

The Conversational Model is designed for the therapy of patients or clients (the words are used interchangeably) whose symptoms and problems arise from defects or disturbances of significant relationships. Closely associated with a general theory of psychoneurotic disturbance, it aims at the promotion of unlearning and of new learning in a dialogue between persons. A situation is created in which problems are disclosed, explored, understood, and modified within a therapeutic conversation.

I have drawn attention to a number of features of the model as they are used in a few minutes of one interview (Chapter 11). In this chapter I repeat and summarize some general principles and concepts which have been developed in Book I in so far as they are relevant to the acquisition and use of basic skills. Then I focus on one very common way in which conversation is impaired or destroyed (i.e. by persecution); and I end with a few brief comments on learning psychotherapy.

GENERAL PRINCIPLES

Personal Problem-Solving

Problems in personal relationships cannot be solved by talking about them, by explaining them from outside. They can only be explored and tackled effectively in the experience of being within a relationship.

'Personal problem-solving' is both a matter of solving personal problems and of solving problems in a personal way.

Psychological problems arise when people use inappropriate ways of dealing with past hurts, especially those involving loss and separation. Means of avoiding pain (avoidance-activities, customarily termed 'mechanisms of defence') can result in actions which hamper personal growth and the development of the dynamic relationship of aloneness-togetherness. These defensive manoeuvres are usually associated with actual or feared conflicts.

Growing up is characterized by a repeated pattern of organization, relative disorganization, and re-organization. There is a recurrent loss of established states of order (characterized by differentiation and integration of experiences and actions) so that new forms of life may develop. There is a need for a balance of stability and change, with a continuity in significant personal relationships. Unreal fears of painful loss, persisting from early childhood, can lead to an inhibition of a process of growth and the realization of potentialities.

The main theme in the stories of Sam and Stephen (Chapter 1) is the adolescent transition from childhood to adult life, a period of relative disorganization. Owing to deep-seated fears (associated, for example, with his unresolved mourning for his father and ambivalence towards his mother), Sam faced a serious threat of disintegration. Leaving childhood seemed a cataclysmic loss. Stephen's drawing with me vividly presented the conflict between the wish to separate from his mother and the fear of being alone on the dangerous voyage of growing up, complicated by the dangers of destruction and forbidden sex.

In both instances, the problem was directly *presented* in the relationship with me. Alone and together, we discovered a mutual *trust* which diminished fear and avoidance actions. We came to share a new language with fresh ways of perceiving and acting in the world. The personal problems were explored and solved *within* a relationship.

Much of the skill (and good fortune) of the therapist lies in discerning and staying with those bits of dialogue which emerge and expand in a shaping 'feeling-language'.

The practical procedures of the model are concerned with problem-solving in a personal conversation. Day-to-day practicalities, emotional memories, and secret individual experiences are important, but they are constantly related to the immediate experiencing of a relationship, here and now. The 'special kind of friendship' of therapy, later termed 'mutual-asymmetry', is directed towards:

1   maintaining a level of anxiety or fear which is necessary for recognizing and solving problems in relationships;

2   providing, and mutually elaborating, a feeling-language in a developing conversation.

The features of personal problem-solving are as follows.

A *diagnosis is made* by the detection, recognition, amplification, exploration, and formulation of problems deemed to be significant. This hypothetical formulation is to some extent based on what is described or 'talked about' (the history); but, of much greater importance, is how the problem is directly revealed and shown in the verbal and non-verbal conversation.

Problems can be arranged in hierarchies. Sam's problem in growing up was associated with sub-problems such as his mixed feelings about his idealized father. Those were directly presented in therapy in his attitude towards me as a great cricketer whom he admired and yet strongly resented. Mr Jones manifested, in a conversation, his ambivalence to his doctor-father and the relation of his stomach aches to fears of leaving home.

The delimitation of what is to be regarded as the central problem for therapy depends upon many factors. Its formulation depends upon the possibility of change, degree of disturbance, strength of motivation, capacity for insight, and time available. Here, I stress that not all defects in personal relationships can be remedied by conversational therapy. To take an extreme example, an autistic child is unlikely ever to grasp the meaning of 'a person'.

A decision about the selection of a suitable client is based on evidence of whether or not the disturbance arises directly from problems in personal relationships, and whether or not he shows himself able and willing to enter into a therapeutic conversation. In making a diagnosis the interviewer is guided by the possibility of discerning and expanding any felt dialogue (however slight and fleeting) which happens during the interview. This evidence cannot be obtained by a description from a case sheet but only by being, or failing to be, in a relationship during the initial sessions. The possibility is experienced, now. It is illustrated by the few minutes with Mr Jones. The *how* is more important than the *what*.

The problem is actively explored. Passivity becomes activity. But sometimes activity serves only to avoid important problems, especially those which are charged with the pain of anxiety and conflict. Avoidance action taken in the past is repeated, often unprofitably, in the present.

The most important fears and conflicts are those connected with separation and loss. On the one hand there is a need for attachment to, and contact with, another significant person; on the other hand there is a need for autonomy and privacy. Aloneness-togetherness in a relationship develops from these basic goals and remains in touch with bodily roots. It is a delicate balance. To be alone brings a dread of loneliness and to be together carries the threat of 'fusion' with loss of distinct identity. Those twin fears, and the conflict between them, can be avoided in diverse ways. The anxiety can be denied or disclaimed. One extreme state can be sought as a flight from the other. There can be a yearning for the delights of eternal union or a withdrawal into the bliss of solitude. Loneliness is often accompanied by compensatory day-dreams of fusion.

Loneliness and fusion can be ways of avoiding pain and uncertainty. They are distressing. Yet they can be creative, and both play a needful part in a developing personal conversation. Aloneness-togetherness is an ideal norm which we glimpse and experience in rare moments. But it remains a goal from infancy to old age. Our personal life is the pursuit of a hope of being an individual-in-relationship.

The basic conflict is one of *approach and avoidance*. It embodies a wish for, and action towards, personal contact, with a moving away out of fear of intimacy: 'I want to be closer but I daren't.' This was evident at various levels in the developing conversation with Mr Jones: in the handshake, in movements towards and away from me, in his retreat into, and emergence from, his overcoat, in the changing rhythms and intonations of his speech, in the ambivalent content of his talk, and in many other ways. The conflicts of action were evident, here and now. They were pointers to problems of personal relationships in his family and in his wider life. In all conflict there is the opposition of the need for stability and order, and the wish for, and fear of, change: a repeated process of organization, relative disorganization, and re-organization.

Exploring a difficult problem demands a capacity to tolerate anxiety and stress, to stand in 'mysteries, uncertainties, doubts'. It means staying with conflict and the acceptance of actions which, hitherto, have been rejected and unadmitted. Psychotherapy requires the maintenance of an optimum level of anxiety, arousal, and motivation. The ideal is a situation of relative safety in which a frank and open conversation can develop. Many structural practicalities (such as furniture and specified time) are necessary, but most important is the reduction of excessive fear by the trust engendered by mutual understanding.

New possibilities for actions and acts are generated. Unrealized potentialities are discovered.

The unfolding of lines of growth are often gradual, but my experience suggests that progress in explorative psychotherapy usually occurs in 'steps'. There are epochs: turning points with sudden changes which are often accompanied by insight.

Consolidation of new attitudes by custom and repeated practice is important but unexpected, and sometimes radical, changes occur in personal conversations in and out of therapy. Unexpected vistas open in a longstanding friendship. Unpredictably, we fall in love – once more, or for the first time – with a companion of years. We see anew a daily view or a well-known face. There is a new look: a freshening of the familiar (Chapters 8 and 9). Our very perception is different; our experience, staled by custom, is re-ordered in a moment of surprise. Our inward eye 'sees' a strange renewed world. The corpse sits up (Chapter 1).

Moments such as these cannot be contrived. They happen frequently in what many people, including psychotherapists, dismiss as ordinary chats. We cannot make them come, but perhaps we can prepare the ground. Disciplined practice in the use of figurative language can provide conditions for the genesis of living symbols (Chapters 5 to 7) which can (but might not) be steps in creative thought and in the deepening of personal meetings.

Such steps occurred in the cricket talk with Sam and in our shared awe in the dream story. Stephen and I saw into a fresh meaning of the rainbow which appeared between and beyond us. The 'shaping spirit' of imagination in relationships intimates a conversation between 'I' and 'myself'.

Moments of vision. They are all very well and, maybe, they are what keep us going in dreary times of enduring what seems to be unchanging. But the daily round of a psychotherapist is just going on, with as much patience as he can muster – detecting, clarifying, and hoping to make obsolete the multifarious means of avoiding the unknown commitments of an encounter with a person. Trying to overcome the timid avoidance of growth. Then, one day, with luck or grace, there might be a step, a shift: a new disclosure. There might be.

A number of key words used in special senses have been discussed in Book I: notably 'conversation', 'person', 'experience', 'action', 'symbol', 'feeling', 'aloneness-togetherness', and 'insight'.

Conversation

'Conversation' has a wide meaning which approximates to the first definition of the word given in the *Shorter Oxford English Dictionary* – 'The action of living or having one's being *in* or *among*' ('For our conversation is in heaven,' *Phil III.*20). It implies a broad conception of language which covers many different modes of being with other people – many 'forms of life', to use Wittgenstein's term (Chapter 4). Language embraces not only overt verbal and non-verbal communication but also 'inner languages' of experience, thought, feeling, and insight. A personal relationship calls for different and yet related 'language games': many diverse kinds of 'action'.

Conversation is reciprocal. Two persons are actively involved in a creative process. There is a progressive increase of mutual understanding which involves negotiation and adjustment: the correction of misunderstanding. This activity is characterized by the emergence of a shared language of feeling.

Sam and I used many different languages in discussing his home life, his school, his aspirations, and his reflections about the cosmos. Much of this talk was 'about' things and situations but we came together as persons in the 'disclosure' language of cricket and of the discovery of the pearl. I met Stephen with mutual understanding in the language of cooperative drawing. Such 'forms of life' are examples of a personal 'feeling-language'. Its beginnings are indicated in the few minutes with Mr Jones.

Problems are directly expressed, presented, or enacted, here and now – not merely 'talked about'. The therapist aims to respond in such a way that the learning can be extended to varied interpersonal relationships in the client's life. Individual self-knowledge achieved within therapy is of importance; but, more significant, is learning ways of relating: learning *how* to converse. The action of being '*in* or *among*' is to live within a personal relationship.

Persons and Things

I said 'Sam and I came together as persons' (p. 7). The model involves a radical distinction between relationships *with* (or, rather, between) persons, and relations *to* things (Chapter 2). Moreover, there is a fundamental difference between 'knowing about' a human being and 'knowing' a person. To recount a long history of Stephen's life, to recite a catalogue of his symptoms and behaviour patterns, or to fix him in a formulated diagnostic phrase, are activities which are not at all the same as knowing and being known by him in a shared smile. The difference is not one of degree (the extent of intimacy, for example). The language of 'knowing' and of 'knowing about' have different forms – different logics. Yet, one mode can enliven the other.

Some people have never learned effective and rewarding ways of knowing, and of allowing themselves to be known by, others. Indeed, we all have deficiencies in our personal relationships. 'Abnormality', here, is a matter of degree. Our notions of human beings as persons are faulty. We have distorted, rigid, or limited notions of other people's experiences, feelings, or reasons for action. We live with inadequate ideas about how to engage in, and what we can expect from, a personal relationship. This is especially so as regards the establishment and on-going development of a dialogue which involves a mutual exchange and sharing of feeling.

In such circumstances, when reciprocity is impaired, the relation to the other becomes more akin to the way we respond to things rather than to persons. It has a quality of 'talking about', 'talking to', 'talking at' rather than a 'talking with' which implies a two-way mutually-adapting conversation. A conversation takes account of the varying responses of the other person, with a continuing reinterpretation of what is attributed to him, especially as regards feelings, motives, and changing meanings. A personal relationship means a maintained sense of the other as an experiencing subject – with unique experiences which are different from and yet related to mine.

Misunderstandings and misperceptions can only be corrected if both parties recognize and accept them, both being willing and able to adjust in aspiring to understanding. 'Understanding' means the mutual discovery of a language in which feeling can be openly expressed, amplified, and modified. The word 'feeling' is a key word which is not to be identified with 'emotion', or 'affect' (Chapter 6). It involves the creation of 'forms', like artistic forms, which have a personal 'meaning'.

Often a disturbance of relationships becomes evident only with those to whom we are close and important emotionally. Someone might relate well (or at least adequately) in many social situations – with colleagues at work, or with acquaintances at a cocktail party. His maladapted behaviour (and substitute symptoms) becomes apparent only with parents, lovers, or intimate friends. The special kind of intimacy of a therapeutic relationship can bring to the fore problems in relationships with significant others.

The fundamental process in the Conversational Model is one of personal problem-solving which aims to achieve a relationship of 'aloneness-togetherness' by means of the creation of a mutual feeling-language. Some significant terms amplified in Book I need to be understood before this complex sentence can be comprehended: 'experiencing subject', 'action', 'symbolical transformation', 'feeling', and 'dialogue'.

Experience, Action, and Act

Experiencing is the sense of my state of being, my existence, of 'how I am now'. At this moment. It is prior to the formation of any distinct conceptions. It is 'felt' from 'within' my body as happening *now*, but as moving, 'flowing' into the future. Ultimately it is indescribable, and can only be intimated in so far as it is expressed in more or less formulated *experiences* which emerge from the stream of experiencing. An important attitude, fostered in therapy, is an awareness of, and a 'staying with', immediate experiencing and a readiness to register what experiences emerge. This means a kind of passivity, a willingness to let things happen, but also an active openness to receive what comes to 'me'. Experiencing is symbolized as experiences with a 'felt-meaning'.

The terms 'activity', 'action', and 'act' are discussed in Chapter 3. I have emphasized the movement from a 'passive state' to an 'active' one.

One of the most important tasks of the therapist is, by his responses, to promote a change from *passivity to activity*. Or, rather, it is a discovery of activity in apparent passivity. Sam's silent, passive resistance was, in effect, very active. In therapy it became directed; for example, when I noted the activity in a new kind of silence before he told me his dream. Stephen appeared, at first, to be a passive victim of an 'illness', but in the creation of the picture, fantasies which first 'came to' him later became an activity of imagination. Joe Jones showed increasing activity in decisively taking off his overcoat and later, without prompting, chose to tell me about his life. There are many kinds of activity and some distinctions are crucial for the psychotherapist.

I use the term *activity* to cover any observable behaviour which is directed towards a goal. In a systems approach (suggested in Chapter 14), it can be applied to the path of a guided missile or the track of a racing rat in a maze. The therapist uses the language of activity in general, but he is concerned with human beings who have intentions and purposes. He needs terms for those activities which are accepted and claimed as 'my own': activities which are responsible and chosen. I distinguish 'actions' and 'acts'.

Although the use of the word *action* is in accordance with a relatively recent philosophical tradition, it may give a wrong impression to the reader. It does not refer only to outward, observable movements but also applies to images, thoughts, and emotions which I regard as 'mine'. In so far as they are inseparably linked with the word 'I', they can be said to be 'willed' ('I think', 'I feel', 'I hope'). This is one, but only one, important reason for the stress I put upon the therapist's use of 'I' in the Conversational Model.

An *act*, a sub-class of action, is an overt deed, action made public. It is given meaning by at least one other person. An important feature of this meaning is the recognition by another that the act is performed by an experiencing subject, a responsible person. Whether in bodily movement or in speech it is always a communication which calls for a responsive action and/or act.

Registering the activity of Stephen's finger movements, I sought for meanings in 'inner' actions and wondered how these could become significant acts.

Some activities are not acknowledged by the person, because they are contrary to his professed attitudes, formulated purposes, self-esteem, or for many other reasons. They are incompatible or in conflict with actions that he has claimed and owned. I term these rejected and denied activities *disclaimed actions*.

Sam disclaimed many fantasies, thoughts, emotions, and wishes which involved sex and aggression. Later, he came to accept the positive values (as actions) in these corner-stones which the builder had rejected.

The term 'disclaimed action' may seem odd and inconsistent since, by definition, actions are owned and willed. It implies that there are activities which *could* be actions if consciously accepted, but there is more to it than that. In an important sense, 'willing' can occur beyond awareness, and to say 'I did not know that I really wanted to go to the party' is not nonsense. (The puzzle of the two 'I's in the last statement calls for an extended discussion.) It should be noted that 'claiming' is not an 'all or none' activity. Some actions are partially claimed: 'I sometimes want to kill you but I don't *really* want to.'

The use of 'action-act' terminology is crucial in a model in which human beings are respected as responsible persons who hope, anticipate, intend, decide, and strive to reach desired ends. They have 'reasons' which cannot be reduced to 'causes' (as is done, for instance, in classical behaviourism and classical psychoanalysis). The main task of the psychotherapist is not, primarily, to unearth causes of disturbance in the past but to promote movement from the present into the future.

By his words and gestures the therapist can himself be a model. He conveys his action of 'owning': of responsibility. To say 'I reckon you are feeling sad' is a vastly different matter from suggesting 'Your depression, or your unconscious guilt, makes you sad.' The transitions from a passive attribution of disturbances caused by 'my illness' to an active 'I feel and do such and such', or from 'an angry mood has come over me' to 'I feel mad', are crucial. Attention to the minute particulars of syntax reveals profound attitudes and should be a foundation-stone of psychotherapy.

Experiencing is symbolized. An expanding personal conversation is a process of symbolical transformation (Chapter 7).

Symbolical Transformation

I have stressed the importance of 'staying with' immediate experiencing using a 'symbolical attitude', 'focusing', 'a wise passiveness', and 'waiting with loving attentiveness'.

I tried to show how as the rainbow picture emerged between Stephen and me there was a progress from passive fantasy, through active fantasy, to imaginative activity. Nascent experiences gave form to, and were formed by, pre-conceptual experiencing. They became owned as meaningful actions and acts.

In Chapters 5, 6, and 7, I distinguished various forms of symbolism. Oversimplifying, I contrasted linear, straight-line, discursive thinking with patterned, imaginative forms of feeling. The distinction is relevant to the differences between attitudes to things and relationships with persons, between 'knowing about' and 'knowing', between 'translating' and 'encountering', and between 'interpreting' and 'showing'. I suggested that both forms emerge from, and need to remain in touch with, a more basic mode of fantasy-thinking which is near to pre-conceptual experiencing. Here, I stress once more the importance of a symbolical attitude towards words, gestures, pictures, or dreams.

A dream of a corpse sitting up can be translated into causal language; as, for example, in terms of infantile necrophilia, or masochistic fantasies. It can be 'explained' – and, at worst, explained away. But with another attitude, it can be confronted as a strange and dimly understood language which is saying something about what is as yet unknown – a language which cannot be put in any other way. It 'presents' a complex feeling, which leads to new discovery.

I term such value-laden presentations *living symbols*. A central feature of personal growth is symbolical transformation. In this process raw 'experiencing' is converted into ordered and organized 'experience', especially in personal conversations.

Experiencing is always 'now' and is always 'in relation to' – especially to persons who stand over and against me. I can never fully enter into the experiencing of another, but I can receive intimations of it by virtue of living symbols which, in Coleridge's term, are 'translucent' to the unknown reality which they express. This philosophizing is most relevant to the therapist's exercise of empathy and striving for understanding.

As a therapist I ask:

1   What is Joe Bloggs experiencing right now?
2   How can I help him to express his experiencing – to symbolize experiences?
3   What kind of language should I use to promote an understanding between us of his experiencing? We need to adjust: to negotiate.

Vital discoveries are made when we *fail* to understand; when we miss the mark.

It is in this gap that new possibilities emerge.

The process of understanding or, rather, correction of misunderstanding, is central in the task of personal problem-solving. It entails the creation of a feeling-language.

Feeling-language

The stories of Sam, Stephen, Freda, Mr Jones and Mr Chip portray the growth of a language of feeling. The problem in establishing and developing a personal relationship is how to discover a language that fits: how to express, how to convey, how to understand, how to share, and how to elaborate feeling within a conversation.

I have tried to say that by the word 'feeling' I do not mean simply an experience or a discharge of emotion, such as anger or gratified desire (Chapter 6). Relatively undifferentiated affects such as these move into more complex, ordered states and languages. The languages have 'meanings' which are akin to those of significant works of art: a symphony, a picture, or a poem. Feeling has its own 'logic'. Living symbols are organized within more embracing heart-felt 'commanding forms'. There is an evolution, a dynamic spectrum, which ranges from sensations (such as touch and sight) to insight and knowing. Feeling words, such as 'love', are growing words: throughout life we 'grow' into their meaning.

The 'disclosure' in cricket body-talk with Sam led on to, and was inseparable from, the shared meaning of the pearl. The drawing with Stephen embodied a progressive shaping of forms which showed, directly presented, a meaning which could not be reduced to other terms. There was a 'fit' between inner and outer forms.

In as much as feeling is an ordering of 'forms of life', it can be called a 'rational' process: a mode of thought. It is a kind of knowing. Like a work of art, it can be technically defective and, hence, inaccurate; and it can lack candour and be insincere. To aspire to exactness and sincerity is to strive for a 'true voice of feeling'.

In psychotherapy, as in creative thought, there is an interplay between imaginative forms and linear discourse. One is tested against the other in the search for truth. Sometimes there is a synthesis. But that is rare.

The guiding theme of this book is the nature and significance of feeling-language. It is the heart of the Conversational Model.

Aloneness-togetherness

Learning to know a person in an expanding conversation involves many varied ways of 'talking' – in words and in various other modes of action. These modes of using language can be conceived in different ways. I shall distinguish 'communication' from 'dialogue'.

Communication means the effective transmission of meaningful 'messages'. It involves a constant modification of what is being said as the speaker hears it, and as he registers the effects on the other participants. Both people are in some way talking at the same time. Cues, verbal or non-verbal, are registered (e.g. a word, a phrase, a lift of an eyebrow, a line on a piece of paper) and translated into meaningful messages. Cues can be described by inspection (e.g. of a videotape), although what counts as a cue depends on what kind of messages are regarded as being significant. Embodied in a message is some information about *how* a communication should be received – what kind of message it is. This is termed 'meta-communication'. In human communication, many messages are transmitted simultaneously through diverse channels and, if they are to be received and interpreted correctly, they should be consistent. A communication has been made when the 'transmitter', A, perceives that his message has been received and responded to, by the 'receiver', B – a perception of the perception. The possibilities for misinterpretation are immense – especially when it comes to understanding expressions of feeling. Reaching understanding involves a continual modification of the conversation by means of a recognition and correction of mistakes. That is 'negotiation'.

Sometimes a person's capacity to maintain intimate relationships is profoundly impaired. Owing to inborn defects or to previous experience (often in early childhood), there is a failure to register the communication of feeling by words, tones of voice, and often subtle facial expressions and gestures. Such 'cues' are frequently not noticed; or, if they are, they are selected in a biased way and misinterpreted. Misinterpretation occurs most frequently when the 'messages' refer to the person who is addressed. For instance, Mr Jones selectively perceived and attended to one of my 'looks' (which, amongst many others, I could detect on a videotape). Ignoring other expressions he took it, wrongly, to mean a constant and unalterable feeling of disapproval. Hence, not surprisingly, he responded with inappropriate fear, anger, and withdrawal. The reciprocity of the conversation was disturbed. In such circumstances, people give cues (of which they are often unaware) which, in turn, are likely to be misconstrued. Thus, Joe Jones, in his irritation, prepared to leave. My immediate impression was that he did not really want help. I misunderstood. If we do not recognize the misunderstanding (Mr Jones did not realize that I construed his behaviour in this way) then we see no reason to correct or change the communication.

The jargon of communication can be applied to tele-communications, computers and biological systems. Such a language can be useful in describing personal conversations, but it has serious limitations. We need the notion of dialogue.

Dialogue entails the recognition of the other person as an experiencing subject. In a simultaneous acting and being acted upon, knowing and being known, there is a mutual creation of a personal feeling-language. 'I and you' becomes 'I-Thou'. Empathy, a one-way apprehension of what Joe Bloggs is experiencing, moves towards a mutual understanding in which Joe and I are at once alone and together. A hyphen is necessary and I term this relationship *aloneness-togetherness*.

I distinguish aloneness from isolation and loneliness; and togetherness from non-differentiation or fusion. Several times, in telling the stories of Sam and Stephen, I used the phrase 'alone and together'. I can only be alone in so far as I can be together with another. I can only be together in so far as I can stand alone.

To be a separate person and also go out to meet another means caring, and it means taking risks. We need trust and we need courage. If we are open to understanding, we are also open to being hurt. Rejection, attack, envy, and persecution can be avoided by withdrawal and alienation or by a superficial cosiness: a 'pseudo-mutuality'.

Personal conversations with Sam and Stephen (and to a lesser extent with Joe Jones) were promoted by a growth of trust. In a climate of increasing understanding, tentative explorations led on to braver ventures and to imaginative play: a togetherness in the 'space-between'. Sam and Stephen emerged from isolated loneliness.

Some security from hurt is provided by the structure of therapy, but trust in a person grows only by mutual understanding and care. In his endeavour to speak a true voice of feeling, the high (and perhaps impossible) ideal of a psychotherapist is to 'penetrate to the core of loneliness in each person and speak to that'.[1]

The words 'alone' and 'together' carry a sense of a mode of being. 'I' stand not only in relation to another experiencing subject, but also to a wider, obscure 'myself'. To be alone means being together in an open dialogue, but it also means an inner dialogue: a conversation with many 'selves' in a society of 'myself'. Sometimes as patient and therapist venture together into unknown regions, there are rare moments of *meeting*. Then perhaps there is a disclosure of a larger 'whole' – a rainbow or a pearl which is 'me in a *sort of way*'.

The broad theoretical notions outlined above are closely related to what we say and do in therapy.

BASIC SKILLS

How we act in psychotherapy depends upon, and derives from, many obscure needs, attitudes, ideas, and emotions. Our feelings on a particular day (worries about the future of an aged aunt or the yellow dawn of a hangover) affect our responses to our clients. But, in order to be coherent, we need to be guided by a general theory.

Risking repetition, I shall spell out some principles of my approach.

1　The Conversational Model is designed for the therapy of patients/clients whose problems lie in intimate relationships, in 'knowing' persons as distinct from 'knowing about' people or things. Past deprivation, hurts, and failures result in:

(a) lack of opportunity to learn a language in which personal feeling can be expressed, understood, and shared.

(b) crippling activities used to avoid feared painful situations (especially loss of 'contact' with another person) are reflected in disorders of behaviour.

2　The process of therapy is termed personal problem-solving. This means the discovery, exploration, and solution of significant problems which are directly enacted, here and now, in the therapeutic conversation.

Learning in therapy involves experimentation with ways of knowing and being known within a relationship. It is extended to other life-situations.

3　A personal conversation, promoted in therapy, involves the differentiation and integration of many forms of language – modes of being with people. The crucial language of 'knowing' is one which expresses, communicates, and shares feeling. It involves:

(a) an apprehension of, and 'staying with', immediate experiencing.

(b) a process of discriminating, symbolizing, and ordering experiences; especially by creative expression in living symbols (using, for example, figurative language and metaphor).

(c) 'owning' experiences (thoughts, wishes, feelings – especially in relation to persons) in a movement from passivity to activity, characterized by accepting responsibility for actions and acts which, formerly, have been disclaimed by means of avoidance activities, usually associated with conflict.

(d) mutual correction of misunderstanding by: adjustment of ineffective communication; promotion of dialogue.

(e) learning different *ways* of achieving personal 'knowing' especially by dealing with misunderstanding.

4   A therapeutic conversation usually progresses by steps with the dawning of new insights, new ways of 'seeing'.

5   The ever-present therapeutic purpose is to facilitate growth by removing obstructions. To free the *vis medicatrix naturae*. Especially important is the reduction of fear associated with separation, loss, and abandonment.

6   A central feature of growth is an aspiration towards an ideal state of aloneness-togetherness. This goes together with an increase of individual awareness with 'inner' conversations between 'I' and many 'selves' in a society of 'myself'.

The discovery of a 'true voice of feeling' by patient and therapist requires genuineness. But sincerity is not enough. There is a need for technical accomplishment. So I shall state the basic procedures of the Conversational Model: a skeleton which, in other chapters, I attempt to clothe with bloody flesh. There are many examples of the following bare statements.

Setting and Structure

The furniture of the consulting room and the limits of time are vital features of the therapeutic language. Two identical chairs set at an angle at which therapist and patient can look at each other or look away without obviously doing so indicate something of the kind of conversation which is expected. Regularity and a statement of limits convey a predictable security. Setting and structure are part of a language. They *say* something of great importance for patient and therapist.

'I' and 'We'

The use of first-person words 'I' and 'we' affirms the aim of a conversation between two separate and yet related responsible persons who, alone and together, claim their actions.

Statements

A one-sided grossly asymmetrical relationship is inimical to conversation. Questions which imply interrogation can inhibit mutual exploration. Statements, if appropriately made, are less likely to put the client on the spot, are more open to correction, and provide a starting point from which diverging themes can be developed. They are often enquiries, but the details of syntax can be vital, especially in early interviews and at times of crisis.

Negotiation

The 'how' of the therapist's talk is crucial. Rather than implying 'this is right', his message should be 'This is the way I see it now . . . but maybe I am not on the ball.' To be tentative is not to be vague. A therapist's statements are definite (i.e. clearly 'owned' by him). He does his best to be accurate but does not know which answers are right for the patient. He conveys his wish to be corrected. He hopes for communication which will lead on to dialogue, with an adjustment of misunderstanding.

Misunderstandings occur. Indeed, they are the stuff of a developing relationship. If perfect empathy could ever be achieved we would get nowhere. A personal conversation is a movement; it progresses not by comfortable agreement but by correction of mistakes. In intimate relationships we constantly miss the mark and it is out of the gap that new possibilities emerge. But the miss must not be too great. Some adjustment must be possible if 'misses' are to be recognized, acknowledged, and clarified. Then it is possible to explore jointly the nature of the misunderstanding.

Here and Now

For the two persons in a conversation the focus is on what the patient is experiencing right now — but with a move forwards. Although the therapist's statements are tentative he is not passive. Again and again he will suggest 'Let's just stay with that . . . just stay and wait.' Especially important are the patient's perceptions of, and attitudes towards, the therapist. Memories of the past are important in so far as they enliven and are 're-composed' in the present with a movement into the future. Dreams, dreamt many years ago, are statements made to this therapist *now*. They can be pregnant metaphors.

Hypotheses

The therapist puts forward hypotheses which are based on cues from the patient, on his own experiences, and on other knowledge, including theory. These are ways of promoting the exploration and organization of feeling. Expressed in a negotiating manner implying openness to correction ('I reckon ...', 'I guess ...', 'I wonder ...'), they are 'tested', not by simple agreement or disagreement, but by whether or not they are extended, amplified, or corrected by the patient. Hypotheses are of three kinds – understanding, linking, and explanatory.

An *understanding hypothesis* involves, first, an expression of empathy, an imaginative statement of what the therapist feels that the client is experiencing right now in the relationship. Empathy is conveyed in such a way as to call forth a response; to achieve a dialogue with increasing mutual understanding: an approach to sympathy. Of particular importance is the communication of a desire to understand. The aim of the hypothesis is to promote a never-ending process: a resolution of misunderstanding.

The extent and depth of understanding is increased by means of ordered forms termed *linking hypotheses*. On the basis of observed recurrent patterns (such as Mr Jones's approach-avoidance behaviour of various kinds) links are made, and parallels are drawn:

(a) between events within therapy at different times; perhaps during one interview, perhaps relating what is happening now to previous sessions;

(b) between patterns in the present therapeutic conversation and those in other areas of life (especially ways in which relationships are defective and distorted).

An *explanatory hypothesis* introduces possible reasons (which may or may not be 'causes') for disturbances in relationships within and outside therapy. It corresponds closely with an 'interpretation' and involves 'because' clauses, usually relating to fear. In its complete form there are three such clauses.

The 'clauses' are given at intervals and it is desirable that the patient should make the explanation himself or, at least, make a substantial contribution. For example, 'I shrink back into my overcoat *because* I am scared of getting too close to you *because*, then, you would cruelly reject me.' A present action is carried out in order to avoid a particular type of relationship which would result in some catastrophe. The fear of the catastrophe may or may not be completely outside awareness. In the conversation, it may or may not be explicitly linked with past experience ('like I was abandoned by my mum').

In the Conversational Model, as distinct from some types of analytical psychotherapy, explanatory interpretations are not the goal of therapy, nor are they essential for 'insight'. They are useful in organizing, in making sense of, immediate experiences and helping the acknowledgement of disclaimed actions; but these formulations are important only in so far as they promote on-going, understanding conversations in a language of feeling which is developing *now*.

Living Symbols and Metaphor

In facilitating personal growth, the therapist deliberately aims to convey and promote a symbolical attitude. This means endowing words, gestures, drawings, and dreams with value; regarding them not only as communications of formulated messages but also as living symbols. They are intimations of, and means of apprehending, what is as yet unknown. By means of figurative language and metaphor, hitherto disparate experiences are welded together. Immediacy and vividness are given to expressions of feeling and, in fresh insights, there is a creation of new forms, new 'wholes'.

Listening and Noticing

First and foremost, a therapist's job is to listen and to go on learning how to listen. He needs to be open to register cues and patterns of cues. Much of this perception occurs beyond his awareness, as shapes and forms arise and are bodied forth in intuition. He needs to become more and more able to listen to himself as well as to his client.

Much of the therapist's receptive activity calls for a relatively unfocused awareness but he also needs to 'notice'.[2] This means a concentrated attentiveness to minute particulars and, at the same time, a readiness to see these anew in a freshening of the familiar. The combination of these two attitudes is difficult to convey, and even more difficult to maintain. It is an ideal which we can aspire to but seldom attain.

In passing, it should be said that the therapist needs to regulate his own anxiety, aiming to maintain an optimum level. We have limits and there are times for *not* listening. Sometimes it is all too much.

Mutual-asymmetry

A conversation moves towards a mutual dialogue. But psychotherapy must be a *special* kind of conversation. It is, perhaps, a mode of friendship but if it is to be therapeutic it must be friendship of a very special sort.

On the one hand, therapy reveals the problems of everyday intimacy and discovers solutions which are in many ways the same as those needed in other life-situations. On the other hand, it provides an unusually safe situation designed to lessen inhibiting fear and to promote personal problem-solving. It requires genuineness and mutuality of feeling in a personal relationship, for only in such a 'real' situation can effective learning occur. Yet, it is asymmetrical (slanted, if not one-sided) in that the ultimate concern is the life of the patient. The therapist does not talk about the same things as the client (e.g. details of his private life) save in exceptional circumstances. Nor is it his job in a professional situation to burden the patient with his own problems and undisciplined emotions. Furthermore, he and the client have different tasks as regards such matters as maintaining structure and necessary detachment.

It is an arduous task for the therapist to establish and tolerate an attitude of involved detachment: openness and mutuality of feeling together with a necessary asymmetry. Self-awareness, personal integrity, and genuine concern are necessary ideals but, in themselves, even these high values are not enough. There is no alternative to persistent, disciplined practice of definite skills.

In psychotherapy I hope for some moments of *meeting*, a genuine dialogue *within the necessary constraints of therapy*. There are diverse ways of avoiding the anxiety of meeting, some of which I have touched upon. In this summarizing section I shall elaborate only one of these. It is the most important because it is the antithesis of conversation: persecution. I am grateful to Russell Meares for the term 'The Persecutory Therapist'.[3]

THE PERSECUTORY THERAPIST

Psychotherapy can do harm. Reports from patients, long study of audio- and video-recordings, and personal experience suggest that the most damaging situation is when so-called 'therapy' becomes a reciprocal, mounting attack. Such a state of affairs is likely to occur with certain kinds of client,[4] but it is often exacerbated, or perhaps even created, by the therapist. Here I am concerned with some ways in which a therapist, often despite good intentions, can become a persecutor and destroy a developing relationship of mutual-asymmetry. I shall make a bare list of four features of the stereotypic 'Persecutory Therapist': intrusion, derogation, invalidation of experience, and opaqueness.

Intrusion

By repeating crude questions, especially as a means of probing into a particular theory, a therapist can be experienced as if he were a prosecuting counsel. Implicitly (or indeed sometimes explicitly) he can demand either a speech in defence or an abject surrender. 'Why?' questions can be especially dangerous, leading to blocking or facile intellectualization. Such interrogations preclude a mutual exploration of unclear, nebulous uncertainties associated perhaps with fear and guilt.

To a beginner I say: 'Make tentative statements, hoping that you will be corrected. There is a fine of five pounds for asking "Why?".'

But intrusion can be of a very different kind. By being too intuitive and empathic we can make a client feel invaded by a magical, all-knowing therapist.

It is important to avoid a forced confession of fragile 'secrets' which, as Meares has cogently argued, are experienced as a 'core of the self'.[5] Secrets should be valued and respected by therapists, by parents, and by husbands and wives. We need an 'inner space' and a 'space-between'.

Derogation

Trying to be helpful, we make interventions which we consider to be 'confronting' or 'insight-giving'. We are often perceived as condemning. Indeed, all unaware, we might be satisfying ourselves by using covert ways to dominate clients, to call them names.

In subtle ways, the patient is made to feel patronized, 'bad', or 'ill'. Self-esteem is lowered; he or she feels alienated, denigrated, and quite different from the therapist who is heard as saying: 'It is all your problem which I do not share.'

Invalidation of Experience

Intrusion or derogation are more obvious forms of attack. Invalidation of the patient's experience is more subtle. It happens when I, as therapist, consider that what the client says does not mean what he or she thinks it does. I am suggesting that the 'real' meaning lies somewhere else. This is not an unusual situation, since psychotherapy is sometimes characterized as a search for 'deeper' explanations. Yet such a quest might be illusory, or even destructive. At its most extreme, it involves the assumption that one piece of behaviour, verbal or otherwise, *stands in place of* another piece of behaviour; that what a patient says means *nothing but* something else – a 'something else' which authorities regard as being more fundamental or causative in a particular theoretical framework. Thus, I can behave as if the patient is communicating in a curious kind of code, which it is my duty to break. Under these circumstances, the client experiences his own words as a cage. However much he strives to find his freedom through them he is imprisoned behind the iron bars of an explanatory stereotype.

The patient may perceive this interpretative behaviour as worse than reductionism, especially if interpretations are directed unremittingly to his 'unconscious'. When he protests that he is unaware of the feelings attributed to him and this plea is dismissed as a 'resistance', he may sense a growing failure and unreality – an alienation from his 'own' thoughts. That which he felt he knew is uncertain, and what seemed substantial becomes a mere figment. He feels more and more bewildered, helpless, unreal, and eventually despairing.

A person's statements should always be respected – whatever they may be. The psychotherapist's job is to *amplify*, to extend awareness, not by implying 'You don't mean that – you really mean this,' but rather, 'You certainly mean that, but maybe you *also* mean something more.' If he treats the patient's experience as if it were part of a cryptic crossword he can be destructive in a way suggested by William James:

> 'Thoughts connected as we feel them to be connected are what we mean by personal selves. The worst a psychology can do is to so interpret the nature of these selves as to rob them of their worth.'[6]

The Opaque Therapist

The therapist is always involved in a two-person situation. Despite inevitable non-verbal messages he sometimes maintains that he is 'neutral'. Perhaps he supposes that by being opaque and faceless he can diminish his personal existence and produce 'pure transference'. To the patient he may feel like unyielding stone.

Since the therapist believes that he is not there as a person, but merely as a 'blank screen', he may respond to all the patient's remarks about him as if they were merely manifestations of other relationships in the past, whether or not elaborated by fantasy. The patient comes to feel that all his productions are unreal distortions. Such a therapist nullifies the patient's attempts to distinguish those responses and attitudes that are illusory from those which are part of an actual situation in the present – certainly affected, and perhaps determined, by the therapist's own characteristics. He impedes the patient's movement towards a healthy reduction of his distorted perception of others, not allowing him to make the comparison between what is 'illusion' and what is 'actual'. Unless at the appropriate time – and this timing is crucial – the therapist reveals what he is like, the patient has no opportunity to test out fantasy against fact. The patient is hindered in his efforts to discover his identity. Since all is illusion he can come to believe that all is distortion – his experience of himself and his perception of other people. Then all his emotional responses are 'neurotic'. There is no healthy bit left.

Above all, psychotherapy is concerned with the development of unrealized potentialities.

Failure to reply to direct questions is a characteristic feature of the 'neutral' or 'opaque' therapist. Not surprisingly, this can be construed as being deliberately frustrating since some questions do concern 'reality', at least in part. They may refer, for example, to the structure of the therapeutic situation. This is not to say that direct questions should always be answered immediately for it is often far from clear what is being asked. The problem is how to explore the possibility – and it is only a possibility – that the question is a signpost to a larger area of the patient's imaginative and emotional life (particularly as it concerns the present conversation) and how to time the reply without being evasive or rejecting. Simple evasion neglects the fantasy which may underlie the question.

As I grow older, I increasingly answer direct questions with direct answers. I find that then it is easier to explore what has not yet been asked.

The opaque mask may put the patient in an untenable, helpless position in various ways: by lack of clarity about the structure of therapy, by imposing impossible requirements, by giving conflicting messages, and by making conflicting demands.

Structure of Therapy

There is reason to suppose that a clear awareness of the task of therapy is beneficial to the patient.[7] A client becomes unnerved and often persecuted if he sits under the eye of a therapist without a notion of what is expected or of what is likely to happen.

We should spell out as far as possible what psychotherapy is about.

Impossible Demands

Although the therapist might give very clear instructions the patient may be unable to comply with them. This is less likely to occur when patients are highly selected; that is, those who can register an emotional response, verbalize it, and relate it to other experience. Since it is not possible to measure outcome or predict suitability with any confidence, those who cannot cope with an 'orthodox' interpretative psychotherapeutic situation often enter treatment. Then, unless the therapist's technique is flexible, persecutory feelings arise.

Perhaps the most important attitude and skill of the therapist is to be willing and able to *recognize signs that he is wrong*, and to modify his approach in the light of such evidence.

My job is to learn how to relate to this particular person.

Conflicting Messages

A most important, but often subtle, way of putting the patient in an untenable situation is by giving conflicting messages. Human beings communicate through many channels and a therapist can say one thing in words and quite different things by tones of voice, gestures, facial expressions, and other non-verbal means – as is apparent from study of videotape recordings. This 'double-talk' is likely to lead to feelings of uncertainty, perplexity, chaos, and persecution. It reinforces maladaptive responses resulting from past experiences of inconsistent behaviour by significant persons, especially parents. A therapist is likely to behave in this way when he attempts to practise a 'technique' which is at odds with his feeling for the patient. Frequently, these 'double-binds' – which indeed can be 'treble' or 'quadruple' – reveal deep-seated personal problems in the therapist. Anxieties, conflicts, and avoidance-mechanisms of which he is unaware can be touched upon by events in the therapeutic relationship. It is relatively easy to detect contradictory messages and demands arising from such difficulties, especially by audio-visual aids, but it is quite another matter to correct them. It is essential that the therapist should have some therapy himself in order to increase his awareness, but often that is not enough. Some people are not cut out to be psychotherapists and even those who are most suited do not 'fit' with, and can be damaging to, some patients.

Conflicting Demands

There are very many ways in which conflicting messages can result in conflicting demands as, for example, when at the same time as encouraging aggression the therapist expresses his own fear of it; or when he recommends independence and, because of his own needs, promotes dependence. These and similar but very diverse 'binds' have been discussed at length by many writers. I shall mention only one which is not often noted. It is related to the types of thinking discussed in Chapters 5 to 7.

The kind of therapist whom Winnicott has characterized as 'orderly' may set down conflicting rules for the therapeutic conversation. He asks the patient to communicate in associative fantasy-thinking, while he, himself, responds only in directed and linear thought. They are two people speaking different 'languages'. This unreal and, indeed, impossible situation may culminate in the therapist remarking, 'I don't think I know what you're saying,' to which the patient may legitimately reply, 'I don't know either.'

The 'orderly' therapist is unreceptive and unresponsive to the images of associative thought. Winnicott writes about this problem in the following way, although in a rather different context:

> 'there are patients who at times need the therapist to note the nonsense that belongs to the mental state of the individual at rest without the need even for the patient to communicate this nonsense, that is to say, without the need for the patient to organize nonsense. The therapist who cannot take this communication becomes engaged in a futile attempt to find some organization in the nonsense, as a result of which the patient leaves the nonsense area because of the hopelessness about communicating nonsense.'[8]

The over-rational therapist, who cannot allow himself to use the presentational language of linear 'nonsense', has a set of rigid expectations based on his beliefs about methods, technique, and theory. He does not enter the state of mind advocated by Freud, who suggests that the therapist should surrender himself in a state of 'evenly suspended attention' and

> 'not to try to fix anything that he hears particularly in his memory, and by these means to catch the drift of the patient's unconscious with his own unconscious.'[9]

This passage suggests that the therapist should allow his imaginative processes to unfurl over the contents of the therapeutic encounter, turning over, in an unfocused way, the matter which is being presented to him. He is not trying to put it into pigeon-holes. Freud writes:

> 'The most successful cases are those in which one proceeds, as it were, aimlessly and allows oneself to be overtaken by any surprises, always presenting them to an open mind, free from any expectations.'[10]

The rhythm and balance of intimacy and distance, of aloneness-togetherness, requires a 'space' in which both patient and therapist can allow fantasy forms and themes to emerge. In this 'play' ideas emerge which when reflected upon can result in imaginative activity.

Serious damage can occur when patient and therapist become locked in an escalating reciprocal persecution which I shall term a *persecutory spiral*.[11] A tragic example is given in Chapter 16.

Feelings of persecution induced in the patient may escalate to unendurable levels. An important factor in the production of this persecutory spiral is the therapist's own anxiety which rises in therapy when there is a threat to the view that he has of himself.

The circumstances in which a therapist can feel persecuted are legion and call for a whole book. Owing to his own personality structure and current problems, he can experience the patient as being intolerably intrusive, derogatory, opaque, inconsistent, and over-rational. He responds by overt and covert attack. In varied ways, therapist and patient persecute each other. Only one important feature will be mentioned – the therapist's sense of omnipotence.

When intrusive, challenging, authoritarian, and sectarian characteristics are overt, the persecutory therapist is not difficult to identify. Frequently, however, his omnipotence is unobtrusive, and he is quite unaware of it. Nevertheless, his implicit role is as the bearer of an esoteric system of knowledge (as a doctor, as an analyst, or as a 'new humanist') which he 'passes down' to the patient, and uses to change him. When the latter fails to improve, is silent, or presents impenetrable defences, the therapist may feel a sense of impotence which he is loath to acknowledge. His anxiety, which he may also fail to recognize, is aroused by the threat to his role and tenaciously held beliefs. He responds by enhancing his omnipotence, and the various modes of behaviour that go with it. The therapist's denial of the two-person situation, together with his opacity and rigidity, is increased. More and more, he emphasizes the patient's 'sickness' and defects. The patient, in turn, experiences growing helplessness. His bewilderment and sense of unreality may become profound. The sense of impotence and persecution, now felt by both members of the dyad, mount to dangerous levels.

Sometimes the persecutory spiral is resolved by ending the therapeutic relationship. Usually, this is done by the patient. It is inconsistent with the therapist's view of himself to accept the failure of his method unless he can label the patient as unsuitable for treatment or as being 'unanalysable'. Not infrequently, reports from therapists explain away failures by means of labels attached to patients, which, however fashionably couched in technical terms, can be roughly translated: 'It is all *his* fault.'

The patient may be unable to leave. His experience of himself at this point is childlike in relation to a dominant parent-figure who knows him to be weak, bad, and resourceless. Yet, he has come to believe that this figure is omniscient – the only one who can possibly redeem him. He is trapped in an unresolvable situation of extreme dependency associated with hostility and rage, often deflected into self-persecuting guilt.

The only possible outcome may be suicide.

Our first concern is not to do harm. We need to go on learning how to learn – about others, about relationships, and about ourselves.

LEARNING PSYCHOTHERAPY

A recurrent theme in this book is the need for the therapist (whether a raw beginner or an experienced expert) continually to clarify, refine, and exercise the basic techniques of his science and art. The above list (pp. 195–200) of the elements in one way of talking with patients needs much elaboration and qualification. The procedures are akin to the scales of notes for a musician or to the words and phrases of a literary artist. Broad theoretical ideas and psychodynamic formulations are of importance only in so far as they are incarnated in the minute particulars of what we do. We need to practise our scales. Technical accomplishment is essential in achieving a unique 'true voice of feeling'.

More than thirty years ago I began to record my interviews on tape. With many patients a portable recorder became a routine part of therapy. I believe that in one year, listening again and again to the minute particulars of the sessions (I heard some interviews more than forty times) I learned more in a few months than I had in long years of previous formal training. We cannot report to others what we do not know has happened.

This book is not concerned with the complex details of training and I shall merely indicate a few ways in which audio-visual aids can be of great value for students. Indeed, in my view, they are indispensable in understanding the general principles and acquiring the specific techniques of the Conversational Model.

There are some things which cannot be talked about but only shown. A reader who wishes to check what I do against what I think I do (as presented in this book) can watch a videotape.[12]

Since 1978 a number of research projects have been carried out in the Department of Psychiatry, University of Manchester, in order to clarify the Conversational Model and to develop a brief teaching method. First, by means of films, the main features and basic skills of the model are illustrated by various therapists. Next, their combination is shown in an on-going interview. After studying these videotapes, aided by a hand-out, trainees can practise the skills with the help of a 'micro-teaching' tape. Preliminary research suggests strongly that at least some of the basic techniques can be learned by most beginners in a surprisingly short time.[13]

The use of such a brief 'package' cannot make a psychotherapist, but the evidence forces me (somewhat reluctantly) to regard it as a useful and, for some people, a most effective introduction.

Demonstrated techniques can be felt as being 'out there', as 'treatments' to be applied. They cannot obviate direct personal experience.

I ask a trainee (or, if I have the chance, an experienced analyst) to record an interview on videotape and to write down, either during or after the interview, an account of the session noting what was important. Later she or he watches the tape first alone; then together with a small group of colleagues; and finally together with the patient.

If this is done scrupulously and with sincerity, few therapists, however naive or however experienced, will fail to learn something more about the prime task of a psychotherapist – *how to go on learning more about how to listen*. By 'listening' I mean an active process of perceiving and paying attention to a multitude of verbal and non-verbal cues and, by an imaginative act, creating possible meanings which can be tried out and modified in a conversation, or dialogue, that aims at understanding. Despite some differences in technique (e.g. regarding the nature of illusions and when they should be corrected) all methods of psychotherapy (as I use that term) assert or imply that the achievement of a meaningful 'realistic' relationship is a central therapeutic factor.

A detailed discussion is called for, but I shall limit myself to a bare list of some uses and possible drawbacks of audio-visual recordings.

1   It is of value to have a library of films of experts at work, particularly to give a flavour of different approaches. However, it does seem that in learning a particular method, *feedback of the trainee's own interviews* is essential.

2   A whole session can be devoted to the minutiae of *a few minutes of tape*, learning to observe more and more verbal and non-verbal behaviours of patient and therapist and to generate possible meanings or hypotheses.

3   *Longer sections* of a whole interview may present a developing process and serve as a basis for discussion of psychodynamic theory (with a multitude of references to the literature).

4   In presenting an account of a *long period of therapy* it is a good exercise to illustrate these with recorded extracts from several interviews.

5   *Role playing* is a most useful technique, both in learning basic technical skills, and in exploring some possible factors of a particular difficulty in therapy, the therapist playing his own patient. The 'therapist-patient' can report his own feelings.

6   To watch a tape *together with a patient* can be a valuable part of therapy as well as of learning. It is often a very enlightening and humbling experience for the therapist and patient to mark on a transcript what each regarded as significant events. The recording often reveals how the therapist misperceives or responds inappropriately because of his own problems. It can be used as a means of increasing self-awareness.

Trainees should be encouraged to *watch in different ways*. A combination of 'objective' inspection and an imaginative 'feeling into' patient and therapist is near to the psychotherapeutic attitude of 'detached involvement', of 'mutual-asymmetry'.

Although for advanced supervision some one-to-one situations are useful experiences, there are advantages in small on-going groups with a constant membership. A climate of mutual trust is of the greatest importance in a situation in which intimate feelings are revealed. My hunch is that three or four members is ideal. Given a flexible basic model, a great deal of 'self-learning' can occur when two or three are gathered together around a videotape or indeed an audiotape (which is often much more practicable). An expert teacher can then be more effectively and economically used.

The use of taped interviews can be criticized on various grounds, e.g. that it makes the situation 'unreal', invades the privacy of an intimate relationship, and leads to emphasis being put upon mechanical techniques rather than on a personal 'meeting'. All these objections have some substance – sometimes. There is an urgent need for detailed investigation with numerous examples.

I shall limit myself to the profound banal-sounding statement that all therapy and teaching should be carried out in the light of a deep respect for people who go on becoming persons in genuine relationships. The greatest danger lies in paying lip-service to such an ideal and then contradicting it in practice. A 'double-bind' makes a damaging psychotherapist.

In the present state of knowledge no one of very many theories can be sufficient. In doing his best to assess what methods are appropriate for what patients, with what therapists, in what situations, a psychotherapist needs to use different frameworks. This eclectic approach calls for a paragon with wide theoretical knowedge, long experience, and a clarity and flexibility of intellect as well as sensitive feeling. However, in the earlier stages of learning a trainee usually needs a clear model with definite techniques. There is an urgent need to elucidate some basic principles which, later, can be questioned, modified, or rejected.

The Conversational Model can be elaborated in many ways using different theoretical principles incarnated in varied personal styles.

Perhaps the most important thing is learning how to go on learning through and by the experiences of a lifetime. In teaching I never fail to read the passage from Rilke quoted on page 36. As I read I seldom fail to discover something new about psychotherapy and about myself.

It is important to make a list of skills. But in a developing relationship, a psychotherapist hears the deep, and often terrible, reverberations of the words 'love' and 'loss'. He is brought face to face with the timid, banal manoeuvres that we all make in order to avoid the dread of being a person-in-relationship.

We love. We lose.
We live. We die.

· 13 ·
LOVE AND LOSS

Alice is desperate and lonely. Her relationships are chaotic and she has made several suicide attempts. But her innocent eye has not been blinded by an excess of classroom education. She writes an account of a therapeutic session:

'I think that I was able to open up to you and express myself so that you could see me raw and all my weaknesses and feelings that torment. I felt obviously that I was opening myself up as much as possible and had given all that I could of my feelings, my truth, but although we discussed them and I saw things in some ways in a different perspective it couldn't go deeper because it was a one-way thing – *I don't want you to tell me all your feelings and thoughts of your own life* but it is difficult when one feels one's giving like one's soul or Being and that it is one-sided. Although I felt you understood most of what I expressed, *I wished perhaps you would reveal your true feelings* and not act out the part of an analyst because I do feel at times that when we are getting somewhere you say the right thing to say instead of what you really feel.' (My italics)

Alice is tormented by a chaotic sense of badness and weakness. She longs to be able to be open and, at the risk of devastating hurt by being roughly handled, she does her best to reveal her weakness and to expose herself raw. She feels safe enough to begin to emerge from her isolation and venture into the unknown, helped by the sympathetic understanding of her therapist. She longs to go 'deeper', but in order to do so she needs to join in a conversation which is much more than a one-sided 'discussion'. The 'right' words of an analyst (as she understands the label) do not speak to her 'soul' or 'Being'. She has been able to enjoy a new view both of herself and of the world around her.

Perhaps she has glimpsed exciting possibilities; she seeks a more profound and transforming vision. Her preliminary discoveries cannot become insight – a passionate 'new look', with movement *into* the world of people and things – unless she receives a response of 'real true feelings'. She has a need to give, and offers as a gift the 'truth' of her own life – her feelings, which are much more than transient emotions. But she can only do this in an intimate, reciprocal meeting, a giving and receiving, a sharing, with another person who opens himself to her and is not only 'playing a part' (although that part might be necessary at times). She asks for a genuine conversation of mutual trust which can free her to explore not only alone but also together with another person. Alice needs to be needed.

She recognizes the special nature of the conversation with its peculiar therapeutic purpose. She seeks a friendship, but it is a friendship of a curious kind. She states clearly the difference between talking *about* and talking *with*. She asks for an equality in the sense of a mutual respect and an honest exchange of feeling in talking with, but accepts an asymmetry with regard to what is talked 'about'. In order to open herself to new experiences, to emerge from her desolate and yet self-protective loneliness, she pleads for help. She longs to express her need for genuineness, for trust, for tenderness – for love.

Our problem is how to find the appropriate sentences with which to respond to the many Alices who sit in the patient's chair. My hope is to discover a true voice of feeling in a mutual personal relationship (Chapter 2).

Alice and I did what we could. I hope that we did. I am not sure. Her circumstances and mine were, or seemed to be, such that we could not continue to meet. About a year later I heard that she had committed suicide. In painful solitude I wondered about psychotherapy – and about the word 'love'.

Love is a growing word. It is not, as was pointed out in Chapter 2, the same kind of word as 'jam jar'. Herbert McCabe observes that we cannot describe what it is like for a man to be loving as easily as we can describe what it is like for him to be walking.[1] 'Love' is an expanding word. Knowing how to use the word 'love' is part of our personal history, of our autobiography. We learn how to use 'jam jar' at an early age, but we are no better at using this and similar words at the age of sixty than when we were six.

We can grasp the meaning of 'jam jar' by being told the rules for its use, but this is not so with words such as 'love'. We cannot *start* with a sophisticated understanding, just as we cannot start with a sophisticated taste in music or literature. In order to live and grow our understanding must reach down to 'primitive roots'.[2]

'Mother's love' can range from being near and giving us what we want, to apparently irrelevant or even hostile acts such as leaving us alone while she cooks our dinner. To grow up is to be open to the possibility of new 'forms'. The meaning of 'love' grows as we grow physically, psychologically, and spiritually.

There are no short-cuts to understanding what love is. If someone has been deprived of the crudest infantile experience of love then he might be permanently crippled or, at least, have great difficulty in learning later what the word can mean. In learning what it symbolizes I need to re-write my autobiography over and over again. To grow is to re-organize the past *now* and to move into the future.

Sandor Ferenczi, a somewhat delinquent disciple of Freud, asserted 'The physician's love heals the patient.'[3] He argued that if psychological problems were due to deprivation of care in infancy, then intellectual interpretations were of little value. I might know 'why' I behave as I do: I have lacked love. But what good is that unless I can feel that I *am* loved, now? Ferenczi came to believe that, if change is to occur, then the infantile situation should be 're-lived', but with a difference – a difference directly *experienced* by the patient. The analyst, as a parent-substitute (unlike the real parent), should supply personal warmth and acceptance. There is a need for an antidote in a new situation, given by a parent who is genuinely and vividly tender.[4]

Ian Suttie, in a sadly neglected book, accepted Ferenczi's dictum.[5] He saw that the anxiety of sadness and separation, deprivation and loss were central in neuroses and psychoses, a view which was later developed by John Bowlby[6] and is followed in this book. He regarded psychotherapy as a quest for a 'companionship' with the patient. He drew attention to the embarrassed 'taboo on tenderness' which scares us all, especially 'scientific' psychotherapists. There is no more effective barrier to treatment. Tenderness is akin to that of the loving relationship between the child and mother which is formed 'with the intention of severance'.[7]

The therapist needs to be a 'mother' (and a 'father'), but he must move towards 'friendship', a more equal personal relationship.

I shall not forget Alice as I make some oversimplified and abstract remarks about attachment and loss in human relationships.

To be a human being, constantly becoming a person, means living and learning in relationships: creating a language. Conversation begins in infancy.

THE GROWING INFANT

From the earliest days there is reciprocal communication between mother and baby. The infant communicates by means of positive cues such as cooing, smiling, and quiescence, and by negative ones such as crying, motor uneasiness, apathy, and refusal. The mother's skill lies in her ways of responding to these *cues*, interpreting them correctly as *messages* of discomfort, satisfaction, hunger, or pain. She communicates to the infant by auditory, visual, and tactile means and there is good evidence that subtle variations in qualities of voice, in ways of handling and of looking, are of great importance in setting the conditions for tranquil behaviour in the growing infant. In this early conversation the child learns *basic trust and hope*, the sense that his mother is reliably there and will be consistently responsive to his needs. Trust arises *between* mother and baby. As important as being gratified, and in my view more important, is the pleasure of giving, of satisfying the needs of the other. This basic *giving and receiving* is vital in psychotherapy. In the security of a trusting conversation the child can begin to explore a world of strange people and unfamiliar things, and is less likely to be overwhelmed by anxiety which, otherwise, will result in ineffective, or even crippling avoidance-activities.

The newborn baby is not an empty container to be filled with experience; he is not a *tabula rasa* on which his biography is written by external hands. He is an active agent who, within the necessary limits set by his circumstances, creates his own life – his own 'world'. But to say I have 'my own' life is not to say I 'own' my life. 'My world' is constructed and re-constructed in 'a world' in which I am alone and yet together with other people.

The infant has potentialities to develop complex modes of experience and diverse patterns of behaviour.[8] These inborn tendencies need to be activated (made 'actual') by people and things in his environment. Of crucial importance is the capacity to form rewarding attachments to particular persons, first to the mother and then to other people. The success of psychotherapy, the well-being of any society, and perhaps the future of mankind, depends upon whether or not, and under what conditions, love can grow.

During the early months a baby progressively learns to control his activities. Experiencing bodies forth experiences, actions, and acts. In

Chapter 7 I have stressed just one theme: the action of looking in a two-way interaction between mother and baby.

To a large extent, the child acquires his knowledge of the world and of himself by doing things. The great French psychologist Piaget has said 'I only know an object to the extent that I act upon it.' No doubt, in the earliest months, the recurrence of regular patterns of sensations in the nursing situation brings some order into a chaos of lights, voices, touches, and tastes. Even then the child's perception of his world is not merely passive; it is greatly affected by his own actions which arise from basic need – his bellowing and cooing and his active seeking and sucking of the nipple. Perception is an *active* creation.

The infant, then, is not a mere recipient of experience. His curiosity and his need to manipulate lead him to explore the environment. Very early on, he pursues things with his eyes and by about the fifth month, he realizes that if he sees something he can also reach out and touch it, move it, and try to taste it. So, by means of actions he begins to integrate separate sensations into perceptions of objects, of his own body, his mother's body, and other external objects. By means of an experimental method he learns how sight, touch, and taste can belong together and how they can help him to reach desirable goals. A personal world comes into being, and in a sense is created, through the *activity of doing*. There is a need to achieve *order and consistency*. Through the child's activity information is elaborated about objects: their colour, form, and weight. He achieves order by discriminating, bringing together, arranging, and counting. He begins to classify the qualities of objects and people, and what can be expected of them, in terms of touching, striking, shaking, pushing, dropping, poking, smiling, crying, babbling, and later talking. So he forms integrated patterns, 'inner plans', 'constructs', or 'schemata' of the world which are constantly developed and consolidated. Each attainment of an organized category or construct is the starting-point for the next one.

As the infant matures, explores, and learns from his experiences, he organizes elements and sub-systems of movements, acts, and actions into larger systems (see Chapter 14). There is a continued coordination. Discrimination and differentiation of skills in adapting to the physical environment and in relating to other people go together with their increasing integration. There is an achievement of hierarchical control, i.e. activities which were formerly 'wholes' become regulated as parts of larger 'wholes'.

Activities become more 'voluntary', i.e. used as means to a new end. Sucking for example is essential in feeding and also is a means of relieving distress. Later it can be used in the service of seeing. Infants will suck in order to increase the illumination of a picture on a screen in a darkened room. An arrangement can be made so that by sucking either quickly or slowly, a motion picture can be brought into focus (brightness being constant). A four-week-old infant can learn to bring the picture into focus and to stop if sucking causes it to blur.[9]

The baby has learned to coordinate sucking and looking. Here perhaps is the basis of metaphor, e.g. a 'devouring look' (p.122).

A similar coordination occurs between hand and eye when the infant's own activity brings reaching and grasping under visual control.

An important point (perhaps relevant to insight in psychotherapy) is that the learning of 'voluntary' actions is not, it seems, achieved by increments. It occurs in steps: it is qualitative not quantitative.[10]

A human being has a need to order his experience and is always 'becoming'. There is a constant progression, the equilibrium is not a static state but a new starting-point for more complex forms of development.[11] A child's world becomes progressively more predictable and organized and he can react more quickly and appropriately, with more assurance about the outcome. Although his conscious concept of time needs to develop, from the beginning he *anticipates* the future in terms of possible satisfaction and dissatisfaction – of *hope* and *fear*.

A young child has a need to explore, to investigate his environment as freely as is consistent with safety. If the novelty becomes too great his trust enables him to relieve his anxiety by running back to the security of mother's arms. If he becomes excessively afraid because of too painful experiences, reinforced by a mother's anxious and over-protective prohibitions, his exploratory drive is inhibited. The development of an attitude of hope with the expectation of rewarding achievement is arrested.

Intimately bound up with hope, fear, and trust is a basic need for attachment, a secure bond with one other person.

BONDING AND LOSS

At some point a baby recognizes his mother (or 'mother figure') and distinguishes her from other people (see p. 122). His nascent perceptions and other experiences – the sound of a voice, the touch of skin, the pressure of arms, and the sight of a face – are organized in a category, made into a whole, a 'construct' of 'mother'. Formerly he responded to other people in similar ways. Now strangers are treated with increasing caution and sooner or later they evoke alarm and withdrawal.

As attachment develops, the infant follows the departing mother, greets her when she returns, and uses her as a base from which to explore. He greets her with *joy*, reacts to her going with *anxiety*, and to her loss with sorrow. Both absence and prolonged loss arouse *anger*.

The most important factor is the mutually entwining patterns of behaviour between the mother and child. In a sequence of interrelation, each, by action and response, modifies the behaviour of the other, and hence strengthens or weakens the mutual bond. There is an emerging conversation.

The infant behaves as if a coherent picture of a complex world is being built up of organized systems with varied goals. Within this 'inner map' the mother is experienced as an independent 'being' existing and moving within space and time in a more or less predictable manner. The baby's behaviour becomes more flexible but for some time remains relatively rigid. In order to learn, he needs a high degree of consistency in his world. States of anxiety, sorrow, or anger occur when the mother's acts do not accord with the infant's implicit predictions.

Attachment-behaviour, characterized by crying when held by others and smiling more when near to the mother, begins at about nine or ten weeks. Later there is crying when the mother disappears. The infant follows her with his eyes, crawls towards and away from her, greets her, scrambles over her, explores her person and clothes, and clings to her as a haven of safety when ill or alarmed.

The above brief and simplified account closely follows John Bowlby.[12]

In summary it can be said that before the age of about four months it is rare to observe patterns of behaviour which denote a differentiation of the mother from other people. They might be present but if so they require special techniques to detect them. The great majority of infants brought up in families clearly show differential responses at the age of six months.

Although attachment is a relatively clear-cut activity it may occur at all ages, is evident in many situations, and can be expressed in a great variety of ways. It appears in many different contexts, varies in intensity over a period of time, and is employed for different purposes. There are general patterns but these are modified by the make-up of a given individual, by age, by the immediate situation, and by the wider social and cultural situation.

The reader might count how many of the patterns he or she exhibits in fact or fantasy when deeply in love, or when a loved person has died.

In *individual* behaviour, when one avenue of expression is blocked, others can be used. Blind infants rely more on auditory and tactile cues. Motor handicaps do not make a relationship impossible; eyes can make up for hands. There are less obvious, though more common, individual differences. For example, there is evidence that there are two types of infant − 'cuddlers' and 'non-cuddlers' − who differ in patterns of activity. The non-cuddlers tend to receive much less physical contact than the cuddlers – they are more restless, they dislike physical constraints such as being dressed or tucked in bed. Although the nature of the relationship of these two types with the mother differs, the ultimate development of attachment and bonding is very similar. By the age of eighteen months, non-cuddlers catch up with the cuddlers. The non-cuddlers use other means of relating; they make more visual contact with the mother. They turn towards her when apprehensive but use less touch, such as holding on to her skirt or hiding their face against her knee.

What might be deprivation for one child is not so for another. The lot of a 'good-enough mother', to use Donald Winnicott's term, is not always a happy one. Stereotyped mothering is not enough. A mother needs to respond with hands, eyes, ears, and voice to the needs of *this* particular child. So, too, the psychotherapist is faced with the problem of remaining 'in touch' with this particular person by means of an appropriate language, whether of eyes, gestures, or words 'spoken' from the right 'distance'.

'Attachment' implies 'to' and I have, perhaps, concentrated too much on the behaviour of the child. The better term for the pattern of early relationships is 'bonding'. A bond is 'between'. The mother also needs to be satisfied in a 'mutual relationship'. When a bond is severed there is loss. A basic theme both in growing up and in the process of psychotherapy is the cycle of loss – relative disorganization – re-organization. Loss and fear of loss of a loved person is the central feature of disturbances in relationships which constitute, or give rise to, psychological disturbance.

The Conversational Model is concerned with the promotion of a state of aloneness-togetherness within which inevitable anxiety associated with loss can be revealed and tolerated. It involves a discovery and resolution of maladapted and unnecessary means of avoiding those conflicts which arise from the fear of damaging separation.

Bearing in mind multifarious individual differences, and the inadequacy of any classification which would do justice to the many Alices, I shall consider very briefly (summarizing the work of J. Bowlby and C. Murray Parkes)[13] loss in early childhood and in adult bereavement in so far as they are relevant to anxiety.

To repeat, love casts out fear, but also fear casts out love.

LOSS IN EARLY CHILDHOOD

When a young child between the ages of about twelve months and three years is separated from his mother (or a person who 'mothers' the child) to whom he is attached, he responds in a characteristic way. Bewildered and isolated with strangers in a strange place, he goes through three phases.

1   His initial response is one of protest. Urgently, he attempts to recover his lost mother. He cries loudly, shakes his cot, throws himself about, and looks eagerly towards any sight or sound which might prove to be his absent mother. With variations this state of disorganization might last a week or more. It seems as if the child is buoyed up by *hope and expectation* that his mother will return.

2   Sooner or later *despair* sets in. Maybe the longing for his mother's return does not diminish but hope fades. Eventually there is *apathy* and *withdrawal*, punctuated perhaps by an intermittent wail. He or she is in a state of misery which I shall call 'grief'. It is as if the mother on whom his life depends has died.

Care-takers wish to believe the child is content. They do not want to see how the child still yearns for the mother's return, although it is evident in bouts of crying and vain searching. He becomes quieter and it is only careful observation that reveals how strongly he remains orientated towards her.

The persistent longing for the mother is often combined with an intense, generalized hostility. There is good reason to believe that in its origin much of the anger is directed towards the missing mother-figure.

As is often the case with a bereaved adult, a child in a hospital or residential nursery at first rejects those who are caring for her. Sometimes clinging to a nurse is accompanied by sobs for the lost mother. After the phase of withdrawal and apathy, there is a search for new relationships. If there is *one particular mother-figure* to whom she can relate and who mothers her with care, perhaps in time she will take to her and treat her almost as if she were her mother. But, if there is no single caring person, the child becomes increasingly self-centred and prone to make transient and shallow relationships with all and sundry.

3   The third phase is one of *detachment*. It is regularly seen whenever a child between the ages of about six months and three years has spent a week or more out of his mother's care, and without being cared for by a single substitute. If the child meets his mother again there is an almost complete absence of attachment-behaviour (although he might respond affectionately when he sees his father).

The duration and degree of the state of detachment correlates highly and significantly with the length of time away from the mother. On return he shows no tendency to cling. He acts as if his mother were a stranger. Sometimes detachment is less pronounced and phases of turning away alternate with phases of clinging.

Bowlby regards detachment-behaviour as the result of a 'defensive process' such as occurs in mourning at any age. The abnormality is not the fact that detachment occurs; all depends upon the form it takes and the degree to which it is reversible. It can be compared to a scar following inflammation. A crippling of personality is not an inevitable result; but the 'scar tissue' can all too often lead to severe dysfunction in later life. The pathological responses made by older persons to loss and threats of loss can be observed in childhood. There is a probable link between psychiatric disturbances of later life and childhood experiences.[14]

Prolonged and severe deprivation due to insufficient, distorted, or discontinuous mothering may have grave and far-reaching effects upon the child's character. It can mould the whole of his future life. There is a large body of evidence about the social effects of such deprivation in monkeys as well as clinical evidence in human beings. It can be said with some confidence that children brought up in impersonal kinds of institutions often have a disturbed, unsocial, or antisocial type of personality. They do not develop a motive for love and affection, forming no close feeling-ties and having little control over aggressive impulses. But there are large variations. People are not born equal and it seems that some infants have less need than others for bodily and emotional care. The quality of mothering may be deficient for this particular child, or there may be distortions and inconsistencies in the early bonding conversation.

Of special importance, most relevant to psychotherapy, is the trans-mission by mothers of inconsistent and contrary cues and messages.

Deprivation and distortion can, then, result in mild or severe disturbances in later life, especially in the realm of personal relation-ships. On the one hand there is an inadequate sense of identity, of myself, of autonomy, and a capacity to be alone; and on the other hand, an inability to be present to, and together with, significant others. It is difficult to achieve a state of aloneness-togetherness.

When a loved person dies we need to mourn. Mourning has phases which, in some ways, are akin to those of loss in early childhood. If early bonding has been deficient, the 'normal' healing process of grieving can be disturbed.

BEREAVEMENT

An attractive girl of nineteen came to ask for my help. For six months Helen had been unable to work because of blinding headaches. She had become more and more solitary and unhappy and eventually took a slight overdose of sleeping pills.

I did not probe with questions. I did not give advice. I tried my best to listen. Occasionally, I attempted to put into words what Helen was experiencing (right *now* in our interview). From time to time I said a few words about the fear which blocked her, which prevented her from saying what she had to say, simple things like: 'You seem to be scared about what I will think about you if you show your feelings.' But, perhaps it was the fine details that mattered most, how I grunted, when I spoke and when I kept my mouth shut; and, maybe, most important of all, the gestures, looks, smiles, and facial contortions.

To state the problem in a sentence: Helen had not grieved when her mother died a year previously. She said: 'Everyone said how wonderful and calm I was. I never cried. I was proud about that.'

During our second meeting Helen dries up.

'I guess you are scared of letting me see how upset you are,' I suggest.

'No. Not that,' she answers. 'It's ... it's ... just too much.'

Silence.

'Look lass,' I say, pointing to her tummy. 'I reckon you're boiling inside and ...'

I am interrupted by her violent sobbing.

During the next few weeks she went through the phases of 'normal' mourning – a phase of *disorganization* characterized by alternating and mixed love, hate, and guilt about her mother. This was followed by a *re-organization* with loss of her symptoms. I do not really know what I did. I suppose that I was someone to mourn *with* – there had not been anybody a year before.

Mourning happens in personal conversations.

Three phases of normal mourning can be distinguished: a state of *shock*; a state of *relative disorganization*; and a process of *re-organization*.

Shock

Helen told me how for a few weeks after her mother's death she had been 'all cold and dead ... or sometimes like a dream'.

A phase of numbing usually lasts for from four hours to a week or so. There is a sense of being stunned and unable to register the news. 'I can't take it in at all', 'I just can't believe it'. During this time the bereaved person may carry on his or her usual life as if nothing had happened.

The mind tends to blot out what is too overwhelming. The death of someone who is deeply loved alters one's life irrevocably. It can be so catastrophic that it is impossible to grasp the inevitability of death. The bereaved refuses to accept the fact and carries on automatically. The *anxiety of separation* is intolerable. There might seem to be a griefless acceptance but the apparent cheerfulness is somewhat flat and the state is rather one of *self-protective numbness*.

This state can, however, be interrupted by outbursts of intense distress, not infrequently accompanied by anger. The bereaved person may be tense and apprehensive, and the calm may be broken by outbursts of intense emotion. Sudden attacks of panic can occur with a flight to the protection of friends. Occasionally a sense of exalted elation can be associated with an experience of union with the dead person.

If the grief-work proceeds then the apparent calm breaks. There are longer periods of disorganized thought and action.

Disorganization

This phase can be separated into two stages which roughly correspond to the states of protest, with yearning, and despair (described above as following loss in childhood). However, there is commonly an interweaving of themes with five characteristics: bodily distress, preoccupation with the image of the deceased, hostile reactions, guilt feelings, and loss of usual patterns of conduct.

Bodily Distress

Waves of distress occur at intervals of about twenty minutes to an hour. These might be manifest in tightness in the throat and chest, choking with shortness of breath, sighing, an empty feeling in the abdomen, weakness ('The slightest effort makes me exhausted'; 'everything is so heavy'), loss of appetite ('Food is like sand'; 'My saliva won't flow'), and insomnia.

Distress is precipitated by visits, by any mention of the deceased and by offers of sympathy. Often there is a tendency to avoid such situations and topics.

Preoccupation with the Image of the Deceased

Within hours or days of the loss, a change occurs and the bereaved person begins to register the reality of the loss. At first this is episodic. There are pangs of intense pining, distress, and outbursts of weeping. Restlessness, preoccupation with thoughts of the lost person are often combined with a sense of his or her actual presence. Signals or sounds, such as a door-latch being lifted, can be interpreted as the return of the dead person. Vivid dreams of the deceased occur with desolation on waking. Sometimes these amount to visions or other hallucinations. ('I saw Jack so clearly. It was dark but the sun was on his face and he was smiling.' 'I wakened up and my mother was bending over me just like she was alive.')

Joan was a middle-aged woman whose husband, Albert, died suddenly and unexpectedly from a coronary thrombosis:

'Nothing ... there is nothing to live for. Just an empty pain. I just wander about looking for him. Searching for nothing. Last week I saw him, just like he was ... in his old tweed coat. For a minute it was lovely ... but then dead and gone. But then he seems to be around again and I hear his steps upstairs. That's worse ... agony when all the memories pour in. In dreams too ... but I waken up and feel for him but he isn't there ... and the morning ... alone and nothing to do.'

There can be vivid hallucinations of the voice of the departed. Many bereaved persons fear insanity. Visions and voices together with some sense of unreality and emotional distance from people are a regular feature of grief. They are in no way abnormal.

During the early phase of mourning a bereaved person alternates between two states of mind: a belief that death has occurred accompanied by pain and hopeless yearning, and a disbelief that it really has occurred. A young woman said: 'When I waken up in the morning I know my mother is dead but then I have to work hard to know that she is still alive.' The disbelief is accompanied by hope and by an urge to *search* for and to recover the person who is lost.

The search is evident in a restless movement and scanning of the environment, by thinking intensely about the lost person, by perceiving and paying attention to anything that suggests the presence of the person, by focusing attention on those places in which the person is likely to be found, and by calling for the lost loved one. Although the bereaved might attempt to dismiss the urge as being irrational and absurd, nevertheless he feels himself impelled to search, if possible to recover the person who has gone.

Hostile Reactions

A common feature of the second phase of mourning is *anger*. As Bowlby points out, it resembles a child's initial protest at losing his mother and his efforts to recover her. Sometimes anger is shown in the form of a general irritability or bitterness together with a loss of warmth in relationships with other people. The bereaved person cannot be bothered with anyone. Sometimes the anger has a particular target: relatives, doctors, and clergy. The very people who are making a particular effort to help are often alienated, especially if they are somewhat clumsy in expressing their good intentions. Accusations of negligence to professional helpers are not uncommon.

There can be *open anger towards the dead person*. ('Why did you leave me like this?')

Anger is often feared and great efforts are made to control it as, for example, by adopting a formal, stiff manner. To the bereaved, loss of control can mean madness.

Joan gazes into space twisting her fingers in agitation.

'Just now, it feels like the end of the world,' I say lamely.

Joan is angry and bitter.

'Just now. Now. You don't understand. You and your smug wife, and patronizing comfort. God, the cruel bastard. And all those dear, good kind friends with platitudes. "Try and do this, dear. It'll help." He isn't here to do anything with. I hate all of you. Go away. Go away.'

I am hurt, really hurt, and yet I also want to understand: to understand in terms of a 'search'. In separations of a temporary nature, anger is frequent and indeed it can serve effectively to bring back the absent person. Maybe this is one of the most important functions of anger. Monkeys throw sticks and stones at those who stray from the group in order to bring them back – and, indeed, do so to a dead monkey for a time. Only when separation is permanent is anger and reproach out of place. But, it is part of our innate repertoire of behaviour patterns and can be understood as the urgent yet fruitless effort of a bereaved person to restore the severed bond, as well as a response to the frustration of a fruitless search.

Guilt Feelings

The bereaved often searches the time before death for evidence of failure to do right by the loved person. ('If only I had not sent her to hospital'; 'I shouldn't have gone out that night, he was upset'; 'If only . . . if only.')

Joan sobs wildly.

'If only I had known. He wanted to go abroad for a holiday. I wouldn't go. I was selfish. Why didn't I . . . why didn't I make him happy? It's too late.'

Self-doubt, self-questioning, self-reproach, shame, and guilt can be associated with suicidal thoughts, despair at life's emptiness, and perhaps fantasies of reunion. Suicidal thoughts with day- or night-dreams of reunion are dangerous.

Loss of Usual Patterns of Conduct

Joan had always been a scrupulous housewife. Now, she became slatternly. The pots piled unwashed and dust lay thick on the Welsh dresser. She dropped her friends and ceased to attend the Women's Institute or the golf-club committee.

Reorganization

Joan's love for Albert had grown over many years. It was many months before she began to shape her life anew. There are times when she still grieves. Perhaps she always will. Maybe a love like hers can confront but never conquer loss.

Yet she picked up. The pots were washed. She played once more in the golf Monthly Medal.

I think that our mourning together was a help. I think so.

One day she told me a dream. 'There was a river. A wide river flowing somewhere ... I don't know where it was going. Albert was there. He smiled. "Goodbye," he said. He went ... over the river. He has gone and yet .... In some way he is here and will be.'

Phrases like 'introjection of the ambivalently-loved object' do not do justice to experiences like that.

ANXIETY, LOSS, AND LOVE

Anxiety and fear lie at the heart of existence. Anxiety about 'being', and fear of losing those whom we love.

I imagine (and we can do no more) that in early infancy there is no distinction between 'me' and 'not me': no capacity to say 'this is inner' and 'that is outer'. Slowly, in an interaction between persons and things, the infant distinguishes his body from his mother's body and from things. Fantasy is differentiated from physical 'reality' and, as an 'I', he or she experiences the rest of the world.

At first perhaps the sense of 'I' (and my body) is unstable. It comes and goes. Therein lies *basic anxiety*, the *Angst* of non-existence, of dissolution, of annihilation. I can only 'be' in relation to another, in a loving relationship which grows from proximity to, and interaction with, a safe face into a shared life-long conversation.

The loss, or absence, of a loved person brings *separation anxiety*. It can threaten my existence, arousing basic anxiety, though it need not do so. In growing up we need to tolerate many agonizing losses − of loved persons and of ideas (and ideals). We need to negotiate periods of relative disorganization in order to attain to new orientations.

Growing up is a matter of learning how to mourn. And of loving with loss.

In the progress from infantile attachment to a relationship of aloneness-togetherness there is a double conflict. An effort to escape from the anxiety of separation (and with it the terror of basic anxiety) can result in a fantasy of oneness, or fusion. But this can bring a fear of loss of identity. Avoidance of this danger can result in withdrawal and a fearful state of isolation.

Loss brings anxiety: the fear of separation and the basic terror of not-being. In growing up we are faced again and again with the pain of mourning: of loss, disorganization, and reorganization. But we can only bear so much, and when anxiety becomes too great we take avoidance action.

We cannot mourn what we have never had: a caring mother. A psychotherapist aims to give what love he can (and it is often not very much) in response to Alice's plea to reveal his 'real true feelings'. Within a trusting conversation, he tries to help to elucidate and to resolve *avoidance-activities* – unnecessary blocks to understanding.

· 14 ·
NEEDS, CONFLICT, AND AVOIDANCE

I have outlined a conception of psychotherapy as a means of facilitating appropriate problem-solving in, and by means of, a conversation. The aim is the solution of a problem in personal relationships evident in disturbances of experience and behaviour, which inhibits personal growth.

A personal problem arises usually (but not always) because of basic and separation anxiety associated with the loss, or anticipated loss, of love as it expands in development. Fear casts out love. We avoid suffering and fear of suffering by activities, actions, and acts which preserve at least some sense of togetherness, a meaningful identity (of I and myself) within a personal language of feeling: an I-Thou 'form of life'.

Love can sometimes cast out fear; but some problems in living can never be solved. Perhaps the most important never are. Therapy is often directed towards bringing about a change of attitude and life style so that the problems become less urgent, or else can be better tolerated with less suffering. To grow up means to live with the pain of conflict and indecision without resorting to crippling avoidance. We never become whole.

Many ways of avoiding pain, learned in early life, are necessary, but they can cease to be useful. Yet obsolete manoeuvres are often maintained. They are repeated because of an apparent short-term gain coupled with a deep-seated fear of change. They foil hopeful exploratory journeys in the quest for love.

Dealing with the devious, subtle, and often unadmitted ways in which we avoid the threat of anxiety and despair is the bread and butter of practical psychotherapy. There is a large literature on the crucial theme of 'mechanisms of defence'. But I do not like the word 'mechanism' and the metaphor of 'defence' seems to me to be appropriate only in certain circumstances.

I shall not attempt to describe and discuss the many so-called 'mechanisms' in detail. They are elaborated in many writings and a beginner can consult other sources to fill out some of my bare statements.[1] There is as yet no coherent classification and there is much confusing overlap in terminology. I do not have a satisfactory answer to this difficulty. I offer one possible way of ordering the many diverse ways by means of which we avoid conflict. It is a schematic and simplified summary in order to indicate some general principles which I find useful in clinical practice. A few instances of avoidance are illustrated briefly in Chapter 15 by an example of short-term therapy.

Problems can be formulated at different levels. Some ways of thinking which are relevant to human beings are also useful in explaining the behaviour of a rat that receives an electric shock whilst seeking food in a T maze. In treating some symptoms, human beings can be regarded as rats. But no person is only a rat. The use of symbols as distinct from signals (Chapter 5) brings new problems which can only be solved by means of language. Perhaps more careful thought about levels of conceptualizing problems might go some way towards making more exciting and productive many sterile and vested-interest arguments. For example, those between 'behaviour therapists' and 'psychotherapists'.

A human need results in activity which is directed towards a goal.

I shall elaborate that basic theme. In considering different kinds of problem, I consider needs as being modes of disturbance in the equilibrium of the system of an organism.

The reader should note that in this chapter I am often talking 'about', using an objectified thing-language which is different from, and yet related to, that which expresses or presents experience from 'inside'.

I have used a key word: 'system'.

SYSTEMS

In the last four decades the notion of a system has had a transforming effect within such diverse fields of knowledge as engineering, biology, sociology, and industry. It has profoundly affected psychology, anthropology, linguistics, and ethics. Perhaps the recent popularity of 'general systems theory' is largely due to its effective use in a world dominated by machines and especially by technological military strategy. Yet, in its language there are key phrases which recall those of St Paul, Nicholas of Cusa, Gottfried Leibnitz, Samuel Taylor Coleridge, Alfred North Whitehead, and many other profound thinkers who have respected the dignity of a human being. It was propounded clearly in about 1730 by Bishop Joseph Butler.[2] A systems approach is in line with a long tradition in psychology – William James, William McDougall, Jean Piaget, and C. G. Jung, are a few amongst many other 'humanistic' psychologists who have recognized the limitations of a positivist, mechanistic, atomistic view of human behaviour which seeks to *reduce* all to elements of chemistry and physics.

Systems theory is complex.[3] The following bald statements are relevant to my immediate concern.

A Whole Is More than the Sum of Its Parts

The description of a human face is not exhausted by a list of elements: its meaning cannot be conveyed by adding separate accounts of the lift of an eyebrow or a twitch of the lips, unless these are used as signals or symbols. In a whole face we are concerned with the *relation* of arbitrarily selected parts. We cannot reduce the action of a whole human being (George walking down the garden) to a list of separate needs, wishes, conditioned responses, or physiological processes.

It is clear that what we regard as a 'whole' or as a 'part' depends upon our purposes. The universe can be a whole and so can a movement of the eyes. A question which faces every therapist is what level we select for study, and what language we use for what ends. In speaking of 'needs' I shall move between different wholes.

A System has Order

A whole system is organized by relations between elements which are *differentiated*, distinguished, and yet are *integrated*, working together in relation. From time to time I have referred to human growth and development as a process of forming wholes by differentiation and integration (e.g. p. 214). In technical language the degree of order can be called 'information'.

A system can be highly integrated and poorly differentiated. For example, a regiment of guards at the Trooping of the Colour move together in a coordinated order but each member does the same thing. An individual can be consistently single-minded yet have a narrow range of abilities, interests, and behaviour (e.g. he can be a highly integrated bore). A marriage can be maintained effectively by keeping within strict agreed limits.

There can be a diverse differentiation and yet poor integration. A very eclectic society of psychotherapists can lack coherent activity: a divergent thinker can have a multitude of fascinating ideas which are never co-ordinated.

In my terms the highest organization (order, information) means a system with a secure integration of highly differentiated parts, e.g. a first-rate football team, a great poem, a genius, a loving relationship, a growing family. I have suggested that development throughout life means a progressive differentiation and integration (p. 214). There is a movement towards wholeness. A language with different and yet related 'games' (Chapter 4) can be regarded as a system. Figurative expressions can lead to increasing order.

Systems Are Organized for Some Purpose

There is an activity directed to an end or goal. The activity (which in human beings, unlike guided missiles, can be a willed action or act) is regulated by its consequences. As I move my pen in order to write this sentence, information is 'fed back' to me from my hand, my eyes, and a multitude of sources about the success or otherwise in approaching my goal. My complex activities and actions are guided by the effects of what I do. A simple straight-line picture of cause and effect is inadequate. My reasons, my envisagement of a future goal, guide my behaviour. Although we cannot conceive of a thermostat or a guided missile as 'envisaging', their activities are guided by feedbacks related to a goal, e.g. regulating the temperature of a room or blowing up a city.

A System Is Maintained in a State of Equilibrium

The *status quo* (such as a room temperature, the amount of sugar in the blood, my level of tension in writing this chapter) is maintained by 'homeostasis': a divergence from a desired optimum is fed back and the error is corrected. Technically, as noted in my talk with Mr Chip (p. 49), such an error-reducing feedback is termed 'negative'. Sometimes things go wrong in guided missiles and in communication between people; then the feedback (termed 'positive') increases the error. This leads to more feedback with further divergence from the goal and disruption of the stable equilibrium of the system. This escalation and threatened disorganization can occur in mutually persecuting interpersonal relationships (p. 205f.).

In living systems a goal of *stability* is balanced by one of *change*: of growth with an increase in order (organization, 'information') by differentiation and integration. Systems constantly change in an optimal *gradual* ordered way but at times there are sudden *revolutions*, with radical changes in organization. Several times I have stressed the importance of 'steps' of insight in psychotherapy (p. 186) and in childhood development (p. 215). In systems jargon, radical changes can be understood in terms of 'catastrophe theory'.[4]

In this book I am using the above ideas only as very general ways of thinking which may be useful in some contexts. I remind the reader of the use of the notion in conceiving of 'myself' as a more or less integrated system with 'selves' as sub-systems (Chapter 10).

Except in some limited highly specialized fields (e.g. experimental studies of some aspects of perception), a systems approach in psychology can hardly be called a theory as that word is used, for example, in nuclear engineering where terms can be expressed mathematically. Cybernetic terms are analogies which can sometimes be evocative metaphors. In previous chapters I have used such notions as parts and wholes, differentiation and integration, stability and change, to talk about such diverse matters as infant development, the use of metaphor, and 'peak experiences'.

To repeat my basic theme. A disturbance of equilibrium in the system of an organism is a *need* (N). A need finds expression in *activity* (A) in fact or in fantasy. Activity is directed towards a *goal* (G) which it is 'anticipated' will satisfy the need and restore the equilibrium (*Figure 9*).

Figure 9

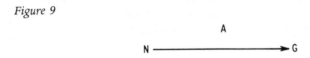

Three points must be borne in mind.

1   For convenience, in *Figure 9* I use a straight line. As I have stated above, this is unsatisfactory. There are multiple feedbacks, and the goal could equally well be shown as leading to the need or to the activity.

2   In this chapter I shall often consider an individual human being as a whole system with various needs as sub-systems, parts related in a hierarchy. But for some purposes an individual can be regarded as a sub-system of larger systems such as a family or a society. Indeed, at some points in this chapter there is inconsistency. The focus of this book is conversation and hence the relevant system is a two-person one. But, as yet, my language is inadequate.

3   The term 'activity' implies force. Sometimes I use the word 'drive' but there is a great danger (evident in much psychotherapeutic literature) of reifying, of treating drives as separate 'things' and asking questions such as 'How many basic drives are there?' In distinguishing different 'needs' for the purpose of this book, I mean to be vague.

NEEDS AND PROBLEMS

For centuries philosophers have been speculating about human needs and motivations and have drawn ethical and political inferences from their views, although often it seems that their conclusions are, in fact, their premises. Whereas Hobbes believed that man was basically selfish and brutish and hence society should be controlled by an absolute monarch, Locke advocated democracy because human nature was essentially peace-loving and co-operative. For many people today, the answers are matters of 'commonsense', personal conviction, logical argument, or the view of the majority. Whatever the assumptions or conclusions, they have a profound influence on our lives and on our futures. There is a great danger in the shrug of the shoulders that accompanies the remark 'It is human nature,' with the implication that some piece of behaviour is therefore unalterable. Expectations and prophecies tend to be self-fulfilling. If it is believed that because man has an aggressive instinct war is inevitable, and that a basic and unalterable acquisitive drive must result in cut-throat competition, then war becomes more likely and the rat-race is promoted.

A human being has marvellous capacities of perceiving, remembering, judging, and solving problems. Yet he can use these capabilities in order to attain very different ends – to make money, to relieve suffering, to wage war, to solve mathematical problems, to save life, or to commit suicide. His activities depend ultimately upon his desires, wants, loves, hates, fears, and values. Despite a paucity of evidence, a psychotherapist cannot but make some assumptions about what in fact are fundamental human needs and aspirations, and how these can be modified in the growth of the individual, the development of society, and the evolution of the race. He must start from some conception of what man is and what he can become.

Needs

Bearing in mind many complexities[5] I suggest a rough, arbitrary, and somewhat naive, hierarchical tripartite division of needs: 'simple', 'complex', and 'existential'.

1   Simple needs include those for food, drink, attachment, sexual satisfaction, novelty, bodily manipulation, and escape from painful stimuli.

2   A person must develop self-esteem with a need to achieve a role and status in society, to love and be loved, to play, and to transform symbols.

3   There is an overall need for a coherent meaning in life with differentiation and integration of experiences, actions, and acts in a sense of 'I' in relation to a wider 'myself', to the world, and to the cosmos.

We can conceive of a hierarchy of systems with 'lower' simple needs being more or less regulated and organized by 'higher' and more complex systems. The Conversational Model puts great emphasis upon the basic need for attachment (bonding) which is elaborated as aloneness-togetherness in the growth of personal relationships.

Frustration

When an activity (A) is blocked and the goal (G) cannot be attained there is *frustration*. An obstruction or barrier (B) gives rise to a *problem*. A rat is prevented from getting food by an electric shock. A patient wishing to get close to another person experiences agonizing fear as he leans towards his therapist (see *Figure 10*).

Figure 10

The frustrating problem increases arousal. The degree of arousal, which moves into anxiety, depends upon:

1   The strength of the activity: the motivation, the desire.
2   The effectiveness of the obstruction, real or imagined.

In a loose way, we can distinguish obstructions as being external or internal, and as occurring at different levels.

An 'outer' barrier can be the shock which halts a rat or the lack of money (and perhaps, more important, of social valuation) which frustrates an unemployed person. It can be the authoritarian refusal of a psychiatrist to grant a patient weekend leave from a hospital. Obstacles can be 'internal' or symbolical: fears of being damaged by getting close to another person, or a forbidding conscience when there is a felt need for rest or for a night out with a lover.

As I have implied, a problem might arise from absence rather than from definite opposition. For instance, a drive for success as a scientist or as a pianist is often frustrated by low intelligence or by poor muscular coordination.

Conflict

The barrier preventing an approach to a goal is often a competing activity or action. I want to go to the party but also I want to finish this chapter. There is conflict. We can describe the situation in outside terms as the vacillating advance and retreat of the rat, or we can present it metaphorically as a conflict between competing sub-systems or as a war between selves (the 'good boy' who has an eye on purgatory and the 'dashing lad' who delights in flirting with Sally). The conflict is between anticipations and expectations, between hope and fear. The competing claims may be immediate and limited ('What shall I do today?') or they can be battles between characters in the drama of a lifetime. Here I am concerned only with a basic pattern. The language of both therapist and patient moves from level to level, from game to game.

We can distinguish three types of conflict.

1   *Approach-approach.* 'I want to play poker and I want to hear Professor Bleaksort's lecture on linguistic analysis.'

2   *Avoidance-avoidance.* 'I can't stand this long silence but I must not make any reassuring noises to this patient.'

3   *Approach-avoidance.* 'I want to get close to you (and to Sally) but I might be hurt, be wicked, or lose myself if I do' (with a few more years in purgatory).

Psychotherapy is most commonly concerned with approach-avoidance conflicts which inhibit problem-solving in personal relationships. The brief examples given intimate something of the complexity of such conflicts.

Personal Problem-solving

In Chapter 7 I outlined six stages of general problem-solving. There is an effort to reach a goal; a felt difficulty (frustration and often anger); a location, exploration, a progressive definition of the problem; an opening up of lines of investigation with generation of alternative solutions; a mulling over and envisaging consequences of possible actions; and a decision to try out some possibilities which are either repeated or abandoned.

In psychotherapy the particular problems are those associated with conflicts of actions and acts in relationships between persons (Chapters 2, 11). They are detected and explored in a conversation between two experiencing subjects. The solution is a way of discovering a feeling-language in a state of aloneness-togetherness, which can be used in other life-situations.

A person is trying to attain a goal of which he might not be fully aware (a hidden change towards a new mode of relating). There are unadmitted actions. Within the relative safety of the interview he can explore the problem.

At first, there is a failure with frustration and stress. ('I just can't talk to you freely just like I can't talk to girls without blushing.') In order to become more aware of the problem, possibilities are explored both in fantasy and in fact. To do this a person needs to be able to bear the anxiety of conflict and the fear of further failure.

It is important to maintain a manageable, and preferably optimum, level of arousal, anxiety, and motivation.[6] The best established law in psychology is that formulated by Yerkes and Dodson.[7] The law can be represented by a graph as in *Figure 11*.

Figure 11

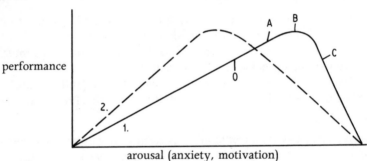

performance

arousal (anxiety, motivation)

The skill in performing any task, ranging from button-pressing and playing golf, to writing poetry, improves with motivation. The aim to achieve a goal is evident in bodily arousal which moves into anxiety. I do better as I try harder – up to a point. I move up curve 1 (continuous line). When I reach B, the efficiency of my performance falls rapidly. Then, I am over-motivated: I am trying too hard. We each have our own optimum for any particular task: about O on the curve.

There is a second important statement of the law. The more difficult is the task the lower is the optimum (dotted curve 2 in *Figure 11*). That is to say that if a child is faced with a new and complex problem a teacher should not say 'Now, here is a hard one, put more effort into it' but rather a casual 'Here, just have a bash at this.'

In psychotherapy it is important to maintain as far as possible an optimum level of arousal and motivation. During an interview I try to make mental drawings of the curves of both the patient and myself (for it is important that neither I nor the patient go over the top). I hope that we can both stay somewhere around O. Occasionally the patient's anxiety-motivation is too low and needs to be increased. More often it is too high. Then it needs to be lowered by means of empathic and understanding statements. Sometimes I need to lower my own anxiety. If need be, if it is all too much, I shut off for a short time. I may even purposely think of something else: such as cricket.

The curve can be thought of as a picture of stress, the degree of discrepancy between the felt means at my disposal and the felt demands of the problem. I have in my mind three Lancashire dialect terms indicated by A, B, and C. At A, I am 'throng', just beginning to feel that I cannot cope with all the pressure of demands (all crowding through a small hole). When I reach B, I am 'thrutched'. There are too many things bombarding me; I attend to one, then to another, and to another: all in disorder. Moving to C, I become 'pow-fagged' (pow – 'head'; fagged – 'fashed, coiled, cumbered'). I cannot cope at all. When I am becoming pow-fagged I must either go off work, perhaps into hospital, or else take avoidance-action.

For effective problem-solving it is important, then, to maintain an optimum level of arousal at which some anxiety and frustration-anger can be tolerated. This means keeping the problem in mind without being compelled to discharge my anxiety in immediate activity. I postpone immediate gratification (acting out). If inner action is not acted upon straight away, then possible solutions can be produced and explored.

In the past, problems have been avoided by various means. These become evident in the therapeutic situation, now. Much psychotherapy is a painstaking elucidation and correction of avoidance-actions which, at one time, may have been appropriate but are unnecessary and damaging in the present.

Before discussing particular methods of avoidance, it is important to recall the difficulties in negotiating the basic, moving pattern of personal growth to which I have pointed in previous chapters: *loss – relative disorganization – re-organization*.

Objectifying intimate and often agonizing experience in terms of systems, we can imagine the loss of differentiated perceptions and activities. The relation of 'parts' is lost and integration is disrupted within sub-systems at different levels and in the hierarchical organization of needs (attachment, self-esteem, and meaning in life). In order to re-organize, new parts need to be discovered and differentiated with the creation of new patterns of order. But there is a need for integration and, in face of chaos, this is often maintained at the cost of further development. Loss of 'higher' complex forms of order results in simpler cruder patterns.[8]

Growing up means coping with the anxiety of separation and the pain of loss – at birth, weaning, adolescence, middle-life, and old age. I have chosen to discuss bereavement as one important instance of a loss of established relationships and attitudes. In pre-literate peoples there are rituals to relieve the anxiety of separation, transition, and of disintegration of the group. They promote the re-incorporation of the individual into the tribe and the re-establishment of relations within the social system.[9] Symbolical transformation, as a healing ritual, can be a creative way of dealing with the anxiety of dissolution. But sometimes ritual can be stunting: a means of avoiding further development.

Throughout life there is an interplay, and maybe a conflict, between change and stability, a drive to grow up and a drawing back from the anxiety of separation. Complete or partial solutions lie in the discovery of new ways of action; with new reasons we explore and adapt to new situations. We learn and create new languages, new symbols, new forms of life. Old conflicts, with goals which are no longer relevant, can be transcended. But the fear and pain might be too great. Then avoidance action is taken.

AVOIDANCE ACTIVITIES

The word 'defence' is sometimes used in this book as a metaphor. It carries the ordinary-language sense of warding off, repelling a threatening 'enemy'. But I do not wish to imply that there are necessarily 'unconscious' or hidden impulses.[10] The term 'mechanisms of defence', used even by some existentially orientated therapists,[11] suggests a restriction to mechanistic causal explanations. That way of thinking can sometimes be useful, but in speaking of activities, actions, and acts (Chapter 3), I put the emphasis upon *reasons* rather than upon causes. Some of the avoidance activities outlined below can be observed in amoebae, rats, dogs, and man, but to speak of *actions* or *acts* entails a language of choosing, willing, and intending.

Avoidance activities are undertaken when the problem is, or seems to be, insoluble, when the goal (e.g. bodily contact, talking on social occasions, reunion with a dead person) cannot be attained. Such activities are necessary for all of us. They can be called 'abnormal' and lead to disturbance when they come into play too early, when they are too extensive and when they are unrealistic. Some activities may have been appropriate in early childhood, but are no longer adapted to changed circumstances (e.g. withdrawal from all social contacts in order to avoid severe hurt which was experienced in infancy).

Of particular importance is the detection and resolution of inappropriate avoidance manoeuvres as these become evident within a conversation (e.g. by resisting exploration or by seeking an immediate collusive warmth and agreement out of a fear of loss). The structure of the interview and the difficulty in establishing trust in a mutual-asymmetrical personal relationship, highlight avoidances: they aim to promote a safe situation (O on the stress curve in *Figure 11*) where avoidance is no longer necessary.

If the conflict engendered is too great to be borne – especially when the problem is, rightly or wrongly, judged to be insoluble – then there is an overwhelming sense of being 'thrutched' and a danger of becoming 'pow-fagged'. Increasing stress threatens disorganization. We are driven to seek some means of reducing the 'overload' and conflict-stress (as distinct from lack-stress).

I shall order various means of reducing stress in terms of modifications of the conflict, of the goal, and of the activity. The distinctions are useful up to a point but they are somewhat artificial. Activity and goal are not clearly separable ('I am writing a book'). Yet there can be a goal without an appropriate activity ('I shall write a book – one day').

In general terms, modes of reducing conflict are as follows. Specific examples will be given later.

1 We can avoid the *whole conflict*; as, for example, by withdrawing from a situation in which conflict occurs, or by pretending that it does not exist.

2 We may *relinquish the goal* either by:

(a) consciously *giving it up* with regret, deciding instead to seek other goals;

(b) *modifying* it in some way, either by remaining satisfied with a *part* of the goal, or by *changing its reality*, attractiveness, desirability.

3 The pain engendered by conflict can be lessened by:

(a) *separating and isolating* the previously (or potentially) conflicting activities so that they do not clash;

(b) modifying the *relative strengths* of activities by either *reducing* or abolishing one activity, and/or *increasing* the opposing or incompatible activity.

An *incomplete solution* (or inadequate avoidance) results in vacillation, ambivalence, neurosis.

The following working classification is far from satisfactory. There are logical inconsistencies which I have been unable to resolve. Sometimes I use an information-processing systems-model which is not wholly compatible with action-act concepts (Chapter 7). Moreover, as mentioned above, an individual is taken as a whole system, with other persons or things regarded as external systems; ideally, there should be formulations of dyads, groups, and societies as systems with individuals as sub-systems. I stress that the essential conceptual framework for a theory of conversational psychotherapy is one of persons-in-relationships which was elaborated in Book I.

Terminology is a large problem, especially with regard to existing classifications e.g. within psychoanalysis or those derived from learning theory. For instance, the concept of 'repression' is mentioned along with other terms which are part of psychoanalytical theory and method. But I try not to use such words if they are inseparable from a model of the psyche which entails notions of reified unconscious 'drives', and structures such as 'ego' and 'superego'. Nevertheless this way of thinking, if not in every detail, is compatible with what many psychoanalysts do in practice, and it can be developed in many different ways within different general theories.

Fundamental Principles

We need to achieve certain basic goals.

Of paramount importance is a sense of a worthwhile *identity*, an assertion of 'I' in relation to a wider myself. This means an integration of experience and action: of control, autonomy, choice, achievement, coherence of meaning, self-determination, responsibility, and self-esteem. In coping with basic anxiety and the fear of separation, loss, and abandonment, we need to respect ourselves (Chapters 10 and 13). Bishop Butler used the large word 'reverence'.[12] Loving ourselves depends upon loving and, to some degree, being approved of, and cared for, by significant other persons within a conversation.

The preservation of a valued relation, I-myself (which can, for some limited purposes, be objectified in terms of relatively differentiated and integrated systems) is at the heart of avoidance actions.

Identity is not static. Moving and growing we need a secure stability (an organization of self-systems) within a process of change. Increasing organization means going through periods of relative disorganization without complete loss of stability (disintegration).

My formulation distinguishes between avoidance of situations, and avoidance by means of disclaiming actions and acts.

Avoidance of situations in which it is anticipated that intolerable conflict would occur (e.g. social gatherings) can be observed and described by outside inspection of behaviour patterns.

Disclaimed actions and acts can be somewhat arbitrarily distinguished one from the other, although there is a good deal of overlap.

1 *Perceptual*. We can fail to see and hear what we anticipate would disrupt the sense of ourselves in relation to others (e.g. we might not register the hostile behaviour towards us of a person which is inconsistent with our cherished image of him or her as an all-loving person). But such unregistered perceptions can be processed as 'information' in systems of which we are unaware. Then, there is inner 'unconscious' conflict.

2 *Private actions*, such as thought and fantasies. We may experience them passively as activities (e.g. fleeting images, ideas, fantasies, or dreams) but avoid conflict by disowning, failing to own them as being 'ours', as belonging to 'me'.

3 *Actions of varied selves*. An important instance of private actions is the avoidance of Richard III's inner civil war. We can accept private actions as being 'mine' without recognizing and acknowledging the claims of other identities, other selves, which play a responsible part in the creation of meaning in and by the society of 'myself' (Chapter 10).

4 *Overt acts*. Most important, we avoid the pain in the act of getting to know, and developing a relationship with, another person who is met as an experiencing subject.

In relationships we often cut out the recognition of, and adjustment to, the 'feedback', or perhaps we misinterpret it.

An avoidance action, a 'defence', always says something about what is being defended. That statement is crucial in psychotherapy. Our defences are never to be regarded as just mechanisms we have to get rid of or to break through by gross and violent means. They are messages which say something important about what is as yet not clearly recognized and owned. The therapist's aim is to hear what is being said, to discover action in apparent passivity, and to promote a developing sequence of experience, activity, action, and act (Chapter 3).

I shall discuss three methods of defence: avoidance of a whole conflict, modification of goals, and change in the strength and relation of competing activities and actions.

Avoidance of a Whole Conflict

We can avoid a particular conflict by *withdrawal*, a retreat from the physical and/or social situation in which it occurs. Or we can *regress* to a less organized state, a mode of experience and identity which no longer gives rise to a problem.

Withdrawal

Rats, having experienced severe electric shocks when seeking food in a maze, will learn to avoid certain areas or in certain circumstances cease to run at all. A psychiatrist who has experienced agonies of sea-sickness and air-sickness may cease to attend overseas conferences. The withdrawals that concern a psychotherapist aiming at a therapeutic conversation are mainly avoidances of actions and acts in significant personal relationships.

Withdrawal can be *situational*, as in the case of the rat, the country-bound psychiatrist, or a person who avoids social gatherings. Or it can be *symbolical*. In order to obtain relief from an urgent, and seemingly impossible sexual conflict I can choose (wittingly or unwittingly) to occupy myself with a critique of the *Summa* of St Thomas Aquinas or Freud's metapsychological adventures. Most of the avoidance actions listed below are special means of effecting symbolical withdrawal. I suggested above that occasionally a psychotherapist needs to withdraw for a time by choosing not to listen.

Regression

If we adopt or return to a less organized or childlike state, then a conflict arising from a more developed mode of adaptation may no longer be experienced as a problem. Let us begin with rats.

In a classical experiment N.R.F. Maier[13] somewhat unkindly put hungry rats in an insoluble problem-solving situation. The rat was on a stand faced with two cards. Behind one card there was food (goal). The rat had to jump (activity) in order to satisfy its need. If it 'chose' correctly the card fell over and it had a good meal. If it jumped at the wrong card it received a painful bump to the nose. If the food was placed consistently behind one or other card the rat could learn which way to jump.

Maier latched and unlatched the cards at random. There was now an insoluble problem. The rat, unable to learn, understandably withdrew and ceased to jump. But when it was subjected to a short but painful blast of air on the backside there was an avoidance-avoidance conflict. Then the animal developed various aberrations of behaviour. There were abortive partial activities. Perhaps it jumped to one side or the other in a stereotyped fashion which persisted whether or not the food was now put consistently behind an unlatched card. The rat could now not learn.

Often the frustrated animal became aggressive, its movements became uncoordinated, and it ceased to control such bodily activities as defecation. It became disorganized, it regressed.

There are many methodological and other questions raised by these experiments and Maier's findings have been questioned.[14] I am using them as pictures or metaphors to illustrate what I observe in psychotherapy. I am anthropomorphizing rats. A child or adult regresses when frustrated by an important insoluble problem. An infant who is repeatedly given inconsistent or contrary messages (double-binds) cannot learn. It is of interest that, in his original report, Maier claimed that the rats could be cured by continued manual guidance through the right card and also (an evocative image!) by gentle fondling.

Human or other animals regress when they are in a situation of severe stress. Four conditions are important. Regression occurs:

1   when an animal is highly motivated to attain a goal (food for the rat, love for Elsie);

2   when there is no escape from an insoluble conflict because of environmental circumstances (a rat being blown from behind and anticipating a broken nose; a child forced to take a feared examination) or of personal choice with, perhaps, public commitment (a student who feels battered by interpretations from his training analyst but who needs to maintain his self-esteem and to qualify);

3   when there is experience or threat of severe hurt and punishment;

4   when, owing to the complexity or lack of clarity in the situation, there are inconsistent consequences of, and responses to, activities and actions.

The psychotherapist's job is to provide a situation for new learning, conditions for growth. He wants to minimize the threat of hurt and yet he strives to be consistent in his verbal and non-verbal messages. If he, or the milieu, gives contradictory double- or treble-binds then Elsie can be made to regress with temper tantrums, clinging, and disorganized behaviour. She cuts her wrists or takes an overdose of sleeping pills.

A less ordered state of regression is often characterized by experiences and behaviour which resemble those of an earlier phase of development such as childlike wailing and helpless dependence.

In most instances marked regression is a regrettable and unfruitful consequence of severe frustration-stress. It is suffered passively by Maier's rats and by deprived children. But in certain circumstances it has a pay-off. Instead of bearing the painful responsibility for making a decision Elsie can regress. She has learned that people will respond by caring for her as a child and temporarily gratify her unsatisfied infantile needs – even though there is no lasting satisfaction. She learns and repeats a way of avoiding adult problems.

Regression becomes an action and act. Sometimes it is a deliberate and owned way of manipulating others in order to gain immediate care and bodily gratification by cuddling and/or advice. More often, it is a disclaimed round-about action, with the implication of helpless passivity: 'I can't help it'.

We are fallible human beings. Regression is appropriate at times in our intimate relationships with spouses, friends, and colleagues. It is a frequent and characteristic way of reacting to difficult problems. It can result in lack of growth or, indeed, serious hurt. The demand can become intolerable to others, who have their limits, and result in a damaging rejection which only serves to increase the demand. An error-increasing positive feedback, a vicious circle, can end in catastrophe. Yet regression can be a positive phase in development.

As a psychotherapist I am in a dilemma. How can I give this person what he or she needs, whilst promoting growth and not encouraging a persistent childlike mode of relating?

In classical psychoanalysis it was considered that frustration was necessary in order that regression should occur in fantasy (without childish 'acting out') to a point of 'fixation' in early childhood at which a significant trauma had occurred. This may indeed be an important feature of re-writing our autobiography; but, in using the term regression, I do not suppose that childlike behaviour is necessarily a return to a point in a person's historical idiosyncratic childhood. It can be a way of moving forward, a phase of relative disorganization necessary for re-organization. As Jung puts it, there can be a *reculer pour mieux sauter*,[15] becoming as a little child in order to envisage and implement a new stage of life.

There are times when, in personal relationships from infancy to old age, we are frustrated. Sometimes we cannot bear the pain. We regress. In psychotherapy, as in child-rearing, we need to recognize and clarify the frustration. But there is no justification for increasing it (unless we aim to create a tough master-race in a Nazi state or on the playing-fields of Eton). In striving to become a little more self-aware, we have quite enough frustration-stress. Most of us have far too much. Our task is to accept, judge, and value regression as a possible way forward: as a means of realizing potentialities. Regression can be a stultifying avoidance or it can be a creative movement.

I have so far focused upon regression as a disorganization of overt behaviour. Perhaps more important is *symbolical regression*, a falling back on more archaic, childlike modes of fantasy and forms of language. In earlier chapters, I have argued that in much creative thought there is a temporary loss of directed, discursive, linear thought, with an indulgence in a more presentational, mythical, magical way of fantasy-thinking (Chapter 7). This regression *can* be productive but it may not be.

I have argued that there is a basic human need for *symbolical transformation*. That necessitates a continued contact with, and occasional return to, a mode of thinking-feeling which is evident in childhood. There is a division of images into 'all-good' and 'all-bad', a polar splitting between idealized and persecutory people and things, a non-differentiation between self and others, and a mode of thought ordered by *condensation* of images and *displacement* of emotions.

Fantasy-thinking can be indulged in as a retreat from, and avoidance of, a present problem. It can be manifest in activities such as *undoing*, i.e. performing some action with the magical aim (admitted or unadmitted) of abolishing the feared or forbidden consequences of some other act. For instance, as with Lady Macbeth, compulsive, ritualized hand-washing might use a lot of water in an attempt to rid us of a terrible deed. At a less obvious level, I have an obscure belief that my compulsive over-indulgence of Fred's immediate demands for reassurance about his problems at work might in a magical way propitiate – make amends for – the disastrous consequences of my damaging and reprehensible gossip about him yesterday.

Some features of schizophrenic thought-disorder can be thought of as avoiding a problem at one level, but as creating some order at another (lower) level. Harold (Chapter 10) could not cope with the conflict of separation from me. He fused our identities and, with a sense of 'mystical participation'[16] felt that my head was on his shoulders.

One of the most important forms of activity, action, and act is *play*. Donald Winnicott speaks of psychotherapy as a means of bringing someone into a state of being able to play, when previously this had been impossible.[17] In play, there is a childlike (but yet also adult) dissolution, reconstruction, and re-organization of memories, experiences, and events. There is a satisfaction of the need for symbolical transformation and, at the same time, a possible re-orientation towards and exploration of a present problem. Play can be defensive, at least for the time being. But in the process of movement through a pre-metaphorical figurative language towards metaphor, it can be a vital means of creating a feeling-language: the central action and act of personal problem-solving.

A psychotherapist is faced with a crucial, and often life-saving question: when is regression a reaction to unnecessary frustration, when is it a learned way of avoiding a soluble problem, and when is it a necessary phase in on-going growth? Psychoanalysts have talked of 'regression in the service of the ego' and, after the event, have distinguished 'benign' and 'malignant' regression.[18] We must face the facts. We do not know how to predict accurately. We can only guess.

I have made, and undoubtedly will continue to make, many mistakes, one way or another. There is only one attitude, although it is very fallible: respect what any person says or does. In some way (as yet to be discovered) whatever anyone says is important. I hope that something new and valuable might emerge – for my patient.

But I must be alert. There is a danger. I might gratify my own needs either by firmly keeping her or him as a child (whilst justifying my actions as 'proper technique') or else indulge my ungratified needs at his or her expense whilst claiming to act as a warm human being.

Modification of the Goal

When we cannot attain a desired goal, we might relinquish it altogether or else modify it in some way. The goal might be located in the physical and social world or in the personal 'inner' world of myself.

A decision to relinquish a goal can be appropriate or inappropriate. The hope of attaining all our goals is an illusion, although it is cherished by all mankind. Somewhere, deep down, most of us long for the bliss of union with an all-loving mother and for life in a peaceful, exciting Utopia. I need to recognize that some goals are realistic for others but not for me: I cannot become a world-famous barrister with a verbal IQ of 95.

There are many ways of giving up a goal.

Change in Attractiveness or Reality of Goals

In order to change our actions, relieving frustration and conflict, we can change the value or nature of the goal.

By *belittling* we reduce the attractiveness of what we seek ('Difficult lectures are a waste of time', 'Jane really isn't as pretty as all that'). The 'sour grapes' manoeuvre is often well concealed. In extreme circumstances we *de-realize* ('Everything is unreal').

The reality of the goal can be altered by *wish-fulfilment fantasy* when we partly satisfy a need in day- or night-dreams in which we can be superstar heroes, sex idols, or great cricketers hitting sixes over the pavilion at Lords.

Another way of substitute achievement is by *identification*. We can consciously or unconsciously imitate, feel into, and in a sense 'be' another person who has achieved the goal. We may take on the characteristics of a master (e.g. a training analyst) and as a disciple share his success, or we may look for self-fulfilment in the success of our children.

Belittling becomes more effective when other achievable goals are made more attractive. Having finally committed ourselves to buying a house because it is cheap we discover woodworm. Then we may justify our choice by exaggerating the beauty of the view.[19]

Choice of Other Goals

When a goal is unattainable we can satisfy our need and maintain self-esteem to some extent by making other goals more desirable.

There can be *displacement* of the activity. (If Alice is not willing I turn to Betty. Not able to be openly angry with the boss I kick the cat.)

I can *deflect* my action to a part of the goal. (I cannot go to bed with Alice and so I write a laudatory critique of her book on women's fashion. I am not up to writing a *Summa* but I can enjoy composing a highly original review of a book on 'God and Science'.)

There can be a *transformation* of a forbidden action by re-direction towards a different socially acceptable goal, e.g. my sexual activity can be satisfied in art or religion. This is akin to what Freud termed 'sublimation'. It is to be noted that although this process is in one sense an 'avoidance', yet symbolical transformation is a basic human need.

The above brief discussion of how goals are changed and modified has focused on activities. Need, goal, and activity are inseparable. The distinction is very arbitrary and the ambiguity is more evident when we turn to changes in action.

Modification of Action

By means of displacement, deflection, and transformation, the direction and aim of activities and actions is changed. Conflict can be avoided by various means of disclaiming or disowning the conflict of particular actions.

Conflicting wishes can be separated by splitting and *dissociation* into different isolated compartments of life. Some examples are evident as, for example, in Sunday religion which is not applied to the workaday world, and in various types of amnesia. Dissociation can be thought of as the divorce of different 'I's or of systems of self (Chapter 10) and is striking in the rare cases of multiple personality (Dr Jekyll and Mr Hyde). A dissociated action may be *converted* into a bodily symptom-language: the 'hearts' of Freda and of Mr Chip.

A special instance of splitting (evident in belittling) is negation or *denial*. I disclaim that an action is 'mine'. I can become unaware of its existence or attribute it to others ('repression' and 'projection'). Denying my own sexual desires or racial prejudice I can condemn these traits in others. The recognition and correction of such false attributions is a central feature of psychotherapy (the positive and negative 'transference' of 'unconscious wishes'). This *external attribution* is almost always a matter of selective perception; we see and hear what supports our pre-determined belief. In an extreme form it becomes a systematized paranoid delusion. It is always to be remembered that such attributions, like most avoidances, are efforts to maintain order in the face of a threat of chaos.

Exaggeration of some action may be a *compensation or over-compensation* for a felt inadequacy (e.g. body-building, writing an obscure novel).

By means of *reversal* a feared or forbidden action can be made relatively acceptable. By adopting a general attitude ('reaction formation') of cleanliness I can disown my enjoyment of playing with dirt and faeces. A consistently meek and compliant person may be disowning anger.

An extreme example of reversal is a *turning against myself*. I hate and damage myself as a means of avoiding attacking others.

An important manoeuvre is *idealization*. I have suggested that the infant originally experiences the mother as split into 'good' and 'bad', perhaps as two distinct figures (pp. 85, 243). Later these are joined. But if bad overcomes good then destruction and chaos ensue. In order to maintain a bond with a loving person badness must be disclaimed – so we idealize. The mother and the beloved are seen and related to as near-perfect, until the scales drop from our eyes.

Painful loss of a loved person is mitigated by taking him or her inside, by *introjection*. That process of converting someone 'out there' into an internal other is a feature of normal childhood development and of bereavement (see p. 123).

The above far from exhaustive list of avoidance-actions includes some of the ways in which we (patients and therapists) attempt to maintain our identity and self-esteem in the face of chaos and pain, especially from conflicts associated with separation and loss.

In the next chapter I shall tell a simple story which illustrates a few of those activities as they are revealed in conversational psychotherapy.

· 15 ·
A SHORT CONVERSATION

Mary Brown sits upright. Rigid. Her face is a mask and her arms are tightly folded over her stomach.

I say something about how difficult it is to talk freely in such a situation, exposing herself to a psychiatrist with a television camera 'watching' us.

She does not look at me. She does not speak.

I prefer to have no information before a first interview (I usually read a referral letter either during or after the session). But I have been telephoned about Mrs Brown. For two years she has been miserable and socially isolated, reproaching herself for unforgivable sins. A diagnosis has been made of 'biological depression'. This so-called 'illness' has not responded to anti-depressant drugs or to a course of electrical convulsive therapy.[1]

I decide to ask about her problem. I do not want to raise her anxiety too early and I guess that, having been labelled as a patient and 'trained' by psychiatrists, she is used to answering questions.

'I would like to know about you . . . about the problem.'

I use the word 'I' and stress 'you' before 'the problem'.

Mrs Brown haltingly gives me a 'good history'.

In order to illustrate some features of the Conversational Model in brief psychotherapy, I am telling a success story. In the next chapter, I tell a very different tale.

A BEREAVEMENT

Mrs Brown whispers. I can hardly hear (I am a bit deaf) but I try to listen, attending to the minute particulars while, at the same time, half-listening, allowing my imagination to range.

From what she says and how she says it, a diagnostic hypothesis emerges. Two 'facts' stand out.

1 The depression 'closed' on the first anniversary of her husband's death.

2 When Mrs Brown talks about her 'wonderful' husband, her eyelids widen and her lips close into tight thin lines. 'She looks damned angry,' I think. Yet, I remind myself, I am not sure that I have received rightly the message of those transient cues.

My general theoretical framework gives a possible shape, a meaning. I tell myself, 'Remember you might be quite wrong,' and write down a hypothesis:

'After the death of her husband the normal course of mourning was arrested in a perpetuated depression because she could not bear the pain of recognizing that she greatly resented her idealized spouse.'

Any hypothesis implies a prediction (if X is done under conditions Y, then Z should follow). If the problem of conflicting feelings is revealed, expressed, and explored within a relationship (at first with me) then the depression and social isolation should be relieved. In the first interview I make some preliminary tests.

In attempting to report what happened, I shall stay close to a transcript (I am *R.F.H.* She is *M.B.*).

R.F.H.   I think ... am I right? ... that you began to feel low, really low ... just a year after Henry died. Exactly a year, I think.'

I am making a link based upon an idea. It seems that Mrs Brown has not made this connection and I want to find out if I am on the right track. Mere agreement or disagreement is not enough. The important point is whether or not she extends, amplifies, my suggestion.

M.B.   'Well I suppose ... well ... this feeling in my head ... it did come when I got home and made a cup of tea after putting flowers on his grave.'

There is a pause. She clenches her fists and then bursts out in a tone of voice which sounds angry to me.

M.B.   'I shall never get over it. *Never* ...'

Mrs Brown's voice changes. I am ashamed to say that I wince as I now hear the strains of violins in a tea-garden orchestra.

M.B. '... he was so wonderful.'

This and other hints (they are no more than that) seem to suggest that my guess could be near the mark.

I suggest that we should meet once weekly for eight interviews.

R.F.H. 'Look, you must choose. I reckon that your feelings about Henry's death ... well, they are mixed up. Do you want to get a line on them ... sort them out more? Maybe it will help, maybe it won't. I don't know. But I wouldn't suggest going ahead if there wasn't ... well ... some hope of finding something ... well something *new*. But it won't be easy ... and painful too.'

I do not put it well and later I try to spell out the problem, the hope, the difficulties, and the pain. If Mrs Brown can commit herself wholeheartedly to a course of action which involves conflict and suffering then she is more likely to discover something in it that she feels to be worthwhile.[2] Like Garibaldi, I offer blood, sweat, and wounds.

Mrs Brown decides to make the contract.

I shall sketch some features of the next eight sessions. 'Some' should be emphasized because I am far from sure which factors were important in the change. I only know that we got together in some important way.

Session 2

Mary Brown talks at length about her ideal marriage.

M.B. 'I miss him all the time – all the time – and night and morning I really feel him there with me.'
'... a very good man.'
'... we never had a wrong word.'
'... he was so good ... so good at times that I felt so lazy and no good for him.'
'... I never cried when he went ... I couldn't somehow, and can't now ... but then ... he hasn't gone – not from *me*.'

There is a suggestion of denial, of not accepting separation and loss ('I really feel him there with me ... he hasn't gone from *me*'). There are hints that Mary is avoiding (not owning) anger, as, for instance, when she clenches her hands and tightens her lips at the words 'I felt so lazy and no good for him'. Perhaps she is also saying '*he* made me feel bad'. Her bland assertion that never in her life has she felt angry could be a 'reaction formation'.

So far Mrs Brown has given few cues of her feeling in relation to me.

Session 3

Themes evident in the first two interviews are repeated and, to a slight extent, elaborated. At one point Mrs Brown tells me about an acquaintance.

M.B. 'A neighbour . . . not a friend really . . . said "You really must pull yourself together." '

As she speaks I once more see her clenched fists and tightened lips. I note a recurrent pattern. It looks like anger, and I decide to try out my hunch.

R.F.H. 'I wonder whether . . . well, you looked a bit cross just now to me. Just a hint in the way you talked about Mrs X. I wonder whether . . . '

M.B. (interrupts) 'Oh no! No. She's quite right.' (Long pause.) ' I wish you wouldn't get at me.' (Definite irritation.) 'Doctors . . . always questioning things. They didn't help my husband . . . not at all. Oh . . . (abrupt change of voice tone) . . . oh, I'm sorry, I didn't mean to be *rude*.'

R. F. H. 'Mmm.'

My ambiguous 'Mmm' is long drawn-out.
Mary Brown goes on to say how useless the doctors were when her husband died. But, although a doctor, I, Bob Hobson, am different.

M.B. 'You are so helpful . . . (she smiles for the first time) a bit like my husband in some ways. Did you say you were away next week?'
R.F.H. 'Yes, I get a feeling that worries you a bit.'
M.B. 'Oh no! Not at all. You will be here a week on Tuesday.'
R.F.H. 'Yes, I'll be back. But you meant Wednesday, our regular time.'

I seem to detect once more a denial of anxiety about separation, occurring here and now as she associates me with her husband. Maybe there is anger towards her friend, me, and perhaps her husband which is *displaced* on to the nameless 'doctors'. We do not meet for two weeks as I am on leave.

Session 4

There is an opening silence. Mary does not look at me. I wait.

M.B. 'A bad week, really depressed . . . . I was helpless, the neighbours had to do everything for me. Really helpless . . . just couldn't move.'

R.F.H. 'You seem very upset about being so helpless ... a bit like a child I suppose.'

M.B. (vigorously) 'I *hate* it. Childish. And Henry not there to comfort me. So useless ... useless and bad. And those neighbours. Not that they pry into things. But really they are good and bring me meals. But I don't fancy food except ... well ... at times I get so hungry. Then I am so empty. I do miss Henry.'

The patterns are becoming clearer. There is a mixed anger and denial with ambivalence. I suggest that the helplessness is like becoming a child – a *regression*. Perhaps there is a significant association between eating and mourning, maybe a need to 'introject' Henry. We need to bury our loved ones with the actual and/or symbolical ham of a funeral tea.[3]

So far little has been said in words about the significance of the relationship between us. It is my practice to focus on the present relationship at a very early stage as in the examples given in previous chapters (e.g. Freda, Chapter 2; Joe Smith, Chapter 3). I do so 'as soon as possible'. But that is a vague statement. I do not know how I judge the precise moment when my suggestions will not be experienced as either intruding or alienating. I can say only that, up to this point, I had felt that if I confronted Mrs Brown with the significance of what was happening in the relationship with me now, she would probably become too scared. I do not want to push her over the top of the stress curve. If I do she will block and fall back on avoidance manoeuvres which will then be strengthened.

Session 5 is a turning point.

Session 5

Mary does not give me her usual 'Hello!' Perched on the edge of her chair with clenched fists, she stares at the floor in dumb misery. I desperately want to help and search for words which might articulate her experience.

R.F.H. 'I guess you are upset ... really upset ... somewhere deep down in your middle ...'

Mary's hand twists on her tummy. I go on, slowly and tentatively, eventually choosing a hackneyed metaphor.

R.F.H. '... sort of ... well ... maybe ... screwed up.' A few tears trickle down Mary's cheeks.

M.B. 'I do miss him so ... But I coped so well for a year ... He'll never come back ... I want ... I want to be with him.'

Suddenly Mary sobs. Not her usual weeping: her sobs are convulsions from somewhere deep down. I do not know how long they go on. (To say that, listening to the tape, I time three-and-a-half minutes, does not answer my question about time.)

Abruptly the sobs cease. I now sense a still sadness. I hope to sit with her in the silence, just being there, *with* her. When I feel it is right I lean forward allowing my hand to rest on her arm. I mutter, almost inaudibly.

R.F.H.   'I feel ... I really feel you *need* to weep for Henry.'

There is a long, long silence (three minutes, I am told by independent observers) before Mary, weeping in a flow (not sobbing, now) speaks through her tears.

M.B.   'I have ... never ... cried for ... for him (pause). He's gone now.'

Her last words are desolate. Then, suddenly, Mary's tone changes. There is a very different register. It is as if the words are thrown at me with a staccato fire of resentment, just as earlier she criticized 'doctors' (Session 2). I shall stay with the bare transcript.

M.B.   'He's gone.'
R.F.H.   'We can't help feeling mad ... sort of angry inside when someone goes away ... even if we don't want to. Like when I went on holiday.'
M.B.   'Yes I did think ... (angry tone) well, why should he go away just when I need him ... you, I mean. But I didn't do anything silly – to myself. But I was no good. I really am wicked.'
                              (Silence.)
    Wicked.   Well ... there was something ... I can't say it. *I can't.*'
R.F.H.   'Maybe ... I don't know ... but from the way you look at me ... I get a hunch that you're scared. Maybe what I'll think of you.'
M.B.   'No ... yes ... well. You would hate me ... well ... if you knew. No one knows. *What I am really like I mean*' (in a rush).
R.F.H.   'Sort of ... well ... that I might not want to see you again.'
M.B.   '*No*. I know you would. It's your job' (bitterly).
R.F.H.   'Yes, I do a job. But well ... I don't know how to put this really but ... I am human (defensively?). And not God.'
M.B.   'You act like God sometimes.'
R.F.H. (in a twist)   'Oh ... ah ... but there *is* something you really want to say but are scared' (demonstrating conflict with hands – falling back on safety mechanisms?).
M.B.   'It's what I did ... I had forgotten ... I really had ... forgotten.

I mean. Well (gulps) I threw a kettle at Henry when I was making tea. I threw it at him. I wanted (weeping) ... I wished I could hurt him. Really mad I was.'

R.F.H.   'I want to know more. Really more I mean. Can we get into it ... perhaps as if it's happening *now*?'

M.B.   'He had looked at a young girl ... the way he looked ... *you* know ... That sort of look.'

R.F.H.   'You must have been really boiling' (unaware of the pun-metaphor). 'Jealous.'

M.B.   ' "Damn you," I said. I had forgotten it ... really I had.'

R.F.H.   'Maybe ... well ... perhaps Henry wasn't *absolutely* good ... and all the time. Not Jesus Christ.'

M.B.   'Well, he *was* good and I had to be too ... try to be. But I couldn't. The other day, I had a wicked feeling. I found myself saying ... not really me saying it – "You *shouldn't* have left me, Henry." I shouted it. But of course he didn't really ... not like that. It's silly.'

R.F.H.   'Well, when someone dies a part of us ... like a child ... can feel mad at being left.'

Those few minutes express the complex sufferings of a lifetime.

Mary weeps for her loss. Experiencing some sense of finality in separation, she begins to mourn. She must be alone with her grief. I can only hope to maintain some space for her solitary task. But, perhaps, there is a fragile bridge over the gulf.

The job of mourning is hard and bitter agony. It is much more so when we also hate the person whom we love. There is guilt: 'For each man kills the thing he loves'.[4] Maybe (and it is only a 'maybe'), I can help by linking Mary's loss of Henry to her resentful loss of me when I go on leave. (I feel rotten about comparing these incommensurable losses, and yet ...) Mary admits some anger about my going away but she cannot even bear that. She turns the anger against herself ('I really am wicked').

I try to tell her how I hear what she is saying. Maybe, I suggest, she is scared of what I will think of (feel about) her. She rejects my intended offer of concern ('It's your job'). I am hurt and respond defensively ('I am human. And not God'). Mary has got me on the raw ('You act like God sometimes'). I feel attacked.

In such situations we need fall-backs. Rightly, in my view, I do not pursue the 'God' theme but verbally and non-verbally try to express, in a well-practised way, how I experience conflict. Mary then goes on, in vivid language, to tell the story of how she threw the kettle at Henry.

I urge Mary to stay with the feeling, not to explain it. She has her eye on my eye as she tells me about Henry's roving eye ('... *you* know').

We do not talk explicitly about my seductive looks but the message is clear. Perhaps I blush.

Maybe, with an accurate diagnosis, other very different therapeutic methods could have helped Mary towards a healing mourning. I am using this example only as an illustration of how the Conversational Model, with its emphasis upon a personal relationship here and now, can be of value in the short-term therapy of long-standing unresolved bereavement.

Sessions 6 to 9

In the last three interviews Mary and I explore and amplify the following themes which emerged earlier in therapy within a relationship:

1   Jealousy: both a very human assertion and yet also a constricting evil.
2   Resentment in the face of impossible demands to be 'good'. (Henry had cast Mary in the role of a saint.)
3   A position of childish dependence mixed with hostility, arising from a wish for autonomy and freedom. (Henry and Mary had colluded in a parent-child relation.)
4   Anger, and aggression moving into destructiveness when we feel rejected and abandoned.
5   Ways of avoiding destructive aggression especially by turning it against 'myself' in self-disgust.

These themes together with various sub-themes remain as personal problems which both Mary and I can continue to explore for the rest of our lives.

BRIEF PSYCHOTHERAPY

I have told a neat story. It is true and yet, if it is taken as a typical sample of what psychotherapy means in a psychiatric out-patient clinic, in a student-counselling centre, or indeed in the plush settings of Harley Street, Devonshire Place, or the recesses of Hampstead, it is false.

Usually, life is not like that.

It is easy for an experienced therapist to tell many anecdotes similar to that of Mrs Brown. They are of great importance. When I have seen, within short time, such a marked change in a patient after years of drugs and ECT, it is difficult to say that psychotherapy (whatever that means) is of no value. Abstruse statistical calculations seem to be irrelevant. Yet I do not claim to know what it was that 'worked'. I can only report as best

I can (recognizing my bias, as far as possible, in selecting what I choose to describe and to present).

'Experience' is fallible. Nevertheless, I shall make make a few comments on brief and long-term psychotherapy, if only to confess doubts and confusions which I share with not a few other psychotherapists. There is much that we do not know. In the last resort my statement about the heart of psychotherapy, and indeed of all helping relationships, is an assertion of values.

Case reports similar to that of Mrs Brown can give a completely false impression. We make a formulation of a specific problem, we agree upon a contract, we explore using a clear notion of conflict and hey presto: the problem is solved. The accounts are true, and yet they can be false.

Mrs Brown and I focused on a fairly circumscribed problem: her inability to cope with loss, to mourn the death of her husband. But that difficulty brought to light a wider, long-standing disturbance, a repeated seeking for a childlike relationship in which dependence was interfused with resentful hostility. The death of her husband made manifest a lifelong search for, and failure to attain, a personal relationship.

Following and during the nine sessions (just a small part of her living) Mary changed her ways of acting. She felt more able to cope – at least as well as most of us can. She made social contacts, and tried out new friendships. Yet she still found herself making unsatisfactory child-parent relationships and, at times, being over-demanding and thus inviting rejection.

After eight sessions I asked myself whether or not we should go on meeting. Maybe Mary Brown's *real* problem had, as yet, hardly been touched upon. Should we go on for x years elucidating and working through her basic separation anxiety? A psychotherapist is constantly faced with the problem of when to end formal interviews.

Some writings on brief psychotherapy give an impression of a happy ending of sweetness and light when the dynamics of a formulated problem are 'worked through'.[5] It is seldom like that in practice. We are compelled again and again to change our initial formulation. Our carefully considered interpretations do not work. At the end of our agreed course of say eight or twelve sessions we still do not know what to do.

I am not saying that formulations and contracts are of no value. They are. Indeed, I now consider that they are the best way of proceeding in short-term or long-term psychotherapy. But often, indeed more often than not, we are left with agonizing questions.

The most important ideal (and it is an ideal) is not to do harm. It is not a psychotherapist's job to break through avoidance manoeuvres. Then he may uncover problems which cannot be dealt with, and even promote an addiction to therapy as if it were the goal of life – which it is not.

Such general statements are all very well. But what shall we *do*? There are no clear answers, either from clinical accounts or from experimental research.[6] We cannot predict what will happen in a personal relationship.

What seems to be a minor link made in a conversation within a few sessions (or even one) can have far-reaching consequences. What would be dismissed as of little significance by an analytical psychotherapist with her theories of personality, or by a researcher with his sophisticated measures of change, can open up new vistas to a person who, in a moment of gentle surprise, sees and confronts his problems anew.

The important question is whether or not a client, patient, person can continue to explore, discover, and commit himself in actions and acts. Can she or he go on and on experiencing, learning, gaining and losing, in work, in friendships, in learned societies, and in chats over a pint or two in the 'Royal Oak'?

It is 10.30 a.m. in Oxford Street, Manchester, on 24 October, 1940. The conductor speaks to me as I get off the tram.

'Nay, lad. Stop for a minute. Tha' art (thou art) in too much of a 'urry (hurry).'

I have not yet learned the lesson but I still go on looking for a meaning: for an answer to a profound question: about making haste slowly!

Brief psychotherapy can be spectacular. (I am narcissistically pleased to be able to recount the case of Mrs Brown.) And not only in its immediate effects. It can open up avenues for continuing development. Life is not to be lived in a consulting room. It seems odd that so-called advances in psychoanalysis should so often result in more and more years of frequent visits to a 'professional'.

I have sympathy, and yet no use for, psychiatrists and analysts (and I include myself) who, when faced with impossible problems say or imply: 'I can't do anything, personality problems aren't "illness",' or 'Nothing can be done unless this client undertakes an analysis of about fifteen years.'

There is a real dilemma. Some basic anxieties can only be experienced and developed creatively in a relatively safe two-person relationship which may have to last for many, many years. 'Brief psychotherapy' can be a pretentious vogue (a denial of wider problems). But so can 'deep analysis'.

Looking back, I see many mistakes. Sometimes I have ended too soon. More often I have gone on too long. That is how it seems. But I do not know, and I doubt whether anyone else does. When to stop? I do not know the answer. The literature is of little help. The decision usually emerges from considerations of time, other personal demands, individual exhaustion – and money. Maybe those are not such bad criteria. My subjective anecdotal examination of results seems to indicate that those patients who have done best are those who have had to break off because of practical considerations (e.g. moving to another part of the world).

A personal relationship never ends. That is the problem raised in this book. Perhaps we should not call it 'therapy'.

BOOK · III ·
THE HEART OF A PSYCHOTHERAPIST

'if way to the Better there be, it exacts a full look at the Worst'
(T. Hardy, 'In Tenebris II',
Poems of the Past and Present, 1901)

'*Negative Capability*, that is, when a man is
capable of being in uncertainties, mysteries, doubts,
without any irritable reaching after fact and reason,'
(J. Keats, Letters, 32.
To G. and T. Keats, 21 December, 1817)

· 16 ·
THE HEART OF
DARKNESS

It is Monday morning. Washing day.

Sue's voice is dull and monotonous.

'It is all a waste of time . . . we just go around in circles . . . nothing changes . . . just the same. Now Jim has dropped me . . . . Oh, I know, I know, I made him reject me, but knowing is no damn use. We were talking like this twelve years ago . . . You are fed up with it too . . . . And then I give you hell ringing you up ten times over the weekend . . . and taking those pills . . . sleeping in your garden and throwing stones through your windows . . . I can't cope . . . I really can't cope . . . I'm no good . . . You are fed up too. I know you are.'

Sue is right. I am fed up: but that is to put it too mildly. Psychotherapy is no good. *I* can't cope. Sue's vicious attacks have gouged out my inside and all the weekend my family life has been in chaos. Today my wife has a big wash, and I have to get through a day of difficult interviews and interminable committees. Sue has failed and feels that she herself is a failure. I have failed. I am a failure.

There are no fresh words. No words to carry on the 'mutual, asymmetrical conversation' of psychotherapy. Just the same sounds growing colder in a repetitive round of empty phrases.

It is often like that: nothing more to say.

Sue speaks in her gentle voice. She has many voices.

'You would be happier if I was dead . . . . I could do something for *you* . . . be out of the way. You can't stand much more.'

She is right. But I hastily reassure. My words are hollow.

Sue died suddenly. Since she had no available relatives I was asked to identify the body. The Coroner's verdict was 'Accidental Death'. I knew that it was suicide. On leaving the mortuary, I wrote a piece of doggerel:

> I often said
> 'I wish her dead'
>
> Cold on a slab
> Bruised lips askew
>
> A twisting stab
> And my guts knew
> That I died too
> That day.
>
> In a way.

The words 'In a way' came with an ironical shrug. Maybe irony is necessary in order to cope with a nightmare. Only many years later did the words come together with Sam's reference to his dream pearl – 'I suppose it's me *in a sort of way*' – (p. 6) and with the dream that came to me in the void of Holy Saturday (p. 8).

When I first met Sue I was a successful, fairly experienced psychotherapist. Again and again I repeated my mistakes. I knew that what I said and did was wrong – according to the principles that I taught and tried hard to practise. My 'head' told me one thing but somewhere, deep down, I was deaf. I had to face it: I knew very little about psychotherapy and despite a long and expensive 'training analysis' I did not know the depths of myself.

Some techniques and skills of the Conversational Model can be taught to beginners fairly quickly (Chapter 12). They can, up to a point, be defined in formulated phrases for the purposes of experimental research.[1] But learning how to become a psychotherapist is the never-ending task of a lifetime. It means going on hoping to become more of a person in relationships. It means the painful recognition of how we use patients for our own ends: how in our 'professional' work we seek satisfaction of our own limited needs, and how we avoid deep-seated fears, of failure, guilt, destruction, meaninglessness, loneliness, and death.

I cannot tell the whole story of Sue. I cannot yet make a whole of it; nor do I expect that I ever shall. She was a remarkable person. Some readers, classifying her as an unusual instance of a 'borderline personality', might not consider that she is a suitable example for a book about the basic features of psychotherapy. Yet, her problems in living are presented by most patients in a routine diagnostic clinic, by many clients in a one-off counselling session and, indeed, by many of us in our friendships. They trouble the hearts of many psychotherapists. If we are to respond to other persons we need to 'come home' and 'your fading fire/Mend first and vital candle in close heart's vault'.[2]

Sue was a psychotherapist.

The first concern of a therapist must be not to do harm. If, as I have argued, psychotherapy is concerned with learning and growth in genuine relationships then, hoping to respond as persons, we must recognize that, despite our expertise, we know very little. We do not know ourselves. In justifying our mistakes (in behaving as saviours, lover-heroes, as scientific investigators, and as persecutors) we maintain our timid defences, indulge our addictions, and, even as we honestly strive to rewrite our autobiography, we fearfully avoid the darkness.

In this final chapter (which I hope is another beginning), I am taking a small step into the mystery that lies at the heart of one psychotherapist. Obscurity is inevitable. It is intimated by the story of George and Joe, vainly searching under the lamp-post (Introduction, p. xvf.). We are left with the challenge of commitment in face of 'mysteries, uncertainties, doubts'.

I do not know how to put words together. We can die of thirst in an arid desert of intellectual definition. Yet more dangerous, perhaps, is to suffocate by indulging ourselves in the lush pastures of melodramatic sentimentality. I want to stay with my limited experience. If I do not, then this book is a lie.

My meeting and parting with Sue remain for me moving moments. They are at the heart of every diagnostic interview and every conversation in brief or long-term psychotherapy. Maybe, they have not been adequately 'worked through'. But I do not know what that phrase means. The important thing is whether or not my word-shapes resonate with the experiencing of you, my reader.

I shall try to say something about the problems of the psychotherapist (and all of us) in facing loneliness. I want to maintain one important distinction. It is between saying 'I have failed' (a necessary recognition of mistakes and limitations) and the blasphemy '*I* am a failure'.

A DEATH

Sue's story is one of loneliness, guilt, destruction, and meaninglessness. It is also a story of courage and of love.

She was an abandoned child. I shall not attempt to give a detailed account of the terrible deprivation of her early life secluded, in squalid filth, with a sexually perverted nanny in an English country village, nor of the girlhood fantasies about her absent parents (an idealized aristocratic father and a loathed alcoholic mother). I do not want to talk 'about' Sue, nor to describe my mistakes in the failed psychotherapy of a 'borderline personality'. I give only a few hints of how I experienced living within a 'therapeutic relationship'.

Sue grew up with nanny in an opaque glass case shut off from persons. Forced to leave school at the age of thirteen, she worked in a local pub and learned the vocabulary of bar-life without understanding its meaning. At sixteen she decided that she was going to become a doctor. With ability and courage she won an Open Scholarship for a Cambridge college. Sue was brilliant and she was ruthless. And she certainly had charm.

She trained as a psychotherapist. Attractive, vivacious, and professionally successful, Sue used her social skills at cocktail parties and at meetings of learned societies. But she lived in secret, dumb loneliness. There are some who would label her 'persona' as being merely a mask, a 'false-self'. But the 'self' that most people saw was real enough and, certainly, revealed her courage. Yet it was partial. She was aware of a chaos of other 'selves' (Chapter 10). She searched for a 'wholeness' at first in the Church, with the measured beauty of the Gregorian Chant, and later in Jung's psychology. Her efforts to cope began to fail and she began to have severe disabling panic attacks. That was when she and I met.

The first two years of psychotherapy (with three or four interviews weekly) were a model of what analysis should be. We kept strictly to the structure and technique and (as it seemed) with emotion, explored the ramifications of a complex oedipal situation, and the deviant sexual fantasies associated with defective bonding. The anxiety symptoms quickly subsided, and Sue's career progressed. All seemed to be well. (If at that time a research worker had used a symptom check-list, the outcome would have been classified as 'very good'.)

It is Saturday, November 1961, five minutes before the end of a session.

There is a brief silence. Then Sue murmurs:

'Are you glad I finished with Hector?'

I am puzzled. Hector is her boyfriend: I do not know what I am saying in my vague grunt.

To my amazement, Sue's face changes. It changes. During the analysis, I have experienced a good deal of what I have labelled 'aggression'. But nothing like this. Tight lips, spitting venom. I know that she sees me – literally *sees* me – as a hostile attacker. A destroyer.

'You don't want me all for yourself. You *don't*.'

Today I am wearing my lime-green waistcoat with delicately coloured buttons. Sue is out of her chair; her hand rips and the buttons ricochet from the four walls. She glares, stalks out and I am left feeling that I have done a dreadful thing.

> 'God save thee, ancient Mariner!
> From the fiends, that plague thee thus! –
> Why look'st thou so?' – 'With my cross-bow
> I shot the ALBATROSS.'[3]

Sue and I have conscientiously explored and interpreted such themes as abandonment and rage, and the disillusionment of seeing her idealized father as a cruel monster. I have done my best to 'analyse the transference'. But I have missed the important fact. Despite all the talk, Sue has *felt* that she and I were merged in a loving union which excluded everyone else. And she has *known* that that was all *I* wanted. A state of idealized blissful non-differentiation was quite split off from another level of being, a state of destroying and being destroyed.

During the next nine-and-a-half years states of idealized fusion alternated with periods of black isolation and loneliness. Yet, Sue continued her professional career with courage and determination. Was it a facade? With her sensitivity and courage she helped, in an amazing way, very many difficult patients. But, herself she could not save.

Sue committed suicide. On a grey Thursday.

'Love is not enough,' I said to myself.

I said the words, but it was, and is, one of those moments when the world changes. I shall never know how lonely her death was.

It was not just the fact that she committed suicide. Suicide can be a good death. It was not only that we had tried and failed. We had tried again and again – for ten years. Sue died in despair and isolation. Failure? There were times, very many times, when she talked of 'love' and was gay. Oh yes, Sue could be gay. But, not for long. 'How I have changed,' she would say and feel something good inside; a 'something' to do with my love, she told me. Then, *I* felt good too. But not for long.

She could never keep a hold on my love and respect, not to keep it warm and lasting inside and between. Not for more than a day or two, or perhaps a week.

I shall mention only one of the bad times.

One evening, Sue pointed a loaded revolver at me. 'You have ruined my life,' she said. It was not easy to keep to the analytical structure. The session, in my house at the children's bedtime, went on for three hours. Repeatedly and vainly, I pointed out the complex vicissitudes of 'projected and introjected destructiveness'. Suddenly she flung herself down the stairs of my house, spitting murder through tight lips. I

followed her down the suburban road at midnight. The peace was
shattered as she smashed every milk bottle outside each detached and
semi-detached villa.

Donald Winnicott blandly states that the death of the analyst is not as
bad as the loss of intactness of the analytic technique and the attitude
towards retaliation.[4] But there are limits. Again and again Sue and I
became more and more lost in a chaos of attack and counter-attack. It only
ended when she suddenly switched to being a desolate little girl
lacerating herself with self-accusations and begging for forgiveness. I
gave in and we were back in the state of collusive cosiness.

I say 'collusive cosiness' in retrospect. It may not be right. I hope it is
wrong. It did seem that sometimes (for a week or two) there was a
relationship of separate-togetherness.

It sounds melodramatic to say that hell was let loose, but that was
what it was like. I don't mean mere events like a brick thrown through
my front window, being almost blinded by a table hurled at my head, or
even trying to smile at a wobbling revolver. None of these express what I
mean by 'hell'. Nor does the uneasy apprehension of knowing that Sue
was pacing all night in my back garden, watching and waiting. Nor the
hate and the wild rages.

It was the envy that I couldn't stand: the vicious attempts to destroy or,
at least, spoil all the 'good' in my life from which she was excluded; my
domestic 'bliss', my 'successful' career, and all my 'normal' friendships.
The worst is impossible to describe – a sensation of all that was warm and
solid inside being wrenched, gouged out, and torn apart. The tempest
would pass but, in some ways, it was then even worse. 'Guilt feeling' is a
poor name for the vicious mutilating attacks that Sue made upon herself
and the terror that she had destroyed me, the only person who stood by
her.

I did feel destroyed. Not simply being no good as an analyst. *I* was a
failure.

My abbreviated account could be discussed in many different ways.

There is now a large literature on 'psychotic splitting', 'delusional
transference', and 'borderline personality'.[5] In a book on basic principles
a long discussion of complex dynamics would be out of place – although,
in my view, they apply to all of us. I point only to the persistence of
intense rage, destructive envy, and fantasies of fusion associated with
early deprivation referred to in earlier chapters.[6] Perhaps if I had known
more of such matters at that time, the outcome might have been different.
Perhaps. Sue brought home to me that deep down I shared her chaotic
splitting. At times, my counter-attacks were more vicious (because more
disguised) than her attacks.

We might consider the effects of abandonment in infancy, and to what extent damage is irreparable. We could formulate urgent questions about our personal relationships and our wider society. They are questions which, as yet, we are quite unable to answer.

There are soul-searching issues about the limits of a psychotherapist's work and personality. How can we recognize and maintain them? Where do we draw the line? What about the disruption of, and damage to, our families and to ourselves?

Here, I am concerned with how Sue, and many other patients, have compelled me to acknowledge the hidden regions of my own heart. It is an experience shared by many therapists, counsellors, teachers, spiritual directors, and friends who commit themselves to a personal relationship. I came to see once more how, despite a long training analysis, I had only a passing and casual acquaintance with myself. I was faced with meaninglessness and with the essential loneliness which lies at the heart of psychotherapy and of all personal relationships.

LONELINESS

In 1901, when working on *Principia Mathematica*, Bertrand Russell saw Mrs A. N. Whitehead in a severe bout of pain. He writes:

> 'She seemed cut off from everyone and everything by walls of agony, and the sense of the solitude of each human soul suddenly overwhelmed me. Ever since my marriage, my emotional life had been calm and superficial. I had forgotten all the deeper issues, and had been content with flippant cleverness. Suddenly the ground seemed to give way beneath me, and I found myself in quite another region. Within five minutes I went through some such reflections as the following: the loneliness of the human soul is unendurable; nothing can penetrate it except the highest intensity of the sort of love that religious teachers have preached; whatever does not spring from this motive is harmful, or at best useless; it follows that war is wrong, that a public school education is abominable, that the use of force is to be deprecated, and that in human relations one should penetrate to the core of loneliness in each person and speak to that.'[7]

In loneliness we are inarticulate. There are no words. That is the agony. We cannot speak our loneliness, but perhaps (a large 'perhaps') if we are able to discover and to rest in our loneliness there might emerge some fragments of a language in which we can speak *out* of it, and maybe our speaking will find an echo in the loneliness of another.

When imprisoned in the deepest loneliness, I am dumb. Walled around by terror, I assume that no one else can ever be like this. Only me. Often, there is intense shame – for in our society, however much we may talk of heroic or creative solitude, it is not at all acceptable to say 'I am lonely'. We keep our secret from others – and from ourselves.

If there are no words to express the deepest sense of loneliness how can we speak out of it and speak to it? How can a psychotherapist penetrate to the core of loneliness in each person and speak to that? It is an impossible task.

'Loneliness' is a large word. I shall use it vaguely to mean the pain of a felt inability to satisfy that urgent need for relation with other persons: a basic need of a human being. It is a subjective term. Strictly, I can say only 'I am lonely', not 'he is lonely'. The meaning of loneliness cannot be exhausted by descriptions of 'symptoms' of sensory and social deprivation and isolation. The situations of old people in tenements and attics, of prisoners in solitary confinement, of shipwrecked sailors, of single middle-aged women, and of leaders making world-shaking decisions, are some among many other conditions which can, but do not always, result in loneliness. It is important that they be studied by social and experimental psychologists and they are of great importance for psychotherapists. In touching on a large subject, I am not concerned with what can be inspected from outside.[8]

Loneliness as experienced by me, and only by me, can only be dimly apprehended by another in an imaginative act within and beyond a conversation. It is only then that I can say, 'you are lonely', or rather 'thou art lonely'. Loneliness is a word appropriate to the 'grammar' of a personal relationship – of conversation (Chapter 13).

I shall distinguish, very arbitrarily, two modes of loneliness, 'no-being' and 'cut-offness'. They are associated with the two types of anxiety discussed in Chapter 13: basic (or existential) anxiety, and separation anxiety.

In infancy, the sense of 'I' is at first transient or evanescent. The 'I am' comes and goes; it seems to be established, then it is lost. The terror of ceasing to be persists throughout life. It is experienced as the loneliness of no-being, the heart of darkness.

That basic anxiety can be lived with only in a relationship with at least one other person. The fear of losing a significant other is separation anxiety, expressed in (and defended against by) the loneliness of cut-offness.

If early mothering is defective, as it was with Sue, then existence is fragile. The sense of 'I' is tenuous and continually threatened. We need other persons who are reliably 'there', who can be with us. We need basic trust. If we are threatened by abandonment, the sudden and unpredictable loss of contact with a human body, then we are constantly faced with horror of no-being. No body is there.

In *cut-offness* I have a sense of 'my own world', of fantasies, thoughts, and ideas. It is 'within' but it also extends beyond me. I am me but unless I have contact with others – a contact which is (actually or symbolically) bodily – my existence is intolerable. Unable to communicate, I long to move into relation with others – to be understood and to share.

Jung's involvement in psychotherapy forced him to face his own lonely cut-offness. He writes:

'We must first tread with the patient the path of his illness – the path of his mistake that sharpens his conflicts and increases his loneliness till it becomes unbearable – hoping that from the psychic depths which cast up the powers of destruction the rescuing forces will also come.'[9]

Jung is stressing the positive, creative meaning which is hidden in the self-centred ('narcissistic') egoism of many neurotics. His hope – and it is only a hope – is that in a growing realization of isolation, as well as powers of destruction, 'rescuing forces' will arise. Jung felt that he should mend his own fading fire. According to his testimony, he decided to abandon a successful academic career in order to explore himself.

'The consequence of my resolve, and my involvement with things which neither I nor anyone else could understand, was an extreme loneliness. I was going about laden with thoughts of which I could speak to no one: they would only have been misunderstood. I felt the gulf between the external world and the interior world of images, in its most painful form. I could not yet see that interaction of both worlds which I now understand. I saw only an irreconcilable contradiction between "inner" and "outer".

However, it was clear to me from the start that I could find contact with the outer world and with people only if I succeeded in showing – and this would demand the most intensive effort – that the contents of psychic experience are real, and real not only as my own personal experiences, but as collective experiences which others also have. Later I tried to demonstrate this in my scientific work, and I did all in my power to convey to my intimates a new way of seeing things. I knew that if I did not succeed, I would be condemned to absolute isolation.'[10]

Jung endeavoured to learn and to speak, however haltingly, phrases of a language which were common to all the lonely members of mankind. In an imaginative grammar of 'archetypal symbols' he sought to discover a bridge – a rainbow – between the apparently irreconcilable contradiction of 'inner' and 'outer'.

But sometimes there are no fantasies, no thoughts, no ideas. I do not know how to express a state of being which is also not-being. I shall refer to it as no-being.[11]

No-being is dimly expressed in the terrible paradox 'I am no one'. There are no images that I can call 'me', 'mine', or 'my own'. Beneath a chaos of disconnected fragments lies an abyss of nothingness. The odd sentence 'I have no being' carries with it the implication 'no one is there'. I have no sense of contact with another person who might confirm that 'I am me', with an identity separate from the world of people and things 'out there'. Even my body is alien. There is a threat of non-being, of not being able to speak the word 'I'. Non-being (like death as distinct from dying) cannot be experienced directly but in no-being there is a strange mysterious uncanny sense of the unknown, of an annihilation in which 'I cease to be'. This disintegrating anxiety is the basic problem in all psychotherapy.

It is now the fashion to ascribe this mode of existence, bordering on non-existence, to persons who are conveniently classified as being 'borderline' or 'narcissistic'. For me, it lies at the heart of everyday living. We live at the edge of a void, the heart of darkness. Yet, it is the Black Hole that gives depth to personal relationships.

THE DARKNESS OF MYSELF

In the month before Sue died, I sat for long hours with Frankie, an attractive girl of seventeen, whilst she was 'shooting' heroin. It is happening now.

I feel that I am taking part in a religious rite. The elaborate preparation of the syringe, the careful opening of the phial (emptied to the very last drop), the solemn choice of a vein: Frankie performs all these actions with scrupulous care in accordance with the canons of her junkie culture. She uses the correct words in a language that, as yet, I only dimly understand. Then there is the moment as she draws up a stream of blood and gazes at it as if in awe. I am strangely moved by the kind of numinous terror that I have once or twice experienced in a Latin Mass. Frankie tells me vividly how, for her, the ceremony is most powerful when performed and shared with other junkies who have an intense loyalty to each other.

As up to a point – and it is always only up to a point – I imaginatively enter into Frankie's world, I am faced with the darkness of myself – an abyss that is beyond 'me'.

Using the word in a broad sense, most of us are 'addicts' in one way or another. We are devoted to compulsive actions which are ultimately damaging to our integrity as persons – to food; to tranquillizers and sleeping pills; to the images on a television screen; to erudite scholarship; to committee activities; to dependence on friends, spouses, or analysts; to recording our dreams; and to 'religions' such as 'Christianity' or golf.

And we get 'withdrawal symptoms' when we cannot pursue those activities by means of which we deny the terror of non-existence, the void of no-being.

As I talk with Frankie or as I watch an alcoholic sliding down skid-row, I say 'There am I.'

Twenty-five years ago, the great psychotherapist Frieda Fromm-Reichmann said that psychiatrists were reluctant to consider the problems of lonely patients because of their own fear of loneliness.[12] Talking *about* loneliness in general terms, however well illustrated by clinical descriptions, can be a way of avoiding it. 'It is they who are lonely, not really me.' Or perhaps we explain it away with euphemisms: it is a depressive affect or a schizoid problem: it is 'really' this, that, or the other.

As psychiatrists and analysts, and as friends, husbands, wives, and parents, we do everything possible to avoid being confronted by the terrifying depths of loneliness. In going on learning to become psychotherapists we learn skills, we practise our scales, we study psychodynamics; but we need to advance a little (and, at best, it is only a little) towards self-awareness. That means remaining in touch with our own cut-offness but, more important, the threat of no-being.

From no-being there emanates a weird threat of contagion or contamination. We look the other way; we interpret glibly or else we maintain a collusive, idealized intimacy which I call 'pseudo-mutuality'.[13]

Lonely people are afraid lest they frighten others; their misgivings are justified. Those of us who have experienced the pangs of the most profound loneliness prefer not to talk about it. We do not wish to be reminded of our terror. We are reluctant to face again the inner void which we fear to acknowledge. We look the other way. Perhaps we do not know and do not want to know what lies within us, although there is a dim and undetermined sense of an unknown danger. The lonely person is further ostracized by others who fear his condition.

We feel helpless as we apprehend the loneliness of another. We do not know how to speak to 'the core of loneliness'. We can 'interact' to some extent. We can 'communicate' about this and that. But it is immensely more difficult to *converse*. Conversation is especially embarrassing because it calls for body-language – the tenderness of a caress or of a shared look. There is still a deep and widespread 'taboo on tenderness' about which Ian Suttie wrote so penetratingly nearly fifty years ago.[14]

In many diverse and complex ways, we strive to deny our loneliness and our ever-present fear of separation, loss, and death: and, by roundabout paths, seek gratification of our longings for togetherness and mutuality.

By hypochondriacal complaints and pathetic overdoses we coerce doctors to touch our bodies. In promiscuity we attempt, and fail, to achieve a union, 'past reason hunted', and, having had, 'past reason hated'.[15] Whisky warms the chill of inner emptiness, and in an interminable analysis there is an unfulfilled belief in the possibility of an everlasting fusion. We avoid the void by noble fights for success, by abstruse and recondite scholarship, by distractions of the social round, by accumulating rusting treasures, and by the desperate duty of good works. We can take refuge in the defiant cry of Richard III – 'I am myself alone'. We can lose ourselves in disembodied, romanticized day-dreams. Or we can commit suicide – usually by default rather than by choice.

In striving to express what I mean by no-being, I am attempting the impossible. It is indescribable. Perhaps a calm acceptance of silence is the ideal. But, in our isolation, most of us can only either fall into despair, madness, or suicide; or else, in halting sentences, we can attempt to move from crude metaphor to the curious clarity of poetry in the hope that we will evoke a glimmer of comprehension in another, and be rewarded by the gift of a sad smile of friendship.

For no-being there are only phrases such as 'frozen isolation', 'empty silence', 'naked horror', 'mere existence', 'being neither dead nor alive', 'in a Black Hole'. I turn to artists.

The title of this chapter is taken from Conrad's tale, *Heart of Darkness*, a story which had a great impact upon me and helped me to face my failure to reach Sue and Frankie.

The narrator is Marlow (Conrad's *alter ego*, who appears in many of his writings). He is an honest, quirky, down-to-earth sailor who believes himself to belong to a world of 'straightforward facts'. On a long twilight journey into the vast depths of nineteenth-century Africa, we are confronted by the horrors of colonial exploitation, of negro chain-gangs, and of disease and starvation. But, more disturbingly, we feel small and fearful in a mysterious unknown 'immensity of earth, sky, and water'. Our journey into the dark land is a venture into our own darkness. There we meet death.

Marlow is looking for a famous man who has disappeared: Kurtz, a distinguished, liberal, eloquent scholar who is studying conditions in Africa. (He could well be an analytical psychotherapist.)

After a perilous journey Marlow finds him. Kurtz has accumulated precious ivory, has made himself into a god for the natives, and has become caught up with unnamed 'abominable rites'.

Marlow arrives in time to be in at the death – Kurtz's death. Kurtz talks. Dying, he talks on and on. All about his grandiose, humanitarian plans. Yet, at the same time, Marlow feels that he is under 'the heavy mute spell of the wilderness'.

Kurtz is a sham. Marlow sees that. The famous writer, charismatic orator, and distinguished musician is contemptibly childish. Yet Marlow maintains that Kurtz is a remarkable man. Kurtz dies. His final cry is:

'The horror! The horror!'

Marlow puts out the candle. In the dark we hear a black boy's idle comment:

'Mistah Kurtz – he dead.'

Marlow, in the impenetrable gloom, reflects upon the greyness of life and death.

'The most you can hope from it is some knowledge of yourself – that comes too late – a crop of unextinguishable regrets.'[16]

Yet, he is determined to be loyal. Kurtz has achieved a 'moral victory'. In his cry 'The horror!' he has the courage to say something, to make a statement – about life, and about death.

Marlow disapproves of Kurtz. But he is humiliated to discover that in the face of death he, himself, has nothing to say. That is why he affirms that the addicted, 'borderline personality', Kurtz, was a remarkable man. He could look into the heart of darkness. Marlow's words express what I feel as I listen again and again to Sue, Frankie, and many others who have died by overt or covert suicide.

'He had something to say. He said it. Since I had peeped over the edge myself, I understand better the meaning of his stare, that could not see the flame of the candle but was . . . piercing enough to penetrate all the hearts that beat in the darkness . . . he had stepped over the edge, while I had been permitted to draw back my hesitating foot.'[17]

Suicide can be a powerful statement: a statement about our bourgeois society, about our personal values, and about the human condition. Sue had something to say and she said it. That is how I now hear the language of her death.

Darkness lies at the heart of psychotherapy.

Conrad, the solitary master-mariner, looked long into the void of lonely no-being. His novels are penetrating psychological analyses of the multitudinous forms of mental isolation in which the heroes, in their various ways, attempt and usually fail to discover an identity by conquering or accepting the hostile, annihilating darkness which lies at the centre of existence. In another novel, the onlooker Marlow affirms that despite his exalted egoism and romanticism, 'Lord Jim' achieved greatness, the ultimate loneliness: 'It is as if loneliness were a hard and absolute condition of existence.'[18] Few artists have expressed so starkly the sense of isolation and in his own life Conrad experienced profoundly the loneliness which most of us, most of the time, try to avoid.

Conrad continued to write with a passionate concern for humanity. He hoped to help to knit together 'the loneliness of innumerable hearts'.[19] Yet he was deeply pessimistic. In a letter quoted earlier (Chapter 9, p. 146) he says that the 'fate of a humanity condemned to perish from cold is not worth troubling about'.[20] Sometimes, I feel that he is right. But more often, in facing no-being, I am sustained by a pregnant metaphor: the black hole.

The Black Hole

For many years I have lived with and, when I have dared, explored a metaphor which has been suggested by astronomers and physicists. It is personal, but that is not to say that it is idiosyncratic.

The inspired work of Albert Einstein, developed by many other scientists, has forced us (experts and laymen alike) to question our accustomed 'puny boundaries'.[21] We are no longer safe in distinct categories of 'space' and 'time'.

The recent notion or discovery (and it is no longer clear which is which) of black holes in the universe has faced physicists, astronomers, and readers of science fiction with the unknowable. A heavy star collapses and condenses. Matter disappears and a vast amount of energy is liberated. Our accepted laws no longer apply. We are confronted with the mystery of pure energy.

Concepts and findings of physics arise from personal experience. What is 'out there' is also 'in here'. William Blake cried, 'Energy is Eternal Delight.'[22] But energy can only be harnessed at a very great risk. It can destroy. A physicist, John Taylor, writes:

'Black holes are dangerous. Once swallowed up by one it would be impossible to escape from it. If there are any in the Universe, and we've seen that there is a high probability of this being so, they should be avoided like the plague.'[23]

I know little of physics and astronomy and stay with the metaphor which is evocative for many people today.[24]

Sarah has a black hole. She almost died by refusing food and was classified as a case of 'anorexia nervosa'. Her life was dominated by a compulsive preoccupation with eating. One theme, amongst many others, was refusing food as a way of avoiding an intolerable impulse to indulge in orgies of gorging herself. She was addicted to food which was 'charged' with ecstatic excitement. It had to be kept in reserve as a delightful experience which could be looked forward to. So long as it was there the future was not a void.

Many years after having ended analytical psychotherapy, Sarah's weight is normal and she is now apparently free from psychological symptoms. Yet (as in all the many instances of anorexia nervosa that I have followed up after successful outcomes) food remains a powerful symbol and to some extent a defence (perhaps a necessary defence; we all need defences). Sarah writes of 'my black hole':

'Away from the edge, I *think* the hole – distanced to a penny – and steer my life round it with my food-and-exercise wheel. Laying aside these defences, I foresee boredom, loneliness, pointlessness.

At the edge, I feel it, anxiously dig my toes against the drag, sucked in by orgy or force-feeding, pushed in by physical inactivity. If I lose control now (control of my appetite or control to another) I'm in – swallowed up, disorientated, depressed, laid waste – in bits. Entombed, the darkness closes over my head, closes against the future, trapped in body-presence; still, silent, lifeless. I lie there in eternity. I know (now) I'll come to life again, shaken and shocked, but it feels like death. '

By charging food with solitary pleasure and excitement which I control, I keep something constantly to look forward to, and by physical activity I keep bodily darkness constantly at bay – not wholly committed to the present most of the time, insulated against small anxieties, failures, disappointments, humiliations; protected against nothingness, no-being.

But the price is guilt – I *know* that I am being less than honest and real; that I avoid experiencing the hole and things in it which I do not want to know about, nor let anyone else see.

So don't offer me a biscuit lightly . . .'

Sarah feels that she must live at the *edge* of the black hole 'experiencing' it as far as possible – and that 'feels like death' – but she must not lose herself in it. Yet in avoiding it there is guilt and she gives a strong hint of the dangerous possibility of a renewal, a coming to life again.

Perhaps there is life in the black hole. Perhaps St John of the Cross and other mystics were not so crazy when they sensed the creative activity of God working obscurely in the Dark Night of the Soul.[25]

The painter Edouard Munch writes in his journal:

'My whole life has been spent walking by the side of a bottomless chasm, jumping from stone to stone. Sometimes I try to leave my narrow path and join the swirling mainstream of life, but I always find myself drawn inexorably back towards the chasm's edge, and there I shall walk until the day I finally fall into the abyss. For as long as I can remember I have suffered from a deep feeling of anxiety which I have tried to express in my art. Without anxiety and illness I should have been like a ship without a rudder.'[26]

In the words of a commentator, Munch tried 'with pessimistic tenderness to close the gap between the Self and the Other'.[27] A psychotherapist might do well to meditate upon the phrase 'pessimistic tenderness'.

Perhaps great artists are in great peril. But just as we are all 'borderline personalities' so, as we rewrite our autobiographies, to some extent we are artists. We can never own the hole. We cannot control or assimilate it. The best we can do is to live on its edge and, in meeting others beside it, 'close the gap' even if only a little.

Some para-scientists have extended the metaphor. They suggest that in entering a black hole, out of time and out of space, we might meet ourselves emerging! 'Mueriendo porque no muero' ('I am dying because I do not die').[28]

MOMENTS OF MEETING

Bertrand Russell maintained that his sudden overwhelming apprehension of the loneliness of the human soul (p. 267) had a profound and lasting effect upon him. The sense of 'mystic illumination' (a peak experience: Chapter 9) faded. His 'habit of analysis' reasserted itself. Yet, thenceforward, he continued to feel more in touch with all his friends and with many of his acquaintances,[29] although, for most of his life, he remained an isolated wanderer.

In 1913 he met Joseph Conrad.

Russell writes of the first encounter between these two remarkable lonely men. In his vivid prose a multitude of meanings body forth from the pregnant word 'meeting'.

'At our very first meeting, we talked with continually increasing intimacy. We seemed to sink through layer after layer of what was superficial, till gradually both reached the central fire. It was an experience unlike any other that I have known. We looked into each other's eyes, half appalled and half intoxicated to find ourselves together in such a region. The emotion was as intense as passionate love, and at the same time all-embracing. I came away bewildered, and hardly able to find my way among ordinary affairs.'[30]

They spent very few hours together but their conversation had a continuing effect on both men. Russell called his son 'Conrad'. He writes: 'In the out-works of our lives we were almost strangers.' Yet there remained 'a bond of extreme strength'. Conrad conveyed to Russell his 'deep admiring affection which, if you were never to see me again and forgot my existence tomorrow, would be unalterably yours *usque ad finem.*'[31]

Such profoundly moving moments are rare, and cannot be expected to occur with this intensity in psychiatric practice. Yet I have experienced them in the briefest of brief psychotherapy and have reason to suppose that they can have lifelong consequences. How to be open to receive and respond to them as we endeavour to 'penetrate to the core of loneliness in each person and speak to that', whilst not intruding on his or her creative aloneness? That is the central and unattainable ideal of psychotherapy. It means remaining in touch with and speaking from our own ineradicable loneliness.

Again and again we fail.

We can never *share* loneliness but maybe, in the touch of a hand, in a deep look, in a groping gesture, in a far-flung metaphor, and even in an interpretation worded with care, there can be a Moment of meeting.

Let us look at, see, and perhaps see into, two small cameos. Two Moments.

The first is taken from Frieda Fromm-Reichmann. She confesses that, in writing about the therapy of a schizophrenic girl, she is attempting to break through 'the loneliness of thinking about loneliness'.

'I asked her a question about her feeling miserable: She raised her hand with her thumb lifted, the other four fingers bent toward her palm, so that I could see only her thumb, isolated from the four hidden fingers. I interpreted the signal with, "That lonely?", in a sympathetic tone of voice. At this, her facial expression loosened up as though in great relief and gratitude, and her fingers opened. Then she began to tell me about herself by means of her fingers, and she asked me by gestures to respond in kind. We continued with this finger conversation for one or two weeks, and as we did so, her anxious tension began to decrease and she began to break through her noncommunicative isolation; and subsequently she emerged altogether from her loneliness.'[32]

The second example of a Moment in psychotherapy is taken from my own experience – it is 'my own' although I do not own it. Frankie has sat rigidly silent, impassively staring at the wall. For four hours a week throughout six months. Suddenly, today at half-past three, I feel really scared – deep down in my middle, I mean. Scared isn't right. It is beyond that. An uncanny nothingness. Do I speak, or do my words speak me?

'Lost . . . like . . . it's like being lost in a nowhere.' Frankie looks up. Our eyes meet and she smiles. Or rather *we* smile. She holds out her hand and I respond. It is a gentle mutual enfolding.

'Lost in a nowhere.' That is a poem. A bodily poem which is born in the space between us. At half-past three? The hands of the clock are creeping and yet they stand still. A Moment.

'Psychotherapy' did not help Frankie with her drug addiction. That was a failure. But *I* did not feel a failure. Nor, I hope, did she.

I have introduced a word, 'Moment': the experience of a meeting in and out of time. The heart of psychotherapy.

What William Blake says of the poet is true for the therapist. He speaks of a Moment which, when found and rightly placed, 'renovates every Moment of the Day'.[33]

> 'For in this Period the Poet's Work is Done, and all the Great
> Events of Time start forth & are conceiv'd in such a Period,
> Within a Moment, a Pulsation of the Artery.'[34]

We can speak to the core of loneliness only by a kind of bodily poetry which is carried alive into the heart with passion. Wordsworth, who knew 'a darkness, call it solitude or blank desertion', writes:

> 'There are in our existence spots of time,
> That with distinct pre-eminence retain
> A renovating virtue, whence . . .
> . . . our minds
> Are nourished and invisibly repaired'[35]

LONELINESS AND LOVE

Joseph Butler was an enthusiastic (but somewhat wobbly) horseman, a gentle bishop, a great philosopher, and an early advocate of general systems-theory (Chapter 14). In the eighteenth century, he summed up his warm, closely-argued formulation of psychology and ethics: 'Reverence thyself'.[36]

At those times when we are able to follow his precept (and he was never a dogmatist) we can shout 'I have failed', but we cannot ever mutter the suicidal words '*I* am a failure'. Butler knew about 'cool self-love'. His powerful adjective 'cool' is a necessary complement to the heart-felt passion which has erupted from time to time in this book. It is the ideal temperature for a psychotherapist − a fiery heat that cools.

The importance of relationships in between persons, as distinct from relations to things (what I have termed a dialogue of aloneness-togetherness) has been reiterated throughout this book. I have suggested that an asymmetrical therapeutic relationship can ripen into a friendship which is never lost, but which expands to others in the client's world. Whether or not this occurs (through creative fusion, separation, and coming together again) depends upon the capacity of both persons to tolerate loss and to bear an inevitable sad loneliness in separation and fear of no-being. In order to relieve the agony of isolation we need to accept our aloneness.

'Alone, alone, all all, alone,
Alone on a wide wide sea!'[37]

Coleridge's evocative image is of stark, isolated despair. Yet, in the poem, it moves on to intimations of love for all creatures – although the guilt of destruction is never expiated (Chapter 8).

The word 'alone' carries overtones and undertones of 'all-one'. I now catch a glimpse of what it might mean to say 'I am myself' – a 'myself' which is an ideal wholeness embracing a togetherness of my 'selves' with those of another; with all others – and perhaps with all nature. I am distinct and differentiated. Yet I am integrated in relationships.

In previous chapters I have attempted, and failed, to say what I mean by aloneness-togetherness. I have approached, and withdrawn from, the word 'love'. I shall try to say something about what I do *not* mean.

Often the word 'love' contracts into sickly sentimentality, burdensome moralistic demands, or subtle ways of coercion. Perhaps the most pernicious and damaging means of avoiding loneliness is not psychosis, neurosis, or Chinese heroin, but pseudo-mutuality.[38] Then, our investment maintains a semblance, an idea, or a sense of relation – an idealization which involves a denial of many experiences in order to maintain a fantasy of togetherness or fusion which does not permit of anything more than minor differences. All our expectations must mesh in with those of the other person. We fail to recognize a divergence, an affirmation of independent identity, as being a temporary, painful, but creative difference: a 'mis-fit' which can lead on to dialogue and to meeting. In cowardice, we avoid a disruption which we fear will demolish the entire relationship.

All of us have unseen capacities for development. Mutual respect means valuing unknown potentialities of the other as a separate, unique person. And it means reverencing ourselves. Platitudes are often pregnant.

In a pseudo-mutual state (it cannot be called a relationship) there is a stifling, static proximity of two isolated individuals – not a relation between persons. The 'goodness' of a 'beautiful friendship', an 'ideal marriage', a 'happy family', or a 'sympathetic' therapeutic relationship is often a collusive fearful glorification of 'fitting in'. It barely conceals, and serves to exacerbate, a resentful, envious loneliness. Pseudo-mutuality seems to offer much, but the 'goodies' do not last. There is a split. What is said in words is contradicted in action.

Love and imagination are closely related. The development of aloneness-togetherness is an imaginative activity which discloses the possibility of creating a kind of loving that lies within and between persons. But it also moves beyond: a movement implied by the initial capitals of Moment, and of Meeting. In states of deepest loneliness direct bodily contact is necessary. In every conversation there are always looks, gestures, movements, as well as powerful sentences, which are carried alive into the heart with passion. Yet the human body always expands beyond the literal, and seeing 'with' the eye always intimates a hope – and a fear – of seeing 'through' the eye; of apprehending a Moment at a crossroad between time and the timeless – a fleeting vision of love in the darkness of despair.

Imagination and love move into religion. Despite all disclaimers, when we formulate techniques of a Conversational Model and engage in research projects, we are making statements about ultimate values. Alfred North Whitehead stood with Bertrand Russell (his co-author of *Principia Mathematica*) beside his wife in her lonely agony. He writes:

'Religion is what the individual does with his own solitariness . . . and if you are never solitary you are never religious.'[39]

Wordsworth, in attempting to express what passed within his own heart, speaks of points within our souls where 'all stand single'.

'The prime and vital principle is thine
In the recesses of thy nature, far
From any reach of outward fellowship,
Else 'tis not thine at all.[40]

Love is a language (Chapter 13). It can only be spoken out of aloneness. With its 'words' of reverence we say, again and again, 'I have failed' but never '*I* am a failure'.

It is proper that a psychotherapist should need his patients to help him tolerate his own loneliness (that is what sympathy means). Sometimes he remains uninvolved because of his fear of separation and loss (with associated rage and envy). But, often, he persists doggedly with devoted dedication rather than experience the pain of loss in a brief encounter. We all sometimes use our patients at their expense either by playing the part of a subtly patronizing, detached, and persecuting observer, or by reinforcing and maintaining states of fantasy-fusion or pseudo-mutuality.

The essential features of psychotherapy are those of any friendship. Psychopathological formulations, reconstructions, or sophisticated inter-pretations may be helpful but they are peripheral. Without tenderness the noise of our talk does harm. The first great task is to stay with no-being and cut-offness, the second is to discover a language in which we can go out to meet and to respond to our patients with honest respect and quiet tenderness, affectionately being-in-touch. In so far as we are poor friends we are rotten therapists and probably damaging analysts – a statement which receives some support from careful research.

'Mysteries, uncertainties, doubts'? Not-knowing or 'unknowing'[41] is a *sine qua non* of scientific enquiry. It is the heart of our personal identity which grows amidst the changing flux of relationships. Phases of distance, periods of necessary absence, clashes of argument, and disappointments of personal misunderstanding, bring the pain of loss and separation. It is agony to be at cross-purposes with someone we love. But it is just when we do *not* fit that there is a potentiality for seeing, hearing, and touching in a new way with a freshening of the relationship (see Chapter 12, p. 197). Changes arising from personal growth and from new social and material situations lead to a non-fulfilment of expectations which, given mutuality, can lead to exploration of differences and the possibility of a deeper but altered mode of togetherness. As we explore the gap we begin to discover and learn the first words of a new language – an unexpected re-creation of friendship. The hoped-for renewal is only a possibility. Some of us never learn and, at best, all our learning is partial.

This book is about how we approach and avoid the joy and pain of understanding: of aloneness-togetherness in personal relationships. I have tried to spell out some technical skills of a Conversational Model of Psychotherapy. I have speculated about the philosophy of psychology of experience, language, symbol, thought, and vision. Above all, I have tried to tell my stories truly. But I have merely talked on and around the periphery of a mystery: the odd word 'love'.

To avoid loneliness is to make a mockery of love. To go on growing up to be a person means to explore new ways of resting in and speaking out of our loneliness. Then, there is the hope of a meeting in the space *between* lonely persons.

> 'When love, with one another so
> Interinanimates two soules,
> That abler soule, which thence doth flow,
> Defects of lonelinesse controules.'[42]

NOTES

Acknowledgements

1 *Russell A. Meares* is now Professor of Psychiatry, Westmead Centre, Sydney, Australia. He has published a book and many papers on psychotherapy (e.g. Meares 1976, 1977, 1983).

2 *A. Hobson*, sometime Head of the English Department, Sir Hugh Owen School, Caernarfon. See Hobson, A. (1972).

3 *S.H. Burton*, a scholar and teacher of English literature and language, sometime of Blundell's School, and St Luke's College, Exeter; the author of numerous books on varied topics (e.g. Burton 1972, 1974, 1980).

4 *Herbert McCabe*. O.P. Blackfriars, Oxford. Priest and author (e.g. McCabe 1968).

5 *I.T. Ramsey*, philosopher and theologian. Late Bishop of Durham (e.g. Ramsey 1957).

6 *D.E. Jenkins*, Lord Bishop of Durham, philosopher and theologian, has published widely (e.g. 1967).

7 *J.M.M. Mair* is Director of the Department of Psychological Services and Research, Crichton Royal Hospital, Dumfries (Mair 1976, 1977).

8 *R.P. Hobson* is Consultant Psychotherapist, Bethlem Royal and Maudsley Hospitals, and Senior Research Fellow, Medical Research Council. He has written on autism and child development (e.g. Hobson, R.P. 1982, 1985).

9 *N.E.C. Coltart*, Vice-President, British Psychoanalytical Society.

10 *D.A. Shapiro*, a clinical psychologist and skilled psychotherapist, is now

leader of a research team in the MRC/ESRC Social and Applied Psychology Unit at the University of Sheffield. He has published widely (e.g. Shapiro 1980, Shapiro and Shapiro 1982).

11 *D.P. Goldberg* is Professor of Psychiatry, University of Manchester. One of his many outstanding and varied achievements has been the development of the practice and teaching of psychotherapy at Manchester and throughout the North West Region. He has devised and led research projects in psychotherapy (e.g. Goldberg *et al.* 1984).

12 *M.S. Towse*, Consultant Psychiatrist, North Manchester General Hospital.

13 *F.H. Margison*, Consultant Psychotherapist, Manchester Royal Infirmary and the University Hospital of South Manchester, Regional Adviser in Psychotherapy.

Introduction

1 Three videotapes comprise a package, *A Conversational Model of Psychotherapy*. (See Chapter 12, Note 12.) Tape 2 – 'Developing a Therapeutic Conversation' – demonstrates my personal style.

2 Quoted from an unpublished Notebook in Coburn (1974): 30.

3 See Note 1.

4 See Hobson (1959, 1964, 1979) for some comments on groups and communities.

5 Eliot (1944) *East Coker* I: l. 202.

BOOK I

Chapter 1

1 Wordsworth (1850) *The Prelude*: ll. 349–50, in Wordsworth (1971).

2 Ruesch and Bateson (1951).

3 At that time I did not know about the work of D.W. Winnicott (e.g. 1971: 121–23) who composed 'squiggles' with younger children.

4 See e.g. Jung (1983) and Hobson (1971).

5 Hobson (1971): a critical review of Jung's ideas.

6 Coleridge (1817): 48.

7 van Gennep (1960).

8 Wittgenstein (1967) – discussed in Chapter 4.

Chapter 2

1 Buber (1937): 3.

2 See e.g. Ramsey (1957), Hamlyn (1974), Peters (1958), McCabe (1968).

3 Buber (1937): 4.

4 Buber (1937): 3.

5 The existential-phenomenological approach is clearly put by May *et al.*

(1958) and Yalom (1980). Classic expositions are Binswanger (1963) and Boss (1963).
6 McCabe (1968): 17–20.
7 Buber (1937): 11.
8 The example was given to me by my son, Dr R. Peter Hobson. I am deeply grateful to him for germinal ideas and for personal conversations over many years. See e.g. Hobson, R.P. (1982, 1985).
9 Blake (1966): 545. From the MS Notebook of 1808–11, No. 29: l. 2.
10 Wittgenstein (1967): 178.

Chapter 3

1 Quoted by Buber (1963): 30.
2 e.g. Gendlin (1962, 1973).
3 e.g. Schafer (1973). Because I adopt and adapt, Schafer's 'action' terms does not mean that I accept all of his ideas (e.g. regarding 'self'). I do not. For a critical assessment see Meares (1985) (in press).
4 Wittgenstein (1966, 1967).
5 e.g. Austin (1965).
6 e.g. Hampshire (1965).
7 Harré and Secord (1972). Harré (1984) puts forward a strong case for reformulating psychological concepts in social, interpersonal terms.
8 Powys (1944): 205.
9 I use some of Gendlin's terms but in a somewhat different sense (e.g. Gendlin 1973).
10 See Chapter 1, Note 4.
11 The translation of this passage from Rilke (1966): 124, closely follows that of Linton (Rilke 1972): 19. There is however, a significant alteration. The line 'Denn die Erinnerungen selbst *sind* es noch nicht' is rendered by Linton 'For it is the memories themselves that matter'. The German is literally 'For the memories themselves are not yet it'. The 'not' is crucial. Herter Norton (Rilke 1964) translates the sentence as 'For it is not yet the memories themselves'. I have inserted the word 'experiences' since 'it' evidently refers to 'verses' which are 'experiences'.
12 S.T. Coleridge, *Ode to Dejection*: l. 87. 'For not to think of what I needs must feel' (Coleridge 1912: 367).
13 Jung, C.G. (1948).
14 It should not be assumed that I follow Schafer in all, or even most, of his reformulations of psychoanalysis.
15 Schafer (1973): 177.

Chapter 4

1 Wittgenstein (1966): 2, Footnote.
2 Wittgenstein (1967) P.I. p. 2f (1). The following notes are all references to *Philosophical Investigations* (P.I.). They give page numbers in English and

paragraphs in brackets. Readable introductions to Wittgenstein's thought are
provided by van Peursen (1969) and Pears (1971).

3 P.I. p. 3 (2). also pp. 8–10 (19, 20, 21).
4 P.I. p. 5 (7).
5 P.I. p. 3 (3).
6 P.I. p. 32 (67).
7 P.I. p. 11 (23).
8 The Word Association Test was probably first developed by Francis Galton
   (1879) and developed by other psychiatrists in the nineteenth century (see
   Lewis, A.J. 1957). C.G. Jung used it to study individual motives and
   developed his notion of 'complexes', clusters of emotionally-toned images
   and ideas, which are often unconscious (see *Collected Works*, II).
9 There is a vast literature on metaphor. A great deal is summarized in Ortony
   (1979). I draw on Richards (1936), Mair (1976) and Ortony, Reynolds and
   Arter (1978).
10 Richards (1936).
11 A *simile* states the comparison more evidently by the use of 'like' or 'as'. In
   synecdoche a part stands for a whole thing, e.g. the 'hands' (men) on a ship,
   metonymy means the use of one thing to refer to something else with which it
   is associated, e.g. in referring to 'the Crown' rather than to the queen. A
   catachresis is when something without a name is given a name belonging to
   something else, e.g. in using the ordinary word 'information' in a highly
   technical sense to refer to measurable processes of computers. In an
   oxymoron two incompatible or contradictory terms are linked – 'the cold fire
   of his eyes'.
12 I seem to recollect that the phrase is used by George Bernard Shaw but cannot
   find the reference.
13 The word 'in-dwelling' is used by Mair (1976): 277–81, who relates it to the
   psychology of G.A. Kelly (1963) and M. Polyani (1958).
14 Richards (1936): 135f.
15 John James Haworth of Crawshawbooth, Rossendale, Lancashire.
16 Hobbes, T. (1962).
17 Rilke (1952) Introduction (J.B. Leishman and S. Spender): 20f.

Chapter 5

1 Keller (1936).
2 Ibid.: 23–24.
3 See Chapter 10.
4 Langer (1951 and 1953).
5 Morris (1946). In her preface to the second edition of *Philosophy in a New Key*
   (1951: viii), Langer states that she has altered her terminology to accord with
   that of Morris. I adopt his meaning of 'signals', 'signs', and 'symbols'.
6 Ogden and Richards (1944).
7 Coleridge's use of the word 'symbol' develops (not always clearly) throughout his voluminous works. A readable exposition is made by Prickett (1970),

especially in Chapter 7: 175–204. Coleridge's later view is expressed, somewhat obscurely, in *The Statesman's Manual* (1816): 28–31.

8 Jung's views, elaborated in his voluminous writings, are summarized in *Man and his Symbols* (1978).

9 Tillich (1957), Chapter 3.

10 See Note 5.

11 The phrase is coined from the writings of Coleridge and Wordsworth about poetic genius, e.g. 'so to represent familiar objects as to awaken the minds of others to a . . . freshness of sensation concerning them' (Coleridge 1818: 110). See Chapter 7.

12 Ogden and Richards (1953).

13 Langer (1951): 55–6.

14 Modified from Ogden and Richards (1944): 11.

15 Langer (1951).

16 Modified from Langer (1951): 69.

17 Frisby (1979): 156.

18 For clear expositions of the evidence and some speculation see Springer and Deutsch (1981) and Blakemore (1977). A good summary is given by Meares (1977).

The evidence at present suggests that the right and left cerebral hemispheres in most people 'think' in different styles. The usually dominant left hemisphere is verbal, sequential, analytic, and mathematical, whereas the right is non-verbal, visuo-spatial, simultaneous, synthetic, intuitive, and musical. The role of the 'lower' older 'reptilian', and 'paleo-mammalian' parts of the brain is less clear. MacLean (1969) speculates that our lowest reptile brain is visceral and has instinctual 'memories' based on ancestral behaviours. The paleo-limbic system generates those behaviours which, concerned with such crude affects as hunger, thirst, cold and warmth, subserve self-preservation, e.g. feeding and fighting.

Some writers (e.g. Ornstein 1972) have argued that the verbal ordered culture of the Western world is dominated by the left hemispheres and that there is a need for a development of the right side with those more artistic and mystic activities which are more evident in cultures of the East. This view is consistent with the approach of this book. It suggests that in psychotherapy we need to pay closer attention to the importance of visual arts and music. Maybe, as was believed in ancient Greece, the cadences of a flute are more healing than the most elegant verbal formulation. But, as I shall suggest, the ideal is a union of the two in imagination. Blakemore (1977) puts it well:

> 'What we should be striving to achieve for ourselves and our brains is not a pampering of one hemisphere to the neglect of the other (whether right or left), or their independent development, but the marriage and harmony of the two.' (p. 165)

Two points are important.

(a) The activity of the emotional, 'reptilian', 'paleo-mammalian' parts of the brain must not be forgotten. Blakemore's 'marriage' is part of a 'family'.

    (b) There are some persons (e.g. perhaps stammerers, like myself) in whom the lateralization is not clear-cut and there is no definite dominance.
19 Shakespeare, *A Midsummer Nights Dream*, V, i: 4–6.
20 Wordsworth (1805), *The Prelude*, II, ll. 208–9, 222–4, in Wordsworth (1971).

Chapter 6

1 Mill (1873) The following page numbers refer to Columbia University edition (1960).
2 94.
3 95.
4 96.
5 97.
6 99.
7 36–7.
8 99.
9 104–05.
10 106–07.
11 MacLeish (1960), Chapter 3: 52–65; Chapter 4: 66–86.
12 Ibid.: 53, 55.
13 Ibid.: 67.
14 Ibid.: 64.
15 Wordsworth (1798), *Tintern Abbey*: l. 48. In Wordsworth (1936): 164.
16 Coleridge (1827).
17 Wordsworth (1798). See Note 15: l. 28.
18 Asch (1958) and Watts (1978)
19 Pollio *et al.* (1977)
20 Köhler (1925): 99.
21 See e.g. 'Transitional Objects and Transitional Phenomena', Winnicott (1971), Chapter 1: 1–25.
22 The metaphor is from Jung. A critical review of Jung's concept of archetypes is to be found in Hobson (1973). A recent discussion is by Samuels (1983).
23 Jung uses the metaphor of the symbol as a transformer. See e.g. his essay 'On Psychic Energy' (1948) *Collected Works* VIII: 3–66.
24 The terms are taken from Langer (1953).
25 *Troilus and Cressida*, V, iii: 63.
26 The notion is developed by Read (1948), Chapter 1: 15–37.
27 The borrowings and modifications have been discussed by many critics. A few examples are Read (1948): 20; Richards (1962); Prickett (1970); Barfield (1974): 213.
28 The notion of 'structures' in the organization of human experience and behaviour, with a 'fit' between 'internal' and 'external' forms, was a concern of the Romantic movement in the late eighteenth and early nineteenth centuries. A pattern-making tendency, a dynamic equilibrium of 'inner' and 'outer' shapes, has recently been a focus of attention in different fields. Lévi-

Strauss in anthropology (Leach 1970) and Chomsky in linguistics (Lyons 1970, Chomsky 1972), have emphasized the importance of innate potenti- alities or 'deep structures' in shaping human experience and behaviour. As argued by Meares (1977, Chapter 2), their speculations have affinities with Jung's notion of archetypes.

29 Read (1948): 10.
30 Letter to J.H. Reynolds, 21 or 22 September, 1818. In Keats (1954): 168.
31 Letter to J. Taylor, 27 February 1818. In Keats (1954): 84.
32 Collingwood (1963). See especially pp. 283–85, and Langer (1953): 388.
33 Blake (1966): 596. From the 'Public Address'.

Chapter 7

1 Readable summaries are by Boyle (1971) and Gilhooly (1982). In focusing on problem-solving I have been much influenced by Bourne, Ekstrand, and Dominowski (1971).
2 Bourne, Ekstrand, and Dominowski (1971): 8.
3 Many other similar striking accounts are given in the literature of creative thought. See e.g. Gruber, Terrell, and Wertheimer (1962), Koestler (1964), and Storr (1972).
4 Kekulé Memorial Lecture (Japp 1897).
5 Ibid.
6 Ibid.
7 Ibid.
8 Ibid.
9 Dewey (1010).
10 Coleridge (1817): 167.
11 Jung (1928): 214.
12 Coleridge (1817): 174.
13 Galton (1879, 1907). A long extract is quoted by Lewis (1967) to which most of the following page numbers refer.
14 Lewis (1967): 57.
15 Freud recommended an attitude of 'evenly suspended attention'. This meant that the therapist should 'avoid as far as possible reflection and the construction of conscious expectations, not to try to fix anything that he heard particulary in his memory, and by these means to catch the drift of the patient's unconscious with his own unconscious' (Freud 1922: 239). See also Freud (1912): 111.
16 Lewis (1967): 57.
17 Free association, the 'fundamental rule of psychoanalysis', means reporting everything that comes to mind, that 'occurs to . . . self-perception' and 'not to give way to critical objections' by rejecting associations as 'not suffi- ciently important', 'irrelevant', or 'meaningless' (Freud 1925: 40). See also Freud (1909): 31–2.
18 Lewis (1967): 59.
19 Lewis (1967): 59 60.
20 Hobbes (1651): 69.

21 Ibid.: 69.

22 Ibid.: 69f.

23 Some examples are Freud (1916–17) – primary and secondary process; Jung (1952: 7–33) – directed and fantasy-thinking; Piaget (1959) – linear and non-linear; and McKellar (1957) – 'A and R' thinking. Meares discusses the question (Meares 1977: 93–110).

24 Neisser (1967).

25 Coleridge (1802), *Dejection: An Ode*: l. 86. In *Poems* (1912): 366. Coleridge's reflections on imagination and the symbol have been discussed by very many critics. See e.g. Richards (1962), Prickett (1970), and Coburn (1974). Key extracts from his writings are ordered with comments and notes in Hill (1978).

An important discussion of the nature of imagination is by Warnock (1976). She critically presents the thought of Wordsworth and Coleridge together with that of Hume, Kant, Sartre, and Wittgenstein.

26 For a brief, scholarly account drawing upon unpublished material see Coburn (1974). A short, clear, and readable account of Coleridge's life and work is provided by Grant (1972).

27 Every student of method in science and art should read Coleridge's 'Essays on the Principles of Method' (Coleridge 1818, I: 448–542).

28 Coleridge (1817): 48–9.

29 Ibid.: 49. See also Coleridge (1818) I: 110.

30 Wordsworth (1805), Preface to *Lyrical Ballads*: 21. In Wordsworth and Coleridge (1805).

31 Coleridge loved coining, or, better, constructing words (See Barfield 1974). He says that he devised the word 'esemplastic' by conjoining Greek words which might mean 'shape into one'. Writing of his word 'esemplastic', he says 'having to convey a new sense, I thought that a new term would both aid the recollection of my meaning, and prevent its being confounded with the usual import of the word imagination'. At that time 'imagination' was often used for facile adornments, which Coleridge relegates to 'fancy'. He somewhat aggressively states that the man of the world who insists that we employ only terms as occur in 'common conversation' is a pedant: 'pedantry consists in the use of words unsuitable to the time, place and company' (Coleridge 1817: 91).

In writing this book I have found it difficult to avoid the pedantry (or worse) of 'he' and 'she'. One example is the use of 'mankind'. I do not know what is suitable to my time, place, and company; or, indeed, where I, myself, stand.

32 Coleridge (1817):167.

33 Ibid.: 167.

34 Ibid.: 167.

35 Ibid.: 169.

36 Ibid.: 174.

37 Ibid.: 174.

38 Coleridge (1827).

39 Coleridge (1817): 174.

40 Blake (1966), *Jerusalem*: Plate 5: ll. 18–20.

41 From an unpublished Notebook. Quoted by Coburn (1974): 32.

42 I have been influenced by the great weight given to the word 'notice' by Thomas Hardy in the fine poem *Afterwards* (Hardy 1928: 521):

> 'When the Present has latched its postern behind my tremulous stay,
> And the May month flaps its glad green leaves like wings
> Delicate-filmed as new-spun silk, will the neighbours say
> "He was a man who used to notice such things"?'

A 'gazer' regards 'a dewfall – hawk' or a 'wind-warped upland thorn' as familiar sights but ' "He was one who had an eye for such mysteries" '. After his death, a 'crossing breeze cuts a pause' in the bell's 'outrollings': ' "He hears it not now, but used to notice such things" '.

43 ll. 204–05.

44 Coleridge (1816), CC, vi: 30.

45 Coleridge (1794–1819) *Notebooks*, Entries II, 2546 17. 104.

46 See discussion by Coburn (1974): 21–5.

47 Tillich, *Theology of Culture*: 56–7, quoted in Prickett (1970): 15.

48 Tillich (1957): 43.

49 Whalley (1974): 16–17.

50 Whitehead (1925): 89.

Chapter 8

1 Conrad (1897): Preface.

2 Conrad (1897): Preface.

3 Magnus (1885).

4 Perhaps there is evidence of affiliative eye-to-eye looking between animals other than man. I have discovered none. Without doubt this occurs between dogs and human beings.

5 Most blind children do not achieve 'I' in a stable form. Fraiberg, in a careful study, remarks that our scientific imagination is 'strained to reconstruct this process' and goes on:

> 'The blind child's route to "I" and self is a perilous one. Many blind children do not make it. In the blind child population a very large number of children at school age or later do not have "I" or other self-reference pronouns in their vocabularies.'
>
> (Fraiberg 1977: 270).

Fraiberg comments that we have no difficulty in understanding why the use of the pronoun 'I' is delayed in blind children. 'The more difficult problem is to understand how the blind child achieves this prodigious feat' (p. 270).

Bee (1981) underlines the importance of mutual gaze for the creation of a feeling bond between mother and baby.

6 In English there are metaphors with regard to higher-order conceptions in which vision and looking are vehicles (e.g. a 'far-seeing idea') but I have not

discovered any relating to more elementary sensations.

7 See e.g. O.K. Bouwsma, 'Moore's Theory of Sense-Data', in Warnock (1976): 18–19.
8 Tomkins (1963), especially chapters 16, 17, 18, 19.
9 Quoted by Tomkins (1963): 161.
10 Quoted by Tomkins (1963): 166.
11 Hobson (1984).
12 Coleridge (1794–1819) *Notebook*, Entries I, 848: 4.123; I, 1250; 21.214.
13 Discussed at length by Tomkins (1963): 512–29.
14 Coleridge. *The Rime of the Ancient Mariner*, 1834 version (in Coleridge 1912), hereafter referred to as *A.M.*, ll. 257–62.
15 Lifton (1965): 16.
16 *A.M.*: ll. 263–66.
17 Coleridge (1818): 109–10.
18 *A.M.*: ll. 354–66.
19 Conrad (1897): Preface.

Chapter 9

1 Ellenberger (1970). See especially Chapter 4: 182–215.
2 Blake (1966), *Jerusalem*: Pl. 5: l. 20.
3 I follow Tomkins (1963), chapters 16 and 17: 118–203.
4 Tomkins (1963): Chapter 16.
5 Quoted by Tomkins (1963).
6 Blake (1966): 154. 'The Marriage of Heaven and Hell':

> 'If the doors of perception were cleansed every thing
> would appear to man as it is, infinite.'

7 Shaw (1907), *Major Barbara*: Act III.
8 Lao Tzu (1973).
9 Wordsworth (1850), *The Prelude*, Book I. In Wordsworth (1971); ll. 340–50.
10 Wordsworth (1850), *The Prelude*. II: ll. 401–05. In Wordsworth (1971).
11 Franck (1973): 10–11.
12 I draw mainly on what, in my view, is his clearest exposition of peak experiences (Maslow 1959). Maslow's general approach is given in Maslow (1968) and (1970).
13 Hamsey (1957).
14 Maslow (1959).
15 Ruskin (1903): 76–162. Discussed by King (1966): 88–94.
16 Coleridge. See Note 36 to Chapter 7.
17 Bruner (1962).
18 Coleridge, See Chapter 7.
19 A. Hobson (1963) has modified Blake's (1966) original 'Till we have built Jerusalem/In England's green & pleasant Land' (Blake 1966, *Milton*: Pl. 1: ll. 15–16). The phrase 'builded here' comes earlier.
20 Otto (1936).

21 Tillich (1977).
22 Wordsworth (1936): 377. *The Tables Turned*: ll. 21–4.
23 Conrad (1897): Preface.
24 Conrad, letter to Cunninghame Graham, 14 January 1898, quoted in Baines (1971): 537.

Chapter 10

1 Shakespeare, *Richard III*, V, iii: 180–91 (Arden edition).
2 ll. 202–03.
3 Wordsworth (1805), *The Prelude*, I: ll. 360–61. In Wordsworth (1971).
4 The puzzling notion of 'self' has been discussed in very many different ways since the times of William James. In 1910, James (1962) distinguished 'I', the knower and doer, from 'me' or 'myself' as being 'known', 'experienced' (James 1962).

A current fashion (not discussed, but taken account of in this book) derives from the ideas of Kohut (1971, 1977).

The problems are discussed well by Redfearn (1983) and by Meares (1977 and 1985 in press).

I deliberately bypass the many practical, linguistic, philosophical, and indeed metaphysical problems. Some are real issues: many are verbal confusions. Returning to William James, I speak of 'I' and 'myself'. For James 'myself' embraced my body, my family, my social self, and also a 'spiritual' self.

Although he is unlikely to agree with my position, I am deeply grateful both personally and professionally to the outstanding work of Michael Fordham (e.g. Fordham 1979).
5 Jung's notion of 'the self' is elaborated throughout his works. Some extracts which discuss the mandala (referred to in this chapter) are presented in Jung (1983): Part 7.
6 Morris (1972).
7 Jung (1952), *Collected Works* V: xxv; and 1963; Chapters 6 and 7.
8 Blake recounts how Isaiah and Ezekiel dined and conversed with him.
9 Mair (1977).
10 Jung (1963): Chapters 6 and 7.
11 I have given a brief personal account in 'Living with Stammer', *Changes*, 1984.
12 Jung has been mentioned. There are affinities in a number of other approaches to psychotherapy. A succinct account is given by Rowan (1983) who has developed a therapeutically relevant concept of 'sub-personalities'.
13 Bowlby (1980): 44–74.
14 Hilgard (1973, 1974).
15 Hilgard quoted in Bowlby (1980): 58–9.
16 Shakespeare, *Henry VI Part III*, I, i: 30.
17 Shakespeare, *Richard III*, V, iii: 193–5.
18 A. Hobson (1972): 99–123.

19 The question interested Jung and perhaps too little attention has been paid to his early studies on the psychology of *dementia praecox* (Jung 1907). See Freeman *et al.* (1958) for a discussion of the psychodynamics of schizophrenics.

20 Mair (1977).

21 See e.g. Meares (1977).

22 The problem of 'internal' and 'external' has been discussed by phenomenologists. See Chapter 2, Note 5.

23 Meares and Hobson (1977).

24 See Note 22.

25 Winnicott (1971): 68.

26 See Chapter 16.

27 A.N. Whitehead, a sadly neglected philosopher, conceived of a continuous organic process of creation, a balance of 'law' and 'novelty', in which 'mind' and 'matter' were not distinct. Consciousness is not all or none. It is a matter of degree, of organization. Maybe a stone has a germ of 'consciousness'! A good summary of his 'process' philosophy is given in Barbour (1966): 439–63.

Chapter 11

1 What I term an 'explanatory hypothesis' is very similar to H. Ezriel's concept of an 'interpretation'. Ezriel (e.g. 1952, 1856–57) regards an interpretation as making a connection between three types of relation: (a) a 'required relationship 'which a person adopts in order to escape from (b) a dangerous 'avoided relationship' which he or she believes will result in (c) a catastrophic 'calamity'.

2 Research on teaching on the model has begun in Manchester (Goldberg *et al.* 1984, Maguire *et al.* 1984). This is being continued by F. Margison in the North West Region. At the Medical Research Unit, Sheffield, D.A. Shapiro and his co-workers are studying the short-term effectiveness of the model as compared with other more prescriptive methods of therapy.

Chapter 12

1 Russell (1967): 146. The passage is quoted at length in Chapter 16 p. 267.

2 See Note 42 to Chapter 7.

3 Meares and Hobson (1977).

4 It is most common with persons who are termed 'borderline' but in my view can occur in any interview.

5 See Meares (1976, 1977, 1980).

6 James (1962): 168.

7 See Meares and Hobson (1977).

8 Winnicott (1971): 56.

9 Freud (1922): 239.

10 Freud (1912).
11 Meares and Hobson (1977).
12 Videotapes: *A Conversational Model of Psychotherapy: A Teaching Method* can be obtained from Tavistock Publications. Three tapes make up this training package. 1: 'Basic Therapeutic Skills' shows examples of techniques. 2: 'Developing a Therapeutic Conversation' demonstrates the progress of one interview by me. 3: 'Structured Teaching of Psychotherapy' can be used by a student with a trainer or alone.
13 Goldberg *et al.* (1984), Maguire *et al.* (1984).

Chapter 13

1 McCabe (1968): 17.
2 McCabe (1968): 19.
3 Ferenczi (1930, 1950).
4 Freud, fearing excesses, took exception to Ferenczi's view. The dangers appear to be evident in some recent psychotherapeutic movements.
5 Suttie (1935).
6 Bowlby has developed his findings and ideas in three large scholarly books (Bowlby 1969, 1973, 1980). An excellent summary is Bowlby (1979).
7 Suttie (1935).
8 See Note 28 to Chapter 6.
9 Bruner (1969).
10 Bruner (1969). My schematic and naive comments about infant development take too little account of a complex, rapidly developing field of knowledge. An exhaustive and exciting account is given by Bower (1979), who gives not only a catalogue of facts but also suggests an overall framework. For instance, he goes beyond bland general terms about 'social behaviour' and distinguishes 'I-thou relations and 'I-it relations' (p. 294). He raises, and discusses, the question of whether or not the infant has a set of behaviours that are specific to people, as distinct from things.
11 See e.g. various essays in Koestler and Smythies (1969).
12 See Note 6 above.
13 Parkes (1972). See also e.g. Worden (1983).
14 Discussed by Bowlby (1980). An earlier work which raises questions still worthy of consideration is Rutter (1972).

Chapter 14

1 Freud (1984) first introduced the term 'defence'. His daughter Anna wrote the classic account (Freud, A. 1963). The beginner will find short and clear accounts of psychoanalytical approaches in Brown and Pedder (1979: 25–33) and in Malan (1979, e.g. p. 8).
2 Butler (c 1736) writes that 'any particular anything' is 'a one or a whole,

made up of several parts; but yet, that the several parts even considered as a whole, do not complete the idea, unless in the notion of a whole, you include the relations and respects which those parts have to each other. Every work, both of Nature and of art, is a system; . . . (it) is for some use or purpose out of and beyond itself' (pp. 340–41). There is 'a conduciveness to this one or more ends' (p. 341). Butler uses the notion in his penetrating formulations of psychology and of ethics.

3 The literature is immense. There are good summaries in Koestler and Smythies (1969) and Waddington (1977).

4 See Waddington (1977): 111. A suggestion of support for the notion of 'steps' in psychotherapy is given by Shapiro and Hobson (1972).

5 The definition of what constitutes a 'need' is arbitrary. I find Bishop Butler's (c 1736) hierarchical classification just as helpful as many modern specul- ations (and they are no more than speculations). In many aspects Butler's system is similar to, but better than, that of Maslow (1970).

6 The terms 'arousal' and 'anxiety' are used in a broad sense.

7 Yerkes and Dodson (1908).

8 The word 'regression' is used for this process. It does not necessarily imply a return to an earlier state.

9 See van Gennep (1960) and Hobson (1965).

10 A great danger is to reify 'drives', 'impulses', or psychological 'contents'.

11 e.g. Yalom (1980).

12 Butler stressed the importance of 'cool self-love' and his great commandment was 'Reverence thyself'.

13 Maier's work (1949, 1956) is critically discussed by Yates (1962): 4–65.

14 See Yates (1962).

15 Jung (1948).

16 Jung (e.g. 1948) uses the term *participation mystique*, taken from the anthropologist Lévy-Bruhl.

17 Winnicott (1971): 38. He states, 'Psychotherapy has to do with two people playing together'.

18 Balint (1968).

19 Festinger's (e.g. 1959, 1964) concept of 'cognitive dissonance' and its resolution as one formulation of 'conflict' has greatly influenced my thinking.

Chapter 15

1 In certain cases, when carefully selected (Hobson 1953) convulsive therapy is necessary and appropriate. In my view, certain drugs are not antithetical to psychotherapy.

2 See Note 19 to Chapter 14. A commitment in a state of dissonance results in a search for experiences which will justify the choice.

3 Funeral meals are a means of strengthening the bonds between the survivors but also are a symbolical taking-in of the dead person (Hobson 1970).

4 Wilde (1966: 843–60) *Ballad of Reading Gaol*. See 1, verse 7, and 6, verse 3.

5 Some of Malan's (1979) examples give this impression.
6 The problems of research in this and other areas of psychotherapy are made evident by a brief look at the voluminous review edited by Garfield and Bergin (1978).

Chapter 16

1 Goldberg et al. (1984), Maguire et al. (1984). See Note 2 to Chapter 11.
2 Hopkins (1931), *Candle Indoors*: 46.
3 Coleridge (1912), *A.M.*: ll. 79–82.
4 Winnicott (1971): 92.
5 A few examples are Little (1958, 1966) and Kohut (1977).
6 Perhaps I have put too little emphasis on the importance of infantile destructive rage which has been elaborated by Klein and her followers. See e.g. Segal (1979).
7 Russell (1967): 146.
8 A comprehensive account of the literature on loneliness is presented in Peplau and Perlman (1982). There is a paucity of hard data. Personality characteristics, cultural norms, social changes (such as death, divorce, physical separation), and varying desires and capacities during the life-cycle, precipitate, contribute, or predispose to loneliness. But they do not necessarily cause it.
9 Jung (1932): 344–45.
10 Jung (1963): 186.
11 Paul Tillich usually speaks of 'non-being' (see Macleod 1973) but I do not think that he uses the term 'no-being'.
12 Fromm-Reichmann (1959): 14f.
13 Wynne et al. (1958).
14 Suttie (1935).
15 Shakespeare: Sonnet 129.
16 Conrad (1902): 150.
17 Conrad (1902): 151.
18 Conrad (1900): 180.
19 Conrad (1897) Preface, p. xi.
20 Conrad, letter to Cunninghame Graham, 14 January, 1898. Quoted by Baines (1971): 537.
21 Wordsworth (1805) *The Prelude* II l. 223. In Wordsworth (1971).
22 Blake (1966) *The Marriage of Heaven and Hell*: Plate 4.
23 Taylor (1974): 81.
24 In an interesting paper 'A Black Hole in Psyche' Giles Clark (1983) describes a patient's experience of a black hole and, if I understand aright, Clark suggests that this is an 'archetypal image'.
25 The 'Dark Night of the Soul' is an evocative phrase which is often used in a vague and indiscriminate way. Although a long argument is called for, I consider that I am staying close to the kernel of meaning in the writings of St John of the Cross (1953). In reading his poetry and prose concerning

different kinds of 'dark night', it is important to remember his extreme ascetic practices.

26 Quoted by Hughes (1980).
27 Hughes (1980): 281.
28 St John of the Cross (1953). I prefer the literal translation of this line.
29 Russell (1967): 146.
30 Russell (1967): 209.
31 Russell (1967): 207.
32 Fromm-Reichmann (1959): 1.
33 Blake (1966) *Milton*: Plate 35, l. 45, p. 526.
34 Blake (1966) *Milton*: Plate 29, l. 1–3, p. 516.
35 Wordsworth (1850), *The Prelude*: XII: ll. 208–10, 214–15. In Wordsworth (1971).
36 Butler (c. 1736): 345. Preface to 'Fifteen Sermons'. He stresses that by 'conscience' he does not mean 'to abstain from gross wickedness', but to live as a 'whole'. 'This', he says, 'is the true meaning of that ancient precept, *Reverence thyself'*. (See Chapter 14, Note 12.)
37 Coleridge (1912), *A.M.*: ll. 232–33.
38 Wynne *et al.* (1958).
39 Whitehead (1926): 16f.
40 Wordsworth (1805) *The Prelude*. XIII: ll. 194–97. In Wordsworth (1971).
41 'Unknowing' has a more positive implication (like 'no-being'). As, e.g. in *The Cloud of Unknowing* (1956).
42 Donne (1633), *The Extasie*: ll. 41–4, 71–2.

A NOTE ON SOURCES, REFERENCES, AND FURTHER READING

In the Introduction I have said that this book is a personal statement of *some* basic ways in which I engage in, and conceptualize, two-person psychotherapy. I believe that my view has some generality but I do not argue the case. I do not engage in controversy, nor do I, overtly, take proper account of contrary opinions.

Sadly, I do little justice to many pioneers whose work has 'turned to blood' within me. I mention only the achievement of Sigmund Freud who is hardly quoted. His careful observations, brilliant insights, and far-flung speculations are, as W.H. Auden (1939) put it, a 'climate of opinion'.

The references are highly selected as being strictly relevant to my theme. They are merely signposts for future dialogues.

I hope that a raw beginner, facing the problems of varied clinical situations, will find practical help in what I have to say. But there are large lacunae. I dislike reading lists. I have never followed one and I find recommendations for 'Further Reading' irritating and often exasperating. I hope that the young reader will explore those avenues which she or he finds exciting. But perhaps a critical perusal of some balanced introductions to individual and group psychotherapy (e.g. Brown and Pedder 1979, Zaro *et al.* 1977) will be of help to some students. Personal approaches, with many technical points neglected by me, are well presented by Storr (1979) and Cox (1978). Malan (1979) clearly outlines a psychoanalytically-based conflict model for brief psychotherapy. Expositions of varied current systems, written by exponents of the different methods, are to be found in Corsini (1973). The summary of Ford and Urban (1963) is still important in that it pays tribute to Alfred Adler and Harry Stack Sullivan who have both been potent influences in my development.

Jung, as a person, a thinker, and a brilliant short-term psychotherapist, has profoundly influenced me. A somewhat different approach to Jungian psychotherapy is clearly presented by my esteemed teacher, Michael Fordham (1978). His book gives many important references which, for reasons of space, I have not included.

A psychotherapist should be acquainted with the history and present scene of academic psychology. There are many overviews and I suggest only those which I have found most helpful: Beloff (1973), Hall and Lindzey (1978).

Literary, philosophical, and religious matters present a great problem. I trust that the notes are sufficient pointers to areas which the reader, if he wishes, can explore for himself, e.g. the thoughts of Coleridge, Butler, Wittgenstein, Tillich, and St John of the Cross.

I hope that any reader, without specialized knowledge, can with some diligence, follow and question my assertions, ideas, and attitudes.

I write a book about personal relationships. That being so, there is an inevitable bias, evident in the references, towards ideas which have arisen in conversations with friends.

REFERENCES

Asch, S.E. (1958) The Metaphor: A Psychological Inquiry. In R. Tagiuri and L. Petrullo (eds) *Person Perception and Interpersonal Behaviour*. Stanford: Stanford University Press.

Auden, W.H. (1939) In Memory of Sigmund Freud. *Collected Shorter Poems, 1927–1957*. London: Faber & Faber.

Austin, J.L. (1965) *How to Do Things with Words*. Oxford: Clarendon Press.

Baines, J. (1971) *Joseph Conrad*. Harmondsworth: Penguin Books.

Balint, M. (1968) *The Basic Fault*. London: Tavistock Publications.

Barbour, I.G. (1966) *Issues in Science and Religion*. London: SCM Press.

Barfield, O. (1974) Coleridge's Enjoyment of Words. In J. Beer (ed.) *Coleridge's Variety*. London and Basingstoke: Macmillan.

Bee, H. (1981) *The Developing Child*. New York: Harper International Edition.

Beer, J. (1978) *Wordsworth and the Human Heart*. London and Basingstoke: Macmillan.

Beloff, J. (1973) *Psychological Sciences*. London: Crosby Lockwood Staples.

Binswanger, L. (1963) *Being-in-the-World*. (Selected papers of Ludwig Binswanger.) New York, London: Basic Books.

Blake, W. (1966) *Complete Writings*. Oxford: Oxford University Press.

Blakemore, C. (1977) *Mechanics of the Mind*. Cambridge: Cambridge University Press. (BBC Reith Lectures, 1976.)

Boss, M. (1963) *Psychoanalysis and Daseinanalysis*. New York, London: Basic Books.

Bourne, L.E., Ekstrand, B.R., and Dominowski, R.L. (1971). *The Psychology of*

Thinking. Englewood Cliffs, NJ: Prentice-Hall.

Bower, T.G.R. (1979) *Human Development*. San Francisco: W.H. Freeman.

Bowlby, J. (1969) *Attachment*. Vol. I. of *Attachment and Loss*. London: The Hogarth Press and Institute of Psychoanalysis.

—— (1973) *Separation: Anxiety and Anger*. Vol. II of *Attachment and Loss*. Harmondsworth: Penguin Books.

—— (1979) *The Making and Breaking of Affectional Bonds*. London: Tavistock Publications.

—— (1980) *Loss, Sadness and Depression*. London: The Hogarth Press and Institute of Psychoanalysis.

Boyle, D.G. (1971) *Language and Thinking in Human Development*. London: Hutchinson University Library.

Breuer, J. and Freud, S. (1895) Studies in Hysteria (Standard Edition. Vol. II.)

Brown, D., and Pedder, J. (1979) *Introduction to Psychotherapy*. London: Tavistock Publications.

Bruner, J.S. (1962) The Conditions of Creativity. In H.E. Gruber, G. Terrell, and M. Wertheimer (eds) *Contemporary Approaches to Creative Thinking*. New York: Atherton Press, London: Prentice Hall, pp. 1–30.

—— (1969) On Voluntary Action and Its Hierarchical Structure. In Koestler and Smythies (1969): 161–79.

Bruner, J.S., Goodnow, J.J. and Austin, G.A. (1956) *A Study of Thinking*. New York, London, Sydney: John Wiley & Sons.

Buber, M. (1937) *I and Thou*. Edinburgh: T. & T. Clark.

—— (1963) *The Way of Man, According to the Teachings of Hasidism*. London: Vincent Stuart.

Burton, S.H. (1972) *The West Country*. London: Robert Hale & Co.

—— (1974) *The Criticism of Poetry*. London: Longman.

—— (1980) *People and Communication*. London and New York: Longman.

Butler, J. (c 1736) Fifteen Sermons. In J. Angus (ed.) *The Analogy of Religion to the Constitution and Cause of Nature, also Fifteen Sermons*. London: The Religious Tract Society (no date).

Chomsky, N. (1972) *Language and Mind*. New York: Harcourt Brace Jovanovich.

Clark, G.A. (1983) A Black Hole in Psyche. In *Harvest* (Analytical Psychology Club, London) **29**: 67–80.

The Cloud of Unknowing (1956). 'A Book of Contemplation the which is called THE CLOUD OF UNKNOWING in which a soul is oned with God.' Edited from the British Museum MS. Introduction E. Underhill. London: John M. Watkins.

Coburn, K. (1974) *The Self Conscious Imagination*. A study of the Coleridge notebooks in celebration of the bi-centenary of his birth 21 October, 1772. Riddell Memorial Lectures, Oxford University Press.

Coleridge, S.T. (1794–1819). *The Notebooks of Samuel Taylor Coleridge*. Ed. K. Coburn. Vol. I 1794–1804 (1957), Vol. II 1804–1808 (1961), Vol III 1808–1819 (1973). New York: Pantheon Books. (Bollingen Series L.)

—— (1816) *The Stateman's Manual*. *The Collected Works of Samuel Taylor Coleridge* VI. London: Routledge & Kegan Paul, Princeton: Princeton University Press.

—— (1817) *Biographia Literaria*. (Everyman Library No. 11.) London, Dent:

New York, Dutton 1956.

—— (1818) *The Friend. I. The Collected Works of Samuel Taylor Coleridge* IV. London: Routledge & Kegan Paul.

—— (1827) *Specimens of the Table Talk of the late S.T. Coleridge.* London and New York: Oxford University Press, 1917.

—— (1912) *The Poems of Samuel Taylor Coleridge.* London: Oxford University Press.

—— (1967) *The Collected Works of Samuel Taylor Coleridge.* London: Routledge & Kegan Paul, Princeton: Princeton University Press. (Bollingen Series LXXV.)

Collingwood, R.G. (1963) *The Principles of Art.* London: Oxford University, Press.

Conrad, J. (1897) *The Nigger of the Narcissus – a Tale of the Sea.* London: Dent, 1946.

—— (1900) *Lord Jim – a Tale.* London: Dent, 1946.

—— (1902) *Heart of Darkness.* London: Dent, 1946.

—— (1904) *Nostromo – a tale of the Seaboard.* London: Dent, 1946.

—— (1921) *Notes on Life and Letters.* London: Dent, 1946.

Corsini, R. (ed.) (1973) *Current Psychotherapies.* Itasca, Illinois: Peacock.

Cox, M. (1978) *Structuring the Therapeutic Process: Compromise with Chaos.* Oxford: Pergamon Press.

Dewey, J. (1910) *How We Think.* Boston: Heath.

Donne, J. (1633) *The Poems of John Donne.* London: Oxford University Press, 1939.

Ellenberger, H.F. (1970) *The Discovery of the Unconscious.* London: Penguin Books.

Eliot, T.S. (1944) *Four Quartets.* London: Faber & Faber.

Ezriel, H. (1952) Notes on Psychoanalytical Group Therapy: Interpretation and Research. *Psychiatry,* **15.**

—— (1956–57) Experimentation within the Psychoanalytic Session. *British Journal of the Philosophy of Science,* **7.**

Ferenczi, S. (1930) The Principle of Relaxation and Neocatharsis. *International Journal of Psychoanalysis* 11: 428–43.

—— (1950) *Further Contributions to the Theory and Technique of Psychoanalysis.* London: The Hogarth Press, pp. 214f.

Festinger, L. (1959) *A Theory of Cognitive Dissonance.* London: Tavistock Publications.

—— (1964) *Conflict, Decision and Dissonance.* London: Tavistock Publications.

Fisher, M. and Stricker, G. (eds) (1982) *Intimacy.* New York and London: Plenum Press.

Ford, D.H. and Urban, H.B. (1963) *Systems of Psychotherapy.* London, New York: John Wiley.

Fordham, M. (1978) *Jungian Psychotherapy: A Study in Analytical Psychotherapy.* Chichester, New York: John Wiley. (Wiley Series on Methods in Psychotherapy.)

—— (1979) The Self as an Imaginative Construct. *Journal of Analytical Psychology* 24: 1:18–30.

Fraiberg, S. (1977) *Insights from the Blind*. London: Souvenir Press.

Franck, F. (1973) *The Zen of Seeing*. London: Wildwood House.

Freeman, T., Cameron J.L. and McGhie, A. (1958) *Chronic Schizophrenia*. London: Tavistock Publications.

Freud, A. (1936) *The Ego and the Mechanisms of Defence*. London: The Hogarth Press.

Freud, S. (1894) *The Neuro-Psychoses of Defence*. Standard Edition III. London: The Hogarth Press and Institute of Psychoanalysis.

—— (1900) *The Interpretation of Dreams*. Standard Edition IV, V.

—— (1909) *Five Lectures on Psychoanalysis*. Standard Edition XI: 31–2.

—— (1912) *Recommendations to Physicians Practising Psychoanalysis*. Standard Edition XII.

—— (1916–17) *Introductory Lectures on Psychoanalysis*. Standard Edition XVI, III: 372ff.

—— (1922) *Two Encyclopaedia Articles*. Standard Edition XVIII: 239.

—— (1925) *An Autobiographical Study*. Standard Edition XX: 40.

Frisby, H.P. (1979) *Seeing*. Oxford: Oxford University Press.

Fromm-Reichmann, F. (1959) Loneliness. *Psychiatry* **22**:1.

Galton, F. (1879) Psychometric Facts. In *Nineteenth Century*, March. Quoted by A.J. Lewis (1967) *The State of Psychiatry*. London: Routledge & Kegan Paul.

—— (1907) *Inquiries into the Human Faculty and its Development*, 2nd edn. London: Everyman, New York: Dent.

Garfield, S.L. and Bergin, A.E. (eds) (1978) *Handbook of Psychotherapy and Behaviour Change*. New York, Chichester: John Wiley.

Gendlin, E.T. (1962) *Experiencing and the Creation of Meaning*. New York; The Free Press of Glencoe (a division of Macmillan).

—— (1973) Experiential Therapy. In Corsini (1973): 317–52.

Gennep, A. van (1960) *The Rites of Passage*. London: Routledge & Kegan Paul.

Gilhooly K.J. (1982) *Thinking. Directed, Undirected and Creative*. London, New York: Academic Press.

Goldberg, D.P., Hobson, R.F., Maguire, G.P., Margison, F.R., O'Dowd, T., Osborn, M. and Moss, S. (1984) The Classification and Assessment of a Method of Psychotherapy. *British Journal of Psychiatry* **144**: 567–75.

Grant, A. (1972) *A Preface to Coleridge*. London: Longman.

Gruber, H.E., Terrell, G. and Wertheimer, M. (1962) *Contemporary Approaches to Creative Thinking*. New York: Atherton Press, London: Prentice Hall.

Hall, C.S. and Lindzey, G. (1978) *Theories of Personality*. New York, Chichester: John Wiley.

Hamlyn, D.W. (1974) Person-Perception and Our Understanding of Others. In T. Mischel (ed.) *Understanding Other Persons*. Oxford: Basil Blackwell.

Hampshire, S. (1965) *Thought and Action*. London: Chatto & Windus.

Hardy, T. (1928) *Collected Poems*. London: Macmillan.

Harré, R. (1984) Social elements as Mind. *British Journal of Medical Psychology* **57** 127–35.

Harré, R. and Secord, P.F. (1972). *The Explanation of Social Behaviour*. Oxford: Basil Blackwell.

Hilgard, E.R. (1973) A Neodissociation Interpretation of Pain Reduction in Hypnosis. *Psychology Review* **80**: 306–411.
—— (1974) Toward a Neo-dissociation Theory: Multiple Cognitive Controls in Human Functioning. *Perspectives in Biology and Medicine* **17**: 301–16.
Hill, J.S. (1978) *Imagination in Coleridge*. London and Basingstoke: Macmillan.
Hinshelwood, R.D. and Manning, N. (eds) (1979). *Therapeutic Communities*. London: Boston and Henley.
Hobbes, T. (1651) *Leviathan*. Ed. J Plamenatz, London: Collins, 1962.
Hobson, A. (1963) *Symbols of Transformation in Poetry*. London: Guild of Pastoral Psychology. (Guild Lecture No. 120.)
—— (1972) *Full Circle*. London: Chatto & Windus.
Hobson, J.A. and McCarley R.W. (1977) The Brain as a Dream State Generator: An Activation-synthesis Hypothesis of the Dream Process. *American Journal of Psychiatry* **134**: 12.
Hobson, R.F. (1953) Prognostic Factors in Electric Convulsive Therapy. *Journal of Neurology, Neurosurgery & Psychiatry* **16**: 275.
—— (1959) An Approach to Group Analysis. *Journal of Analytical Psychology* **4**: 2.
—— (1964) Group Dynamics and Analytical Psychology. *Journal of Analytical Psychology* **9**: 1.
—— (1965) *The King Who Will Return*. London: Guild of Pastoral Psychology. (Guild Lecture No. 130.)
—— (1970) My Own Death. *New Blackfriars* October: 469–79.
—— (1971) Imagination and Amplification in Psychotherapy. *Journal of Analytical Psychology* **16**: 1.
—— (1973) The Archetypes of the Collective Unconscious. In M. Fordham, R. Gordon, J. Hubback, K. Lambert, and M. Williams (eds) *Analytical Psychology: A Modern Science*. The Library of Analytical Psychology. London: Academic Press.
—— (1974) Loneliness. *Journal of Analytical Psychology* **19**: 1.
—— (1979) The Messianic Community. In Hinshelwood and Manning (1979): 231–44.
—— (1984) The Curse in the Dead Man's Eye. *Changes* **2**, 2: 40–4.
Hobson, R.F. and Shapiro, D.A. (1970) The Personal Questionnaire as a Method of Assessing Change during Psychotherapy. *British Journal of Psychiatry* **117**: 541.
Hobson, R.P. (1982 unpublished) On People and Things: The Enigma of Autism. Paper presented to Manchester Medical Society, 23 November, 1982.
—— (1985) Piaget: On the Ways of Knowing in Childhood. In M. Rutter and L. Hersov (eds) *Child and Adolescent Psychiatry: Modern Approaches*. Oxford: Basil Blackwell.
Hopkins, G.M. (1931) *The Poems of Gerard Manley Hopkins*. Oxford: Oxford University Press.
Hughes, R. (1980) *The Shock of the New*. London: British Broadcasting Corporation.
James, W. (1962) *Psychology: Briefer Course*. London and New York: Collier.
Japp, F.R. (1897) Kekulé Memorial Lecture. London: Chemical Society.

Jenkins, D.E. (1967) *The Glory of Man*. London: SCM.

John of the Cross (1953) *The Complete Works of Saint John of the Cross*. London: Burns, Oates & Washbourne.

Jung, C.G. (1904–07) Studies in Word Association *Collected Works* II. London: Routledge & Kegan Paul.

—— (1907) The Psychology of Dementia Praecox. *Collected Works* III.

—— (1928) The Relations Between the Ego and the Unconscious. *Collected Works* VII.

—— (1932) Psychotherapists or the Clergy. *Collected Works* XI.

—— (1948) On Psychic Energy. *Collected Works* VIII: 3–66.

—— (1952) Symbols of Transformation. *Collected Works* V.

—— (1963) *Memories, Dreams, Reflections*. London: Collins and Routledge.

—— (1978) *Man and His Symbols*. London: Picador.

—— (1983) *Selected Writings*. London: Fontana.

Keats J. (1954) *Letters of John Keats*. London; Oxford University Press.

Keller, H. (1902) *The Story of My Life*. Garden City: Doubleday, Doran & Co., 1936.

Kelly, G.A. (1963) *The Psychology of the Unknown*. Columbus: Ohio State University (unpublished).

King, A. (1966) *Wordsworth and the Artist's Vision*. London: The Athlone Press.

Koestler, A. (1964). *The Act of Creation*. London: Hutchinson.

—— and Smythies, J.R. (eds) (1969) *Beyond Reductionism*. The Alpach Symposium 1968. London: Hutchinson.

Köhler, W. (1925) *The Mentality of Apes*. London, Kegan Paul.

Kohut, H. (1971) *The Analysis of Self*. New York: International Universities Press.

—— (1977) *The Restoration of the Self*. New York: International Universities Press.

Lambert, M.J., Shapiro, D.A., Bergin, A.E, and Berman J.S. (1985) The Evaluation of Therapeutic Outcomes. In Garfield and Bergin (in press).

Langer, S.K. (1951) *Philosophy in a New Key*. London: Geoffrey Cumberlege, Oxford University Press.

—— (1953) *Feeling and Form*. London: Routledge & Kegan Paul.

Lao Tzu (1973) *Tao Tê Ching*. London: Wildwood House.

Leach, E. (1970) *Lévi-Strauss*. London: Fontana/Collins.

Lewis, A.J. (1957) Jung's Early Work. *Journal of Analytical Psychology* 2: 2: 119–36. Reprinted in Lewis, A.J. (1967) *The State of Psychiatry*. London: Routledge & Kegan Paul, pp. 54–70.

Lifton, R.J. (1965) Psychological Effects of the Atomic Bomb in Hiroshima: The Theme of Death. In R. Fulton (ed.) *Death and Identity*. New York: John Wiley.

Little, M. (1958) On Delusional Transference (Transference Psychosis). *International Journal of Psychoanalysis* 39: 134–38.

—— (1966) Transference in Borderline States. *International Journal of Psychoanalysis* 47: 375–413.

Lyons, J. (1970) *Chomsky*. London: Fontana/Collins.

McCabe, H. (1968) *Law, Love and Language*. London and Sydney: Sheed & Ward.

McKellar, P. (1957) *Imagination and Thinking*. London: Cohen & West.

MacLean, P.D. (1969) The Paranoid Streak in Man. In A. Koestler and J.R.

Smythies (eds) *Beyond Reductionism*. London: Hutchinson, p. 258–78.

MacLeish, A. (1960) *Poetry and Experience*. Harmondsworth; Penguin Books.

Macleod, A.M. (1973) *Tillich: An Essay on the Role of Ontology in his Philosophical Theory*. London: George Allen & Unwin.

Magnus, H. (1885) *Die Sprache der Augen*. Wiesbaden.

Maguire, G.P., Goldberg, D.P., Hobson, R.F., Margison, F., Moss, S., and O'Dowd T. (1984) Evaluating the Teaching of a Method of Psychotherapy. *British Journal of Psychiatry* **144**: 575–80.

Maier, N.R.F. (1949) *Frustration: The Study of Behaviour without a Goal*. New York: McGraw-Hill.

—— (1956) Frustration Theory: Restatement and Extension. *Psychology Review* **63**: 370–88.

Mair, M. (1976) Metaphors for Living. In A.W. Landfield (ed.) *Nebraska Symposium on Motivation* Vol. 24. Lincoln, Nebraska: University of Nebraska Press.

—— (1977) The Community of Self. In D. Bannister (ed.) *New Perspectives in Personal Construct Theory*. London: Academic Press.

Malan, D.H. (1979) *Individual Psychotherapy and the Science of Psychodynamics*. London: Butterworth.

Maslow, A.H. (1959) Cognition of Being in Peak Experiences. In *The Journal of Genetic Psychology*. Reprinted in B.H. Stoodley (ed.) *Society and Self*. New York: The Free Press of Glencoe, 1962 pp. 645–68.

—— (1968) *Toward a Psychology of Being*. New York: Van Nostrand.

—— (1970) *Motivation and Personality*, New York: Evanston, London: Harper & Row.

May, R., Angel, E., and Ellenberger H.F. (eds) (1958). *Existence, A New Dimension in Psychiatry and Psychology*. New York: Basic Books.

Meares, R. (1976) The Secret. *Psychiatry* **39**: 258–65.

—— (1977) *The Pursuit of Intimacy*. Melbourne: Nelson.

—— (1980) Body Feeling in Human Relations: the Examples of Brancusi and Giacometti. *Psychiatry* **43**: 73–82.

—— (1983) Keats and the Impersonal Therapist: A Note on Empathy and the Therapeutic Screen. *Psychiatry* **46**: 73–82.

—— (1985) Metaphor and Reality: A Response to Roy Schafer. *Contemporary Psychoanalysis*. (in press)

Meares, R. and Hobson, R.F. (1977) The Persecutory Therapist. *British Journal of Medical Psychology* **50**: 349–59.

Mill, J.S. (1873) *Autobiography*. In Helen Taylor (ed.) *The Autobiography of John Stuart Mill*. New York and London: Columbia University Press, 1960.

Morris, C. (1972) *The Discovery of the Individual. 1050–1200* London: SPCK.

Morris, C.W. (1946) *Signs, Language and Behaviour*. Englewood Cliffs: Prentice Hall.

Munroe, R.L. (1957) *Schools of Psychoanalytic Thought*. London: Hutchinson.

Neisser, U. (1967) *Cognitive Psychology*. New York: Appleton-Century-Crofts.

Ogden, C.K. and Richards, I.A. (1944) *The Meaning of Meaning: A Study of the Influence of Language upon Thought and of the Science of Symbolism*. London: Routledge & Kegan Paul.

Ornstein, R.E. (1972) *The Psychology of Consciousness*. San Francisco: W.H. Freeman.

Ortony, A (ed.) (1979) *Metaphor and Thought*. Cambridge: Cambridge University Press.

Ortony, A., Reynolds, R.E., and Arter, J.A. (1978). Metaphor: Theoretical and Empirical Research. *Psychological Bulletin* **85**: 919–43.

Otto, R. (1936) *The Idea of the Holy*. London: Humphrey Milford. *Das Heilige* was first published in 1917. This translation is of the 9th German edition.

Parkes, C.M. (1972) *Bereavement: Studies of Grief in Adult Life*. New York: International Universities Press, London: Tavistock Publications.

Pears, D. (1971) *Wittgenstein*. London: Fontana/Collins.

Peplau, L.A. and Perlman, D. (1982) *Loneliness*. New York, Chichester: John Wiley.

Peters, R.S. (1958) *The Concept of Motivation*. London: Routledge & Kegan Paul.

Peursen, C.A. van (1969) *Ludwig Wittgenstein. An Introduction to his Philosophy*. London: Faber & Faber.

Piaget, J. (1959) *The Language and Thought of the Child*. London: Routledge & Kegan Paul, p. 43.

Pollio, H.R., Barlow, J.M., Fine, H.J., and Pollio, M.R. (1977) *Psychology and the Poetics of Growth*. London: Lawrence Erlbaum.

Polyani, M. (1958) *Personal Knowledge*. London: Routledge & Kegan Paul.

Powys, J.C. (1944) *The Art of Growing Old*. London: Jonathan Cape.

Prickett, S. (1970) *Coleridge and Wordsworth*. Cambridge: Cambridge University Press.

Ramsey, I.T. (1957) *Religious Language*. London: SCM.

Read, H. (1948) *The True Voice of Feeling*. London: Faber & Faber.

Redfearn, J.W.T. (1983) Ego and Self: Terminology. *Journal of Analytical Psychology* **28**: 91–106.

Richards, I.A. (1936) *The Philosophy of Rhetoric*. London: Oxford University Press.

—— (1962) *Coleridge on Imagination* London: Routledge & Kegan Paul.

Rilke, R.M. (1952) *Duino Elegies*. London: The Hogarth Press.

—— (1964) *The Notebooks of Malte Laurids Brigge*. New York: W.W. Norton.

—— (1966) *Die Aufzeichnungen des Malte Laurids Brigge*. In *Werke in sechs Bänden* V: 124f. Frankfurt am Main: Insel Verlag.

—— (1972) *The Notebook of Malte Laurids Brigge*. London: The Hogarth Press.

Rowan, J. (1983) Person as Group. In H.H. Blumberg, A.P. Hare, V. Kent, and M. Davies (eds) *Small Groups and Social Interactions*. New York, Chichester: John Wiley.

Ruesch, J. and Bateson, G. (1951) Communication. *The Social Matrix of Psychiatry*. New York: W.W. Norton.

Ruskin, J. (1903) *Modern Painters*. Library Edition. London.

Russell, B.A.W.R. (1967) *The Autobiography of Bertrand Russell (1872 – 1914)*. London: Allen & Unwin.

Rutter, M. (1972) *Maternal Deprivation Reassessed*. Harmondsworth: Penguin Books.

Samuels, A. (1983) The Theory of Archetypes in Jungian and Post-Jungian

Analytical Psychology. *International Review of Psycho-Analysis* **10**: 429.

Schafer, R. (1973) Action: Its Place in Psychoanalytic Interpretation and Theory. In *The Annual of Psychoanalysis*, Vol. I (1973). Quadrangle/New York Times Book Co.

Segal, H. (1979) *Klein*. Glasgow: Fontana/Collins. (Fontana Modern Masters, ed. F. Kermode.)

Shapiro, D.A. (1980) Science and Psychotherapy: The State of the Art. *British Journal of Medical Psychology* **53**: 1–10.

Shapiro, D.A. and R.F. Hobson. (1972) Change in Psychotherapy: a Single Case Study. *Psychological Medicine* **2**, No. 3: 312–17.

Shapiro, D.A. and Shapiro, D. (1982) Meta-Analysis of Comparative Outcome Research: A Replication and Refinement. *Psychological Bulletin* **92**: 581–604.

Shaw, G.B. (1907) *Major Barbara*. In *The Complete Plays of Bernard Shaw*, London: Odhams Press, 1937. Harmondsworth: Penguin Books, 1945: 131.

Springer, S.P. and Deutsch, G. (1981) *Left Brain, Right Brain*. San Francisco: W.H. Freeman.

Storr, A. (1972) *The Dynamics of Creation*. London: Secker & Warburg.

—— (1979) *The Art of Psychotherapy*. London: Secker & Warburg, Heinemann.

Suttie, I. (1935) *Origins of Love and Hate*. London: Routledge & Kegan Paul.

Taylor, J. (1974) *Black Holes*. Glasgow: Fontana/Collins.

Tillich, P. (1956) *The Religious Situation*. New York: Meridian, London: Thames & Hudson.

—— (1957) *Dynamics of Faith*. London: Allen & Unwin.

—— (1965) *Further Explorations*. London: Chatto & Windus.

—— (1977) *The Courage to Be*. Glasgow: Fontana/Collins.

Tomkins, S.S. (1963) *Affect, Imagery, Consciousness* in Vol II, *The Negative Affects*. New York: Springer Publishing Co., London: Tavistock Publications.

Vogel, G.W. (1978) An Alternative View of the Neurobiology of Dreaming. *American Journal of Psychiatry* **135**: 12.

Waddington, C.H. (1977) *Tools for Thought*. St. Albans: Paladin.

Warnock, G.J. (ed.) (1967) *The Philosophy of Perception*. London: Oxford University Press.

Warnock, M. (1976) *Imagination*. London: Faber & Faber.

Watts, F. (1978) Beyond Metaphor. *New Forum* **5**: 2.

Whalley, G. (1974) Coleridge's Poetic Sensibility. In J. Beer (ed.) *Coleridge's Variety*. London: Macmillan.

Whitehead, A.N. (1925) *Science and the Modern World*. New York: Macmillan, Cambridge: Cambridge University Press.

—— (1926) *Religion in the Making*. London: Cambridge University Press.

Wilde, O. (1966) *Complete Works of Oscar Wilde*. London and Glasgow: Collins.

Winnicott, D.W. (1971) *Playing and Reality*. London: Tavistock Publications.

Wittgenstein, L. (1966) *Lectures and Conversations on Aesthetics, Psychology, and Religious Belief*. Oxford: Basil Blackwell.

—— (1967) *Philosophische Untersuchungen*. (Philosophical Investigations.) Oxford: Basil Blackwell.

—— (1970) *Lectures and Conversations on Aesthetics, Psychology and Religious Belief*. Oxford: Basil Blackwell.

Worden, J.W. (1983) *Grief Counselling and Therapy*. London and New York: Tavistock Publications.

Wordsworth, W. (1936) *The Poetical Works of William Wordsworth*. Ed. T. Hutchinson, revised E. de Selincourt. London: Oxford University Press.

—— (1971) *The Prelude*. A parallel text. Harmondsworth: Penguin Books.

Wordsworth, W. and Coleridge, S.T. (1805) *Lyrical Ballads*. London and Glasgow: Collins. (Collins Annotated Student Texts.)

Wynne, L.C., Ryckoff, I.M., Day, J., and Hirsch, S.I. (1958). Pseudo-Mutuality in the Family Relations of Schizophrenics. *Psychiatry* **21**: 205.

Yalom, I.D. (1980) *Existential Psychotherapy*. New York: Basic Books.

Yates, A.J. (1962) *Frustration and Conflict*. London: Methuen, New York: John Wiley.

Yerkes, R.M. and Dodson, J.D. (1908) The Relation of Strength of Stimulus to Rapidity of Habit-Formation. *Journal of Comparative Neurology & Psychology* **18**: 459

Zaro, J.S., Barach, R., Nedelman, D.J., and Dreiblatt, I.S. (1977) *A Guide for Beginning Psychotherapists*. London: Cambridge University Press.

NAME INDEX

Note The names of patients in the stories are to be found in the Subject Index.

SUBJECT INDEX